design and designing

D1634987

design and designing

a critical introduction

edited by
steve garner and chris evans

London · New York

English edition

First published in 2012 by

Berg

Editorial offices:

50 Bedford Square, London WC1B 3DP, UK

175 Fifth Avenue, New York, NY 10010, USA

Berg is an imprint of Bloomsbury Publishing Plc.

Library of Congress Cataloging-in-Publication Data

Design and designing : a critical introduction / edited by Steve Garner and Chris Evans.

   pages cm

Includes bibliographical references and index.

ISBN 978-1-84788-577-7 (hardback) —

ISBN 978-1-84788-576-0 (paper) —

ISBN 978-0-85785-220-5 ( )

  1. Design. I. Garner, Steven W. (Steven William), editor of compilation.

II. Evans, Chris, 1947– editor of compilation.

NK1510.D4722 2012

745.4—dc23   2012002799

British Library Cataloguing-in-Publication Data

A catalogue record for this book is available from the British Library.

ISBN 978 1 84788 577 7 (Cloth)

    978 1 84788 576 0 (Paper)

Typeset by Apex CoVantage, LLC, Madison, WI, USA.

Printed in the UK by the MPG Books Group

www.bergpublishers.com

contents

tables and illustrations

tables

plates

figures

Acknowledgments

The editors gratefully acknowledge the service of Ryan Cox in redrawing many of the diagrams and artwork in this collection.

editors and contributors

Editors

Steve Garner has led some of the United Kingdom's most innovative and popular design programmes, most recently as professor of design at The Open University and formerly as programme leader for Industrial Design and Technology at Loughborough University. He has examined design at secondary, undergraduate, masters and PhD levels. He was a designer in the furniture industry, but more recently he has developed research into e-learning in design, the use of representations in design (particularly sketches), usability in product design and computer-supported collaborative designing. He has published widely, including the edited collection *Writing on Drawing* in 2008.

Chris Evans is course director for MSc Product Design Innovation and BSc Product Design at Aston University in Birmingham. He has been creating and coordinating a wide variety of design courses since 1989. This is underpinned by nearly twenty years of professional design and management with leading manufacturing organizations, including Mettoy Ltd (Corgi: die-cast toys); Ogle Design (toys, consumer electronics, transport systems, vehicle design); Prestige plc (cookware, kitchen equipment); Crown House Tableware (glass, ceramics) and Hasbro Europe (toys). Chris's teaching and practice reveal his core design philosophy: that successful design can only come about through a melding of creativity and innovation, appropriate engineering

and technological knowledge and an effective understanding of markets and user requirements.

Contributors

Katerina Alexiou joined The Open University as a Research Councils UK academic fellow. Her research is in the area of design theory and methods, including design cognition, design computing, collaborative design, learning, creativity and social aspects of design. She also has a special interest in the intersection between complexity science and design.

Jonathon Allen is associate professor in design at the University of Western Sydney, Australia. He has a BA(Hons) in Industrial Design and Technology and a PhD, both from Loughborough University, United Kingdom. He has over fifteen years of teaching experience at universities in the United Kingdom, New Zealand and Australia, supervising many international award-winning students.

Liz Anelli is a freelance illustrator. She contributes widely to creative learning programmes in the United Kingdom and international learning settings and is a champion of the Campaign for Drawing. Focusing on visual narratives and sketchbook travelogues, she provides annotated illustrative solutions for a diverse range of clients.

Maureen Carroll is the research director of Stanford University's REDlab (Research in Design and Education), a partnership between Stanford's

Hasso Plattner Institute of Design and the School of Education. She is co-founder of Lime Design Associates, whose mission is to catalyze innovation in the education and corporate sectors. Carroll has a PhD in education (language, literacy and culture) from the University of California, Berkeley.

Leticia Britos Cavagnaro, PhD, is adjunct faculty at Stanford Technology Ventures Program, co-teaching the Creativity and Innovation course at the Hasso Plattner Institute of Design. She is a member of the REDlab (Research in Education and Design) at Stanford's School of Education and co-founder of design consultancy Lime Design Associates.

Andrew Collier, MCSD, is joint managing director of the international consultancy SMC Design. He has over twenty-five years of experience in the planning, styling, interior and graphic design of cruise ships and ferries. He has worked with many leading shipping lines on new-build projects and major refurbishments.

Philip A. Davies is a mechanical engineer and a senior lecturer at Aston University. His research interests focus on the development of new products, especially in the areas of solar energy, purification of water for drinking and technologies for growing and processing food crops.

Emma Dewberry is a senior lecturer in design ecology at The Open University. Her work draws out different design dialogues and practices that reflect ecological contexts. She contributes to design courses and she has spoken nationally and internationally at exhibitions, conferences and invited lectures.

Michele D. Dickey is an associate professor at Miami University. She holds a joint appointment in instructional design and technology and interactive media studies. She teaches classes in game design, educational/serious game design, three-dimensional animation as well as courses in instructional media. Her research concerns design and production of games.

Bryce T. J. Dyer is senior lecturer in product design at Bournemouth University, where he lectures on both product design and design methods. His research interests concern the ethical implementation of technology used in elite sports. He writes for both mainstream magazines and academic publications.

Bob Eves is a senior lecturer in product design in the School of Design, Engineering and Computing at Bournemouth University. He has led a range of student design projects exploring the structural and free play of semiotics in design and has published research internationally in this field.

Shelley Goldman is professor at the Stanford University School of Education and holds a courtesy appointment in Mechanical Engineering–Design. She works at the nexus of learning, design and technology. She is the principal investigator of REDlab (Research in Education and Design), which conducts research and development to bring design thinking to education.

Luiz Vidal Gomes has been working with design education in Brazil since 1983 and has developed research on design language as a structural model for teaching. He is an editor for design publications and author of books and papers on the subject of creativity, design methodology and design pedagogy.

Tom Greenwood is a designer and marketer focused on understanding how business can be used as a tool to achieve environmental and social improvement. He is the creator of the online sustainable design resource www.espdesign.org, a contact for the O2 global sustainable design network and currently a director of www.Whole grainDigital.com.

David Heathcote has degrees in critical theory, history of design and history of architecture by research. He is an independent lecturer, writer, curator, filmmaker and broadcaster. He currently is a visiting tutor at Middlesex University and the Royal College of Art.

Jon Hewitt is a practising designer, experienced in working within various business sectors. Contributing to both current and future streams of development, he actively works with blue-chip brands and start-ups alike. His profession has taken him around the world, working alongside like-minded professionals creating and exploring design scenarios and experiences.

Claire Howell is a barrister and a senior lecturer in law at Aston Business School. She has written extensively on intellectual property law issues. She is a founder member of the European Intellectual Property Teachers Network and has acted as a consultant for the European Patent Office.

Jack Ingram is emeritus professor of product design at Birmingham City University. He is a fellow of the Design Research Society and co-founder of *The Design Journal.* The role of design in the evolution of our consumer society is explored in *The Design of Everyday Life,* published by Berg.

Terence Kavanagh is a graduate of the Royal College of Art. He was head of textile design at Loughborough College of Art and Design, becoming principal in 1998. He was director of Loughborough University School of Art and Design until 2002 and is currently dean of the faculty. His research concerns the impact of emerging technologies on the applied arts.

Paul Kouppas began his professional life as three-dimensional medical animator, later designing medical patient three-dimensional simulations using haptic devices and stereoscopic displays. He has worked as a university lecturer in industrial design, and is chief technology officer of an augmented reality and interactive media company in Sydney, Australia.

Tatjana Leblanc is designer and professor at the University of Montreal. Before joining the academic community as an expert in context-sensitive design approaches and transdisciplinary thinking, she pursued a successful professional career in European and US internationally renowned design consultancies. Her expertise has been recognized with several design awards.

Alison McKay is professor of design systems and director of the University of Leeds product design programme. Her research centres on sociotechnical aspects of two kinds of design systems: the networks of people and organizations that develop and support products through life and computer-aided design systems to support design synthesis.

Ligia Medeiros is a Brazilian industrial designer with interests in design education, design research and innovation. She has been engaged in the development of a taxonomy of graphic representation to assist teaching and learning in the creative stages of the design process.

Clyde Millard studied industrial design under Naum Slutsky, who had taught at the Bauhaus. Clyde's first job was designing light fittings in Finland. He worked for several UK design consultancies before setting up Clyde Millard Design in 1975. Clyde is a fellow of the Chartered Society of Designers.

Barbara Millet is an assistant professor in the Department of Industrial Engineering at Texas Tech University. She joined Texas Tech in 2009, after twelve years of working in industry. Her research focuses on usability engineering with an emphasis on human–computer interaction, text entry and handheld devices.

Mario Minichiello was formally academic director, Loughborough University School of Art and Design, and head of school, Birmingham Institute of Art and Design. He has numerous international links, including to Sydney University and Newcastle University in Australia. A widely published international conference speaker and author, Minichiello continues to work in mass media.

Brigid O'Kane is associate professor of design at the University of Cincinnati's College of Design, Architecture, Art and Planning. She has worked for General Motors as a senior lead creative designer and at the General Motors Advanced Concept Center in California developing running prototypes of advanced concept vehicles.

Patrick Patterson is chair of the Department of Industrial Engineering at Texas Tech University and a professional engineer, a certified professional ergonomist and a fellow of the Institute of Industrial Engineers. His research and teaching interests include safety engineering, rehabilitation engineering, user-centered product design and errors in complex systems.

Stephen Peake is a senior lecturer in the Design Group at The Open University and a fellow in management science at the Judge Business School, University of Cambridge. He has used design and business thinking to facilitate corporate leadership and creativity events in the fields of sustainability and health care.

Sharon Helmer Poggenpohl taught in notable design programs in Asia and the United States with a focus on postgraduate design education, both masters and PhD, as well as design research. She edits and publishes the international scholarly journal *Visible Language* and co-edited *Design Integrations* (2009).

Dorothea Strube has a degree in arts administration from the Berlin Technical University. She is an independent arts administrator in the area of art in architecture and public art competitions funded by local, regional and federal governments. She also lectures at the Kunsthochschule Weißensee in Berlin.

Randall Teal is an assistant professor of architecture at the University of Idaho. His pedagogical and research interests are in design fundamentals and architectural theory with a significant influence from continental thought. His writing focuses primarily on understanding and promoting situated dialogue between creative processes and the built environment.

Michael Tovey is professor of industrial design at Coventry University. He was responsible for the establishment and development of Transport Design achieving international prominence and centre of excellence status. He was dean of the Coventry School of Art and Design for eighteen years, pioneering design research, contributing publications and holding a number of research council grants.

Richard Woolley has led numerous projects for Land Rover. His work has been recognized through Design Council and Car of the Year awards. In the past, he has worked for Ford in the USA, BMW in Germany and Honda in Japan. He is currently studio director for Land Rover Advanced Design.

Theodore Zamenopoulos is a lecturer in design at The Open University, and he leads the second-level design course. His research interests include the neurological basis of design thinking, mathematical and computational models of design and the role of new technologies in design learning and design support.

introduction

This collection has been written for all those students who are, or are considering, embarking on a university or college education in design. It presents a broad portfolio of expert design 'voices' that provide key insights to design practice and design theory today. It doesn't seek to reproduce the content that a design course might present you with, but it does aim to provide you with a clear road map to help you make sense of the experiences to come. Whatever your design career ambitions might be, there are important messages for you in this book.

Design is a mature, confident and economically valuable discipline in higher education around the world. It is enriched by its interface with numerous other disciplines including art, technology, the human sciences and business. One of the key characteristics of design today is the variety of specialist fields or subjects that collectively form the parent domain. Some of these, such as architecture, typography design and the crafts in wood, fabric, ceramic and metal, possess an extensive history of education and practice. Other fields are relatively new, such as the design of digital games, interaction design and service design. In reality design is a disparate collection of subjects linked by some important threads. This book is about these threads that bind the discipline of design together.

At the outset of any analysis of design, it's useful to draw a distinction between the *outputs* of design—the various products, pages, services, patterns, sets or buildings—that result from design activity and the *process* of designing that has given rise to these outputs. Hence, the title of this book, which attempts to flag up very clearly that we all commonly use the word *design* as both a noun and a verb. Also flagged up in the title is the aim to provide an introduction. This collection will help you understand design and designing. The content has been written to be understandable by those with no design expertise or knowledge, but it should also appeal to readers with some design experience. The twenty-eight chapters are structured as seven parts, and each presents a close scrutiny of a particular design theme such as design process, sustainability and designing for people.

Both design and designing are in a state of continuous and dynamic evolution. Today one of the major drivers in this international evolution is the imperative for designers to work across boundaries—to apply their skills and knowledge across traditional lines of demarcation taking them into, for example, business, marketing, management, production and user satisfaction. Designing today is less a craft and more a component of the knowledge economy. Designing today is about knowing how to acquire knowledge and how to creatively apply it. This collection of original writing by authors from the United States, United Kingdom and other design-focused countries aims to illuminate the transferable skills and knowledge of world-class designing. It can be used to support university-level design teaching, and it can be read by those with a more general interest in the principles and processes of designing today. It can be used to support learning in specialist subjects such as graphic communication or product design, and it should also appeal to those with broader interests in subjects such as design studies

---

Defining Design and Designing

The word *design* has become variously used—some might say overused—in our modern media-dominated, globalized culture; so what does design mean and what is designing? Here are the definitions from a design course of The Open University.[1]

Design (noun): specific plans, drawings or instructions that contain all the necessary information for the manufacture of a product, process or system; a particular physical embodiment of a product or device.

Designing (verb): the process of converting generalized ideas and concepts into a *design* as defined above.

Designing is a process that takes us from the 'what is' to the 'what might be'. It is a process of change through intervention. Clearly intervening isn't limited to professional designers—we all do it. For example we might decorate our homes or create personal Web pages. Does that mean we are all designers because we intervene in this way? No, because designing is more than simply changing or improving our own personal world. Designing is the planning and delivery process by which artefacts, services, environments and systems are brought into being and which address the needs of the producer, users and many other stakeholders.

---

1. *Design and Designing* (T211), The Open University, Blk 1 (2010), p. 76.

---

or those taking a design foundation course. This collection seeks to inform and stimulate as well as develop a range of cognitive design abilities related to the aesthetic, moral, ethical and social contexts of human experience. A number of information boxes are distributed throughout the collection, and these provide bite-sized insights into principles and practices of design. They provide their own unique narrative thread throughout the book. Put together, the information boxes and the chapters provide the theoretical underpinning of an essentially practical subject.

The title also flags up that this collection provides a 'critical' introduction because it seeks to develop readers' critical abilities. Typically today the undergraduate learning experience in design is studio-based, where imagination, creativity and practical skills are developed alongside intellectual powers and the ability to communicate. But new learning environments are emerging with greater emphasis on independent and social learning. This book can be used for self-directed study or with your own online community. The chapters presented here will foster your creative design inquisitiveness; they will help you develop design thinking skills of analysis, synthesis and judgement; they will raise your awareness of environmental, social, cultural and economic issues and they will help you achieve your career goals through an understanding of generic and subject-specific principles and practices of designing today.

As well as learning ***about*** design, this book provides opportunities to learn ***through*** design. Each of the seven parts includes a modest design project that allows readers to stretch their abilities at questioning, creating, reflecting and communicating.

This book offers stimulating insights to design and designing today. It explores how, where, why and when design operates in the twenty-first century, it challenges notions of supply and consumption of design and it plots a new road map for design education and the practice of designing.

part i

the designing process

introduction to part i

It can be confusing when authors use the word *design* as both a noun and a verb. Of course they are quite correct in that design can be used to mean the process of resolving problems or addressing opportunities, and it can also refer to the outputs of this process—the various products, buildings, Web pages, services and so on. To overcome this potential confusion, this book adopts the word *designing* when referring to the process, and it's the process that forms the focus for Part I.

At the core of Part I is an apparently simple question: are there any common characteristics to the designing process? It's a good question because the numerous professions of design can seem so different. Can there really be significant similarities between, say, the process of designing jet engines, postage stamps, Web-based interactive services and furniture? The four authors in Part I who seek to illuminate this matter address the question in different ways, but it seems clear there are indeed unifying features across a disparate community of practitioners. One of the purposes of design education would seem to be the development of core skills and knowledge as well as subject-specific skills and knowledge. In Chapter 1 Michael Tovey refers to these as the 'passport to practice'.

Perhaps one of the most significant steps in the search for a common design process has been the identification of common thinking styles across various design professions. Chapter 2, by Maureen Carroll and colleagues, addresses this head-on with a discussion of 'design thinking'. Interestingly, design thinking is not held to be some special skill of designers—it's shown to consist of some quite ordinary approaches that can be learnt and applied by anyone. These include letting problems and solutions emerge together, testing ideas using representations, embracing ambiguity and learning from failure. It's not that designers have a monopoly on these, but they do seem to successfully combine them to create powerful approaches. Designing is about applying different types of skills to understand and to create. Sometimes a design job requires skills be applied sequentially, but at other times you need to apply skills simultaneously. Design thinking particularly seems to require the simultaneous application of analysis and creation. Perhaps designing simply requires a certain attitude in order for thinking skills to be effective. It certainly seems to require confidence, motivation, resilience and a willingness to question, and these elusive capabilities need to be nurtured and fostered. In Chapter 3 Tatjana Leblanc provides some practical examples of how design process skills have been developed by students.

Designing is also a disciplined activity. The pressures of constraints and deadlines mean we have to manage ourselves and others. Few designers have the freedom to indulge themselves, and knowing when and how to draw to an end each stage of the design process is a vital skill. In Chapter 4, Alison McKay documents the discipline of design thinking—that is, how creative thinking can be controlled so that it delivers appropriate outcomes.

As you might expect, Part I is not the end of the process story. It is picked up throughout the collection by several authors. But by the end of Part I you should have acquired an understanding of a generic process of designing and be able to represent it in simple diagrams. How you apply such a design process and the tools you might use to assist you is the subject of later parts.

chapter 1

the passport to practice

michael tovey

ABOUT THIS CHAPTER

In our universities and colleges there is a long tradition of teaching design through design practice. For most students, their end goal is achieving a level of capability to function as designers in the professional world. That is, they wish to become part of the community of design practitioners. Today it is vital that their education helps them construct a 'passport' to enter this community.

For many design students, the physical manifestation of their passport to design practice is their portfolio of design work. It is in this assemblage of work that they demonstrate that they can tackle design problems to a standard that is recognisable as appropriate in a professional arena. In this they show that they can think in a 'designerly' way. The communication is primarily through visual means, and good drawing and modelling skills are very important. But it can be argued that demonstrating the ability to engage in creative thinking—and more particularly the creative synthesising of ideas and problems through design thinking—is the most important capability required to acquire this passport to enter the community of practice.

> **"The ability to engage in creative thinking—and more particularly the creative synthesising of ideas and problems through design thinking—is the most important capability required to achieve this passport to enter the community of practice."**

This chapter is about creating an effective passport into the communities of practice that make up the professional design world. The context used here is automotive design, but the lessons are transferable to many other fields of design. The chapter asserts that you can achieve your passport by developing design thinking skills and communicating these through appropriate evidence.

communities of practice

A community of practice is typically a group of professionally qualified people in the same discipline, all of whom negotiate with, and participate in, a mutually understood discourse. This discourse is both explicit and, very often, unspoken or tacit, but the signs of membership are usually unmistakable. It is possible to understand this shared discourse in terms of Community of Practice Theory. This was devised by Jean Lave and Etienne Wenger about twenty years ago[1] and has provided an innovative foundation for many researchers since. The social theory of learning highlights the value of our 'lived experience of participation in the world'.[2] That is, our learning takes place through a deepening process of participation in such a community of practice. Even our identities are formed from this participation. Wenger defines the major principles of a community of practice in three separate, but related, quotes:

- Communities of practice are groups of people who share a concern or a passion for something they do and who interact regularly to learn how to do it better.
- A community of practice is not merely a community of interest—people who like certain kinds of movies, for instance. Members of a community of practice are practitioners. They develop a shared repertoire of resources: experiences, stories, tools, ways of addressing recurring problems—in short, a shared practice.
- In pursuing their interest in their domain, members engage in joint activities and discussions, help each other, and share information. They build relationships that enable them to learn from each other.[3]

Learning within a community of practice is an experience of identity formation. It is not just an accumulation of skills and information, but also a process of becoming—in this case a certain kind of creative and critically minded design practitioner. It is through this 'transformative practice', as Wenger calls it, within a professional community of creative design practitioners that learning can become a source of motivation, meaning and personal and social energy. Wenger provides a

> **"Learning within a community of practice is an experience of identity formation."**

number of indicators that a community of practice has formed:

1. sustained mutual relationships—harmonious or in conflict
2. shared ways of engaging in doing things together
3. the rapid flow of information and propagation of innovation
4. absence of introductory preambles, as if conversations and interactions were merely the continuation of an ongoing process
5. very quick setup of a problem to be discussed
6. substantial overlap in participants' descriptions of who belongs
7. knowing what others know, what they can do and how they can contribute to an enterprise
8. mutually defining identities
9. the ability to assess the appropriateness of actions and products
10. specific tools, representations and other artefacts
11. local lore, shared stories, inside jokes, knowing laughter
12. jargon and shortcuts to communication
13. certain styles recognized as displaying membership
14. a shared discourse reflecting a certain perspective on the world.

The source of coherence in the community is the emphasis on practice. It is this which distinguishes such communities from, for example, a community of interest, including as it does both explicit and tacit knowledge and information. Often unarticulated, this emphasis on practice includes all the implicit relations, tacit conventions, subtle clues, untold rules of thumb, recognisable intuitions, specific perceptions, well-tuned sensitivities, embodied understandings, underlying assumptions and shared world views.

Members of such a community develop, share and negotiate their identities in relation to their shared practice. The process of assimilating newcomers is initially through peripheral engagement. This is progressively legitimized by established members who induct newcomers in much the same way that they were in their turn inducted. However, communities of practice are not havens of peace. Relations between members are constantly evolving, and each new generation can cause disagreements with more established members as they introduce new ideas and different ways of looking at processes and practices. Indeed such friction is essential to maintain the energy and vibrancy of the community. Also, involvement in a community of practice can go beyond the concern with the professional activities to include social interaction. There can be an emphasis on not only staying in contact with professional developments within the discipline, but also the latest gossip and rumour. The joint enterprise is based on ownership, and members can develop economies of communication and shared understanding. This can lead to common responses and shared practices.

design communities

Designers come in many types. There are architects, industrial designers, design engineers, graphic designers, interaction designers, fashion designers, interior designers, craft designers, furniture designers, jewellery designers and many more. Each of them represents a significant group of practitioners and each could be regarded as a community of practice. Some of the categories are sufficiently large that they subdivide into groups of more specialist designers. Thus, for example, graphic designers might distinguish between those concentrating on corporate identity, media graphics or information design. Similarly, industrial design contains the large subcategories of product design and automotive design and smaller groups such as boat designers.

For major groups there are formal national bodies to which entry is by examination. Thus, for example, for architects there is the Royal Institute of British Architects in the United Kingdom, and the Society of American Architects and the American Institute of Architects in the USA. Many countries have their own national equivalent. For a wide range of design professions in the United Kingdom there is the Chartered Society of Designers, and in the USA there is the Industrial Designers Society of America. Some designers find the Institute of Engineering Designers more appropriate. Most such societies are national and tend to have national membership. The less formal groupings can be international in scope. A powerful example is that of the community of practice of automotive designers.

The community of practice of automotive designers

Key to the development of the community of practice of automotive designers was the contribution which Harley Earl, head of design at General Motors (GM), made to the development of automotive design.[4] The striking appearance of the company's vehicles from the 1930s until the

Figure 1.1 Harley Earl had a huge impact on the style
of cars emerging from Detroit in the 1930s, 40s and 50s.
(Getty TR006163 RF)

end of the 1950s was created by Earl and the people working for him. In retrospect this can be regarded as a period of self-confident extravagance, which is vastly different from the economic realities facing the car companies and their designers today.

A lasting legacy of Earl's approach is the structure of the automotive design process and the activities which designers engage with in designing new vehicles and presenting their proposals. Much of this has evolved from the systems that Earl set up. However, this is not his only legacy. He made an important contribution to General Motors' becoming the biggest car manufacturer in the world

for much of the twentieth century. He managed not only five separate car design studios—one each for Chevrolet, Pontiac, Buick, Oldsmobile and Cadillac—but also twelve specialist studios. During his period at GM, his designs accounted for more than 50 million vehicles. Inevitably this scale of operation required a significant number of designers, clay modellers, engineers and managers. Many of these were trained in-house. But many joined from elsewhere, and they stayed at GM for different periods. Many left to take up jobs with other car companies throughout the world. Some became leading designers in these other companies. This collection of designers came to function as a community of practice. Many of them had a shared experience of design studios where they had worked alongside one another. They had a shared vocabulary, shared enthusiasms and often similar attitudes. This community naturally was initially a predominantly US-based phenomenon. However, as General Motors was itself increasingly developing as an international and multinational company, its designers were becoming international too. And they communicated and shared experiences with designers from other companies and other countries.

General Motors' dominance is now over. It is no longer the biggest car company in the world. Communications across the globe are instant, and travel is much easier. The community of practice of car designers is international and multi-company. There are car design studios in all of the major industrial countries of the world. The designers who work in these studios typically share their passion for vehicles, and each time a new concept is revealed by one studio it causes interest and excitement in the other studios. There are many opportunities for them to stay in touch with developments through the many Internet resources and publications. Although during the development of a new design there is usually great secrecy in the company concerned, a great deal of information is shared throughout the industry, and companies often move in similar directions, responding to common pressures from the market and government policies. Each design studio will have its own team of designers, engineers and other specialists. These designers will often pursue individual career paths which take them from one company to another. Collectively this body of people constitutes a community of professional practice. To those in the community, it is visible and high-profile, and it is a community

which many students of transport design aspire to join.

For an international community to function, it is important that there is communication between its members. For automotive designers today, this is supplemented by online resources such as *Car Design News.*[5] This was created by three car

---

Creative Design

What is creativity, and what distinguishes the products or works of exceptionally creative processes and people?

Creative design displays novelty or originality in work that represents an (apparent) break or discontinuity from what has gone before, anywhere in the world. Exceptionally creative works are generally accepted as being of great value to many people in the world. They have a major influence on the work of others and may be of importance in shaping whole cultures or technologies. They may provide the foundation of new businesses or industries or even affect the performance of economies and nations.

Creativity: A goal-directed human activity that results in novel or original work that is perceived to be of value to individuals or society.

Novelty: Being new or different from what was previously known or usual.

Originality: Being the first example of something; not derived from anything that has appeared before.

Value: Having importance, significance, worth, utility or desirability.

There is clearly a spectrum of originality, novelty and value—from breakthroughs of significance to the whole world (e.g. the first powered aircraft, the Internet) to the products of everyday creativity of value mainly to their creator and immediate group (e.g. a flower arrangement, a room interior). Even so, how creative something is considered to be is a matter of judgement and thus will vary in time and place.

From: R. Roy, *Design and Designing* (T211), The Open University, Blk 3 (2010), p. 12.

designers from the United States and the United Kingdom. It contains news from a designer's perspective of developments in car design, with in-depth reviews, an extensive online gallery from all of the major car shows and student exhibitions and competitions, discussion forums, resources and job listings, a large online collection of car designer portfolios, a paid-for members editorial and a car design taxonomy. With over a million hits a year, it is a highly effective device for facilitating the community of practice.

designerly thinking

Design practice, in any of the various specialist fields, calls on a range of technical capabilities, shared enthusiasms, understanding of the operational culture and other domain-specific skills. These are extremely important in the identity of each community of practice. One of the distinguishing characteristics of the designers within a particular area is that they exhibit qualities which mark them out as designers. Thus they function differently from other specialists such as legislators, planning controllers and civil engineers in the process of designing buildings or as marketers, product planners, production engineers and others in product design. What designers do is design; they create designs and solve design problems. Thus, in this most obvious sense, they are different from other professionals. The contention in this chapter is that in order to function effectively as designers, they must engage in designerly practices. At the core of this is design thinking, which includes tackling vague problems, thinking in a constructive and solution-focused way and homing in on concrete propositions. In so doing, design thinkers typically employ an object

language, often in the form of drawings or other visual models. This is a core capability which is shared across different types of designers.

For each specialist field of design there is a range of domain-specific knowledge and expertise which is crucial to its functioning. Thus fashion designers must know about both fabric technology and clothing manufacture and, most importantly, must be able to key into the latest trends in catwalk style. Similarly, there is an equivalent area of expertise for architects in planning controls, building technology and regulation and understanding current thinking on architectural practice. All of the other types of designers have their own equivalent areas of specific expertise and knowledge which distinguish them from each other. What they share is their ability to employ design thinking. In the process of creating a design there is clearly a place for both logical analysis and creative thinking. In fact they are both essential. For a number of types of designing the analytical activities such as data acquisition, problem definition and solution evaluation need to be tackled in an explicit and objective manner. The design brief and specification can be the initiating force which both precedes the development of design proposals and functions as a checklist to evaluate them. Such an approach is particularly useful in managing the design process and could be described as a specification-driven strategy.

Designers are also responsible for the creative component in the strategy, which could be seen as a solution-led procedure in which the emphasis is on the identification within the design problem of whatever will allow the generation of a solution conjecture at the earliest possible moment—in other words, before the problem has been fully analysed and understood. This solution proposal is derived from those elements within the problem which will permit the creation of the physical form of the design idea. Thus thinking is converted from an abstract problem definition to a piece of visual thinking. Draft ideas are then offered to the problem as a way of both evaluating the design and analysing the problem. This reveals where more design thinking needs to be done and what more information is required. Visually conceived design conjecture in the form of an undetailed design concept can be used to give direction to the analytical thinking, which will either simultaneously or subsequently propel the development of the design proposal. Where this is applied, it is usually externalized as a drawing, model or computer-aided design (CAD) model.

Both the specification-driven design strategy and the solution-led approach emphasize the interaction of analytical–evaluative processes and synthetic–visual processes, but they differ in the sequence. To simplify, the first approach begins with analysis, and in the second the synthesis happens first. The specification-driven strategy emphasizes the production of a detailed definition of a design problem in words and numbers. The solution-led approach, by contrast, emphasizes the early representation of a design solution proposal in the form of a drawing, CAD or three-dimensional (3D) model.

types of intelligence

All of the types of designers we are considering concern themselves with the design of objects, either in two dimensions or three. They all work in the real world where people have three-dimensional bodies and senses linked to sophisticated mental processes. Howard Gardner's theory of multiple intelligences[6] fits well with the notion of design thinking and has enabled educators to create innovative materials for engaging learners. Gardner identified seven distinct attributes of personal intelligence: linguistic intelligence, logical-mathematical intelligence, musical intelligence, bodily-kinaesthetic intelligence, spatial intelligence, interpersonal intelligence and intrapersonal intelligence.

Spatial intelligence or spatial understanding has many different points of relevance here; architects may concentrate on values such as positive and negative spaces defined by buildings and with navigation through them; cartographers will have interests in representing the earth's topology and manufactured features. Gardner's work also draws attention to more abstract and elusive spatial capacities. These include a sensitivity to the various lines of force that enter into a visual or spatial display and the identification of resemblances that may exist across seemingly disparate forms. The metaphoric ability to discern similarities across diverse domains also derives from spatial intelligence and is a crucial attribute of professional design practitioners. In order to develop what Gardner terms the 'language of space' and 'thinking in the spatial medium', design students are required, through the activities of drawing and modelling, to gain more sophisticated visuospatial understandings of the complexity of surfacing and three-dimensional form. Drawing and modelling are key ingredients in developing visuospatial capability, graphically speaking the language of objects, and, since they provide evidence of competence, they are vital to acquiring a passport.

thinking as dual processing

There has been much research into how the brain functions. Some of this has focused on the different characteristics of the two halves of the brain, or cerebral laterality. Many researchers in this field have characterized the two hemispheres of the brain as separate information processors and encoders. There is strong evidence that underlying the left hemisphere's dominance for expressive speech and the right hemisphere's dominance for manipulating objects in space are different processing modes. Typically the modes are characterized as analytic–synthetic, linear–holistic, serial–parallel or focal–diffuse for the left

and right halves of the brain, respectively. This dichotomy is attractive as it seems to correspond with the different types of cognitive style identified by psychologists in problem-solving procedures. It also seems to correspond with the analysis–synthesis dichotomy which has been identified as the basis of the design process.

It is clear that for anything other than very simple mental operations both halves of the brain are involved, as has been shown in magnetic resonance imaging maps of cerebral activity during

Figure 1.2 Dual processing model of the design thinking process. (Copyright author)

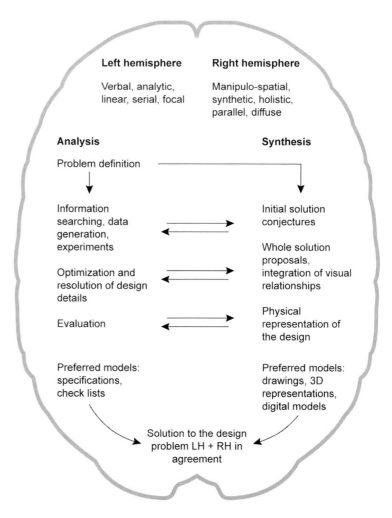

Left hemisphere

Verbal, analytic, linear, serial, focal

Right hemisphere

Manipulo-spatial, synthetic, holistic, parallel, diffuse

Analysis

Problem definition

Information searching, data generation, experiments

Optimization and resolution of design details

Evaluation

Preferred models: specifications, check lists

Synthesis

Initial solution conjectures

Whole solution proposals, integration of visual relationships

Physical representation of the design

Preferred models: drawings, 3D representations, digital models

Solution to the design problem LH + RH in agreement

experimental tasks. It would seem that the two processing modes are typically employed at the same time and interactively and that a more complete understanding of any particular problem arises from the matching of initially separate simultaneous mental operations. It is possible that design thinking may be organized in a similar way, with two simultaneous interacting cognitive styles being employed. Thus it would be expected that an analytic, linear strategy would be at work in the process of data generation and organization to yield a design specification, and also in the evaluation of design proposals. In parallel with this, a synthetic–holistic strategy, used in the generation of solution conjectures, would be the integration of visual relationships and the physical representation of a design as drawings or 3D models.

These two interacting lateralized mental operations can be used to map out design thinking and help understand it. I have called this the *dual processing* model of the design process.[7] In it there is the assumption that the two halves of the brain will both be involved in solving design problems, each half working in its own preferred information processing mode and each tending towards its favoured modelling language—the left in words and symbols, the right in drawings, 3D constructions and/or digital CAD models (see Figure 1.2). The design process will be concluded successfully when the two processors are in agreement over a solution.

The essence of this model is the interaction of the two modes of thought, each stimulating and modifying the other, both crucially involved in the evolution and resolution of a fully detailed design proposal. Although such a model is of course speculative, it does provide a framework within which different design approaches can be accommodated. The relative emphasis given to serial–analytical and to simultaneous–holistic thinking varies between designers and between types of design problem. For example engineering designers may give first priority to analysis and the derivation of a specification, whereas product designers may concentrate more on the holistic processes used to derive a design concept presented as a drawing or a 3D model. Nonetheless

---

Four Stages of the Creative Process

An old but still widely used model of the creative process is that formulated by the psychologist Graham Wallas based on accounts by scientists and mathematicians of the stages they went through when trying to solve difficult problems. Wallas identified four stages in creative problem solving: preparation, incubation, illumination and verification.[1]

Preparation: This is the stage in which necessary facts are gathered and initial attempts may be made to solve the problem. Preparation might require considerable effort searching for information, experimentation and exploring and redefining the problem. It may also rely heavily on existing knowledge and experience.

Incubation: At this stage the problem is set aside, deliberately or otherwise, and no longer given conscious attention.

Illumination: This is the inspiration or 'flash of insight' in which the solution (or at least a key idea on which part of the solution might be based) suddenly occurs in the mind of the creator, often when he or she is not working on the problem. This is thought to be the result of the relaxed brain repatterning information absorbed during the period of preparation.

Verification: This final stage involves checking the validity of the idea or solution, working out the details and generally developing it for practical use. This may take days or years of effort without any guarantee of success.

From: R. Roy, *Design and Designing* (T211), The Open University, Blk 3 (2010), pp. 38–39.

[1] G. Wallas (1926), *The Art of Thought,* New York, Harcourt.

it is assumed that the design process will always involve both modes of thinking and that it is their relative proportions which will vary.

thinking about thinking

In any analysis of thinking there are many dichotomies which seem to parallel the dual processing model. These include the distinctions between convergent and divergent thinking and that between reflective and impulsive thinking. One of the most fundamental is that between verbal and nonverbal thought, and as I noted above, design thinking contains a high proportion of nonverbal thinking. Those who have contributed most to productive techniques in thinking seem to have had a need to describe it in terms of such dichotomies, and one of the most useful has been Edward de Bono's split between vertical thinking and lateral thinking.[8] This has much in common with the left hemisphere/right hemisphere split of the dual processing model. *Lateral thinking* is a term invented by de Bono in the 1960s, which he contrasts with traditional, logical thinking—what he calls *vertical thinking*. Vertical thinking is very useful, particularly when analysing a problem or putting forward an argument. Typically it involves making yes/no decisions at each stage, selecting and discarding material. Although it is powerful and useful, it can also be limiting. It is the equivalent of digging a hole by making deeper the hole you already have. Lateral thinking is concerned with digging as many new holes as possible, for the solution may not be in the direction in which you are already digging. There are many techniques for facilitating lateral thinking. Some are concerned simply with overcoming the limiting effects of vertical thinking, by challenging assumptions or by suspended judgement. Others are more provocative, creating

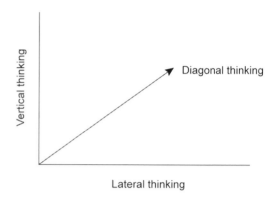

Figure 1.3 Diagonal thinking as a combination of vertical and lateral thinking. (Copyright author)

new combinations, concept changes and idea reversals to encourage innovation.

A recent and very fruitful development of de Bono's ideas has emerged from the Institute of Practitioners in Advertising (IPA) in the United Kingdom. The idea for *diagonal thinking* was initiated by Hamish Pringle[9] who has a senior role in the IPA. The concept underpins a tool designed to aid the recruitment of talented people into the creative industries. A self-assessment psychometric test is offered as a way of signalling whether the applicants are able to employ the appropriate combination of capabilities. The core notion of diagonal thinking is that to be effective in creative professions a combination of both linear and lateral thinking is required. This is characterized in Figure 1.3. It is an attractive and useful way of depicting the relationship between linear and simultaneous thinking which is proposed in the dual processing model. It would seem to play a fundamental part in design thinking.

thinking with drawing

All designing involves representations of one type or another. These might range from diagrams quickly drawn on the back of an envelope to digital images created on screen to three-dimensional models or prototypes. The making of representations that are fast, economical and effective are vital to design thinking because this enables the maker to both communicate with others and to reflect on his or her own thinking. Freehand drawing has traditionally been the bedrock of representation-making in design. In skilful hands, a few lines and perhaps some tone can evoke a concept of complexity and sophistication as in the vehicle illustrations shown in Figure 1.4.

Design sketching is quite different from the process of producing a drawing of what you have in front of you. Drawing from the object is a matter of reproducing and interpreting something which exists in the physical world and which you can see.

Design sketches, whether on paper or computer, are not drawings of something 'out there', but are the attempts by the designer to give external form to something which is imagined, existing only in the designer's mind. As such it may be conceived incompletely with hazy details.

Sketching is a necessary process in design thinking, and today new CAD tools and software offer exciting new ways to digitally externalize creative design thinking. Just as when using a pen or pencil on paper, new digital tools allow creative people to tap into their mind's eye and give external expression to their mental images. The activity can be relaxing, which can, in its turn, reduce the inhibitions to the flow of thought and original thinking. Whilst the designer is sketching there can be a mental sifting and re-organization of information,

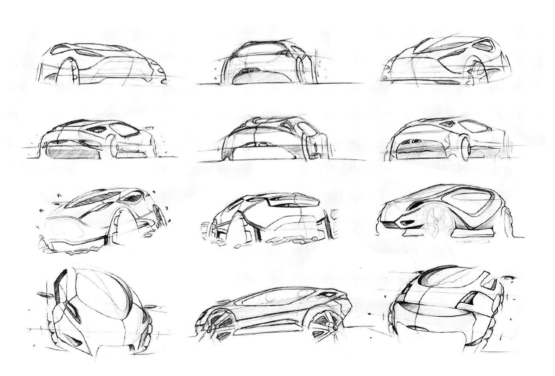

Figure 1.4 Concept car illustrations (Seesing, Coventry University). (Copyright author)

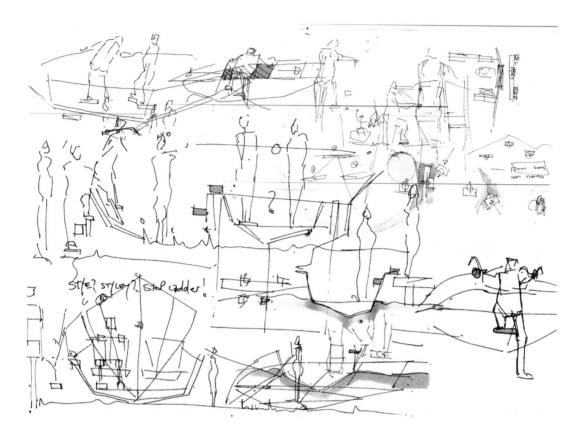

Figure 1.5 Deliberate ambiguity in sketches. Exploring a
relationship between people, place and product (Houghton,
Coventry University). (Copyright author)

stimulating more design ideas. Even as images are
being made they become part of the information
being absorbed and evaluated to help create the
next idea. It is a process of interactive generation.
Relatively unstructured and ambiguous sketches
tend to occur early in the conceptual stages of
design, which is typically characterized by vague
knowledge and shifting goals.

Most designers use drawing in some form or
other. However, the nature of the drawings and
other representations will vary between different
fields of design and for different stages of the design
process. As noted above, drawings and models are

the physical manifestation of visual thinking. They
provide a language for handling design ideas. A
drawing is the manifestation of right-hemisphere
thinking, just as writing is the manifestation of
left-hemisphere thinking. Some design sketching
does not follow the ideas in the mind, but instead
precedes them. Thus designers may engage in
sketching not to record an idea, but to help generate it. This is visual thinking. The purpose of this
early sketching activity is primarily to enable the designer to identify clues which can be used to form
and inform emerging design concepts. The designer uses a series of rapid sketches to transform

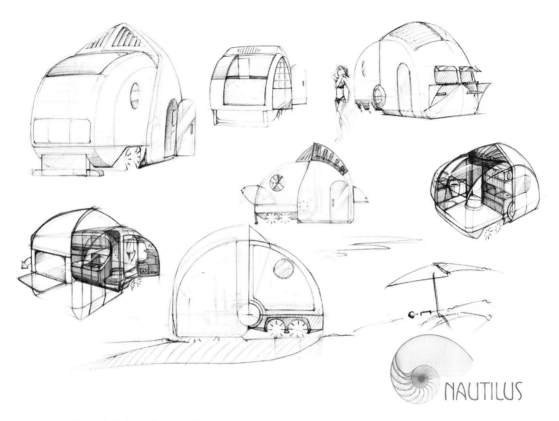

Figure 1.6 Concept sketches for a mobile home
(Hawken, Coventry University). (Copyright author)

images in a cyclic manner; each sketch generates images in the mind, which drive the development of the themes embodied in the design. In turn this leads the designer to transform the previous images by additions, deletions and modifications. Because such sketches don't seek to support communication with others, the designer can be extremely brief and vague, applying a personal graphic shorthand. In the hands of skilled practitioners, sketching on paper or using digital tools can be fast, clear and creative (see Figure 1.6).

The making and using of effective graphic representations can be regarded as a key component in creative problem solving, and thus it forms a vital part of design thinking. Such representations range from personal thinking sketches through a range of images and constructions devised for external consumption such as concept pictures, diagrams of usability or drawings depicting component detail (see Figure 1.7).

Today, the distinction between the digital and the tangible has become blurred as designers repeatedly move between different techniques for making drawings. Whatever your personal preference for ways of making drawings, their exploitation still lies at the core of designing. Thinking and communicating with drawing will be used as an indicator in your journey towards a passport to practice.

Figure 1.7 Digital models of a pill dispenser (Goulding, Coventry University). (Copyright author)

CHAPTER SUMMARY

- Central to the notion of a passport to design practice is the recognition of the existence of groups as communities of design practitioners.
- For each specialist group of practicing designers there is either explicitly or implicitly a community of professional practice, each having its own specialist history, technology, skills, knowledge base and expertise.
- Gaining entry to a community of practice requires familiarity with generic skills and capabilities in design plus others that are domain-specific.
- Designing involves the application of solution-focused creativity in tandem with analytical thinking in a dual processing approach. This is design thinking.
- Design thinking exploits visual thinking, the use of visuospatial intelligence, to resolve design problems. Visual thinking is externalized as design drawings and other representations.
- Representations can be seen as evidence of competence in design thinking. Such evidence is vital to obtaining a passport to a community of design practice.
- Expertise in design thinking is crucial to all sorts of design activity, but because it is generic it also has wide application outside design. It is a highly transferable skill, meaning designers can be highly effective members of teams tackling a range of different problems.

chapter 2

design thinking

maureen carroll, leticia britos cavagnaro and shelley goldman

'One can't believe impossible things.'

'I daresay you haven't had much practice,' said the Queen. 'When I was your age I always did it for half-an-hour a day. Why, sometimes I believed six impossible things before breakfast.'

Lewis Carroll, Alice's Adventures in Wonderland

ABOUT THIS CHAPTER

This is a chapter about design thinking. It describes both the process and the mindsets that support a way of thinking that is both creative and analytical. Design is not linear in the way characterized in many diagrams of design. It is convoluted and complex, requiring designers to loop backwards and forwards between the present and past stages in cycles of iteration. At the core of this chapter are some practical pointers and insightful observations on what characterizes good design thinkers. The chapter is supported with references to some of the leading design thinkers in design practice and design education today.

---

what is design thinking?

Why are some people able to believe in what seems unachievable? It once seemed impossible for a machine to fly through the sky, but Leonardo da Vinci and the Wright brothers thought differently. It once seemed impossible to breathe underwater until Jacques Cousteau invented the aqualung in 1943. Few imagined they would see the day that a man walked on the moon, and even fewer a generation ago envisaged the scale of today's Internet. A remarkable opportunity awaits you as you enter the field of design; you have the opportunity to contribute to the changes you want to see in the world. The problems we face in the twenty-first century are increasingly complex and nuanced. As a designer, you have a say in what is possible. Perhaps taking Lewis Carroll's advice and practising believing the impossible for half an hour a day might be a very sensible idea because design thinkers can make the seemingly impossible real. But as Nolan Bushnell, entrepreneur and founder of Atari Inc. noted, 'Everyone who's ever taken a shower has had an idea. It's the person who gets out of the shower, dries off and does something about it who makes a difference.'[1]

Design thinking is an orientation toward learning that encompasses active problem solving and believing in one's ability to bring about change that has impact. It engenders a sense of creative confidence that is both resilient and highly optimistic. Tim Brown, the chief executive and president of global design consultancy IDEO, describes the design thinking process as an approach that uses the designer's sensibility and methods for problem solving to meet people's needs in a technologically feasible and commercially viable way. In other words, design thinking is human-centred innovation.[2] As you become a design thinker, you jubilantly reframe how you see the world. Problems become opportunities, failure becomes simply a means to learn and intuition becomes a beautiful accompaniment to analysis.

Design thinking starts with divergence—the deliberate attempt to expand the range of options rather than narrow them down. Two fundamental kinds of thinking coexist and often collide in our world: analytical thinking and creative thinking. Achieving a balance between them is critical. Design thinking focuses on asking the right questions, challenging assumptions, generating a range of possibilities and learning through targeted stages of iterative prototyping. Using ethnographic tools and contextual inquiry, design thinkers learn how to uncover real needs and empathic insights that lead to transformative and innovative solutions to complex problems. These problems might range

> **"Design thinking focuses on asking the right questions, challenging assumptions, generating a range of possibilities and learning through targeted stages of iterative prototyping."**

> **"As you become a design thinker, you jubilantly reframe how you see the world. Problems become opportunities, failure becomes simply a means to learn and intuition becomes a beautiful accompaniment to analysis."**

from how to create access to clean water, how to re-envision children's education, how to create effective work/life balances, how to make the world a kinder place or how to motivate people to exercise regularly. In sum, the design thinking process provides a scaffold that can be used to solve complex problems in robust, creative and holistic ways. David Kelley, founder of IDEO and Stanford University's Hasso Plattner Institute of Design (the *d.school*) sums up his mission thus:

> My contribution is to teach as many people as I can to use both sides of their brain, so that for every problem, every decision in their lives, they consider creative as well as analytical solutions.[3]

the design thinking process

There is general agreement that design thinking comprises both a process and a series of underlying mindsets, but there are different opinions on this process and the precise number of stages it involves. Dubberly[4] describes an extensive collection of ways that design thinking may be conceptualized. IDEO envisages the design thinking process as inspiration, ideation and implementation. At Stanford University's Hasso Plattner

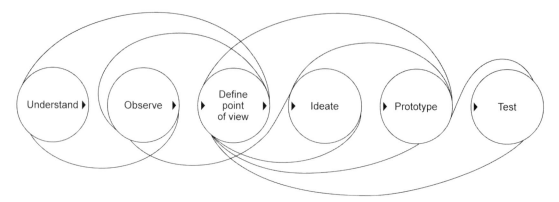

Figure 2.1 Diagram of stages in the design thinking process. (Hasso Plattner Institute of Design, Stanford University)

Institute of Design, design thinking is described as a six-step process: understand, observe, define point of view, ideate, prototype and test.[5] It is represented in Figure 2.1 and is examined under the following subheadings.

Understand

Understanding is the first stage of design thinking. Time is spent gathering data through multiple sources, such as talking to experts and conducting research. The goal is to develop a meaningful framework of background knowledge about the problem you want to solve.

Observe

The goal during the observation stage is to generate deep insights in your framework of understanding. You might, for example, uncover deep insights to the needs and wants of consumers or users by observing and interviewing. In order to do so, it is important to get out into the world and engage with new ideas, become a keen people watcher and observe how people behave and interact in a variety of spaces and places.

Define point of view

In this stage the emphasis is on synthesis. One way to achieve clearer definition is to create a point-of-view statement. This seeks to consolidate and shape the 'problem space' that was formed in the earlier stages. For example it might capture vital user needs or novel insights to usability issues from observing people. Try filling in the following template to construct your own point-of-view statement (you will need to relate it to a particular design problem you have observed).

       _____ (Your user) needs a way to _____ (a verb) because he/she _____ (your insights).

The point-of-view statement is used as a springboard for ideation, the next stage of the design thinking process.

Ideate

Ideating is a critical component of design thinking. The goal of ideation is to generate a large number of alternative proposals and ideas without considering what is feasible or practical. No idea is too far-fetched and no one's ideas are rejected. At this stage it's vital to suspend judgement. Brainstorming is one technique that can be particularly effective in ideation. It is a technique that originated from the work of Alex Osborn.[6] Here are eight guidelines for framing a successful team ideation session.

Rules of Brainstorming

1. Defer judgement
2. Go for quality
3. Have one conversation at a time
4. Encourage wild ideas
5. Build on the ideas of others
6. Be visual
7. Stay on topic
8. Headline

Prototype

A prototype can be a sketch, a construction, a digital model—it can even be as simple as a cardboard box. It is a means of envisaging an idea, a way of giving an idea a tangible form. This has benefits for the creator, who can assess and develop his or her idea, and it allows an idea to be communicated to others, which is essential. Prototyping can be a rough and rapid activity in the design thinking process, or it might be more precise—particularly if it takes place later in the development process when the time and cost can be justified.

Test

Testing is part of the iterative process that provides feedback. The purpose of testing is to learn what works and what doesn't. Testing might take place very early in a design task, perhaps to explore the problem space defined earlier. It can also take place much later, perhaps to evaluate a

---

Models and Modelling

Designing is an iterative process where both the problem and the ideas for resolving the problem frequently evolve together. Such a process depends on the integration of some mental capacities and some physical tools that collectively can be referred to as *modelling*.

The term *model* encompasses a wide range of applications. You may be most familiar with its use to describe, for example, a new car (the most recent model) or as a name for those men and women who display the latest fashion creations (fashion models). In design activity, the term model can refer to three-dimensional constructions such as an architect's scale model of a proposed building. The term can also refer to drawings and sketches—in this case, they are simply two-dimensional models.

One thing these models have in common is that they are simplifications of reality. The weather map we see nightly on television is an example of helpful simplicity. This capacity for models to simplify reality can be very helpful in designing. It can enable us to simplify problems and ideas so that we can begin to work on them and communicate our ideas. Some models have a primary function to *communicate* information, while other models are used to *explore, develop* or *test ideas*.

---

detailed design idea. Feedback leads to new understanding, which in turn leads to new development. We refer to this cycling between stages as 'iteration', and it provides an effective means of improving ideas.

improving your design thinking

Following this six-stage model effectively requires some important design thinking skills. It requires a mix of creative and analytical thinking. This section offers six key pointers for those who wish to combine design process with design thinking.

Be human-centred

Design thinking is a human-centred process. People are frequently the source of inspiration and invariably the focus for solving design challenges. Design thinkers seek to interpret complex human needs, often in novel and creative ways. Develop your ability to be human-centred.

Be mindful of process

This is the ability to know where you are in the design process. Some writers refer to this as a metacognitive awareness or 'knowing what you know'.[7] When you are mindful of the process, you are able to make informed decisions about where you need to be in the process at different times.

Embrace prototyping

In a culture of prototyping, you build to think. Your prototypes not only communicate what you think, they can be used to help you create ideas themselves. This strategy can lead to highly experimental outputs. It can help build resilience to criticism and assist designers to embrace failure as a source of new learning.

Show, don't tell

Design thinking requires us to be image-oriented, frequently rejecting verbal expression in favour of graphic strategies. Expressing ideas in a nonverbal way can make ideas more compelling. It can help you see problems and opportunities that discussion may not reveal and often leads to positive and fruitful misunderstandings.

Act

In design thinking it is often better to act than to think. Do, don't plan. Move, don't sit. Try something, and if it doesn't work, try something else. This capacity is characterized by movement.

Seek radical collaboration

Working in diverse multidisciplinary teams will usually lead to greater innovations than teams that come from the same discipline. Seek out radical or diverse voices; the journey may be frustrating and painful, but the potential rewards are greater and such collaborations can lead to innovative insights and outputs.

Becoming a design thinker

So how does one become a design thinker? By being reflective and turning the process on yourself. Because it is an iterative process, becoming a design thinker needs to be an ongoing process that you continually refine. You become more skilled and fluent in your ability to apply the process to an ever-broadening range of problems. One truly becomes a design thinker when the process and the capacities listed above become a core part of your being. To be effective, such a core needs to be supported with other characteristics, and these are discussed below. They consolidate this chapter's key points on developing the skills and mindsets essential to becoming a design thinker.

characteristics of design thinkers

Design thinkers are comfortable lingering in ambiguity

In a society that is driven towards finding quick solutions, we eagerly race to solve problems, often before we have fully explored the problem space or even fully defined the problem to be solved. Yet in a world of increasing complexity, being able to define the problems worth solving can be the greatest challenge of all. A skilled design thinker knows the value of staying in the problem space for as long as it takes and is not reluctant to revisit it when needed. Just how long to remain is a judgement call that is based on assessing whether or not you have been able to gain pertinent insights to your problem.

Being comfortable with ambiguity is what truly distinguishes a design thinker. When you are willing to stay in the problem space for a long time, you become increasingly comfortable with the idea of not knowing. The unknown presents opportunities rather than limitations. One way to think about lingering in ambiguity is to consider the notion of a fermata. A fermata, shown in Figure 2.2, is an element of musical notation that indicates that a note should be sustained for longer than its note value would indicate. How long to sustain the note is at the discretion of the conductor or the musician. A skilled design thinker becomes able to judge just how long to linger in ambiguity, just as a skilled musician decides how long to sustain a note. One thing that is certain, though, is that one must stay in the problem space as long as it takes to develop strong empathic insights about your stakeholders. Only then will you be able to design meaningful and impactful solutions.

Another important element of lingering in ambiguity is the idea that we often are attempting to address questions that already have solutions embedded in them. Consider the story of the National Aeronautics and Space Administration (NASA) space pen. NASA was interested in solving the problem of how astronauts could write in space. After a significant investment, they created the space pen. The Russians, however, decided to give their astronauts something different—a pencil. The lesson from this is that it is important to stay in the problem space in order to ensure that you are asking the right questions. The question for NASA was not 'How might we create a pen that could write in space?' It was 'How might we find a way for astronauts to record written information in space?' or even 'How might we find a way to support communication between astronauts in space?' Since the initial question already contained a solution (the pen), there was a missed opportunity to design a better and more innovative solution. Instead of worrying about not knowing all the answers, focus on asking the right questions.

Figure 2.2 A fermata instructs a musician to sustain a note.

Design thinkers fail forward

Design thinking reconceptualizes failure and focuses instead on celebrating it. This is tricky to do in education and organizational cultures where celebrating failure is considered an oxymoron. Schools want students to succeed. Businesses want their workers to succeed. What does it mean to celebrate failure? It doesn't mean rejoicing in the fact that you fail; it means that you celebrate

Figure 2.3 Take risks, learn from mistakes, fail forward.
(Getty 85660547 RF)

that it is okay to fail in the pursuit of knowledge and that you use failure as a tool to get to success. If you try to do something bold and new, you are going to fail. Admit that, confront it and learn from it. This is the direct opposite of a 'whatever' mentality, where one fecklessly fails and moves on to another idea.

This ability not to be overwhelmed with not getting things right immediately is essential to the notion of 'failing forward'. When you embrace the notion of failing forward, failure becomes a powerful springboard to learning. You say to yourself, 'Yes, I failed. Failure happens. Let me think about why this happened, and move forward.' This is important because if ideas are shut down too early, or deemed failures or left unexplored, then

so is the willingness to take risks. In life, you often hear people say that they have learned the most from their failures. Perhaps little was learned during the actual failure itself, but the subsequent reflection can be very revealing and a cause for celebration that you are failing forward.

Professor of psychology Carol Dweck describes the notion of a growth mindset as a belief that your abilities can expand over time. This is the opposite of a fixed mindset, which is when you believe you were born with all the intelligence and abilities you will ever have. In an article in the *New York Times* in 2008 she is quoted as saying:

> Society is obsessed with the idea of talent and genius and people who are 'naturals'

with innate ability…people who believe in the power of talent tend not to fulfil their potential because they're so concerned with looking smart and not making mistakes. But people who believe that talent can be developed are the ones who really push, stretch, confront their own mistakes and learn from them.[8]

Failing forward is an essential element of having a growth mindset. Educational psychologist Guy Claxton describes the importance of resiliency and the ability to think with a mix of creativity and clarity. He describes how powerful learners exploit experimentation and have an attitude that is characterized by seeing what happens, making adjustments and continually modifying their efforts by asking 'what if?'[9] Similarly, leading author Betty Edwards[10] describes how one's self-perception as a creative and artistic person is an important element of creativity and confidence and how being willing to continually reframe and rethink is critical to learning. Having a growth mindset is essential to being a design thinker. If you believe that you have innate capabilities that are fixed, you are probably unwilling to take the risks that will enable you to learn and to grow. You limit what you will try and what you might achieve. When you have a growth mindset, you are confident in your ability to learn new things, and you are willing to embrace challenges without fear. You know that if you are not successful, it is not a reflection of your lack of abilities. It is, instead, an opportunity to learn. You can't wait to try new things. You look at the world with wonder and see it as a joyful place. When you have a growth mindset, it opens up new avenues for you to think creatively and reflects a belief that you have the power to try and try again to change your world. Design thinkers are not afraid to work

hard. They see that making a change in the world is not a function of their own capabilities but rather a function of how hard they are willing to work to make that change happen.

There is an interesting connection between being innovative and having a growth mindset. If you are less willing to take risks because you believe that if you fail it will reflect poorly on people's perception of your abilities, you are not going to be willing to be an innovator. Being comfortable admitting that you make mistakes is essential, and it is important not to hide what you perceive as deficiencies. In a poll of 143 creativity researchers, the ability to learn from experience was cited as the most important ingredient for creative achievement.[11] Being an innovator and a design thinker means you don't want to pass up the opportunity to learn and grow, two essential elements of failing forward.

Design thinkers challenge assumptions

Seeing with fresh eyes is an essential part of being a design thinker. Don't assume that things must be done a certain way. Instead, dig deeper and try to challenge what you assume to be true. Observe people as they go about their daily life activities. It is important to seek out extreme users, so try to look for people who seem to be doing the unexpected. Looking at the world with an eye towards challenging assumptions is very similar to the way an ethnographer works. You come to a study with a very broad notion of what you are studying, but you do not have specific questions or answers early in the process. You want to stay in the moment of heightened observation. Your fresh eyes give you the ability to open new possibilities. The goal of ethnography, and design thinking, is to generate deep insights that lead to more informed questions, more critical reflection,

Figure 2.4 A design thinker scrutinizes the world and might see it differently each day. (Getty 91805950 RF)

and solutions that pay close attention to people engaged in real-world contexts. This happens when you challenge your assumptions.

Cirque de Soleil challenged assumptions about what a circus can be by creating an experience that borrowed from the world of theatre, opera and music and significantly expanded their audience. iTunes challenged our assumptions about whether it was necessary to buy an entire CD when purchasing music. When you challenge your assumptions, you discover untapped opportunities and spaces for creativity and innovation.

Design thinkers view the world with empathy

The most striking 'aha' moments in design thinking happen when you realize that you have created something meaningful for someone else. You realize it's not about 'me'. As author Daniel Pink suggests, developing this capacity is preparing

you for a future world that makes new demands on designers:

> The future belongs to a very different kind of person with a very different kind of mind. The era of 'left brain' dominance, and the Information Age that it engendered, is giving way to a new world in which right-brain qualities—inventiveness, empathy, meaning predominate.[12]

How do you become more empathic? You can begin by understanding what empathy isn't. Empathy isn't feeling sorry for someone, a sense that you have had a similar feeling or simply being compassionate. Instead, empathy requires looking closely and letting the words of another wash through you without barriers. It requires being still enough to sense motion and sensing connections that often don't require words. It is about finding patterns with no apparent rhyme, being able to ask questions about what you think you see and being a caring discerner of what isn't being said and what story isn't being told. Being empathic is essential to a design thinker.

Interviewing is one of the many techniques commonly used by design thinkers. However, there is a critical distinction between being a good interviewer and an empathic interviewer. Being an empathic interviewer requires that you truly care enough to understand what the other person is expressing. Your questions must be probing and genuine. It is important not to fill in silences after you ask a question; let the other person take the time to reflect and revisit his or her responses. Empathic interviewers hear discrepancies and ask for elaboration. They understand that the stories people tell might not always be truthful or accurate, but they are always meaningful because they reveal how people view and interpret the world. They are aware of the subtleties in a person's body language and facial expression, because they know there are stories that are not told in words. In 2009, *Metropolis* magazine published a list of ten ways that classrooms might change in order to address the priorities of the twenty-first century. The list came from the leading design consultancy IDEO. It included:

> Be an anthropologist, not an archaeologist. An archaeologist seeks to understand the past by investigating its relics and digging for the truth of what was. An anthropologist studies people to understand their values, needs, and desires. If you want to design new solutions for the future, you have to understand what people care about and design for that. Don't dig for the answer—connect.[13]

An example of how empathy resulted in innovation occurred in 'Design for Extreme Affordability', a class that is offered at Stanford University's Hasso Plattner Institute of Design. An inexpensive incubator was on the wish list of international challenges posed to the class. Graduate student Linus Liang visited Nepal and found that while urban hospitals had standard incubators, rural women, who had their babies at home with the assistance of midwives, had no access to incubators. Instead they sometimes wrapped hot water bottles around their babies. The project team decided to try to build something that would work without electricity and which would meet the needs of rural communities. What they created was the Embrace infant warmer, a baby-sized sleeping bag with a removable heating pouch (see Plate 2). The design incorporates an innovative material to regulate a baby's temperature.

Four Types of Associative Thinking

Some argue that creative thinking is a matter of forming new associations between elements of existing knowledge. Here are four types of associative thinking:

Adaptation: This is probably the most common form of associative thinking. In this a technical principle or solution from one field is used to provide an idea for a solution in another. For example, the roll-on deodorant container was adapted from the ballpoint pen.

Transfer: This is a similar, but less direct, form of adaptation in which the technologies, manufacturing processes or materials in one field provide the stimulus for a concept design in another. An example would be the transfer of laser technology to applications ranging from navigation and surgery to welding and sound reproduction.

Combination: This is where two or more existing devices are combined to produce a new concept, which can then be embodied in different designs. For example the combination of a digital camera with a telephone stimulated new types of communication devices.

Analogy: This means drawing on similarities in ideas or designs. We can find Web cams whose shape is inspired by cartoon characters, cars that have similar characteristics to the form of insects and buildings that suggest an analogy with living systems.

From: R. Roy, *Design and Designing* (T211), The Open University, Blk 3 (2010), p. 41.

The development of Embrace was an example of empathic need-finding.

Design thinkers live life in 'beta'

Design thinkers believe in the power of prototyping. Prototyping—or making physical, experiential or virtual representations of ideas—is a critical activity in a design process. Giving prototypes to potential users can be very revealing. Watch how the user interacts with it, listen to the questions asked, ask questions to gain additional information and then use the insights you have gained to refine your prototype.

Tom Wujec, a leading innovation strategist, ran a series of experiments called the Marshmallow Challenge (http://marshmallowchallenge.com), which provided an interesting example of how prototyping is used by different kinds of people. Teams were assembled and were asked to build a free-standing structure in eighteen minutes using twenty sticks of spaghetti, one yard (approximately one metre) of tape, one yard of string and one marshmallow. The instructions stated that the marshmallow needed to be on the top of the structure. The winning team would be the one with the tallest structure. What is most interesting about this task, which Wujec has conducted with over seventy groups of students, designers, architects and business people, is the difference between groups on how much time is spent planning versus how much time is spent building. The majority of teams wait until the end of their time before they place the marshmallow on top, and more often than not, the structure collapses. The youngest children, the kindergarteners, do not work like this. Instead, they build, test and repeat until they find a structure that works. They learn from early failure, and most times, they build the tallest and most interesting structures. In the Marshmallow Challenge, it turned out that kindergartners are very good at prototyping.

When you approach problems in ways like the children in the Marshmallow Challenge, the

Figure 2.5 Young children build, test and repeat until they find a structure that works. (Photo by Steve Garner)

world becomes a prototyping playground. You begin to live your life in 'beta'. For example you might prototype how you get to work, how you arrange your closet, how you plan a Saturday night party or how you will schedule a new project. You frame your activities as prototypes, and you are always looking to improve the ways you live your life. Rather than this being a state of continual dissatisfaction, it can be a positive and empowering search for improvement and learning. You become a joyful and exuberant learner. When you live life in beta, you don't always know exactly where you are going or how you will you get there, but you are confident in your belief that you will get somewhere worth going. As the author Warren Berger notes:

> Design is a way of seeing the world with an eye towards changing it. To do that, you must be able to see not just what is, but what might be. And seeing is only the beginning: designers are also makers. They sketch and build, giving form to ideas. They take that faint glimmer of possibility and make it visible and real to others.[14]

The characteristics of a design thinker are worth developing, but you need to unlock your creative confidence. Having a capacity for design thinking doesn't mean you have every answer, but that you have both a process and a strategy to find answers to complex problems. As you approach the world as a design thinker, there will always be someone who will tell you that the numbers don't add up, your idea won't work, and change is just too risky. It is important, as the Queen in Lewis Carroll's story suggested, to believe in impossible things. Only you can amplify your inner voice to find the perfect equilibrium between what is and what might be.

CHAPTER SUMMARY

- Questioning the impossible is a vital foundation of design thinking.
- Design thinking is an action approach to problem finding and problem solving. It's about doing as well as thinking. Prototyping is core to doing.
- Design thinking is a process and a mindset.
- The skills of reframing problems and creatively generating and testing ideas underpin design thinking.
- Design thinking develops creative confidence.
- Design thinking is a way of addressing user needs, technological feasibility and commercial viability.
- Design thinkers value ambiguity, embrace failure as a learning opportunity, challenge assumptions, believe in the power of empathy and prototype their ideas to test them.

chapter 3

problem finding and problem solving

tatjana leblanc

ABOUT THIS CHAPTER

Design means different things to different people. As a verb, I like to think of design as a *creative process of envisioning a better future in which people's needs and desires are addressed.* In order to envision better products, including systems and environments, one needs to be mindful of the existing ones and how they have evolved. We need to acknowledge their positive characteristics and address the weaker ones. It is important to look not only at making a product desirable, but also to examine how people choose a product, how they interact with a product, how they experience it, how it impacts their life, how it withstands time and, importantly, how it is disposed of. The knowledge gained helps not only pinpoint genuine needs, it allows designers to establish design criteria that guide them through the creative process. Studying the user context, observing and asking the right questions are all fundamental to design, and they condition the success of a designed output. So, how do you ask the right questions? How do you identify problems and select the right tools to solve them?

This chapter addresses these questions and introduces various techniques for problem finding and problem solving. The reader will also gain a better understanding of how to move from an information-gathering mode into an idea-generation mode and how user-centred approaches impact the design outcome.

---

understanding the design mandate

While many people frequently spot opportunities for design activity, design students and design professionals alike often wait for an instruction or mandate before beginning. The mandate is partly an authorization to begin work, but it is also a written outline of what the person paying for the service expects. The mandate is often accompanied by other documents such as a design brief, and it is well worth spending time to understand these.

There can be a variety of reasons why mandates are issued. A manufacturing company may want to add a new product to its existing range, or it may feel the need to rejuvenate its brand by modernizing and updating features. Other companies are more ambitious, perhaps wanting to stay ahead of the competition, to introduce product innovation, promote their know-how or open up new market niches. Many in the mobile communication sector illustrate this ambition. Their design outputs have included the Blackberry, applications for the iPhone, text messaging and Twitter. Of course, some companies pursue a goal of creating needs and encouraging consumption rather than responding to existing market needs and wants.

Designers today need to combine an understanding of what motivates a design project with an understanding of the context in which a problem occurs. Understanding the needs and wants of the end users is critical, and the success of a design is increasingly measured by the degree of satisfaction of the user. The very first task any designer should tackle, once he or she has received the mandate instruction, is to dissect the initial design brief, interpret it and rewrite it. Some can be highly detailed with a number of technical and economic constraints, marketing-driven specifications, norms and standards, performance requirements, components layout, accreditation requirements, manufacturing capacity, price range of the new product and so on. Such assignments can appear overwhelmingly constraining. Therefore, a designer needs to learn to filter the information—to structure and prioritize. When faced with a detailed design brief, take care not to fall into the trap of neglecting the information-gathering phase that is fundamental to finding the right problem and making the *fuzzy front end* of a project clearer. If the design task is more exploratory in nature, one that inspires more innovative alternatives, the scope and design criteria might only be established later in the process, once

> "Designers today need to combine an understanding of what motivates a design project with an understanding of the context in which a problem occurs."

problems or needs have been defined and new design opportunities identified.

Many people still see design as a purely form-giving activity. In fact, some of the people involved in producing a design brief are not necessarily familiar with the creative process. Where this is the case it is advisable to carefully study the design mandate, gather facts and additional information independently and reformulate the design brief by including a report on the task from your own perspective. This will not only substantiate a designer's understanding of the task and the challenges, it also explains how a designer intends to approach the task. This can provide invaluable material for discussion and communication with clients that might prevent wasted time later down the line. Thus, the designer needs to assume the role of 'expert' in the process of design, even though many other specialists will need to be involved in the resolution of the design problem.

It's possible to summarize in ten steps the process of interpreting a design mandate.

TEN STEPS IN INTERPRETING A DESIGN MANDATE

1. Scrutinize the design brief you've been given. Break it apart, for example into overall demand, scope, expectations, limitations and time frame. Question the limitations and constraints.
2. Organize and prioritize information. Exclude what isn't pertinent to the design process.
3. List questions. For example are necessary resources available, is there access to experts or information?

4. Gather preliminary information. Consider gathering data independently, for example by testing products and talking to users or sales people about likes or dislikes or by observing users interacting with a product.

5. Document and summarize preliminary findings, problems observed and new questions.

6. Determine the best approach to finding answers to your questions. This might include further observation, interviewing users and other stakeholders, analysing and comparing existing solutions and consulting experts.

7. Reformulate the design brief in your own words. It should include a problem statement, design intent, desired outcome and constraints.

8. Discuss the design intent with the primary decision makers.

9. Clarify expectations, limitations and creative latitude.

10. Establish the scope, time frame, critical milestones and deliverables.

design process

A design process is a nonlinear sequence of phases during which different activities are performed. The design methods often depend on the nature of the mandate, and a certain level of flexibility is vital. One of the leading design thinkers of our time, John Christopher Jones, noted 'Methodology should not be a fixed track to a fixed destination, but a conversation about everything that could be made to happen.'[1]

Such a conversation may bring different modes of actions into play:

The mode of thought

This mode involves *critical thinking* while analysing the subject matter and *divergent thinking* while synthesizing or elaborating new ideas. This mode exploits creative thinking techniques such as concept mapping, categorization and brainstorming.

The mode of expression

In this mode designers engage in representing and communicating thoughts and ideas using various media such as sketches, scenarios, physical or virtual models and mock-ups, prototypes, virtual images and simulation.

The mode of implementation

This is the mode of physical embodiment of concepts into artefacts. Table 3.1 outlines the typical phases and activities a creative process involves, plus some of the techniques and tools that might be employed. However, one needs to keep in mind that each project is different, and a design approach needs to be tailored to the specific context.

Some projects may require in-depth user studies. In this case specific design research methods such as ethnographic studies or participatory studies which involve end users or other stakeholders should be considered.[2] Typically, such studies are conducted independently by experts or experienced designers and precede a design project. The outcome can be very unpredictable. Nevertheless, more and more design consultancies specialize in this type of design research, especially those that have adopted human-centred

Table 3.1   PHASES OF A TYPICAL DESIGN PROJECT

Phases	Activities	Techniques and tools
Information gathering	familiarization with context gathering information who, when, where, why, how? analyzing information identifying problems and needs	observation surveys, interviews product value analysis user value analysis
Problem definition	stating the problem(s) prioritizing design objectives defining the scope, design criteria	concept mapping and mind mapping product categorization design brief
Concept development	ideation visualizing ideas selecting promising ideas developing ideas into concepts	group ideation and brainstorming individual idea search sketches, mock-ups, user scenarios drawings with detail preliminary 3D modelling
Design development	elaborating a coherent concept elaborating principles of use validating volume and proportions defining materials and processes revision, refinement and detailing defining design details	drawings, virtual models, 3D modelling drawings of interface, functions, parts drawings of working principle, parts shop drawings design models, prototypes design refinement and revised drawings
Design evaluation	evaluating the design solution testing the design solution	feedback from users (focus group) input from experts
Transition into research and development	refining and revising the design generating dimension drawings and 3D files	

approaches. Such studies can generate detailed data about people's perceptions, attitudes and behaviour, but skill is needed to interpret the data if it is to make a useful contribution to clarify the task, rectify presumptions or reorient design efforts.

design problems

Before a problem can be solved, it needs to be identified and articulated. However, the problem stated might not be the one that needs fixing. Metaphorically speaking, a doctor will not necessarily treat a patient's immediate problem (a symptom such as fever). Instead he or she would want to find out the initial causes (perhaps an infection or virus). In design, the initially stated problem might only be a symptom and not the actual root of the problem. The success of the design process will depend on a designer's ability to recognize and address the real problems and needs.

> **"The problem stated might not be the one that needs fixing"**

Constructive Discontent

One of the noticeable characteristics of professional designers in a variety of fields is their inquisitiveness and frequent
dissatisfaction with the way things are. They are always exploring things, testing them out, seeing how things work and
looking for new opportunities.

Most designers possess an attitude of discontent towards existing products or systems and they deliberately
cultivate this. Constructive discontent means having a critical attitude of looking at our built and manufactured world
to spot weaknesses in designs. But it also means being
motivated and able to find ways of improving what exists.

Constructive discontent might lead to improvements in
usability, manufacturing efficiency, sustainability, assembly,
pleasure in ownership or use, cost savings, repairability and
many other characteristics of designs.

Adapted from: N. Cross, *Design and Designing* (T211), The
Open University, Blk 2 (2010), p. 22.

What makes a problem a problem?

In general, a problem can be anything that does
not meet someone's expectation; a condition or
a situation that people disapprove of or disagree
with. In design it refers to an issue that requires
improvement or transformation, in other words,
from one state to a preferred one. Notice here that
a design problem does not have to have a negative connotation. In design, a need, a purpose or a
goal that designers pursue creatively can also be
referred to as a problem.

There are a number of ways of looking at a
problem, and every discipline will have its own
preferred emphasis. Some involved in design engage with the technical characteristics and product performance, while others may be concerned
with costs and benefits. Ideally, designers should
take all perspectives into account and seek other
disciplines' expertise throughout the design
and decision-making process. It is important to

underline the direct relationship between a problem statement and the solutions proposed. The
pertinence of a solution will depend on a person's
ability to target the right problems and ask the
right questions. Therefore, the goal of the processes of inquiry is to identify the right problems
and to view them as design opportunities.

Stating a problem

Successfully formulating a design problem is vital
to successfully resolving it. Thus, successful designing depends on how we frame our design
problems. The approaches for designing (creating
a completely new artefact, feature or service) or
redesigning (improving an existing one) may not
necessarily be the same, but they both rely on a
foundation of good problem formulation. For example if a design task is phrased as 'Design a new
chair', it seems to elicit an *object-focused design
approach:* how it is made, how it can be improved,
optimization of parts. Such an approach is likely
to produce different shapes, perhaps improved
details, a new feature or an eco-friendly solution.
However, if the problem is stated as 'How to accommodate people's need for sitting?' designers
tend to opt for a more *human-centred design approach.* In other words, it sets off a whole different
set of questions: What do we understand by sitting? In what circumstances is sitting required?
How long, how comfortable? What defines comfort? What might someone do while sitting? Who
are we talking about? How has this need been
addressed before? How has the object evolved?
Why? One can expect the outcome to be different
using such a human-centred approach, because
ideas are likely to emerge while seeking answers
to these questions. The latter is more likely to give
rise to creative idea generation. For example people do not always use an object as intended. A
chair might be easily used as a ladder, a pedestal,

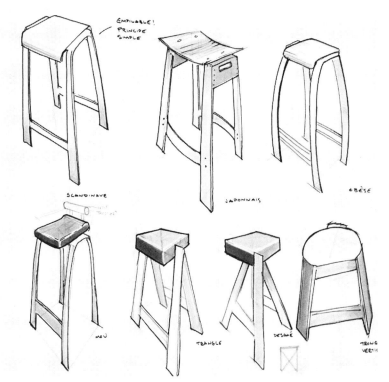

Figure 3.1 (a) Object-focused approach: how to improve a wooden stool through shape exploration. (Photo copyright Claudie Rousseau) (b) User-centred approach: stool concept derived from observing how people sit. (Photo copyright Anne-Sophie Therrien)

(a)

(b)

or a side table. The initial phrasing of the problem can be a catalyst to such creative reinterpretations or it can suppress creativity.

information gathering

This section is concerned with the questions concerning what, who, when, where, how and why. In order to expose problems, we need to collect data on the subject matter. We need to observe, question and gather all kinds of information that relates directly or indirectly to our topic. Exploring problem situations means trying to define 'real' needs. We need to know who is directly or indirectly involved or affected by a particular problem. When and where does it occur? Why is it considered a problem? It means developing skills to look at unfamiliar things, and it means looking at familiar things in new ways.[3] The best way of approaching an information-gathering task is by grouping questions in categories such as the user(s), the context of use, the experience of use

and the characteristics of the object, service or environment. This is summarized in Table 3.2 and explored in the following subsections.

Users

A common mistake designers make is taking their personal experience as the primary reference and assuming that others feel the same. Personal experiences can matter greatly, and they can play a significant role in establishing a hypothesis. Yet by observing other people, we learn how perception, attitudes and values can differ. We need to do more than think of the wide diversity of users who might come into contact with our products— we need to adopt a user-centred or user-focused design approach, one that puts the user and potential user at the core of our design thinking.[4]

The context of use

Each user context has its own set of challenges. Outdoor furniture, for instance, needs to be durable and resilient to various weather conditions or perhaps vandalism. A bench made from metal

Table 3.2   CATEGORIES OF QUESTIONS FOR GATHERING INFORMATION IN DESIGN

The user(s)	The context	The user experience	The object
Who are the:	Where and when do people use the	How people choose a product	Its purpose
Primary user(s)	object?	What are they looking for?	Its features
Secondary user(s)	How they interact with it	What matters to them?	How it works
Stakeholder(s)	Why they use it	How they interact with it	How it is made
What is/are their:	What are the different circumstances?	How it compares to other products	How it has evolved
Lifestyle	Are there alternatives?	What do they like or dislike about the	Its advantage and
Habits	Are there adaptations?	product or service?	disadvantages
Values	What is the environment like?	Does it meet their expectations?	Its value
Feelings	What is the product/ environment	What does it mean to them?	Competitive products
Perceptions	relationship?	What is memorable?	Trends
Preferences	Different user scenarios	What would they change if they could?	
Expectations			

can be quite uncomfortable on a hot summer day and uninvitingly cold during the winter season. Therefore, analysing the context of use is crucial before establishing design criteria and product specifications, because this knowledge will influence decisions such as the use of certain materials, weight, height or shape.

The user experience

User-focused designing demands techniques that help designers evaluate how people interact with a product, how they experience a product, what are the steps involved and what in the process can be improved. Using scenarios can be a very useful way to get to know the potential market for a new design.[5] Creating a scenario of use involves observing how people interact and experience a particular product. You need to document the process step-by-step, and to do this you might want to use video, photos or sketches as well as written notes. Data gathering is followed by analysing and commenting on each step. Annotation is particularly useful for noting observations such as feelings, actions, movements and so on. Creating a user scenario obliges a designer to be very attentive and analytical. Experience prototyping or re-enacting the process of interaction with the product fosters critical thinking.[6] It helps focus on the actions of the primary user, plus it provides insight into influential factors such as secondary users, ambiance, distracting elements and sequence of interactions. Figure 3.2 shows a scenario revealing the stages of preparing a hot chocolate drink. Although the steps are simplified, the scenario illustrates the complexity of the task. Such process representation makes it easier

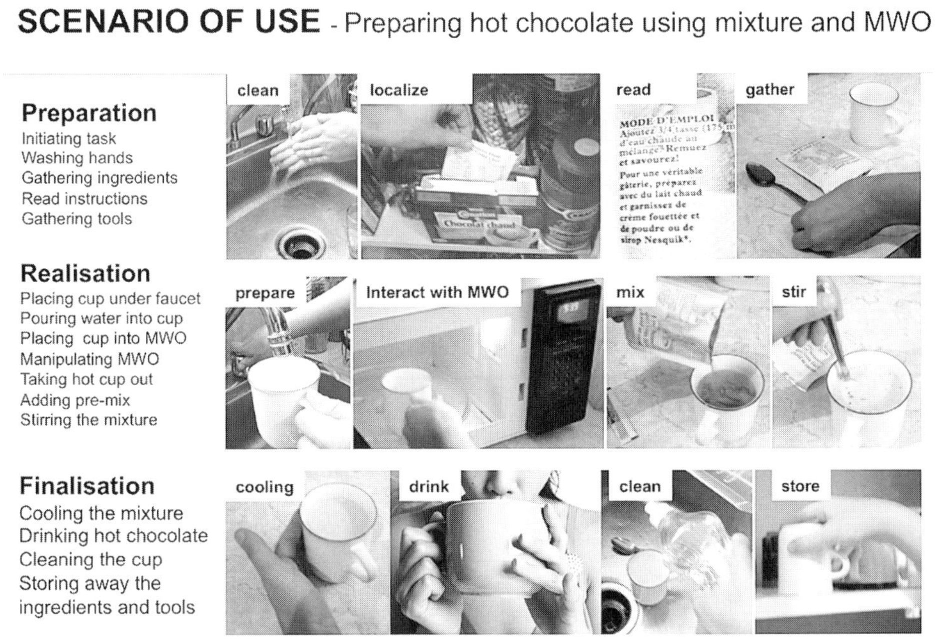

SCENARIO OF USE - Preparing hot chocolate using mixture and MWO

Preparation
Initiating task
Washing hands
Gathering ingredients
Read instructions
Gathering tools

clean · localize · read · gather

Realisation
Placing cup under faucet
Pouring water into cup
Placing cup into MWO
Manipulating MWO
Taking hot cup out
Adding pre-mix
Stirring the mixture

prepare · Interact with MWO · mix · stir

Finalisation
Cooling the mixture
Drinking hot chocolate
Cleaning the cup
Storing away the ingredients and tools

cooling · drink · clean · store

Figure 3.2. Simplified user scenario for preparing hot chocolate. (Copyright author)

to isolate certain challenges that a person might encounter. Other scenarios might look at interactions with a specific product interface.

User scenarios help the design team to investigate each aspect of a process. As well as supporting the process of identifying problems, scenarios can assist ideation by revealing how to make interactions intuitive and more pleasant and meaningful.

The object

Not only do people expect an object to serve its designated purpose, they understand that it reflects certain values. When choosing a product, people consciously or unconsciously manifest their life principles and standards. In fact, our decisions to buy products are frequently based on meaning rather than function. Some prefer one brand to another because it represents values they can relate to (eco-friendly, durable, efficient), or because it has a reputation for well-engineered and well-designed products, such as some German cars. Of course, others may favour a product because it simply fits their budget, without putting more thought into it.[7] In general, analysing objects involves looking at some important characteristics:

> *Physical characteristics:* these might include the components that constitute the object (screen, keyboard, on/off button, etc.) and how it is configured (that is, the relationship between its components) and its physical description (slim, light, efficient, etc.).
> *Technical characteristics:* the way a product functions, its actions or the way it is made.
> *Communicative characteristics:* the object's semantic quality—that is, what it expresses or denotes to the user (e.g. utility) and what it evokes and connotes (image, origin, value, symbolism, etc.).

Comparing objects and their features and examining the way they have evolved can be informative and inspiring. We may learn how technological progress has changed a product category or how the needs have been addressed before. Designers often (re)discover significant notions that have been forgotten over time or learn the origins of others that have persisted. Chairs, for instance, derive from thrones, and some symbols of the power of a chair are still incorporated

---

Technology Push and Market Pull

Many new product designs are rooted in innovations in new technologies such as biotechnologies, communication technologies or material technologies. In contrast, many examples of new designs owe their success to a recognition of what people want or need—whether that be safer vehicles, social networking or recyclable packaging. There are, therefore, two strong drivers to new product development—the push that comes from new technologies and the pull of market needs and wants.

These two aspects are usually called *technology push* and *market pull.* Technology itself, of course, does not do any market pushing—that comes from the developers and suppliers of the new technology and from the makers of the new products. In practice, a lot of new product development is influenced by a combination of both technology push and market pull.

Many companies aware of market pull use market research to identify customers' wants and needs. Where technology push dominates, applications of new technology can create new demands among consumers and open up new markets. Market research usually cannot identify demands for products that do not yet exist.

From: N. Cross, *Design and Designing* (T211), The Open University, Blk 2 (2010), p. 15.

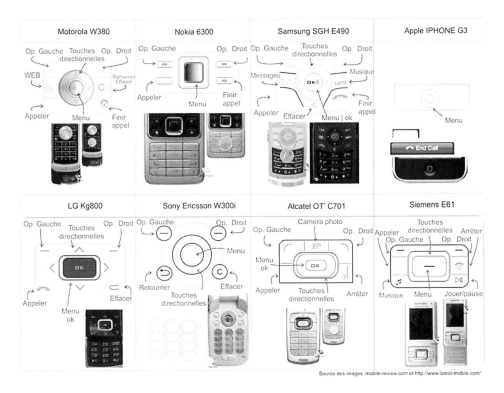

Figure 3.3 Product and interface comparisons using image boards. (Copyright author)

today. For example consider the hierarchy of office chairs from the humble stool to the largest executive chair. A wide range of products lend themselves to visual documentation of design evolution (see Plate 3).

Product analysis is often best represented on image boards or posters. These can help designers and other participants visualize and compare existing products and their features (Figure 3.3).

techniques and tips for creative researching

Information relevant to design can be gathered in many ways. This section reviews some useful techniques, but try to adopt a strategy that seeks to employ multiple ways of gathering information. First consider this checklist:

- Test products, services or environments yourself. Imagine yourself in the shoes of the potential users or stakeholders.
- Examine how products are presented to their respective markets and how this compares to competitor designs.
- Observe how different people choose and use these designs.
- Question users and stakeholders, perhaps using interviews or questionnaires, about why they chose a product and not others, how they use it and why.

- Consider visiting shops or other points of sale. Talk to sales staff.
- Review scientific literature and consumer reports. Search the Internet for testimonials.
- Manufacturers can provide a range of information. A visit to a factory can be informative and inspiring.

Surveys

Exploring problems will bring you into contact with users, experts, manufacturers and many others. Surveys of these key stakeholders can be quite an efficient way to collect information, opinions or feedback. Many of the who-why-where-when-how questions can be asked either face-to-face in an informal conversation or in a more formal or semi-structured way such as a consultation or interview. For a larger sample consider the use of paper questionnaires, online questionnaires, texting or phone interviews. Questionnaires can allow people to respond anonymously, which is especially useful when questions might touch on personal issues. Design increasingly uses social networking tools such as Facebook to gain broader access to information rapidly. Overall, a questionnaire should convey neutrality. It should leave room for respondents to explain certain aspects in their own words.

Designing good design research is vital, and you need to balance expert input and user input. Surveys with questions that are poorly phrased don't elicit the necessary feedback. Always take time to prepare your questions. Test them in pilot trials and rewrite them if necessary. Keep in mind that some respondents will tend to overanalyse things, others may try to hide things, particularly any perceived failings on their part, and some people will try to give you what they think to be the right answers—that is, how a situation should be, not how it actually is. Any of these can skew your research findings. A question can set a tone or be perceived as judgemental. Aim to achieve questioning that is neutral and provides people with options. Not all questions can be answered with a yes or no. Sometime an answer might depend on certain circumstances. Therefore, some topics may need to be introduced gradually, and others may require multiple choices to express nuances.

Interviews

Interviews or consultations can be conducted in a formal and structured way or in a semistructured conversational form. They offer some useful advantages over a questionnaire; for example they facilitate follow-up questions and the interviewer can encourage the interviewee to elaborate. It is not easy to formulate verbal questions without insinuating, hinting, implying or suggesting. As with written surveys, errors are common and they can dramatically influence the findings. Depending on the context, there can be more than one stakeholder so designers often have to spread their investigative efforts. When questioning a cleaning crew, we might learn about challenges such as cleaning around chairs, moving them and materials that are easier to clean and disinfect. Asking the right questions can be as much of an art as analysing the answers.

Observations

Not all questions can be answered through surveys or interviews. Researchers frequently find inconsistencies between what people say and what they actually do. Observations are therefore used as a complementary investigative method. Observations can be written in a logbook, sketched, photographed, recorded or filmed. One design student for instance had spent an afternoon in a park observing how young people interacted with each other, individually, as couples, in groups, what they sat on, how they sat, how long, how they interacted with the outdoor furniture (picnic tables, benches, playground furniture, stairs) and observed what they seemed to be drawn to. These observations were recorded in a sketchbook for later analysis (Figure 3.4).

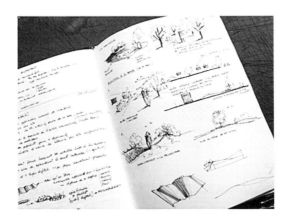

Figure 3.4 Example sketchbook documenting observations, thoughts and ideas. (Copyright author)

In other circumstances, snapshots can be worth a thousand words. Photos can capture a problem without exaggeration or bias. They can be shared, analysed, used for comparison, even inspire. In general, observations captured through sketches or photos help answer the who, what, where and how questions, and surveys, interviews and focus groups provide insights into why something is done or perceived a certain way.

Observations are a tremendously rich source for ideas and inspiration. Figure 3.5 illustrates some typical uses of furniture in a cafe. One person uses a stool to lean her bag against or place a glass of wine on, another person uses a chair as a step, and other people sit on their stools in different ways, one holding his jacket. Each observed situation points towards a design opportunity: the need to support something, to view something, to suspend something, to be stable. These snapshots trigger ideas which can then be externalized so they can be assessed against the perceived problems. In this way research leads to innovative ideas and innovative ideas can be measured against real problems.

Figure 3.5 Observing when, where and how people use café chairs. (Copyright author)

Concept mapping

Concept mapping is a technique developed to visually represent, organize and share someone's understanding, vision or interpretation of something. The term *concept* is generally understood as designating a thing, a notion, an idea or a problem. Figure 3.6 illustrates the technique of *concept mapping.*[8]

Designers use concept mapping for various purposes: to collect preliminary thoughts and

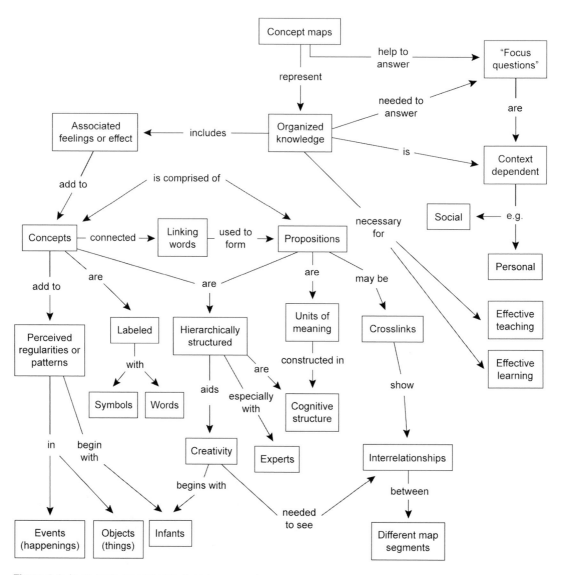

Figure 3.6 An example concept map. Based on example from IHMC *CmapTools* at http://cmap.ihmc.us/Publications/ ResearchPapers/TheoryCmaps/Fig1CmapAboutCmaps-large.png (accessed 30 April 2011).

illustrate the initial understanding of a problem, to organize and plan design activities (what to observe, ask, test, compare), to sort gathered information such as facts, feelings, observations and assumptions and to help create ideas. Designers start by producing several simple diagrams which serve as a basis for discussion, planning and ideation. To this initial structure, designers keep adding information in the form of facts, photos, sketches and articles. Concept maps can be produced individually or through group effort during brainstorming sessions. To keep the process flexible, some prefer using different-coloured sticky labels, index cards or pushpins. Such maps can

be quickly produced by hand, but for more elaborate maps the use of dedicated software is recommended to make reconfiguration, renaming, and colour coding easier.[9]

Categorization

Categorization is a form of classification that is useful to creative researching. Essentially it is a technique of hierarchical layering. For example a *dining chair* belongs to the category *chair,* which in turn belongs to a higher level that can be called *sitting furniture.* This in turn is part of the overall category of *furniture.* This is illustrated in Figure 3.7. The structure uses segmentation based

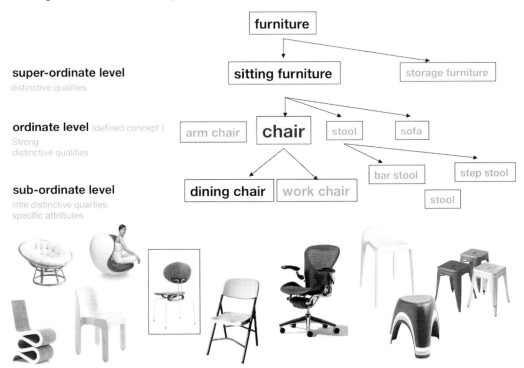

Figure 3.7 (a) Example of chair attribute categorization. (Copyright author)

HOW TO SIT
functional characteristics in a context of use

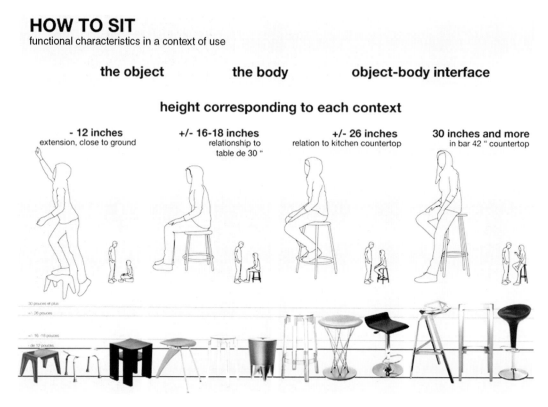

the object   **the body**   **object-body interface**

height corresponding to each context

- 12 inches	+/- 16-18 inches	+/- 26 inches	30 inches and more
extension, close to ground	relationship to table de 30 "	relation to kitchen countertop	in bar 42 " countertop

Figure 3.7 (b) Classification by height/user context. (Photo copyright Claudie Rousseau)

on distinctive attributes.[10] This technique is ideal for cataloguing products, features, experiences or problems and analysing their commonality or distinctiveness.

Study mock-ups

Reduced-scale study mock-ups are an intrinsic part of the creative process. They help explore and evaluate ideas three-dimensionally, encouraging designers to commit to proportions, dimensions and shape. They are used to first visualize the initial design intent, explore alternatives and ultimately define or modify ideas. Reduced-scale mock-ups are quickly made using paper, cardboard, foam core, or any modelling materials that serve the purpose of roughly reproducing the intended shape. Full-size study mock-ups (Figure 3.8) help validate ergonomic, functional and aesthetic aspects, evaluate feasibility and compare an evolved concept with established design criteria. They too can be made from all kind of materials—cardboard, foam core, soft foam, wood, etc. Designers use them to validate various details of a concept in a tangible way, to test and reassess critical dimensions and to take corrective measures. Study mock-ups are critical decision-making tools that help correct unforeseen problems before reproducing the design intent using three-dimensional modelling software.

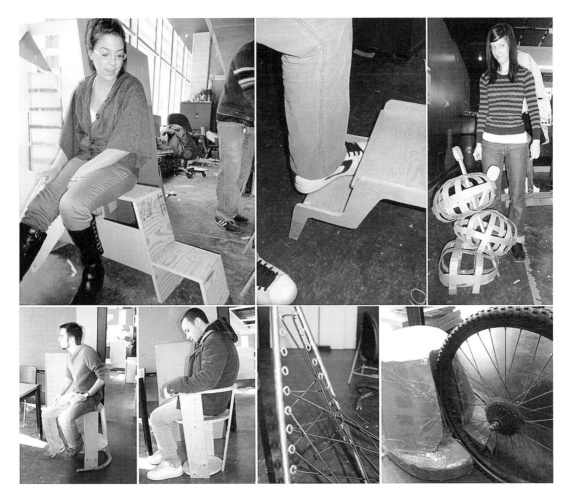

Figure 3.8 Students demonstrating full-size study mock-ups in a studio class. (Copyright author)

combining techniques

The following example is just one illustration of the combining of tools and techniques for the co-evolution of problem finding and problem solving. It is part of the work generated by the student Anne Laliberté-Guitard during her 2009 studio class. Plate 4 reveals how she explored stacking sitting furniture. This idea was inspired by balls of wool and the way they are held together. Figure 3.9 uses photographic analysis of objects that

similarly possessed an intertwined, linear quality. Such images are also used to demonstrate design intent, functionality or desired qualities. These observations were transformed into a proposal for a novel item of furniture that captured the linear characteristics of the source and yet functioned as a device to support a person sitting or lying down. Figure 3.10 depicts various ways of using this item of furniture.

Such doodles—that is, sketches produced by hand or computer software—assist designers

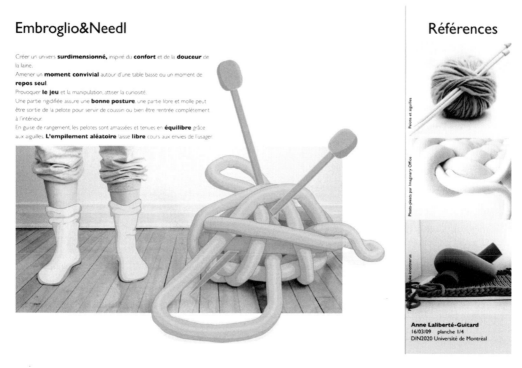

Figure 3.9 A design proposal with source material shown on right. (Photos copyright Anne Laliberté-Guitard)

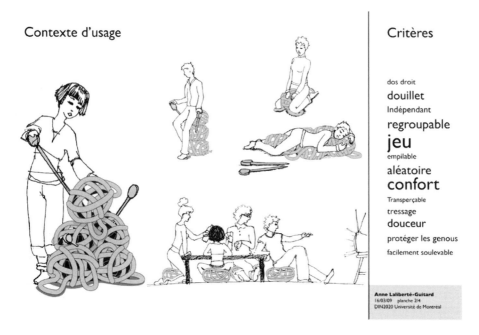

Figure 3.10 Usability explained visually. (Photos copyright Anne Laliberté-Guitard)

in understanding the visual world. They help them to visualize thoughts and ideas and to explore variations. These can serve to support discussions with others, allowing them to react and contribute to the maturing of an idea; or they can be part of a personal, inner dialogue. Later in the process designers develop their ideas by producing more refined and elaborate representations, which might exploit various media.

CHAPTER SUMMARY

- Analyse the design mandate you're given. Clarify expectations and question assumptions.
- Reformulate the design brief to explore the scope and latitude you have within the time frame.
- Designing is not merely the creation of beautiful things. Designing is a dual process of problem finding and problem solving.
- There are many ways of approaching this dual process, and there are a variety of useful tools available to designers. If mastered, these tools and techniques can become a fundamental resource for insight and inspiration.
- Combine techniques to create powerful design approaches.
- Don't lose sight of the problem you are trying to solve, and take care with any shortcuts in the process of solving them.
- Designing requires a thorough understanding of the people and the context for which we are designing.
- Strive to adopt a user-centred approach in all your designing.

chapter 4

---

designing design

alison mckay

ABOUT THIS CHAPTER

Many people outside of the design professions engage in the process of designing, but an education or training in design hones some very particular and important skills and knowledge. This chapter describes these skills and areas of knowledge to help you develop as a designer.

　　If one observes expert designers in action, from a variety of specialist design disciplines, it can be seen that their design processes are partly about successfully understanding the need in a given situation and partly about the creation of an output that addresses this need. This is very different to the activities of people who try to find problems to which they already have potential solutions; designers typically act as if they care more about responding to needs than applying solutions. This dual process of understanding needs and responding through the creation of designs has been called 'design thinking' because at the root of both is skilful thinking. This chapter is a journey into design thinking. It aims to help you be a better design thinker and to apply design thinking in your own work. Perhaps most ambitiously it seeks to help you move from being a consumer of other people's design methods and processes to being a composer and creator of your own approaches to design—that is, designing design. Designing today exploits a variety of computer-based tools and digital processes, and this chapter concludes by reflecting on the need to combine design thinking skills with new technologies to enhance both your illumination of needs and your creative responding.

---

problems and solutions

All design programmes, and particularly those at undergraduate level, agonize over what to include and what not to include in their curricula. Clearly there will be significant differences between different disciplines; for example, a jewellery course must introduce different concepts, practices and vocabularies than, say, a course in textiles design or architecture. Similarly, a Web designer may need to learn about the computational constructs used to realize Web sites, whereas a product designer is more likely to need to know about manufacturing processes and materials. But even within the same discipline there are significant differences between courses. Some seek to develop strong vocational skills and knowledge such as communication, interdisciplinary working and business practices. Other courses try to foster personal and transferable creative skills. There's just too much for any one course or individual to develop a high level of competence in everything.

In addition, different design programmes place different emphases on the balance between skills, knowledge and attitudes. However, there are some common threads between courses and across disciplines. Two of these threads are the existence of a core process for designing and the exploitation of design thinking guided by such a design process. Much of the analysis in this chapter is drawn from the work of engineers and product designers, but the stages and the thinking within these stages can be seen across a variety of design disciplines. There are three parts to this chapter:

- Understanding problems: this section explores the importance of understanding the needs of users and other stakeholders and converting this understanding into design requirements.
- A framework for creative and analytical thinking: this section examines the integration of creative and analytical thinking in the design process, including the construction of stage gates and time lines in the process.
- Computers and design thinking: this final section considers how designers might exploit digital technologies to support their designing.

understanding problems

Designs deliver value by addressing people's needs and providing solutions to problems ranging from the mundane to grand challenges such as how as a society we can live more sustainably. A first essential step in any design process is, therefore, to understand the needs and, if necessary, question and renegotiate the requirements.

So what does this mean for student designers? The first thing to remember is that good designing means solving the right problem. Understanding problems (and so needs) demands curiosity: read around the problem area, speak with people who might know something, even though you may not know quite what, and question the brief. At some point before you start designing you will need to translate your understanding of the problem into design requirements that you can use later in the process to evaluate your designs. This can be tricky, because your own understanding of the problem and the understanding by your stakeholders are likely to evolve as the project proceeds. As a designer you need to be willing to adapt to changing problem landscapes and stakeholder needs.

> **"Your own understanding of the problem and the understanding by your stakeholders are likely to evolve as the project proceeds."**

Understanding through questioning

Designers respond to *needs* but are often presented with *requirements* and *solutions,* so a first essential step in any design process is to understand the needs and, if necessary, question and renegotiate the requirements you may have been given. Ask questions: who are the people involved? Who do these people work with? How are they affected? What do they want to achieve? Who will buy the product, use it, support it, dispose of it? Why do they want it? For example if Dave will use a product but Shirley will buy it, then whose goals, if any, should take precedence? Keep asking why. And be very wary of design requirements that define (if only partially) the solution. An example of how you might do this is illustrated in Box 4.1, which is based on a real project where students were involved in the design of a surgical robot. Note the voice of the hypothetical design thinker who comments on the verbal exchange between stakeholder and designer.

You can see how the designer has to ask all the D questions, but he or she also needs to play the design thinker role. This involves interpretation, scepticism and creativity. Where you stop in this questioning process of course depends on the context. For example if you are working for a robot manufacturer, then coming up with a nonrobotic device may be regarded as inappropriate; however, it might be better to know that there is a cheaper, quicker and more effective solution before you go to the trouble and cost of designing a robot for which there is a limited market. You are also likely to find through such a questioning process that some people's needs conflict with those of others. For example a surgeon may want a robot that is of the highest quality, whereas the procurement department of the hospital may want the cheapest possible solution. Such conflicts are not always easy to resolve, some may not be resolvable at all, but as you become more experienced you will be better able to judge. As you begin on your career, however, stay curious and keep asking questions, perhaps on the basis that if the information is out there, then you, as the designer, are better off knowing sooner rather than later.

BOX 4.1. SAMPLE OF A DESIGN DIALOGUE WITH ADDED 'DESIGN THINKER' COMMENTS

S: stakeholder; D: designer; *DT: design thinker*

S: We want a robot that can carry a camera during laparoscopic (keyhole) surgery. The robot must be no bigger than twenty millimetres by twenty millimetres.

D: Why must the robot be no bigger than twenty millimetres by twenty millimetres?

S: So that it can fit through the incision.

D: So actually the robot needs to be small enough to fit through an incision of a given size...

DT: ...when it is going through the incision, which means it could be bigger at other times — some sort of folding device would then become an option. I need to understand what the story of the use of the robot will be — a day in the life of the robot.

D: Why do you want a robot?

S: So that it can move about inside the patient's abdomen.

D: Why do you want to be able to move about in the patient's body?

S: So that we can look at things from different perspectives.

D: So actually you need a device that can fit through an incision and be used to look around from different viewpoints...

DT: ...some sort of periscope might work then.

S: But that wouldn't use our newly developed technology, which is all about a robot.

DT: aaaahha...

Translate your understanding of the problem into design requirements

There are very few right or wrong answers in design—just better or worse solutions in the eyes of one or more stakeholders. As a designer you need to have some idea of how success might be recognized and, ideally, measured; this is what you capture in design requirements. Design requirements are essential because they give you a systematic way of comparing design ideas and selecting the superior ones to explore and develop. Once you have begun to understand the problem, and so the needs of different stakeholders, you can translate it into design requirements that, in turn, can be used to drive a design process and measure its success. The process of understanding a problem and translating it into requirements is iterative; it goes round in loops. Your understanding of the problem will evolve as you try to specify requirements. In turn, as your understanding evolves, you are likely to find that you need to rephrase earlier requirements. This is especially important because, even with the best will in the world, you may have misinterpreted a need—or a need may have changed by the time you have a solution, or it might have changed in response to your solution.

Needs evolve

Not only do needs evolve, but our understanding of needs is likely to develop as we progress through a design project. Designers need to stimulate this learning process. At the beginning of a design project, you're unlikely to know everything about a problem so it is important to gather information and conduct other forms of research. It can be difficult knowing where to start, but you should be more concerned about not gathering enough information than about wasting time gathering the wrong information. Avoid fixating on a specific solution or solution principle too soon. Premature fixation on specific solutions or solution principles can be a real barrier to creativity and innovation. If you have a solution in your mind, sketch it out and then move on to identify other concepts and solution principles. Examples of solution principles in the context of the surgical device introduced earlier might be that the solution must be a robot or must use a particular technology or must be

---

Renewal, Development or Innovation?

Most manufacturing companies face a dilemma in product planning: should they merely renew existing products, should they develop and improve the ones they have, or should they attempt some radical innovation? Each option has its advantages and disadvantages.

Radical product innovation occurs when new technology is developed to meet, or create, new markets. It might involve new product types or new manufacturing systems. This is almost certainly going to require expensive research and development. The acceptability to the market is unknown, but potential commercial rewards are high.

Alternatively, a company might apply an already developed technology in an undeveloped market, or it might translate new technology for an already developed market. Both of these can be described as product development. For example Sony has translated adult products into new markets for children's goods, and Apple transformed the notion of personal music through technologies for downloading, storage and playing.

Despite the perception that new design is everywhere, most product development is in the least risky category of product renewal. There is a constant need for product renewal, through both minor and major product modifications, if companies are to maintain their market positions.

From: N. Cross, *Design and Designing* (T211), The Open University, Blk 2 (2010), p. 19.

made from a particular material; if this happens, keep asking yourself why. Your users' understanding of their own needs is likely to change too, so keep engaged with the stakeholders, especially users, and don't blame them if things change.

a framework for creative and analytical thinking

Designs may be of services or physical products or they may be the means of producing them, such as a manufacturing process. It follows, then, that one can design a designing process, including the one you yourself use for designing. This section explores this idea further.

Most student designers will end up working in either their own or other people's businesses. The primary goal of commercial organizations is to deliver value to their customers and other stakeholders, so ensuring that they make a profit or at least break even. Traditionally, manufacturing companies do this by delivering physical products to their customers whilst service companies deliver value through their services. Increasingly, companies are delivering products with associated services; for example Rolls Royce sells power by the hour to airlines by leasing aircraft engines it traditionally sold and providing support services to ensure that the customer receives the power it has purchased.[1] There are other priorities too, often captured in corporate social responsibility policies; but if a business does not make a profit, then it will not have the resources needed to deliver other societal benefits.

Companies typically conduct design as part of a product development process. Examples include the Rolls Royce Derwent process for aero engines and the Full Service® process employed by ABB, an international leader in power and automation technologies. A number of authors provide idealized general-purpose definitions of the product development processes, such as Ulrich and Eppinger and Cagan and Vogel.[2]

Stage gates

Product development processes are typically stage-gated processes. Stage-gated processes have two key characteristics: *stages* where activity takes place and *gates* where decisions are made. Typical activities include research, concept development and detail design. Performance of product development processes is often measured in terms of four performance indicators: time, cost, quality and responsiveness. *Time* refers to the amount of time it takes to execute the process from start (e.g. when the brief is received) to finish (e.g. when the final design is delivered). *Cost* refers to the resources used in executing the process (e.g. money, energy, people's time). *Quality* relates to how good the result of the process is. The 'goodness' of a design varies depending on who is judging it and can be measured in a number of ways, including with respect to design requirements and/or against the product specification that results from the act of designing. Finally, *responsiveness* relates to how well the process can respond to change (e.g. if the brief changes, then a more responsive process will be able to deliver a solution that responds to the new brief more quickly than a less responsive one).

Despite the many different kinds of products and services and the business models under which they are delivered to customers, there are some commonalities. A general framework that has been used to guide student product design work at the University of Leeds is given in Figure 4.1. In this model the stage gates are

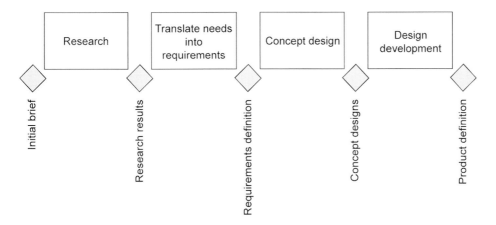

Figure 4.1 General schematic stage-gated product development process. (Copyright author)

vital—it's at these points that decisions are made, either by an individual or group (and typically not the designer) on whether to proceed, stop or go back and rework part of the project. Thus, a key requirement in any design process lies in ensuring that appropriate information is presented at stage gates to support effective decision making.

If you're practising being curious, then a question you might ask about Figure 4.1 lies in what the horizontal axis means: does the fact that, for example, *Concept design* is shown to the right of *Research* mean anything? Different people will give you different answers. From this chapter's point of view, an answer would be, 'Yes, but you might be better asking the same question about the stage gates.' The stage gates are the places where the results of activities are reported. You might think of the stage-gate process as a constraint to your designing, but actually it provides a valuable framework within which to work. It allows designers to break down the overall product development process into a series of activities, and thus it makes the process more manageable. One particular breakdown is shown in Figure 4.2.

It can be seen that the overall activity, *Develop product,* comprises four key subactivities: *Research, Translate needs into requirements, Concept design,* and *Design development.* Details of two of these activities, *Research* and *Concept design,* are then elaborated further. The dashed arrow lines represent part/whole relationships, which means an element at the head of an arrow is part of the element at the tail of that arrow. For example, *Research* is a part of overall *Develop product,* and *Test competitor products* is a part of *Research.*

The horizontal lines in Figure 4.2 represent information flows between the four key subactivities. In this view of the process, the stage gates can be regarded as attributes of flows between the first layer of activities. For example, *Research results* are information that flow from the *Research* activity to the *Translate needs into requirements* activity, and *Concept designs* are information that flow from the *Concept design* activity to the *Design development* activity. Conveniently, the flows in Figure 4.2 are all information; in a real process, there are likely to be other kinds of flow, such as

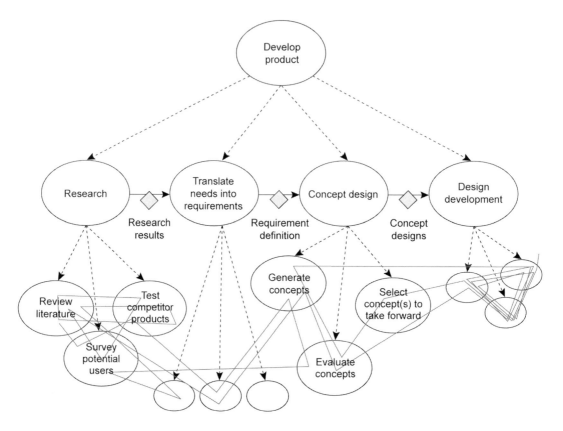

Figure 4.2 Process structures (grey lines show iterations).
(Copyright author)

material and money, which are beyond the scope of this chapter. Suffice to say, the notation used in Figure 4.2 can be applied in other cases with the addition of new line styles and labels.

Time lines

Having thought about the process and the activities and information flows that it contains, we can now think about applying a time line from beginning to end. This is where iteration comes in. The grey lines in Figure 4.2 show an actual path through this process which, as can be seen, is iterative; it skips around, frequently returning to earlier stages, rather than following a sequential

path. A key feature that is missing from the process definition is the inclusion of activities that create information for the stage gates; this will be addressed later in this section when we look at how we might apply design to the communication of information that results from the process. When you create a time line in a project, remember the following recommendations:

Get started

Getting started builds reflection time into your process. The most common mistake students make in design work is that they delay starting and so have no or little time for reflection. So start as soon as you get the brief and do a little each day rather than saving it to the end.

Do the project more than once, but do less each time

This may sound counter-intuitive and time-consuming but splitting the time available and doing the project more than once gives you a chance to both learn about the project from start to finish and use what you learn in the project. As such, it has the potential to dramatically improve the final result. Of course if you take this approach, given that most projects have limited resources, you spend less time on each task each time round. Table 4.1 illustrates how time might be allocated based on a fifty-hour project carried out over a period of five weeks with the effort distributed equally across the five weeks.

Notice that, if using the phased approach, Phase 1 (fifteen hours) would be completed

Table 4.1   COMPARING TIME ALLOCATIONS (HOURS) WHEN DOING A PROJECT ONCE AND TWICE

Week	Activity	One time around	Two times around	
			Phase 1	Phase 2
1	Research	10	3	7
2	Translate needs into requirements	10	3	7
3	Concept design	10	3	7
4	Develop design	10	3	7
5	Produce out-puts for stage gates	10	3	7
	TOTAL	50	50	

Ideas, Concepts and Inventions

The basis of a concept design is an idea in the mind of the designer or team. An idea may involve an existing or a new technical principle for the particular function concerned. Such ideas may emerge during the task or problem clarification phase of designing.

The idea then has to take shape, to be embodied in a specific physical configuration as one or more concept designs. Drawings, computer-aided design representations, three-dimensional models and mock-ups might all be used to help give form to an idea. One characteristic of a successful design is that it perfectly encapsulates the idea that inspired it. But each designer will interpret his or her ideas in different ways. The chosen concept is then developed through the stages of embodiment and detailed design until suitable for production and practical use.

If the idea or concept design is based on a novel technical principle for its particular function or manufacture (even if that principle has been applied in other devices or systems), it may count as an invention. Invention is, however, an imprecise term and only has clear-cut legal meaning if the invention is patented.

From: R. Roy, *Design and Designing* (T211), The Open University, Blk 3 (2010), p. 26.

halfway through the second week and you'd have a far better idea of what needs doing in Phase 2. Given that many students are hesitant about starting a project and few will have devoted much time to it by the middle of the second week, even if this strategy doesn't work, you won't have lost much through trying it.

Avoid getting fixated on one solution

As noted earlier, fixing on a solution, even if it seems to be a very good idea, stops you iterating, it puts a block on your creativity and it hinders your movement through the design process. It's not wrong to have ideas—in fact they are essential—but note them down, documenting any benefits, and then move on to generate new ideas.

Separate your designing from preparing for presentations (e.g. at stage gates)

A typical deliverable from a student design project is a design portfolio, but the value of such a presentation rests heavily on the quality of the designing. The portfolio can only be produced once the design is near completion. So keep a sketch or log book where you record all that you do, and then report from it in your presentation. Be prepared to present your design in different ways for different audiences, and anticipate questions. Don't forget to evaluate and test as well as measure and justify, and capture your design rationale as a means of demonstrating your design thinking.

Designing communications

Applying design to the communication of your process and designs demands that you understand who you are trying to communicate with and what they are going to want to be able to do with the information you provide. Jacques Giard, in his book *Design FAQs,* introduces a design triad, where designers interact with users and manufacturers (see Figure 4.3).[3]

The kind of information that is communicated is highlighted at the interfaces between the different stakeholders. In addition, designers need to communicate with other designers with whom they may be working on the same product development team or perhaps future designers who may wish to understand why a given design is as it is. A common way of communicating with users is through photorealistic rendered images and prototypes (e.g. as shown in Plate 5), while communication with manufacturers or others in the design team might exploit more technical data or computer models.

However, don't ignore the potential of sketching to help explore and generate ideas both with other designers and in the private process of communicating with yourself. When you're designing, keep a sketchbook, and once you have a design, extract material from the sketchbook that is appropriate for the stage gate you're at and the audience you're communicating with. This means that you need to think about the audience you're communicating with and be clear in your mind about what information they might need or want. You need to understand not only the detail of your design but also the detail of how others are going to use it. Don't just think about your immediate customer and supplier; think about the supplier's supplier and the customer's customers too, since this will give you insights into their needs and thus the design of your communications.

computers and design thinking

Although computers play an increasingly important role in today's design processes, designing is, at its heart, still a human activity. Only humans can distinguish between the priorities in a design problem, and only humans can match these priorities and values to innovative opportunities. Having said this, the scope and diversity of new digital technologies means that human decision-making now has access to some sophisticated help. Computer-aided design (CAD) has facilitated the modelling of ideas for many decades, but new

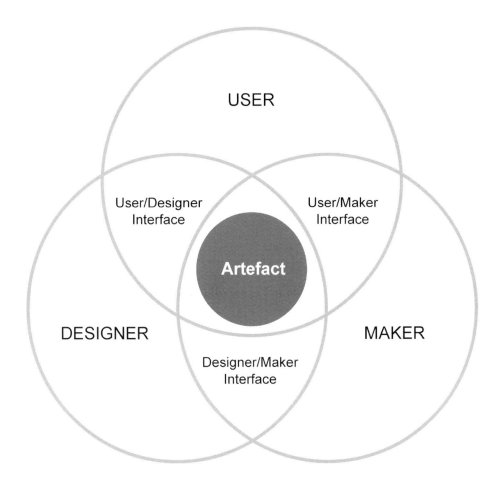

Figure 4.3 Design triad. (After J. Giard, *Design FAQs,* Dorset Group, 2005)

mobile devices linked to online databases allow clearer definitions of design problems. New digital tools allow designers to gather information on users or markets, and various programmes help translate complex data into usable specifications and requirements. Perhaps of even greater significance is the ability of new software to model the design process, allowing the designer or design team to adapt and share unique models of process appropriate to a specific context, whether this be in an advertising agency or for an aircraft manufacturer.

"Although computers play an increasingly important role in today's design processes, designing is, at its heart, still a human activity."

Computers and products

Computer-aided design tools first came into being in the 1960s, when it became possible to present graphical information, as opposed to text, on display devices. The 1970s saw the emergence of computational geometry as a distinct subject area. Since then, computer-aided design tools and systems developed rapidly, and in 1995 Boeing reported the first ever major product that was wholly defined on the computer: the digital design and preassembly of its 777 airliner.

Nearly two decades later, CAD systems are a key part of most industrial product development processes. They range from digital sketching and computer-aided illustration tools used early in a design process through to three-dimensional solid modelling systems, which are typically used towards the end of a design activity to create unambiguous digital product definitions. CAD models have two common uses: they provide data for input to other software tools, such as analysis and manufacturing packages; and they are used to communicate the design embedded within the CAD model. The communication can be for a range of reasons and to a range of people— including suppliers who might manufacture the product, customers who might incorporate the design into a larger model or maintenance teams who support the product through its life.

CAD systems can make a huge difference, positive and negative, to designing. A key challenge for student product designers lies in understanding the roles of different kinds of systems. In essence, once you know what the shape of a part is—that is, after the shape has been designed— today's CAD systems are very good for creating unambiguous definitions of that part. As such, CAD is well suited to supporting downstream

Figure 4.4 Boeing's 777 airliner. (Photo from Getty 871850–001 RM)

activities such as design evaluation and analysis, prototyping and manufacturing. Data exchange technologies are used to communicate designs or to build them through various rapid prototyping technologies. The effective use of data exchange technologies needs CAD models that are well formed, as opposed to those that just look good on screen. Until recently, it's been difficult to apply CAD before shapes have been created—largely because CAD models have, embedded within them, structures that are not easily changed. It has meant that CAD systems have been less well suited to the early, conceptual stages of design, when changes in concept need to be supported. This weakness is being addressed in a new generation of computer-aided design *synthesis* packages, currently in the form of early research prototypes, where researchers are exploring ways in which designers' creativity might be supported and enhanced.

Computers and processes

Major process benefits are reportedly gained from the use of CAD. For example as a result of the digital definition of the 777 airliner, Boeing reported waste reductions of over 50 per cent associated with change, error and rework in the product development and realization process. In addition, once in use, Boeing was able to use the CAD models to produce maintenance manuals and other product documentation; and a knock-on of this was that design changes could be reflected in this documentation more easily than in manual systems. There are many ways to define a given part, and there is typically no right or wrong way. However, if you want other people to share your models, then it's a good idea to ensure that the structure you embed into the model is a reasonable one and one that can be easily seen from the

CAD model itself. Common errors are absence of versioning (when a team shares models and can't tell which version of whose model is in the final assembly) and the inclusion of spurious parts (i.e. parts that aren't used in the assembly but exist in its structure). The key question to ask yourself is, 'Will someone using this model know what I mean and intend without the need to speak with me?' If the answer is no, then the model probably needs improving.

Designing design

This chapter has built on the premise that designing is an imperfect process that we can constantly adapt and improve in the light of various pressures and opportunities. The notion of the professional, and so reflective, designer is crucial. If this chapter is successful, then it will encourage student readers to be constructively critical of the various models of the design process they come across in their studies and practice, and it will be liberating in that it will free them to creatively define their own design processes within accepted norms and the business processes within which they find themselves operating.

Design systems need to support designers in designing for uncertain futures. Design drivers are likely to include changing business climates, changing political and regulatory environments, changing societal demands, and changing human behaviours and expectations. Computer systems will help if used appropriately, but many of the systems that designers work with are human activity systems created by themselves and the people with whom they work.[4] A key future competency of professional designers will be their ability to reflect and adapt the systems they both use and define to respond to opportunities and challenges. As designs are increasingly delivered to market by networks of organizations located around the globe, the need is growing for well-defined design information that leads to more effective communication of designs and, perhaps more importantly, designs that solve real problems and so deliver value to their ultimate users.

CHAPTER SUMMARY

- Designing is a thinking skill as much as a practical skill.
- Develop your ability to understand needs and problems by asking questions. Remember that needs, and understanding of needs, are likely to evolve.
- Translate your understanding of needs and problems into design requirements.
- Begin design projects sooner rather than later, and consider doing a design project more than once, but do less each time.
- Avoid getting fixated on one solution.
- Don't confuse doing with presenting. For example don't start trying to define a design before you have designed it, and remember that you can define the same design in a number of ways.
- With CAD models, what you get is more than what you see, so be systematic in your use of CAD.
- Ensure that you create information that is fit for its intended purpose rather than just convenient and easy to define in the systems you are using.
- Consider the product development process as a framework to work within rather than a straitjacket that constrains you.

introduction to the 24:7 projects

To get the most out of this book, you are encouraged to participate in the guided designing activities. The projects presented here will develop your capacity for understanding design and engaging with the process of designing. They have been created for those who have very little experience of design, but they also aim to stretch those people who have more developed design abilities.

Many designers will say they work 24:7—twenty-four hours a day, seven days a week! Whilst this must be an exaggeration, it's clear that most designers are deeply engaged in looking at, talking about, thinking around and doing design. The projects presented in this collection use the theme of 24:7 across a varied selection of activities. There are seven projects, one at the end of each section, and they all involve the number twenty-four in some way, such as asking for twenty-four ideas or giving you twenty-four hours (one day) to generate a design proposal. Each project seeks to illustrate some of the key points presented in its respective section, and the projects gradually build your ability to think creatively, model ideas, communicate and evaluate. Most of the projects are bite-sized and can be completed in a short space of time. Even those projects that suggest more time or the involvement of more people can be tackled as a short individual design task if you prefer. All projects aim to stretch your investigative or analytical skills as well as your ability to interpret, innovate and meet user or market needs.

All the projects are deliberately unclear in particular ways, because problem finding is just as important as problem solving. If you are to develop design thinking skills, you need to be confident in your ability to interrogate the world, to find the real problems underneath the given problems and to challenge what others think. The skill of commercial design thinking is to combine this with diplomacy, creativity and practicality. In this way you can develop a marketable reputation for redefining problems as well as creating solutions that have real value in today's world.

The materials you require to undertake these projects are very modest. Some require only a cheap pen or pencil and paper. Others invite you to make some simple three-dimensional models using waste cardboard, scissors and adhesive tape. Since the projects are untutored, you are free to take them in any direction you wish. You are welcome to place your own emphasis in the projects, so for example you might interpret a project as graphic communication, product design, design studies or any of a wide range of subdisciplines in design practice. Some readers might prefer to work entirely digitally, exploiting online resources, whilst others might prefer more traditional approaches of sketching, model-making and face-to-face meetings.

However you choose to work, take these opportunities to immerse yourself in the world of design and designing.

Background

Part I has been about the process of designing. Partly it's a linear process, but it's also iterative—the designer loops back to earlier stages if avenues of exploration aren't fruitful or if new information emerges. The design process can be difficult to explain because it involves creative thinking. It can be immensely rewarding, but it can also be messy. It is a process that demands we integrate skills, knowledge and values.

The Project

Create an idea for a design game that can be played by children. This game must help them understand the design process. Make a simple model of your game so that you can try it out with some volunteer players. Use their feedback to help you improve the game. Remake the game and trial it again until you're happy with the result. In keeping with the limited attention span of children, your game must take no longer than twenty-four minutes before a winner emerges. It can be much quicker.

Guidelines

You may decide how long you want to spend on this project. Try to make your game engaging and fun. Decide who your target market is; they might be young or older children. Don't make the rules too complicated. Your game might be aimed at entertainment, education or a mix of both.

You might want to consider a board game or a digital game. How will players progress—will you incorporate dice, will you include questions or activities? You might make the game competitive or collaborative, but how is the game won? What is the aim of the game, and how does it engage the players? How many players do you want to include? The purpose of involving volunteer players is to generate feedback for you. Observe them playing your game, ask them questions and get them to suggest improvements.

part ii

creating and communicating

introduction to part ii

Part I presented designing as an iterative process where both the problems and the ideas for resolving these problems evolved together through various loops and cycles. It also suggested that the process relies on the integration of some mental capacities. Part II highlights some of the tools and techniques that need to be combined with our mental capacities if our designing is to be effective. While our design goals might be creating and communicating, the tools we need to achieve these can be characterized as modelling, drawing and computing.

One thing models have in common is that they are simplifications of reality. The weather map we see nightly on television is an example of helpful simplicity. Imagine having to interpret a sequence of satellite photographs of a region to determine the weather! Instead we are given symbols indicating weather trends in limited but sufficient detail. Two or three variations in the picture allow us to understand the changing weather conditions.

This capacity for models to simplify reality can be very helpful in designing, and this theme is taken up by Jack Ingram in Chapter 5. He provides a useful bridge between Part I and Part II, because he illustrates how models can assist us to understand process and develop product. Three-dimensional constructions and drawn representations are shown to have value, because they assist the tasks of distilling problems, generating ideas and communicating proposals.

Drawing has been associated with human creative expression since the dawn of civilization.

Some cave paintings date back 30,000 years. Drawings made as part of a design process are more difficult to date, but there exists an architectural plan of a Babylonian temple inscribed in stone from 2130 BCE. Drawing continues to have an important function in designing today—it provides a cheap, speedy and safe means of making mistakes. As Mario Minichiello and Liz Anelli discuss, drawing can help us think creatively as well as communicate the outcomes of our thinking. Some controlled styles of drawing allow designers to check relationships between components before going to the much greater expense of having their ideas produced.

Without a doubt, the most significant development in design modelling in recent decades has been the widespread use of digital models and computer-aided design (CAD). In some ways, the new and easily usable CAD systems have superseded the making of three-dimensional constructions and freehand sketching. This is taken up by Jonathon Allen and Paul Kouppas, who reveal the powerful capacity for CAD to communicate and evaluate design ideas quickly, easily and at relatively low cost. There are additional advantages in that digital models offer a seamless interface with downstream processes of manufacture in many fields ranging from fashion design to architecture.

Building narrative into design is frequently overlooked, but it provides a key unifying concept across today's design disciplines. If design is communication, then designing is the creation of narrative. In Chapter 8, Michele Dickey uses game design as the context for an examination of narrative, but the wider implications are significant: brands need to communicate values, magazines need to associate themselves with styles and products need to convey usability. Other types of design might use an embedded narrative to help us express ourselves, follow instructions or enjoy ownership. The challenge for design is how to model narrative during research and development.

Part II focuses on modelling, drawing and computing because, in many ways, these are the external tools of an internal design thinking process. Having a portfolio of digital, freehand and three-dimensional modelling skills is vital to the professional practice of design today.

chapter 5

models *of* design and models *in* design

jack ingram

ABOUT THIS CHAPTER

This chapter is about models. Not just the sorts of representations, artefacts and images that might arise during designing, but models that tell us something about the processes of designing. In this chapter I draw a distinction between three types of models: conceptual, physical and virtual. Conceptual models help us understand processes such as thinking processes, project management processes and processes of product evolution. Physical models help us understand and evaluate ideas at all stages of design processes. These might range from a sketch or quick construction very early in a design process to a working prototype made near the end of a design project. The third type of model, virtual models, overlaps with conceptual and physical models in that this type can represent either processes or products of design. Virtual models have become more important as design processes and products have become more digital.

---

conceptual models of design

In design, as in many aspects of everyday life, it is possible to be successful without realising quite why—it is possible to learn design skills by trial and error or by watching a skilled practitioner at work. Indeed, for much of the twentieth century, this was the normal mode of design education. However, modern practice necessitates that today designers need an understanding of underlying theory. I draw a parallel with the Highway Code, where theoretical knowledge is developed in parallel with practical driving skills, or alternatively in horticulture, where there is rarely enough time to gain all the required knowledge of plants through practice alone.

Even when we do have some theoretical knowledge of design, we may not know a precise theory, but instead have a simplified idea of some rules that should be followed or a mental picture of how activities relate to each other. I view this simplification of theory into something more understandable as a form of 'modelling', the structuring of concepts into a form that facilitates both their comprehension and their application. Modelling is fundamental for understanding the world and our place in it. All of us construct conceptual models that encapsulate our thoughts and ideas, and designers have come to rely on this ability. However, much of the modelling we employ is tacit—that is, we may not be able to describe it or perhaps even be aware that we are doing it.

The cognitive skills to understand the world around us and interpret the raw information we take in through our senses are influenced by the cultural contexts in which we live and our formal education. This mix of the social, religious, economic and moral circumstances that shape the way we think and lead our lives, together with our education and professional training, have a major influence on the way we see the world: a banker is likely to see things differently from a social worker, and designers, because of the models they employ, have a particularly 'designerly' way of thinking. So our understanding of design and designing is partly shaped by who we are and how we think. But it's also shaped by our ability to create simplified representations or models of our processes and the outputs of those processes. This chapter will return to the creation of conceptual models of design, but first I want to develop a foundation of understanding by considering physical and virtual models.

physical and virtual models in design

We live in a real and tangible world—for example the trains we ride in, the seats we sit on and the clothes we wear. Despite the emergence of virtual products and a new focus for design on systems, the overwhelming proportion of design today still concerns the manipulation and shaping of the material world. It is understandable then that if design largely concerns the physical world, the models that are produced as part of a development process can benefit from being physical. Drawings are a particular form of physical model. Clearly they are two-dimensional and not three-dimensional like an item of jewellery or a

prototype of a piece of furniture. All physical models are simplifications in one way or another, and drawings and sketches are merely extreme forms of simplification. Models may have drawbacks when compared to, say, working prototypes, but they can be extremely efficient in their ability to convey information, their speed of construction and their low cost. Designing is not just about having ideas. The ideas need to be given form in ways that are meaningful and relevant for different stakeholders, such as the intended users or the manufacturers. If an idea inside a designer's head is to be communicated by anything more than words, it has to take some physical form, whether as two-dimensional images or some three-dimensional form. Physical models of design proposals are a powerful medium for getting ideas from inside a designer's mind into the minds of others; they allow designers, their colleagues and their clients to evaluate ideas before committing to the expense of producing the real thing.

Recent advances in digital modelling and imaging have made possible a range of techniques that are now accessible to design professionals and students alike. The necessary computing power is affordable, and software is more accessible, both in terms of its cost and its ease of use. Virtual models, particularly computer-generated equivalents of physical models, whilst taking as much time to make as their physical equivalents, have the added benefit of being reproducible and transmissible—a model created in a car manufacturer's styling studio in California immediately can be viewed interactively and simultaneously in Detroit, London, Tokyo and Munich. Some properties of virtual models can be changed very easily—for example colour variations can be made instantaneously. Also, sophisticated virtual models have applications beyond those of physical models. For example complex structures and product components can be 'assembled' in a virtual rehearsal for real-life construction and manufacture, minimising the likelihood of problems at a later stage, when corrections would be costly. Individual virtual components can be tested for strength in a variety of extreme circumstances.

As noted above, the significance of virtual products is increasing. The global market for computer software, games and music grows at a phenomenal rate. The commercial sector concerned with designing and developing business and retail systems looks set to challenge the traditional sectors making tangible goods. Furthermore, the development of virtual products and systems will understandably exploit virtual models in their design process. After all, why would you need to make a physical model if your end product will only exist as a virtual product? However, the opposite is also true; if the end product relies for its success on tactile qualities, how can a virtual model help you make decisions about, for example, its weight and balance, its strength and flexibility? Clothing and furniture, cutlery and jewellery, hand and power tools, sports equipment, lighting and many more products all benefit from physical modelling at stages of the design process. In practice, designers use both physical and virtual models at different stages, and no single model need communicate all aspects of the proposal.

mixing models in stages of design

To provide a framework for showing examples of conceptual, physical and virtual models, a commonly used description of a design project

---

Three Types of Model

At a general level, there are three types of model used in designing:

1. *Iconic models:* These are probably the most familiar type of model. They work by looking like the real or intended object. Thus, a realistic but scale model of a new building, a prototype motorbike or fashion sketches are all variations of iconic models.
2. *Symbolic models:* These models work by using an abstract code to represent a selected aspect of the real world. Mathematical formulae used to determine heat loss in buildings or flow characteristics in plastic moulding are examples of symbolic models.
3. *Analogue models:* These are models that work by means of diagrams that stand for but don't necessarily look like the subject they seek to represent. Harry Beck's diagrammatic map of the London Underground and a drawing of an electrical circuit are analogue models.

---

progression will be our starting point. Two central themes to be developed are:

Iteration—repeated cycles of activity in which ideas are generated, modelled, communicated and evaluated, each cycle integrating the new knowledge from the previous attempt.

Evolution—in addition to the work of designers, there are other influences on the way our world is shaped, and designers can benefit from understanding how technologies and consumer practices change and evolve over time.

When a new technology is first embodied in a product, the designer's task is to help promote the possibilities that the technology can deliver, as when digital cameras were first launched. Now established, digital cameras compete less on the technological possibilities and more on style and convenience of use. Similarly, the first fast-food outlets, and particularly drive-throughs, at first challenged designers to make the concepts acceptable to a sceptical public, but now that the concept is established, the designer's task is focused on detail design and the promotion of brand values. In these examples, we see that often, whilst the current task may be new to a designer, there will have been precedents set by previous designers, and our experience of their designs may inform our thinking. Any design task can be seen as a new iteration within a longer-term evolution of the product or service being designed.

One way of describing design is as a problem-solving activity in which the problems may be stylistic, aesthetic, functional and so on. The language of design processes commonly assumes a progression from a problem to a solution, through at least two essential intermediate stages. Figure 5.1 presents a diagram in which the design process has been reduced to four stages: problem, concept, detailed specification and solution.

The first stage concerns the definition of the problem. Concept generation leads to a preferred concept or concepts, which in turn supports detail development. Once a detailed specification is available, then further modelling, prototyping and evaluation lead to a solution. This basic conceptual model of the design process can act as a guide to design activity, but note that conceptual, physical and virtual models can be employed at any stage. The following sections explore the use of modelling at different stages in the design process.

Stage 1: modelling the problem

Problem definition can be seen as the starting point of the designer's task and the first opportunity for using models to gain a better understanding of what is being asked. Where the work is prompted by a design brief, this stage is concerned with interrogating or challenging this brief—pouncing on every phrase in the brief, looking for every possible interpretation in order to be clear what is being asked. For example, London-based designers Seymour Powell have adopted the routine practice of responding to a brief by producing their own extensive written interpretation, which is returned to the client for comment. In this way, the trigger for design action is discussed or negotiated to a point where the client and the designer share a clear understanding of what is required. Many products are offered as part of a manufacturer's range and in competition with ranges from

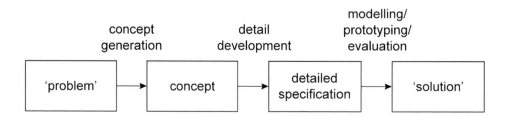

Figure 5.1 A four-stage linear model of the design process.

rival producers. In such cases, the design brief seeks to establish where exactly the proposed outcome fits in the context of its rivals and those products in the client's existing range.

More generally, all design problems are shaped by their context. The designer's task is to create something that fits a particular set of circumstances—a household appliance that can be housed within existing kitchen units, work clothing that will withstand a given range of environmental conditions, a building to stand out from (or blend in with) its surroundings. In many cases, models can help define the context and assist the designer to see the fit between his or her ideas and the context in which he or she must operate. In architectural design, the site determines many features of a design. Its size, contours and orientation will influence the structure, access and aesthetics of proposals as will adjacent features such as existing buildings, roadways and protected trees. Models which successfully capture such contextual information can greatly assist the creative stages that follow.

The detail in a site model can be quite sketchy, and models can be made very quickly. Figure 5.2 shows a site model that uses a stiff base board on which is built up layers of foam core or cardboard to suggest contours of a particular location.

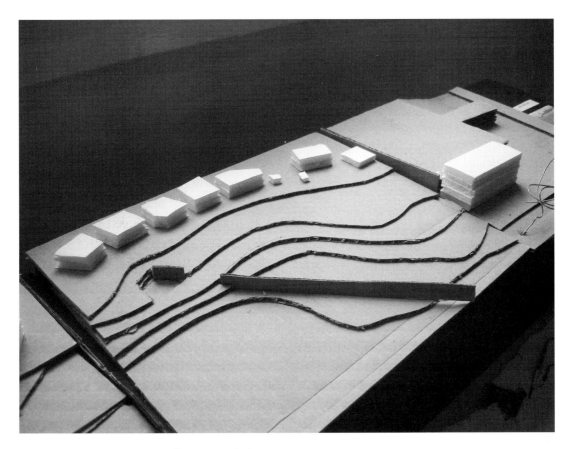

Figure 5.2 Contoured site model. (Copyright author)

Interior designers often find it helpful to create models that reveal the structural elements of a building. These can illuminate the parameters within which the designer must work. The level of detail need not be great, but it should include immovable features and keep to scale. As can be seen from Figure 5.3, even quite scruffy models can be useful— although in this case, the visual intrusion of the sticky tape can distract from the important conceptual information contained in the model.

An alternative to small-scale models when exploring a design problem is to use full-size interior mock-ups. Three students, faced with the task of designing an interior for a mobile home, created an internal space to the limited dimensions given in the brief. Here they lived and worked for two weeks, acting out the requirements of a range of users and keeping a comprehensive photographic record of their experiences. From the several internal layouts they tried, they agreed on the most promising for detail development and used their photographic record as a basis for their sketches. The benefits they gained included confidence in the practicality of their proposals (they had firsthand experience of having used the space), a guide for their freehand perspective drawings and evidence of their design process to support their proposals.

The technique of 'user trips' is well established in design. As a means of heightening awareness of a user's needs in a given situation, it is very powerful and delivers a lot of information in a short time. Also it has uses beyond design. A manufacturer of ironing tables insisted its sales team undertook all their own ironing to gain empathy with its customers. After initial resistance, the all-male team admitted that they felt better able to argue the case for the company's products once they were experienced users. As in the design of the mobile home interior, the process sought to establish the minimum contextual parameters. In the design of the mobile home interior, the students started with an empty space of the specified size,

Figure 5.3 Model used to convey structural elements of an interior. (Copyright author)

Figure 5.4 How much space do we actually need? (Getty 85730719 RM)

then acted out the user activities they wished to design for through user trips, and finally interior features were generated in the light of their experiences in the space. These emerging ideas were not fixed—they were constantly evolving and changing in response to being tried out through further user trips and other testing. The modelling in the mobile home project was both full-size and scaled-down, and it was deliberately sketchy. It is important to keep models, mock-ups or constructions nonprecious so that new opportunities are integrated and any necessary changes are accepted. An important function for design models is that they promote and support problem definition through action as well as through internalized contemplation. The shift from private

thoughts developed with the aid of sketches to the physicality of models that encourage comments, discussion and participation of others can be revealing.

> "An important function for design models is that they promote and support problem definition through action as well as through internalized contemplation."

Stage 2: concept development

Designers translate verbal descriptions of problems into physical realities. To initiate the shift from an idea of a requirement, expressed in words, towards a physical design solution, visualization skills are key. In skilful hands, a written brief can be translated into a range of pictorial expressions that encapsulate the spirit of the requirement without a firm commitment to detailed specification. For example sketching can suggest possible avenues of exploration or development without dominating. This stage is concerned with exploring a range of possibilities, comparing them and developing them, perhaps by combining aspects of different ideas. The generation of concepts can be tricky because, as noted above, designers need to provide clarity in the expression of a concept whilst avoiding fixing too rigidly on an idea. The modelling decisions

for the designer focus on what to include and what to leave out. For example packaging and other graphic design concept mock-ups frequently utilize blocks of content-free text (often Latin) so that attention is not drawn away from the general concept. Similarly, early models of consumer products, interiors and architectural concepts tend to avoid colour and other detail. But including some characteristics can enhance the value of a model. For example some models benefit from being created full-size, even when designing quite large products, while other models mimic product weight as well as size so that they can be used to generate realistic user feedback. It is important that the models stimulate the

Figure 5.5 Modelling to explore, develop and evaluate.
(Getty 975321–002 RM)

imagination, and providing too much detail can suggest a decision already made or direct attention away from the general concept and towards a level of detail that is normally considered at a later stage. At the concept-generation stage of the design process, it is good practice to develop several alternatives for evaluation, even if there appears to be a clearly preferred option.

There are several lessons here. Models can be put into context—full-size mock-ups can assist in the evaluation of user interfaces, a weighted model of a power tool can be checked for balance in a number of work situations by acting out its use in representative tasks, models of packaging can be put onto shelves next to rival products. This putting into context can then be evaluated and is best done by having in advance a set of criteria against which they are to be judged.

It's also important not to overlook the value of models in supporting creative, playful designing. Designing is fun, and happy accidents can be productive, as the following example reveals: In a competition to design the display system for an end-of-year exhibition, students submitted one-tenth scale models of the structure that was to be produced in the university workshops. Models were displayed and votes cast by the student body, leading to a clear winner. Unfortunately, the winning student had been absent and when he returned was at first pleased to hear that he had won, but then distressed that his model had been displayed and judged upside down! When he pointed out the error and tried to insist that the model was righted, he was unanimously overruled, and twenty-five exhibition stands were manufactured to his upside down design. The world of design is littered with such stories. Models encourage playful experimentation, and 'now turn it on its head' is a legitimate technique for

exploring possibilities, whether employed deliberately by the designer or inadvertently by others.

Stage 3: detail development

Choosing a concept for development frequently gives rise to conflicts. Even where a proposal is a combination of features from several concept designs, there is a need to assess and evaluate. Here, too, models can play a vital role. Models at this stage do not necessarily need to represent the whole proposal, and here are some examples of models that address single issues.

A common type of model in product design is the *proof-of-principle* model. In these, a single feature is identified and modelled to allow rigorous evaluation. Figure 5.6 shows a concept for a self-powered wheeled suitcase that can carry its owner. A key characteristic of this 'transporter' suitcase is the ease with which the user can change the product's configuration. The proof-of-principle model looks nothing like the finished product but is robust and well made enough to carry a man's weight, and videos of it in use provided evidence of its practicality. Its existence provides credibility for the otherwise virtually modelled proposal.

Proof-of-principle models are the direct opposite of appearance models, which focus on aesthetic detail without concern for how things work. Increasingly, virtual modelling is replacing physical models for the presentation of detail. Although the time commitment for equivalent physical and virtual models is very similar, virtual models have some advantages. Duplicates of virtual models take no extra time, and small detail changes made for comparison are easy to achieve. As a general rule, every duplicate physical model required means a doubling of time and effort.

Figure 5.6 Proof-of-principle model and virtual model for 'transporter' suitcase. (Copyright author)

In the development of a motorcycle that is adjustable for a range of rider sizes and riding postures, Stephane Garreau used both proof-of-principle models and virtual appearance models. Very simple adjustable seat and handlebar rigs (Plate 6) determined the range of adjustment needed to provide for a wide range of postures and rider sizes. Photographs of several representative riders were then combined with duplicates of the virtual model to produce illustrative images.

If the designer follows this broad sequence of three stages, he or she arrives at the fourth stage, shown in Figure 5.1 and which, at the risk of over-simplifying the case, I've called 'solution'. But of course it's only a solution and not *the* solution. This solution is as much a stage in the process

as the three earlier stages. It requires the use of some particularly refined models that collectively are referred to as prototypes.

an iterative approach to the design process

The design process of Wei Li, a postgraduate student at Birmingham City University in the United Kingdom, illustrates both the iterative and the evolutionary characteristics of an integrated model of design practice. Wei Li was interested in how, compared with the unchanging design of chopsticks in the East, the development of Western eating utensils over several centuries reflected changes in diet and eating practices in both formal and informal dining. He wished to contrast knives and forks with chopsticks for a society in which eating choices are increasingly cross-cultural. Here are some of the key iterations of his design process:

First set of iterations: sketch 'principles' for evaluation

Before embarking on any design activity, Wei Li collected huge numbers of knives, forks and spoons from bargain stores, junk shops and through friends, and he visited museum collections. He constructed a history of European cutlery in relation to diet, cooking and eating fashions, classifying utensils according to their functions of cutting, piercing, scraping and scooping. He hosted a number of events for his fellow students, in which foods of different textures, and morsels of different sizes, served on a variety of plates and dishes, were eaten with a variety of (sometimes inappropriate) utensils. Out of these events there emerged the beginnings of an idea for an implement that might combine some of the advantages of chopsticks, spoons, forks and knives. These first concepts were developed through sketches for his own evaluation (several iterations) into diagrammatic representations of some twenty-one possible configurations (Plate 7a). The proposals were evaluated using a formal rating scale with the students who had participated in the eating events.

Second set of iterations: sketch models

The seven preferred principles that emerged from the first set of iterations were formalized into simple models that shared a common construction (in plain white polypropylene sheet) through a number of iterations that tried different materials and determined the best dimensions. These models (Plate 7b), which had minimal functionality, were

then formally evaluated by an extended range of users.

Third set of iterations: prototyping and proof-of-principle modelling

To test functionality, a single utensil that combined characteristics emerging from several of the previous sketch models was developed through experimentation (Plate 7c). This prototype was sufficiently functional to allow testers to eat a range of foods. It should be noted that full functionality would include being dishwasher-proof and having durability. For this stage, it was considered sufficient to evaluate the central purpose of handling a variety of foods in a range of eating situations.

Fourth set of iterations: appearance modelling (virtual)

In this final stage, Wei Li developed the detail of the form for the product. A computer-generated model of the proposed utensil accommodated manufacturing considerations whilst specifying the form (Plates 7d and 7e), including a finely dimensioned joint for the two component parts that must work either separately or combined in a single product.

Combining iterations

Wei Li's project demonstrates how several different types of modelling can enhance iterative design thinking, each having a specific role at successive stages in the project. Such iterations are not simply 'going back to start again'. The start of each iteration is unique, influenced by the experience of the previous iterations. It is good practice to ask yourself each time, 'What have I learned since I was last at this point?' In preparation for his project, Wei Li had researched a number of theoretical models of design process, on which he based his project planning. In addition to physical and virtual modelling in the form of sketches, sketch models, proof-of-principal models and detailed CAD modelling, he informed his thinking through research into the historical evolution of Western diet and eating utensils, user trips and user research in the systematic evaluation of concepts. His work nicely captures the iterative nature of design. Figure 5.7 offers a simplified representation—another model—of this process. Contrast it with that shown in Figure 5.1. The iterative model of design process characterized in Figure 5.7 reveals an awkward truth. The design process never ends, and the likelihood is that your solution will be seen by some future person as a design problem, just as you see design opportunities in the things that make up the world around you.

Be a modeller

This chapter has started and finished with conceptual models of the design process. Both models are useful in helping you know where you are

> "The design process never ends, and the likelihood is that your solution will be seen by some future person as a design problem."

as you try to progress a design project. The first model will help you plan your time; it was used here as a framework within which examples of physical and virtual modelling could be presented in the context of stages of a design process which progresses from a problem to a solution. The concluding model shows how the starting point is less important than going through many iterations, using appropriate physical and virtual models to evaluate the issues explored in each iteration. It also makes the distinction between parts of the design process that take place in your mind (the world of ideas) and those that are in 'the world of objects'. Remember, we use conceptual models to help us understand issues such as sustainability

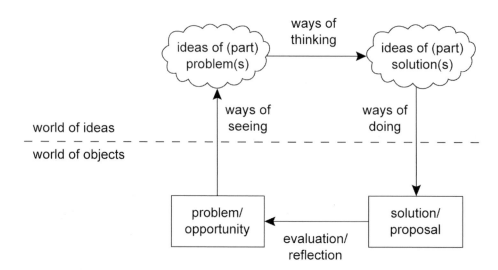

Figure 5.7 An iterative model of the design process.
(Copyright author)

The Danger of Models

There are dangers inherent in any use of models by designers, despite all their usefulness, precisely because models are simplifications and do not possess all the properties of the real or intended designs. A model may not be a true representation—it may fail to match the actual object—not just in trivial or irrelevant aspects but in precisely those crucial features of performance that it is intended to simulate. Thus, a structural model of a building or bridge may omit representation of certain types of extreme occasional load caused, say, by heavy snow falls, side winds or seismic shocks, with obvious potential for catastrophic consequences.

Sometimes models can mislead in more subtle ways. There can be a tendency among those who develop computer and mathematical models for use in design, for example, to include only those factors which are capable of precise description in quantitative terms. Meanwhile they exclude other, perhaps psychological, social or aesthetic factors which are more elusive and complex, and hence very difficult to pin down in any explicit symbolic or numerical formulation.

Another danger is associated with scale and concerns the prediction of performance. Crash-testing a scale model of a car is no substitute for crash-testing a full-size example, because materials and assemblies perform in complex and often unpredictable ways.

or aesthetic taste, so whilst models *of* design process are the most common application of conceptual models in design practice and education, conceptual models are useful *within* design, too.

Although by its very nature, design is goal-directed, deciding what problems to tackle can be difficult. Problems require interpretation. They require the designer to be sensitive to opportunities. Even here, modelling can be a valuable means of defining activity. Conceptual, physical and virtual models can all be used to help shape a problem as well as shape a solution.

CHAPTER SUMMARY

- All models are simplifications. This is both their strength and weakness in the design process.
- Physical and virtual models can make ideas visible. They facilitate creative thinking, communication, sharing, discussion, testing and evaluation.
- Conceptual models of the design process help us realize where we are within a project. They can assist structuring and planning.
- In practice, the design process finishes when evaluation of the outcome of a number of iterations suggests that the solution is viable enough not to require yet another iteration.
- Products evolve continuously, and designers merely influence stages of this evolution. One person's design solution might be another person's starting point.
- Since design models can capture process as well as product, they are extremely useful in education as evidence for assessment.

chapter 6

why do designers draw?

mario minichiello and liz anelli

ABOUT THIS CHAPTER

Drawing holds a special place in human development; it was our first complex language of communication, and it provided a means of explaining the world around us before we learnt to speak, read or write. It is estimated that the earliest images made on cave walls are about 30,000 years old. Our early human ancestors made drawings to document and describe their world and to communicate with each other. Clearly, drawing for them was an important part of their lives, and they went to extraordinary lengths to make drawings. But now we have digital cameras, the computer and its software as well as a host of modern image-capturing devices. Why should we still bother? What does drawing give us that we can't get elsewhere? This chapter sets out to answer these questions.

why draw?

This is a really good question, because learning to draw is not easy. But good things do not necessarily come easily. Drawing is the key to showing as words are the key to speaking—both types of expression externalize our thoughts, knowledge and ideas. Drawing embraces a variety of skills and knowledge with much wider applications than the ability to record what we see. Like speaking, it is rooted in cognitive processes and it can, by practice, be controlled and developed into a diverse and highly sophisticated language.[1] Each method of communication has its place, but just reflect for a moment on the amount of time we now spend giving and receiving information that does not use words. Perhaps drawing is the most relevant and succinct way of doing this. In this chapter we suggest that drawing is universal and does not date.

As anyone who has ever stopped to ask directions in a strange town will know, complicated verbal descriptions are hard to hold in your head. Words are linear, taking place in time, whereas a visual depiction, like a drawn map for example, once made is all present all of the time. The eye can rove between its parts in varying orders to make sense of it. When we ask directions, we commonly need to ask for clarification or to repeat back what we have heard to verify our understanding. A drawn map, once we know its visual codes—rectangles represent buildings, straight lines represent roads, wiggly lines represent rivers, and so forth—is a document we can keep (maybe for centuries) without its understanding diminishing. Language and terminology may change in that time, but lines remain constant. It takes an expert to translate mankind's early written language, whereas older cave drawings can communicate powerfully to the untutored.

Designers and commercial artists need to have a means of explaining ideas to others. Drawing helps by supporting and developing this capability, and it has additional benefits in building confidence and self-esteem. Drawing can also be used as a playful activity; for enjoyment, relaxation and experimenting with ideas. For the purpose of explaining the uses of drawing, we have not separated or sought to make distinctions between different traditions or movements and how they have allied drawing practices to suit particular disciplines. In our view, drawing is, and has always been, the constant element and the ancestor to all. It is inherent in the processes of visual communication, irrespective of discipline. In this chapter, we focus on the generic benefits of drawing and provide some examples of its application to various creative activities.

what practice brings

Drawing, like reading, writing and speaking, is a uniquely human form of communication. In common with other examples of human endeavour, the more you practise, the more proficient you become. Top-level athletes train to develop strength, speed and stamina. Even though their chosen specialism may be the long jump, they do not spend all day leaping into sand or merely perfecting their stride and take-off. A greater amount of time is spent lifting weights, jogging, swimming, and so on to gain all-round fitness and agility so that the whole body is equal to the demands made on it by the sport. Like in so many other disciplines,

practice really does improve your abilities. To play the piano at a professional level requires equally varied practice—not just concert pieces but those that exercise scale and pitch, maybe even posture, flexibility and breathing. To get the best sound out of a piano, it's beneficial to know how it works inside and out, how best to sit at it, how to arch the hand and wrist and, most importantly, for those hands to instinctively be able to fly from note to note without pause to consider where they are. These skills come from hours of practice each day as much as from any innate talent.

The same is true for any visual communicator, be they architect, fashion designer or graphic artist. Alongside a thorough knowledge of the subject

Externalize, Explore, Communicate

Drawings, whether on paper or on computer, provide a cheap and safe means of making mistakes. Relationships between components can be checked before going to the much greater expense of having them manufactured as physical entities.

Sketch drawings can be very efficient. They are often rough, incomplete and ambiguous. They allow an individual to very quickly externalize an idea, perhaps for self-evaluation or to support creative thinking. They also provide an efficient means of communication, and so sketches can assist a design team to creatively share and resolve problems. Furthermore, they act as a record of thinking and therefore make a vital contribution to log books and other formal records of practice.

Sketch drawings and sketch constructions help designers to generate, communicate and develop ideas, particularly when the problem is still being defined or when there are multiple potential directions for exploration. At the other extreme, engineering drawings facilitate unambiguous communication of precise intention. Engineering drawings are not usually produced early in the process. They are time-consuming to produce, and their precision might stifle alternative creative ideas.

area and the creativity to contribute new ideas, the practising artist/designer needs to draw. This is their language, and they must be expert in this if they are to achieve the highest from their specialism. Not only does the practice of drawing enable the designer to convey his or her thoughts on paper, it equips the designer to think differently—some would say more visually. The term *visual thinking* was the title of a seminal book by Rudolph Arnheim[2] in the 1960s, but the principles of thinking with imagery remain powerful today. The visual world provides the grammar of the design professions. Visual thinking is the cognitive basis of how designers see, interpret, translate and transform our constructed world. Can we really understand a complicated object, such as a window frame or a bicycle, until we have viewed it, perhaps from several angles? Even then, how much have we really learnt by just looking? If we make some drawings during our observations, our learning is enhanced. As we go through this process, we soon find we have previously held vague suppositions about scale and proportion, about which surfaces interconnect and at which angles, about shape and texture and about tone and shading.

> "Not only does the practice of drawing enable the designer to convey his or her thoughts on paper, it equips the designer to think differently—some would say more visually."

For the visual thinker, it is also true that in concentrating the mind totally on observing and recording, drawing can bring a freedom to juxtapose unconnected thoughts. Our emerging understanding of the physiology of the brain has revealed that drawing stimulates different parts of the brain to those that support modes of thinking associated with reading, writing and speaking. Some authors have suggested that drawing is predominantly a right-brain activity in contrast to the left-brain preference to work with abstract codes such as numbers and letters.[3] You may have experienced this as a difficulty in quickly switching from one mode of thinking to another or when trying to combine the two. It may explain why a person can comfortably draw whilst listening to background speech or music (on a radio for example) but may have difficulty reading or writing or other left-brain processes while the same sounds are playing. Many formal drawing classes undertake short (three- to five-minute) drawing exercises to help students achieve this switchover. Commonly, in addition to quick studies with the preferred drawing hand, these exercises will include drawing with the hand not usually used, drawing without looking at the paper or drawing from memory. Such exercises deliberately challenge the student about, for example, what is seen and how it is recorded. Another exercise that helpfully challenges accepted thinking styles is drawing with a continuous line—that is, keeping the mark-making tool in constant contact with the paper. When students don't take time to practice, they frequently find making drawings more difficult and, as a result, lose confidence in their ability. The results of such exercises are often discarded because they are only intended as warm-up exercises for the brain, eye and hand. However, be brave and try to keep them in your portfolio—they can be very revealing to you about your development.

The drawings shown in Figure 6.1 are examples of the exercises described above, made by first-year art students attending a British Council–sponsored 'Big Draw' session in Mauritius. Most

Figure 6.1 A display of student drawings.
(Copyright Mario Minichiello)

were surprised by the accuracy of drawings made under unfamiliar conditions. As well as helping develop your ability to concentrate deeply and develop creative thinking, drawing provides a store of visual problem-solving skills. As you start to develop your range of skills (your visual vocabulary), you also become a more confident communicator.

the grammar of drawing

Drawing from reference photographs has a useful place in most fields of design. However, because the camera, not the drawer, has already made the translation from three to two dimensions, it can be difficult for the brain to be stimulated into re-making these decisions. In flattening the image, the camera has deleted much of the information about the object. There is also a loss of scale and impact of its actual presence. Through lines, tones and other marks, we develop a kind of topography of drawing; these skills improve quickly with practice, and a style, or personal language, develops which makes your work more distinctive. This, when arrived at through practice, is a genuine 'signature' as personal and as unconscious as the way you walk or talk. But take care not to seek a signature style as a convenient way of masking inadequacies in your drawing or drafting skills. Affectations are no substitute for a natural and believable style.

In the same way that learning to speak, read and write enables you to think, synthesize ideas and communicate verbally, so learning to 'see well' is the key to learning to draw well and communicate visually to another person. To fully use the potential of drawing, it has to be understood as a series of strategies. Over time we become conversant with the grammar of visual language, its morphology and its elements, such as proportion, space (positive and negative), area, volume, light, tone, texture, perspective and composition. Making drawings requires us to make decisions about the interrelationships between these elements and in turn engages the viewer in decoding and understanding what has been created. This skill can be as relevant to an architect or engineer as a sculptor or information designer. In a mixed group of designers, it is interesting to see how different specialists often prefer drawing in ways that correspond to their discipline. In a life class we know, an illustrator consistently used line whereas a sculptor used tone to describe the same figure. Life drawing, particularly, is an activity where creative people engage in decision-making about how the model looks, how to translate this and how to communicate this thinking through one's drawing style. Drawing gives artists and designers freedom to invent and develop ideas quickly and instinctively, to interpret and render the world they see without resorting to photography or its associated processes.[4] Those who have mastered the key components of drawing enjoy the benefits, including versatile employability. It is a capability which you continue developing for the whole of your life.

> "In the same way that learning to speak, read and write enables you to think, synthesize ideas and communicate verbally, so learning to 'see well' is the key to learning to draw well and communicate visually to another person."

uses of drawing

At a simple level, drawing can be divided into two categories: *objective* (that which captures—perhaps realistically but not necessarily so—what the drawer sees) and *subjective* (imagined, selected or fictitious visualizations). We focus here on the three types of drawing practice where the objective and subjective can coexist.

1. The making of descriptive drawings such as product representations or portraits. The emphasis here is on communication.
2. The making of private drawings, often in sketchbooks, where the emphasis is on the support of creative, transformational thinking.
3. The making of drawings that support invention or imagination.

Descriptive drawing

Description lies at the heart of objective drawing. The outputs can be as simple as a seating plan for a banquet, a diagram of how to make a rabbit hutch or a map of how to get to the shops. They can be as complicated as a magnified botanical illustration or a picture in a medical textbook. Even at their most objective, the means by which the marks are made convey a degree of individuality, a certain style, and they require varying degrees of decoding.

The sort of computer-aided design (CAD) image shown in Figure 6.2 might communicate an existing engine design, or it might seek to convey a new design not yet in existence. Its main purpose is to make the subject accessible to others in a way that words cannot—perhaps to convince, to sell an idea or merely to reveal a potential. The drawing is a combination of complex written and mapped information, synthesized to an easily digestible single image. It takes a shortcut through technically precise specifications of measurements, tolerance and ratios, the order of build and how the engine could be constructed, and it uses the capability of our mind to accept incomplete or partially obscured information. In

short, the drawing is readable. The sequential nature of written language means that to describe the engine by words would result in a long list of features. Drawing it gives a holistic result, a visual representation of all the engine's specifications. To what extent does one need to understand an engine to draw it? Certainly Leonardo da Vinci thought that he needed to understand the workings of the human body if he was to represent people successfully in his paintings. Interestingly, Leonardo used drawing extensively to help him understand the body parts he uncovered in his dissections. The kind of drawing shown in Figure 6.2 is a form of analytical research that investigates how the proposed design—in this case a motorcycle engine—would look, how it would appear in the real world. It also provides a method to explore and explain the engine—to deconstruct

Figure 6.2 Detailed CAD visualization of a motorcycle engine. (By kind permission of Triumph Motorcycles Ltd)

it and alter it—and therefore it links to creative strategies.

Drawing is both a practical and an intellectual process. A drawing of a person is not just a copy of his or her appearance. It is the construction of a representation of the person being looked at by you. You select what you want to record about the person informed by what you see, the ideas you have about what you see and the drawing methods and materials you use. Portraiture is a long-established form of descriptive drawing. Many artists who engage with drawing the human form use a drawing system known as the Slade school method, a measure and transfer system of plotting key points of the object under observation and then transferring these measurements, angles and perspective information onto the drawing surface. Such measuring systems train you to look and sensitize you to proportions and the compositional space the subject or object sits in. This process allows you to consider what marks, lines and media you might need to capture the physical nature of the subject in a representational drawing. In this way you start to see more critically and to be more aware of proportion, shapes and perspective.

Plate 8 is a portrait of two friends drawn in the morning sun outside their house in Italy one summer. The drawing is concerned with the interplay of colour and light in a particular environment. This study of colour set against human forms is a useful way of developing a range of colours for products which may be specifically linked with a place, for example a collection of textile designs inspired by Italian colours. It is also an example of how you can develop a personal style through using unusual materials. For example this drawing was made using fast-drying shellac-based inks because of the intensity of their colour. While the shellac in the inks tends to ruin your brushes, the drawing is waterproof and doesn't fade but takes a long time to dry—in this case, two days. The actual drawing was made in about two hours.

Sketchbook drawing

Sketchbooks are a form of personal diary, and, as such, they can provide a private space for insightful musing about the world and the events in our lives. Drawing in sketchbooks can have many purposes and take many different approaches. A sketchbook allows you to think and plan. But the word *sketch* can be misleading. We don't intend *sketchbook* to mean a collection of drawings that are hasty, rough or poor quality. Nor do we mean a collection of highly finished works. In the field, it is often only possible to make quick drawings of things seen or ideas sparked—maybe through an overheard conversation. Through practice you start to develop a shorthand for making notes about such experiences. For some it might lead to making drawings that are more symbolic than descriptive. The process trains the visual memory, it hones observational skills and extends one's vocabulary of mark-making. Figure 6.3 shows collaged drawn examples from Liz Anelli's sketchbook made during a visit to Tanzania. Gathering quick drawings alongside and sometimes onto scraps of local printed ephemera can lead to an interesting style of illustration.

Generally artists and designers find sketchbooks useful because of the relationship between thinking and capturing ideas. Sketchbooks have traditionally been a place of research and experimentation, a chance to develop a set of practices, and this gives these drawings their own grammar. The notebooks or sketchbooks of most artists and designers remain unpublished—they are places for private thoughts, experiments and

Figure 6.3 Image from Liz Anelli's Tanzania sketchbook.
(Copyright Liz Anelli)

ideas. However, there is also a long and established relationship between illustration and reportage. Personal drawn journals can—as in the case of artists such as David Hockney, John Keane, John Burningham, Quentin Blake, Paul Hogarth, David Gentleman and Rigby Graham, to name a few—result in highly inventive and exciting books. The ever-growing portfolio space available online also affords a place to publish and share work in progress, with online drawing groups established across the world.

In our own sketchbooks, drawing is used as a means by which we explore an issue or event, a mixture of the descriptive and subjective, real experiences and created concepts. In Mario's career in illustration, he has often been sent to report on international conflicts and events for newspapers and other media. He has used drawing to interpret events and bring a sense of narrative

and involvement in a way that is more difficult to achieve through other forms of communication. The relative slowness of the drawing process compared to the speed of mainstream photography and film is turned into an advantage. Like the difference between 'fast' and 'slow' food, the viewer's attention is maximized as he or she is invited to reflect and savour what is presented as well as the way it is constructed. Figure 6.4 comes from Mario's war diaries.

Mario's sketchbooks have allowed him, over a period of time, to develop a process by which he transforms different kinds of information and ideas into personal statements that reflect his concerns. Because sketchbooks provide private spaces with no art director, editor or client to think about, interference is kept to a minimum. The time constraints are all your own, the critiques internal. They allow you to combine memory and visual

Figure 6.4 Image from the war diaries of Mario Minichiello.
(Copyright Mario Minichiello)

decisions in the creative process. Unlike photographs, drawings do not seek to capture one moment of time but many, through the process of looking, transferring and relooking. Figure 6.5 shows drawings for the *Sydney Morning Herald* undertaken whilst Mario was working as visiting fellow at Sydney University College of the Arts, Australia in 2007. The strong sensory experience that Australia provided inspired him to develop a more reflective and contemplative approach to his drawing practice. His objective was to elicit a more ethical response in the viewer, and the drawing books provided the ideal context in that

Figure 6.5 Aboriginal boy and birds. Charcoal on paper.
(Copyright Mario Minichiello)

they created the necessary private space and supported his personal inquiry.

Inventive drawing and the imagination

We have taught drawing for almost thirty years, and in that time we have never found anything that can match drawing as a support for the inventive and imaginative capacities of designers and artists. Drawing and thinking allow us to move through possibilities. It is a process that involves reflection and trial and error, a dialogue between imagination and the world in which a creation will exist.

Daniel has Asperger syndrome, and he was twelve years old when he made the drawing shown in Figure 6.6. His drawing of a future city is pure invention. However, for this fictional world to be plausible, it relies on his recall of real cities seen in conjunction with knowledge that comes from reading science fiction graphic novels. His interest in architectural forms and a comprehension of perspective is combined with an ability to observe closely and critically. This enables him to visualize creative new worlds, allowing his objective drawing to feed off memory and imagination. It is a combination of descriptive drawing and the imagination. It's a potentially valuable capacity for all designers.

Drawing is fundamentally about idea building. One exercise that develops this capacity requires ten A1-size sheets, each divided into 36 rectangles—making a total of 360 boxes to draw within. Participants in Drawing 360 (Figure 6.7) have some basic rules and restrictions: that no two boxes may contain the same images or have the same media used within them and there is an agreed-upon time limit. The task is to fill these sheets with visual interpretations of simple words such as *transport, vacation, murder, start, angry*. The rules force participants to find new ways of using their equipment and, when these options run out, to generate new interpretations and graphic outputs. When we last ran this project, it resulted in students drawing with flour, milk cartons, pipe cleaners and electrical tape and discovering for themselves that limitation can be the spark of invention.

combining drawing types

Whatever discipline you intend to practise in, the designs you develop have to fit a purpose. But often this purpose is not clear at the outset of a project and so drawing takes on the dual roles of problem investigation and idea visualization. It

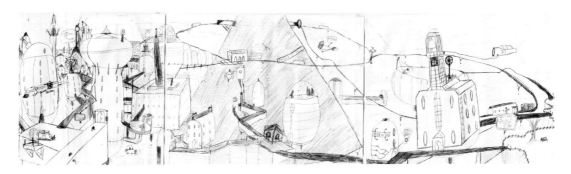

Figure 6.6 Daniel's imagined city. (Copyright Liz Anelli)

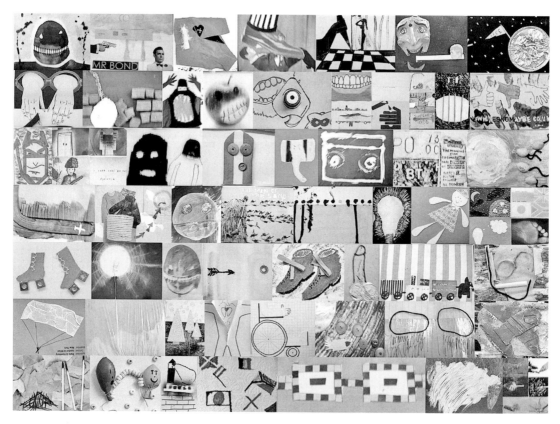

Figure 6.7 Examples from the Drawing 360 project.
(Copyright Mario Minichiello)

becomes a process of graphic inquiry. The facility to visualize accurately what you intend can be a great help in such a process, but speed and progression are vital. The visualization process of drawing ideas freely and rapidly is closely related to the creativity technique of brainstorming. It is a way of encouraging the subconscious to engage in the creative process through lateral thinking.[5]

Most people find it difficult to take risks. Having established a way of successfully making a drawing that looks like the thing you see and that other people acknowledge, it can be frustrating to go in search of new approaches. But it can also be stimulating. In the Body Maps project, illustrated in Figure 6.8, students were asked to reinterpret

elements of themselves and the world around them through imaginative use of scale, media and technique. They had to consider not just how they would use their tools but what they wanted them to say, to ultimately create something new and unique to themselves. In this example, students began by drawing objects using different techniques, from simple line work, textural drawing and frottage, to high levels of rendering and detailed mark making.

The group moved through a sequence of exercises over fifteen weeks, exploring the means and uses of drawing, and culminating in these final two drawings on a grand scale, double life size. They were the largest controlled drawings these students had made, and they found it daunting

How Idea Generation Works

All idea generation techniques work on a limited number of principles: First, they stimulate an individual or group to conduct a divergent search for ideas and to consider odd or zany ideas that otherwise might have been excluded. Second, the techniques often require the individual or group to suspend judgement on the quality or viability of the ideas so as not to converge prematurely and kill off half-formed ideas. Thus, participants diverge widely before converging.

Some techniques work by providing words, images, etc. that stimulate an individual or group to come up with ideas spontaneously. These are usually called intuitive techniques (with some similarity to heuristic methods of designing). Other techniques work by breaking the problem into parts, identifying possible subsolutions and then generating overall solutions by permutation and combination. These are usually called logical or systematic techniques.

These two basic types of idea generation can both operate in two ways:

1. free association, in which new ideas are stimulated in the mind arising from the experience and environment of the individual and by ideas produced by other people (a free association/intuitive technique is brainstorming)
2. forced relationships, where new ideas are produced in the mind by making people consider connections between related or unrelated ideas (an example of a forced relationship/systematic technique is morphological analysis)

From: R. Roy, *Design and Designing* (T211), The Open University, Blk 3 (2010), p. 103.

to have not only their attributes but also their mistakes magnified. They had to use a variety of media and blend objective descriptions with subjective knowledge and narratives about themselves, whilst keeping to the deadline.

Creating stories through drawing

It is clear that drawing has rivals, particularly the camera and computer-based imaging systems. However, much visualization is still reliant on drawing, even if the resultant outputs will be applied through new digital media. For example the advertising and branding industry use storyboarding as a way of developing ideas about a brand and its values before committing to the expensive use of experts and media. Storyboards are used by filmmakers and directors to plan out a film and to sell it (pitch it) to potential financial supporters. And drawn storyboards are still vital in developing animations. Here the relationship between drawing and film finds a unique expression. If you turn a storyboard of (for example) a bouncing ball into a simple flip book, the eye sees the images flicking over as movement—drawing becomes a moving image. However it's applied, the construction of storyboards and storybooks exploiting drawing costs pennies in comparison to the huge expense of film production.

Children's picture storybooks are commonly developed through similar visual narratives, with or without any accompanying text, as the artist tries different ways to make each page work. Submission of a mock or dummy book before commission is essential for editorial consideration of the artist's intention. At this point, the plot and characters might not be finalized. Drawings are not only used because they are cheap and versatile, they function as flexibly as words to form a dialogue between writer and artist. Drawing enables the creator to experiment with page composition, character development, emotional expression, scenic buildup and sensitivity of media.

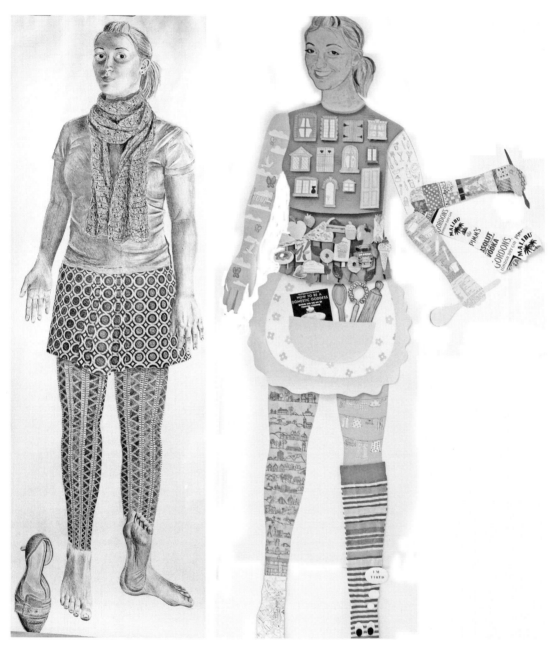

Figure 6.8 Reinterpretation through drawing. Work of
first-year illustration students. (Copyright Liz Anelli)

Figure 6.9 Storyboarding
for a children's book.
(Copyright Liz Anelli)

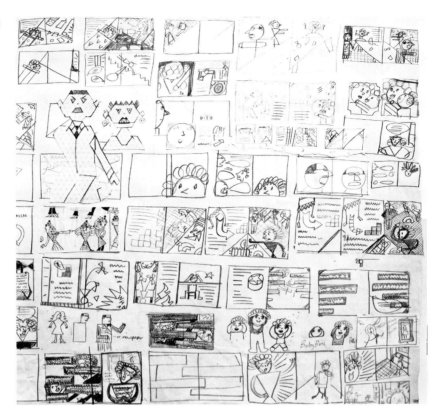

Figure 6.10 Three-
dimensional school
visualization by Liz Anelli.
(Copyright Liz Anelli)

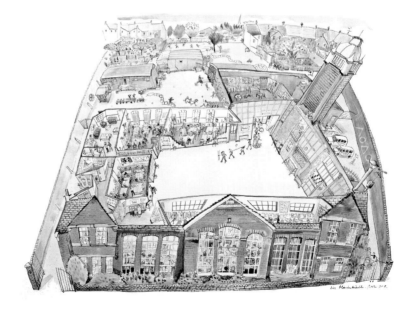

Seek feedback and develop your style

Drawing has a role in the formative processes of design, for example in creating and developing ideas, and in the summative processes such as the visualising and communicating of outcomes and finished ideas. It is the most flexible and versatile process you will ever learn, and all it takes to activate this deep knowledge and highly transferable skill is a pencil and paper.

Every stage of learning in the field of art and design is open to being seen by others—even your private sketchbooks. By definition, your work as a designer is for public viewing. While you may be constantly critical of your own outputs, in much commercial design work, the process of visualization, involving stages of exploratory drawing, is the point when an idea is tested and subjected to critical feedback by a third party.

All visually creative professions have problem solving at their heart. A furniture designer seeks to invent a novel chair that still fulfils all the old remits of sitting comfortably; advertisers are always looking for new ways to sell; fashion, product and indeed vehicle designers need to regularly reinvent the wheel. In some situations, you can literally draw yourself out of a predicament. Humans dominate this planet because of our incurable curiosity and our need to discover things and improve things. Drawing, for all design disciplines, is the deconstruction and reconstruction in our own personal vision of the nuts and bolts of the world.

CHAPTER SUMMARY

- Visual imagery is our most ancient means of communication, and it still provides a very effective way of getting other people to understand our ideas and proposals.
- Drawing helps you to think and work things out by visualising your ideas.
- Drawing is the essential foundation on which artists and designers build their ability to communicate. Particularly practice your descriptive drawing.
- Drawing develops your creative skills. It helps with creative problem finding as well as creative problem solving.
- Drawing helps designers integrate their intellectual process of idea creation, analysis, synthesis and evaluation.
- Keep a sketchbook. Freehand drawings, thumbnail sketches and rough images in sketchbooks help the process of design inquiry.

chapter 7

computer-aided design: past, present, future

jonathon allen and paul kouppas

ABOUT THIS CHAPTER

Computer-aided design (CAD) has evolved at a tremendous pace, from simple two-dimensional (2D) draughting to more complex three-dimensional (3D) modelling to the use of animation and the linking with artificial intelligence. Since the first integrated circuit was developed in 1958, computational processing speed and memory capacity have grown exponentially, doubling every two years or so—a phenomenon known as Moore's Law after Gordon Moore, the co-founder of Intel, who first identified and predicted this trend. The proliferation of ever more powerful and cheaper computers has provided a fertile environment for CAD's growth, but, moreover, the great leaps forward have been when CAD has migrated from one discipline to another. This chapter is about this important migration. The way in which CAD has evolved by jumping between disciplines is indicative of the evolution of the design professions themselves. The resultant cross-pollination of ideas, practices and tools has led to new hybrid design disciplines. Computers are now increasingly mediating design processes and have changed much of design practice itself.

CAD at the core of design practice and design education

The ever-evolving and multimodal nature of the design process means that design students and professionals will necessarily need to be conversant in a wide range of CAD programs and, further, will often be simultaneously learning whilst using software. Knowing which process or software to use, and when, is perhaps the key to addressing today's design challenges and meeting ever-shorter time scales. The new design virtuoso's instrument is the computer, and the designer's virtuosity is in drawing together a range of computer tools to compose designs or perform his or her role in delivering a good response to a brief. The designer at times will perform solo but will typically be working alongside (whether literally or, increasingly, virtually) other specialists as part of a team working on the different aspects of a complex design project. These projects can often involve many people in different parts of the world. The integration and management of these projects pose their own challenges, such as the consideration of file formats and compression to allow for the acceptance and delivery of files, and a suite of computer tools more readily assists this process.

Navigating these challenges can be both exciting and daunting, but if approached in the right way, CAD can help unleash and augment the designer's creative capacity. That creative capacity, of course, must already exist in the designer. CAD can assist in realizing visions and facilitating a greater understanding of concepts but still requires ideas to be worked out via more traditional means such as drawing, argument, critique and research. As with any instrument, CAD requires talent and diligence to master.

From starting a design degree to commencing a professional career in design will take between three and five years. In that time, you will be exposed to a plethora of software applications, from general word-processing, Web-searching and communication tools to more specialist 2D draughting packages for the generation of engineering and plan drawings; 3D modelling software for creating accurate representations of products, buildings, packaging or animation characters; animation applications for the generation of fly-throughs or short movies; digital imaging software for vector and pixel-based image generation and manipulation; multimedia applications and Web authoring tools for interactivity; as well as analytical software to help verify and evaluate design ideas.

You may spend three or four years honing your skills with these packages before perhaps entering the profession you've trained for. An important realization is that the field of CAD will also evolve dramatically in this time, with upgrades and new features—indeed, by the time you graduate, the software you began using may look nothing like it did when you started learning it. The software may not even be available, or new players may enter the market, such is the pace of change and competition in the CAD software market.

This may seem rather formidable, and indeed there is a lot to learn, but understanding how CAD has evolved and how it is being applied to help realize designers' ideas can be quite inspiring. Investing the time to hone design skills—both manual and digital—is vital to your success as a designer. Having an appreciation and understanding of how computers are, or potentially could be, used in the design process, along with some generalizable technical skills in their application is now increasingly important. It matters less what particular software you use. What's more important to employers is your knowledge of CAD, the adaptability of your skills and your ability to learn quickly. Indeed, many companies use their own in-house proprietary software (e.g. Pixar), and so the only way of learning the package is to work there. What is important is garnering the fundamental processes that are the foundation of most proprietary software. So if your dream job is to work at Pixar (whose isn't?), then you need to equip yourself with the principles of traditional animation such as 'squash and stretch', 'timing and motion' and so on. Even if your ambition is not to work for an animation studio, a knowledge of animation and the ability to stage an idea can facilitate a better presentation of your designs and can help you incorporate personality, expression or mood in your design ideas. Increasingly, designers are combining inspiration, skills and techniques whilst adopting tools from outside their primary discipline.

When faced with learning a CAD package, the terminology can be somewhat daunting and alien—from *ACIS SAT* to *splines* and *NURBS,* the terminology used in CAD sounds like something more akin to science fiction—and certainly the field of CAD is guilty of acronym abuse. So what does it all mean, and what do you really need to know to get your head around the subject? In order to answer these questions and anticipate what your future as a design practitioner will be like, it is worth not only looking at current practice, but also how we have got to here. In turn, we can better anticipate how CAD is likely to evolve in the near future.

2D CAD: from draughting machines to machines that draught

The evolution of CAD has followed an interesting path, migrating from aircraft to automotive to architecture to animation to artificial intelligence, gaining richness en route. Computer-aided design also used to be known as computer-aided draughting, and this is an indicator of CAD's two-dimensional origins. The first CAD packages were largely replacements of the drawing board, producing predominantly orthographic and isometric drawings. The huge advantage of CAD was its ability to duplicate elements, allowing for quick modifications of part drawings, easy sharing of files, and dramatic reduction in the time taken to produce and edit drawings. There was also a key advantage in electronic storage of files, meaning that files could readily be duplicated and shared (particularly important when the design team members are working in different locations and manufacture is occurring overseas). The need for plan chests full of drawings in each location quickly became a thing of the past.

It is rare to see drawing boards and draughting machines these days, but not so long ago design studios were full of them—many manufacturing companies, engineering firms and architects offices had vast rooms filled with draughters

> **Computer-Aided Design (CAD)**
> ***
> Today CAD can be used to precisely define design ideas, and it can be used to help sketch out vague, ethereal concepts. It is a core tool in a wide range of industries from film special effects to civil engineering, and it has a variety of applications from idea generation to component testing and user trials. It offers important functionality at most of the stages of a typical design project. Three of the most valuable functions for CAD include:
>
> - *Visualization:* the construction of digital representations ranging from pictorial images to virtual reality installations
> - *Simulation:* the creation of digital models that allow some level of interaction by various stakeholders
> - *Technical assessment:* this includes anticipating manufacturing problems, understanding a site, assembly, testing strength and evaluation of usability.
>
> The linking of CAD with computer-aided manufacture (CAM) has given rise to the term CAD/CAM.

labouring over their technical drawings, with plan chests full of blueprints and detailed drawings of every single part of a product or building. Thankfully, but also sadly for the loss of this artistry, those days are gone and technical drawings are now almost exclusively computer-generated. This has dramatically accelerated the design detailing and development process. Many CAD packages now include standardized parts files, so designers can simply drag and drop items into their design drawings. For instance, standardized items such as doors, windows and various building panels can be retrieved from a directory and dropped into architectural plans; or in engineering, standardized pipes, tubes and mechanical fixings can be quickly inserted into drawing files. This not only speeds up the process of producing detailed drawings and plans but also ensures dimensional accuracy. Many parts manufacturers also provide digital drawing files of their stock so that designers can accurately accommodate these parts in their designs with the assurances that everything will fit.

Importantly, producing drawings in CAD means that the same computer file that produced the drawing can also be used to generate cutting paths for the manufacture of items, thus resulting in a far more efficient and accurate process. This translation from CAD draughting to digital making is often referred to as CAD/CAM, where CAM stands for computer-aided manufacture. Many 2D CAD applications now incorporate 3D capabilities, but the development of 3D CAD systems have, by and large, superseded their 2D cousins.

> **"Producing drawings in CAD means that the same computer file that produced the drawing can also be used to generate cutting paths for the manufacture of items."**

3D CAD: from aircraft to automotive and back

The development of commercial 3D CAD software has an interesting past. Aircraft designers during the 1940s would use small wooden strips called splines to create templates for aircraft. The thin wooden strips were bent and held in place at key points (nodes), and the timber's natural stiffness ensured that a smooth curve resulted. These splines were then traced onto paper to create the templates for the construction of the aircraft. This was very much a hands-on craft technique, but

the principles behind the construction of these spline curves remain the basis of modern CAD systems. In the late 1950s and early 1960s, mathematical definitions of these curves were developed by the French mathematicians Paul De Casteljau and Pierre Bézier. Both worked in the automotive industry (De Casteljau for Citroën and Bézier for Renault) and, as is typical of the secrecy of the automotive industry, worked independently without knowing of each other's work. Bézier published his work in 1962, and his name is best remembered because the early vector-based graphics and animation tools used Bézier curves to generate lines or motion paths in the computer. A Bézier curve consists of a line defined by two end points plus a series of nodes on that line that can be moved using control handles to redefine the curve. Bézier curves are still integral in how computer models in CAD are drawn and defined today.

A mathematical definition of such curves allowed computers to quickly crunch the numbers to generate and manipulate the lines, allowing precise representation of exterior surfaces. Commonly, 3D surfaces in CAD are referred to as parametric surfaces, and they can be mathematically represented by NURBS, or nonuniform rational B-splines, which are like rubber sheets stretched over the surface. Imagine, then, a grid of lines projected over this sheet with control points to allow the surface to be stretched and manipulated by the designer to create complex free-form surfaces. This is how dynamic models can be created: by patching together a series of these NURBS surfaces.

Once the overall surfaces of the object are created, a material editor is used to create textures that can be mapped onto those surfaces for rendering. So once the CAD model has been

Figure 7.1 Wall-E paper mechanics, 2008. UV layout and paper cutout, flat shade render and textured high dynamic range imaging rendering. (Photo copyright Paul Kouppas)

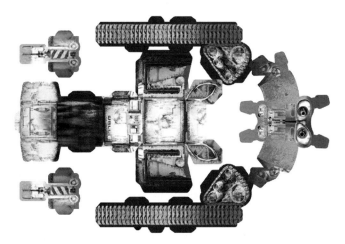

created, the object can be rendered to appear matte or shiny, hairy or smooth, coloured or plain, translucent or opaque. Many animation and visualization packages call their desktop a 'scene', allowing the designer the ability to stage his or her models with cameras, lights, and other digital assets (sometimes referred to as actors). Each of these digital assets must be controlled through a variety of settings to allow for various lighting conditions and viewing angles so that the computer knows how to render the surfaces, cast shadows and add reflections to create lifelike visualizations.

Much of the development of early CAD systems was either in research groups at universities or by in-house teams at large automotive and aircraft manufacturing companies. There were two reasons for this: first, the sheer cost of computers in the 1960s was prohibitive for smaller industries to adopt CAD, and, second, the engineering requirements of both automobiles and aircraft required the ability to manufacture complex 3D

surfaces. The pioneering developers of CAD systems included, from the automotive field, General Motors, Renault and Ford, and from the aircraft industry, Lockheed and McDonnell-Douglas. Throughout the 1970s, many other automotive and aircraft manufacturers developed their own CAD programs, but because of the nature of those industries and the commercial sensitivity of their processes, these CAD systems were specialized and bespoke. It wasn't until 1980 that standardization began, with the introduction of the Initial Graphic Exchange Standard (IGES)—a standard still in use today that allows complex 3D curves and surfaces to be transferred between different CAD systems.

The French aircraft manufacturer Avion Marcel Dassault began developing a 3D CAD application in 1977 for the development of the Mirage jet fighter aircraft. It was soon realized that the software application it had created could have commercial value, and in 1981 a subsidiary company,

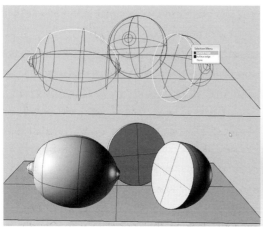

Figure 7.2 Kiwi-lime, 2009. Simple NURBS demonstration surface model constructed from single Bézier curve and revolve or lathe technique, photo textures applied allow for a convincing rendering. (Photo copyright Paul Kouppas)

Dassault Systemes, was established. A year later, in a sales and marketing partnership with IBM, one of the most successful 3D CAD applications, Computer Aided Three-dimensional Interactive Application, or CATIA® for short, was released. Dassault Systemes remains one of the leading CAD software providers and includes Solid-Works® and CATIA® in its portfolio along with several other computer software tools to manage the complete product life cycle.

from aircraft to architecture

Because CATIA was initially developed for handling the complex nature of 3D aircraft surfaces, it was readily adopted by other transport design disciplines, such as automotive, rail and marine craft design. Architects have also utilized the software for its ability to handle complex geometry and surfaces. Most notably, Frank Gehry's Gehry Technologies, has developed Digital Project™, a suite of software for 3D building information modelling, built upon the CATIA engine, precisely because it can handle the complex free-form surfaces typical of his buildings.

Another architect who advocates the use of CATIA, along with several other CAD tools, is Mark Burry, director of the Spatial Information Architecture Laboratory and professor of innovation at RMIT University in Melbourne, Australia. Burry is a pioneering researcher and practitioner in the role of CAD in creative and transdisciplinary projects, and one of many case studies where this best plays out is in his career-long work on Antoni Gaudí's masterpiece, the Sagrada Família church in Barcelona (see www.sagradafamilia.cat/).

Gaudí commenced work on the church in 1883, but by the time of his death in 1926 the church was less than a quarter complete. During the Spanish Civil War, many of Gaudí's models of the building were destroyed, and so the completion of the church has relied on in-depth research, interrogation and interpretation of Gaudí's processes in order to complete the design according to his intent. One of the design processes Gaudí developed was to create physical models by stretching strings across a space and adding weights to the strings at particular points to pull the string to generate complex catenary structures. When the structure (or an image of it such as a photo) was inverted, the form of his buildings was revealed. In essence, Gaudí's process is not too dissimilar to the way in which aircraft designers used splines, adding extra force at particular points to change the curvature of a line. This process can be digitally modelled today using 3D CAD systems where control points are manipulated to replicate the complex surfaces that Gaudí proposed.

Burry first began work on Gaudí whilst still a student, and at that time the complex structures had to be calculated and drawn by hand. This was a very labour-intensive process but perhaps, too, an insightful one, as it afforded a deeper understanding of the complexities of Gaudí's structures and of the processes by which they were generated. Burry is now executive architect for the project and works with teams in Australia and Spain studying the remaining pieces of Gaudí's physical models and drawings in order to interpret and complete the design. Parametric CAD software is used to help generate digital models that resolve some of the details left behind in an attempt to present designs that correlate with Gaudí's intent. Because parametric software allows multiple points of a surface to be manipulated in relation to each other point, the 3D CAD model can be tweaked relatively quickly to best fit with the remaining physical models. With the use of rapid prototyping, the digital model can be reproduced as a physical model to help verify the design.

The use of CAD here is particularly interesting, as it is helping to reveal insights into Gaudí's compositional strategies and is allowing the creative exploration and interpretation of Gaudí's work long after his death. The Sagrada Família church is still under construction, and CAD is used to share information and progress across the world. From an office in Melbourne, the architect can be discussing (via video link) a particular design feature with the stone masons and site architects in Barcelona. In front of them both can be the same CAD model in both digital form (on screen) and as a physical representation (a rapid prototyped part).

the artistry of media and mediation

The ability to use CAD with other forms of computer-based communication was very attractive to the automotive industry because of the industry's need to support international team working. Indeed, the automotive sector has been one of the pioneers of CAD and has also been an early adopter of other technologies to streamline its business. There are several reasons for this. Automotive design and manufacture is a global business, producing vehicles for international markets. Cars and commercial vehicles must conform to different national legislation and design requirements as well as appeal to the nuances of different cultural groups. The complexities of operating such a business with design, engineering and manufacturing teams geographically dispersed around the globe and the necessity to ensure

that all of the teams work toward the common goal, on time and on budget, require very effective management and communication. Increasingly, this management and communication are being mediated with computational tools typically referred to as product life cycle management.

The management of the life cycle of a vehicle not only involves every stage of design, development and manufacture, but also the vehicle's use and service and, ultimately, its disposal and recycling—all of which need to be planned for and accommodated in the vehicle's design from the outset. The development of a new vehicle, from initial meetings and early concept sketches to the time the vehicle is driven off the production line, takes several years and an incredible financial investment. There are many stages in the process of design and development involving teams of specialists in different locations around the world.

CAD has a vital role to play in the styling of vehicle form, and designers work using an array of 2D and 3D computer applications to produce lifelike visual representations of vehicles. The process begins with many sketches, whether traditionally with pen, pencil, marker and pastel or on a digital tablet. After a series of reviews and critiques, refinement of the sketches will translate into exploratory CAD models. Typically, the 2D illustrations can be inserted into the background so that splines and surfaces can be created from them. Programs such as Autodesk Alias® allow designers to capture details of their 2D digital sketches to form the basis of a 3D CAD model. The two-dimensional curves are given a new life, curving and bending as they are shaped into three-dimensional representations. BMW's fabric-skinned shape-shifting sports car concept, the GINA—'Geometry and Functions in N Adaptations'—is the embodiment of such practice. The aluminium wire frame structure accurately represents the NURBS curves used to generate the design, and its stretchable polyurethane-coated elastane skins the NURBS surfaces.

Automotive clay modellers will work alongside the designers to produce physical representations of a vehicle. Both the clay modellers and the designers are after Class A surfaces, where all of the curves on the surface are accurately aligned and congruent. In order to obtain this, often the CAD and clay models are developed and refined concurrently. An initial CAD model may provide the basis for the production of a clay model, which will be refined by hand, digitally scanned and reimported to CAD software to finesse.

CAD and the support of teams

Once the CAD model is produced, others in the design, engineering, manufacture and marketing divisions of the company can work with the CAD data to help plan and develop other essential design tasks. Mechanical engineers can use analytical software tools to assess such things as the vehicle's aerodynamics and drag efficiency, the structural integrity of the vehicle and how it will perform in virtual crash testing and the vehicle's vibration and handling characteristics. Ergonomists can assess the vehicle's accommodation of the particular demographic it has been designed for—this is particularly relevant in a global market where anthropometric data vary from region to region, and cultural factors, such as the wearing of turbans by Sikh communities, also need to be taken into account. Ergonomic software can help assess (preferably early in the design cycle) a vehicle's design based on the 3D CAD model, and the layout of controls, seating posture, ingress

and egress, viewing position, safety and comfort can be resolved alongside the designer. Colour and trim designers will take the CAD model and render different colour and material finish combinations and prepare specifications based upon this. Manufacturing and production engineers can detail a bill of materials from the CAD model that, in turn, can be used to help procure parts, liaise with suppliers, develop manufacturing plants and inform costing and financial analysis of the vehicle's profitability.

Consideration of environmental impact, ecodesign and design for disassembly needs to be factored into the design cycle, preferably as early as possible. Automotive regulatory compliance management tools are now part of many CAD and product life cycle management software packages, providing lists of suppliers, identification of recycled content in parts and even assessing the best and worst manufacturing locations in regard to environmental and financial factors. Different legislation in different parts of the world also needs to be considered, and, in conjunction with the bill of materials, legislative and regulatory compliance can be assessed and changes made accordingly using analytical software. This is an increasingly important factor in automotive design (and in product design more generally) particularly in Europe, where end-of-life vehicle legislation makes it the responsibility of automotive manufactures to consider how the vehicles they produce will be disposed of.

With the proliferation of CAD-based tools, one might think that manual skills such as hand sketching and hand modelling are no longer relevant. This is far from the case. Indeed, sketching is still core to automotive design, as sketching allows relatively quick exploration of form and is also a wonderfully emotive medium that captures the gestural energy, essence and flair of an idea. Physical making is also still prevalent, in the form of clay modelling. Whilst the automotive sector has experimented with the all-digital studio, limitations of this process were observed, and most studios will have a balance of digital and physical processes. The real success of CAD and CAM systems here has been in speeding up the process and facilitating more fluid conversation and design iteration amongst the teams.

Increasingly in the automotive sector, project teams are distributed around the globe, with key divisions of companies located in the United States, Asia and Europe. This has given rise to the twenty-four-hour studio, where designers and engineers will each build upon the work of the other.

> **"The real success of CAD and CAM systems here has been in speeding up the process and facilitating more fluid conversation and design iteration amongst the teams."**

So a project might move from Detroit, USA, to Melbourne, Australia, to Cologne in Germany and then back again. This has the great potential of speeding up the process but also poses problems of management and communication (in the studio described above, language differences mean that the car *hood* becomes a *bonnet* and then an *auto haube* as it travels from team to team). Working from the same CAD model, where the parts are visually represented, provides a more universal language but also necessitates powerful computers and a fast network system to not only transfer the data but to work on it concurrently.

Augmented reality (AR) is an emerging technology that allows for the real-time visualization of CAD over a live video feed. It can facilitate, using immersive stereoscopic head-up displays and haptic devices, the ability for designers to virtually see a CAD model appear immersed in their field of vision so that they can move around it and see it from any angle. Haptics allow the user to seemingly feel and touch the virtual object using three-degrees-of-freedom torque feedback devices. The integration of such technology will allow designers to

Dune concept #1
Front frame gloss black | Rear frame matte black | Grey tint lens

Dune concept #2
Front frame gloss dark bronze | Rear frame matte chocolate | Burnt umber lens

Figure 7.3 Augmented reality glasses, 2011. Renders of 3D solid model for rapid prototyping by Explore Engage. (Photo copyright Paul Kouppas)

step away from their computers and virtually sculpt or verify a design in much the same way as automotive clay modellers do today. Volkswagen currently employs AR for training of technical experts in the field of car service; the digital projections enable the company to convey the complex technical inner life of the vehicles to the trainees much better than conventional methods. Sydney-based company Explore Engage is developing see-through AR glasses; these devices will tether to smartphones and allow the user to experience AR for a range of applications. Soon such devices and the technology will be prolific in the marketplace, so it is quite plausible that augmented reality will be part of CAD systems in the very near future.

story and captivating detail of the film. Making the film took 800,000 computer hours to generate and render well over 100,000 frames, equating to 600 billion bytes of information. Prior to this date, computational hardware would have struggled to produce such a film. A whole raft of full-length computer animated films have followed, and CGI animation has long since overtaken traditional animation to become the industry standard. CGI is also extensively used in live-action films, and, in many cases, the quality is so good that it is very difficult to determine whether some scenes in films are real or not. The advertising industry has been quick to see the advantages.

In 3D computer animation, a character is modelled, and a representation of the character's

from animation to allegory

The discussion of CAD and its evolution cannot ignore the phenomenal development in computer-generated imagery (CGI) and its impact across the spectrum of design. In particular, dynamic CGI in the form of computer animation is perhaps one of the most interesting allegorical stories of the phenomenal rate of progress of CAD capabilities and how computers have transformed an entire industry. The term *animation* perhaps serves as a poignant analogy in the context of this discussion: frame by frame, CAD has moved faster and faster to a point where it appears to be fluid and has come to life.

When *Toy Story* by Pixar hit movie theatres in 1995, a new era in computer animation began. It was the first completely computer-generated feature-length film and was highly profitable; in comparison with traditionally animated films, the film used far fewer animators and was therefore significantly less expensive to make. The box office takings were also a testament to the compelling

Digital Models

Digital models are valuable in many ways. They can be easily stored and modified; they can be electronically distributed to other stakeholders in a design project and some can be tested to explore strengths and weaknesses in components (e.g. using finite element analysis). Sometimes designs are just too big or complex to prototype. Products such as new buildings or passenger aircraft will be developed and proven largely as computer-based models.

The field of product design differs from these large projects in a number of ways. The look and feel of consumer products are vital aspects of their success. Very often, the only way to get early feedback on these aesthetic qualities from potential users is to provide them with models, visual prototypes or fully working representations. Product design, more than most other design professions, requires the fast construction of three-dimensional models. The ability of modern rapid prototyping systems to allow designers to create tangible forms from digital models means that we continue to see the making of both two-dimensional and three-dimensional models. Rapid prototyping systems can produce components quickly, accurately and in tough materials, allowing them to be used in working prototypes.

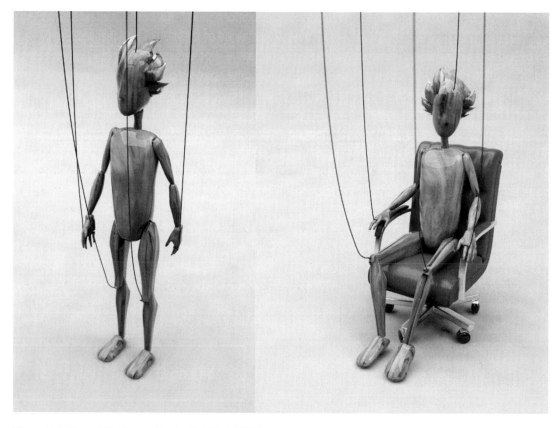

Figure 7.4 Puppet 'No Strings Attached', 2008. NURBS surface model with realistic photo wood textures, rendered using high dynamic range imaging. (Photo copyright Paul Kouppas)

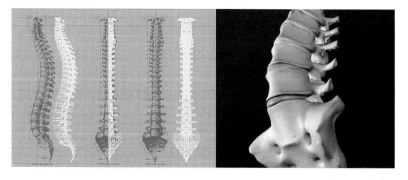

Figure 7.5 Realistic human spine model, 1999. Originally NURBS surface, converted to a polygonal model, materials applied and rendered. Paul Kouppas/Moberg Multimedia Photo. (Photo copyright Paul Kouppas)

structure, or skeleton, is generated. This skeleton consists of a number of animation variables, or avars, that define the character's motion. In *Toy Story,* the central character, Woody, had in the order of 700 avars that could be controlled to bring the character to life. Ten years later, Aslan, the title character in the film production of *The Chronicles of Narnia: The Lion, the Witch and the*

Wardrobe, had as many avars to control his face as Woody had in his entire body. These avars can be considered much like the control points in other 3D parametric models, but, interestingly, the movement of the points can be programmed to move in certain ways. All of these morph and dynamically bend the 3D mesh of the character, each a reflection of a physical nuance or phoneme to give life to the character. Behavioural properties can be assigned to the avars to define how these control points move—for instance the way grass wafts in the breeze can be described mathematically, and then computer models can be programmed to behave in the same way. This is giving rise to fascinating new disciplines and hybrid areas of design, linking such areas as mathematics, computing, biomechanics and biology. Avars can also be controlled through motion capture, whereby an actor wearing a body costume containing numerous reflective marker points acts out the role in front of the camera. The movement of the points is detected, and that movement is applied to the avars of the CAD model to create lifelike movement. This technique has been used very effectively in a number of films, but perhaps most impressively by Weta Digital in its work on *The Lord of the Rings, King Kong* and *Avatar.*

from animation to artificial intelligence

A major breakthrough in CGI films was the enormous scale of the battle scenes in *The Lord of the Rings,* where a hundred thousand characters appeared in the panorama. The characters were predominantly produced by CGI, but each behaved with a degree of uniqueness that hitherto had not been produced. To control and choreograph each character would have been far too time-consuming and would have made directorial changes extremely difficult. A solution came from one of the computer graphics software engineers working at Weta Digital, Stephen Regelous, who gave each character a 'brain'. Rather than treating the characters as particles that move in a uniform or predictable way, the characters were given artificial intelligence that allowed them to react and respond to others around them as well as to the environment they were in. Stephen Regelous received an Academy Award for his work, and the proprietary software he developed, Massive (Multiple Agent Simulation System in Virtual Environment), has since been used on many other films.

Massive software has also been used in real-life applications, to model behaviour of human crowds, traffic and other ecological systems. For instance, crowd planning and emergency evacuations of buildings and urban environments can be simulated entirely in CAD. This allows for architects and designers to become better informed prior to committing to a final design. It can also save an incredible amount of money, save time and, of course, save lives.

Modelling humans—be it their anthropometric form, their dynamic movement or their behaviour—is particularly challenging given the complexities of capturing realistic motion and expression, let alone analysing and synthesize behavioural and attitudinal responses. There are many around the world working on this and perhaps in the not-too-distant future evidence-based avatars will be incorporated into CAD software to help verify, evaluate and even perform the designing for you.

Whilst CAD has changed the way in which designers work, of crucial importance is to ensure that computers are the ones assisting designers

Figure 7.6 Swimmer with goggles, 2008. Face modelled as NURBS surface based on stock photo and then converted to polygonal model. Evidence of organic/NURBS surface present in her cap. Model and rendering by Paul Kouppas. (Photo copyright Paul Kouppas)

in the process of designing. There is a very real danger in being seduced by CAD; that somehow the capabilities of CAD can compensate for a lack of design ability. As with any instrument, to master CAD requires talent and diligence. It requires creative capacity and a particularly capable designer who can use the tool and not be instrumentally designed by it.

CHAPTER SUMMARY

- The way in which CAD has evolved by jumping between disciplines is indicative of the evolution of the design professions themselves. Computers are now increasingly mediating design processes and have changed much of design practice.

- CAD quickly gained a foothold in design because it enabled easy duplication of parts, quick modifications of drawings, the visualization and testing of models and easy sharing of files.

- CAD models can also be used to guide manufacturing. Linking CAD with computer-aided manufacture is referred to as CAD/CAM.

- Knowing which computing tool to use, and when, in the design process is key to addressing today's design challenges and meeting ever-shorter time scales.

- CAD can help unleash and augment the designer's creative capacity.
- A knowledge of animation and the ability to stage an idea can facilitate both a better presentation of your designs and can help you incorporate personality, expression or mood in your design ideas.
- In the designing process there continues to be an important symbiotic relationship between tangible models and digital models.
- Today CAD can be used to model complex systems such as human behaviour in crowds, traffic and ecological systems.
- CAD and CAM systems have speeded up the designing process and facilitated more fluid conversations and iteration amongst design teams.

chapter 8

game design and the importance of narrative

michele d. dickey

ABOUT THIS CHAPTER

Since the 1990s, computer and video games have become an increasingly popular form of entertainment, now generating revenue that surpasses that of the motion picture industry. New types of games combine education with entertainment in so-called edutainment. *Serious* games in a variety of formats are now being used to educate, train, persuade and inform customers of for example universities, health centres and commercial organizations. They are now found in marketing, politics, medicine and even religion. Games can be a very effective tool because, unlike static or motion media, games have the potential to draw in users. As players, we engage through interaction.

While the design of games and interactive media has become hugely popular, it presents many challenges for those who want to work in the associated professions. Interaction designers need to have a working knowledge of programming, digital art, sound design, characterization and the human factors of user interaction. These domains represent a wide variety of skill sets, the sum of which few designers possess. Perhaps most significantly, game designers today need to understand the significance of *narrative,* and this can be particularly challenging. Partly this chapter aims to provide interaction designers with frameworks for creating and integrating well-crafted narrative for both entertainment and serious game design. But there's also a message for those with career ambitions in other design professions about the importance of narrative in engaging users in many fields of design today.

---

the significance of narrative

At a basic level, a narrative is a story. It can take a written form, but it can also be created using visual images or just spoken language. Because design has traditionally been located in the visual arts, the communication of design narrative has heavily exploited drawings, photographs, moving images or three-dimensional form. It's the visual expression of narrative, exploiting shape, line, movement and colour, that can make a design such as a film or a computer game appear attractive, engaging or understandable. For game designers particularly, such visual tools and techniques are vital to the creation of narrative. Narrative plays a key role in human reasoning. The psychologist Jerome Bruner suggests that narrative allows humans to assign meaning to their experiences.[1] Humans use narrative not only to frame thought but to guide actions and to convey knowledge. Narrative within games provides a framework for interaction, and although it is not always necessary for game play (think of the game checkers), it often plays an important role, particularly in digital games. Narrative can provide motivation as well as an explanation for interaction. It can be particularly important in the design of serious games because it serves as a cognitive framework for problem solving.[2]

> "It's the visual expression of narrative, exploiting shape, line, movement and colour, that can make a design such as a film or a computer game appear attractive, engaging or understandable."

To understand the dynamics involved in game narrative, it is helpful to have some knowledge of how narrative functions in different game genres along with the interactions of game mechanics. Therefore, this chapter continues with an exploration of the relationship between narrative, game genres and game mechanics. Following this is a discussion of methods for developing narrative and character design and a short discussion of how narrative can be supported by game environments and spaces.

narrative and game genres

As in film and literature, there are a variety of genres that are used to classify games. Some of

Modelling Serious Fun with Video Games

Why are video games so popular? What underpins an industry currently worth $50 billion a year? One suggestion is that despite them being labelled an entertainment medium, games tap into a fundamental human drive to learn. Video games, like models and prototypes used in design, provide a way of learning through making mistakes. Importantly, games and design models both allow you to make mistakes with very little risk. If your design model breaks during testing or your game character is killed, your real-world self doesn't come to any harm, you probably haven't wasted months of development time (or perhaps you have!) and you haven't had to invest huge sums of money. As Tim Brown of design consultancy IDEO has pointed out, designing is about trying to fail faster because we learn much more from failure than from success. Design models provide a very effective means for learning by failing in controlled, safe and cheap ways.

A good video game, like an effective design model, allows us to experiment and play, to bend and break the rules. It can surprise us with its feedback and we achieve pleasure by learning from it, my mastering and reapplying the lessons it offers us. Both have the capacity to surprise and delight, and there is progression offering opportunities for new learning at new levels. Design modelling, like gaming, isn't always about playing—even if it appears to be to the casual onlooker. They are both forms of serious learning.

the more common game genres include action games, adventure games, role-playing games, simulations (construction, sports, life and vehicle), strategy games and multiplayer online games—often involving many participants in so-called massive multiplayer online games.

Although most games fit broadly within a genre, it is not uncommon for games to incorporate and interweave elements of different genres. Similarly, not all game genres incorporate narrative to the

Figure 8.1 Racing simulation game. (Getty 101263297 RM)

same degree, nor do they always have clearly de-fined attributes. Table 8.1 provides an overview of several of the most common game genres along with generalizations of the standard conventions of *game play, game types* and *examples* as well as the role of *narrative.*

Because games are used for a variety of pur-poses, it is important that designers have a sense of different game genres, the types of game play and the role of narrative provided in different genres. Not all game genres suit all purposes. Action games can be very engaging but may not be a suitable choice for some types of education and training. Similarly, adventure games are rich in narrative but require an investment of time and do not always have the broad appeal that might be

> "Because games are now being used for a variety of purposes, it is important that designers have a sense of different game genres, the types of game play and the role of narrative provided in different genres."

necessary for product marketing. Having knowl-edge of the type of game play involved in each genre is important for designers in matching the purpose and goals of a game to a specific game genre and constructing the game narrative.

Table 8.1   GAME GENRES AND CONVENTIONS

Game genre	Conventions
Action games	• Game play: reaction time and hand-eye coordination under pressure. • Game types: combat games, fighter games, shooter games (first-person and third-person) and platform games. • Examples: range from arcade games such as *Pong* and *PacMan* to contemporary games such as the *Super Smash Bros.* and *Halo.* • Narrative: Action games traditionally did not present strong narratives; however, as action games have become more complex, narrative storyline is becoming more pervasive and plays a greater role in game design.
Adventure games	• Game play: uncovering an underlying narrative by completing various puzzles, collecting and manipulations, mazes and challenges. • Game types: text-based adventure games and graphical adventure games. • Examples: *Colossal Cave Adventure, Myst* and the *Azada.* • Narrative: Adventure games have been characterized as 'interactive narrative'. Storyline is central to game play, and the purpose of game play is to uncover the storyline.
Role-playing games (RPGs)	• Game play: player adopts a role or character within the game and develops the character by completing various quests. Game narrative and setting are a large part of the game play experience. • Game types: table-top RPGs, computer and console RPGs and massive multiple online role-playing games. • Examples: *Dungeons and Dragons, Final Fantasy* and *World of Warcraft.* • Narrative: Like adventure games, role-playing games also rely strongly on narrative; however, depending on the type of role-playing game, the narrative storyline may differ according to a player's role within the game.
Simulation games	• Game play: to simulate real or fictional reality. • Game types: construction games, sports games, life management games and vehicle simulators. • Examples: *Rollercoaster Tycoon* series (construction), the *Madden* series (sports), the *Sims* series (life management) and *Microsoft Flight Simulator* (vehicle). • Narrative: Simulation games vary in the role of narrative. For some types of simulations, the narrative is little more than a framework for game play, but with the adaptation of online simulations, narrative plays a more influential role as the complexity of game play increases.
Strategy games	• Game play: decision-making (both tactical and logistical) and resource management. • Game types: turn-based strategy games and real-time strategy games. • Examples: Chess, *Risk* and *Civilization.* • Narrative: Similar to simulation games, narrative can play a varying role in strategy games depending on the scale and complexity of the game.
Massive multi-player online (MMO) games	• Game play: persistent online game play via a computer, console or mobile device (smartphone, iPod or iPad). • Game types: MMO-RPG, MMO shooter and MMO real-time strategy games. • Examples: *World of Warcraft, Halo,* and *Starcraft.* • Narrative: Like role-playing games, MMOs also rely strongly on narrative; however, depending on the type of MMO game, the depth of narrative may vary. With MMO-RPGs, the narrative is embedded in the environment. While there is typically a broad narrative arc, each player's character will have different experiences and local storylines based on individual game play.

narrative and game mechanics

Like game genre, *game mechanics* is a loosely defined term within the field of game design. Just as there are many different genres and combinations of genres of games, so there are varying types of game mechanics. This can broadly be defined as the type of goal and rule-based interaction provided within a game. Typically, most game play is goal-oriented. The setting and storyline serve as the framework for interaction, while the characters provide differing roles in aiding or impeding a player to achieve a goal. Interaction within game play is usually bound by rules. Rules define what the player can and cannot do, plus they define victory and loss conditions. Because games often blur and blend genres, it is difficult to concretely align game mechanics with various genres. However, at the risk of overgeneralizing, some common game mechanics that can be found within

action, simulation, role-playing, strategy games and massive multiplayer online varieties include the following: collection, elimination, avoidance, resource management, races and construction. In a good game, mechanics are interwoven with the narrative. Table 8.2 presents a summary of these game mechanics along with examples of their application in games and the genres of games where they might be used.

Of course, several of these mechanics may be manifest in various ways in different genres. For example, resource management is a key mechanic for both role-playing games and strategy games, but how it functions can be very different. Within a role-playing game, resource management is used to help a player enhance and develop her or his character—for example by earning money (within the game) to purchase new armour or weapons for the character. Yet resource management within a strategy game may involve land cultivation or the

Table 8.2   GAME MECHANICS

Mechanics	Summary and genre
Collection mechanics	• This mechanic concerns the gathering or collecting a specified amount of objects (points, bounty, territory, etc.). • Game genres: action, role-playing, simulation and strategy games.
Elimination mechanics	• This mechanic requires players to defeat specified enemies, agents or objects. • Game genres: action, role-playing, simulation and strategy games.
Avoidance mechanics	• This mechanic requires players to avoid losing objects or territories. • Game genres: action, role-playing, simulation and strategy games.
Resource management mechanics	• This mechanic requires players to balance and negotiate resources (e.g. tokens, money, health, character attributes and traits) to achieve one or more goals. • Game genres: role-playing, simulation and strategy games.
Race mechanics	• This mechanic requires players to beat an opponent(s) in some type of race negotiating space, time or both. • Game genres: action, role-playing, simulation and strategy games.
Construction mechanics	• This mechanic requires players to build, construct and/or alter an environment. • Game genres: role-playing, simulation and strategy games.

Figure 8.2 Good game mechanics is frequently at the root of pleasurable user experience. (Getty 200122055–001 RF)

acquisition of territory to enhance holdings. The design of narrative supports the plausibility of the game mechanics. Having knowledge of both type and variety of game mechanics is important for interaction designers, because mechanics define the interaction in game play. Much of the success of the user experience of a game can derive from the successful application of game mechanics.

narrative in games

The role of narrative in game design fuels an on-going debate. Advocates of narrative in games argue that a strong narrative storyline can create more immersive and engaging game play,[3] while opponents argue that interaction is the key, not storytelling.[4] People in the latter category hold that narrative is primarily linear and, whilst it might work well in literature and film, games represent a potentially different medium. Games are not necessarily linear in character; they offer opportunities to incorporate storyline whilst permitting a player to impact or even change this story depending upon choices made throughout the game. One strategy for infusing story and plot into game play includes branching stories in which players' choices significantly impact on both the storyline and the outcome. Alternatively, a designer might keep the narrative line intact but allow the players a choice in the order in which they access components of the story.[5]

Narrative often varies in degree from genre to genre. For example, adventure games can be characterized as a type of interactive fiction, where the goal of a game is to uncover the storyline, whereas an action game such as Tetris has very little narrative beyond the goals and mechanics of the game. Typically, narrative serves as an underlying frame for a game. The use of a back story can provide a background or history to a given storyline. Back story can enhance the dramatic context for action and interaction in a game.[6] A back story may be as simple as a brief sketch of the main characters and key conflicts within a storyline (e.g. 'A long time ago in a galaxy far, far away . . .') or it can be as complex as a player's manual containing a detailed history of key characters and conflicts along with maps that illustrate the game's terrain and in-depth explanations of items and actions. The mood and tone of a game can also be established or enhanced by cut scenes. These are elements of storyline dispersed throughout a game and only revealed during the course of play. Cut scenes can take many forms and may be as elaborate as sections of full-screen motion video or as simple as journal entries, book chapters, images, audio broadcasts or even conversations with nonplayer characters.

One of the most common narrative structures found in digital games is the *quest*. This is an age-old device that has been exploited by some of

Figure 8.3 The quest is one of the most common narrative structures found in digital games. (Getty 108270129 RF)

the foremost authors in our culture ranging from Homer, Chaucer, Cervantes and Joyce to the writers of more recent popular films such as *Star Wars, Sleepless in Seattle* and *Finding Nemo*. The classic structure of the quest typically involves a hero or heroine who, for various reasons, must embark on some type of journey. During the journey, this character has to confront various dangers, typically culminating in a large struggle or conflict before returning to everyday life.

This is a popular narrative structure in game design because it affords many opportunities for exploration and battle. One of the more frequently cited sources of guidance on narrative in game design is author and academic Christopher Vogler.[7] In his presentation of the classic quest structure, Vogler draws heavily on the work of foremost scholar of mythology Joseph Campbell, outlining twelve stages of a classic quest which can be found in much contemporary storytelling. Table 8.3 illustrates the nature and purpose of these stages and uses the popular movie *The Wizard of Oz*[8] to set the theory in context.

Once a concept and game genre are decided on, this classic quest can help structure a narrative framework for a game. Narrative can provide a compelling hook, but it doesn't work without effective characterization.

narrative and characterization

In addition to a storyline, many games include nonplayer characters scattered throughout the game play environment. Nonplayer characters may serve a variety of functions within a game. They may play the role of enemies or allies or provide a means of conveying information. Compelling characters can motivate, challenge and even emotionally impact players. As in other forms of media, creating compelling characters can be very challenging, particularly for those without a background in creative writing. Nevertheless, there are strategies for character design for games which can aid novice designers. Prior to the visual design, a designer must first understand the role and function of a character in a game. The following seven character archetypes can typically be found in games built around the classic quest: Protagonist (or hero), Mentor, Threshold Guardian, Herald, Shapeshifter/Trickster and Shadow. These can be traced back to the writings of seminal Swiss psychiatrist Carl Jung, who argues that such archetypal patterns are part of our collective unconscious.[9] However, Christopher Vogler stresses that archetypes should not be considered as fixed roles but rather as a 'function performed temporarily by characters to achieve certain effects in a story'.[10] He proposes that game designers would do better to focus on the psychological function of the archetype and its dramatic function in the progression of the storyline. Table 8.4 presents a short description of the role or purpose of character types and how these roles are manifest in game design.

As with narrative, it is important for designers working in interactive media to have a sense of character design and story development. Knowledge of classic character types and purposes can provide a framework for innovation by inspiring new combinations of type and allowing designers to create new kinds of roles. Once the role and function of a game character has been determined, the next step is to outline visual aspects of a character. If there is motion involved, much information about a character and the role a character plays can be conveyed through animation. Similarly, conventions of attractiveness, agreeableness and dominance can be conveyed through the representations which can exploit shape, line, colour and texture.

Table 8.3   STAGES OF A QUEST (USING THE FILM *WIZARD OF OZ* FOR EXAMPLES)

Stage	Purpose
1. Ordinary world	Stage 1: The hero/protagonist is situated in the ordinary world (or whatever may be construed as ordinary). Example: Dorothy is living on her family farm in Kansas.
2. Call to adventure	Stage 2: Suddenly, the hero/protagonist is presented with a problem, challenge or event which necessitates that he or she leaves the comfort and familiarity of the ordinary world. Example: A tornado strikes Dorothy's house and she lands in Oz.
3. Refusal of the call	Stage 3: The hero/protagonist initially may refuse, balk or have reservations about undertaking the adventure. Example: Dorothy is reluctant to wear the ruby slippers.
4. Meeting with the mentor	Stage 4: The hero/protagonist meets a mentor or someone who may offer advice, guidance or insight into the call to adventure. Example: Glinda the Good Witch convinces Dorothy that the great and powerful Wizard can help her to return home to Kansas.
5. Crossing the first threshold	Stage 5: The hero/protagonist commits to the adventure. During this process or journey, the hero/protagonist encounters a challenge which must be overcome in order to progress. Example: Dorothy is unsure of which path to take. She encounters the Tin Man, who accompanies her on travels along the Yellow Brick Road.
6. Tests, allies and enemies	Stage 6. The hero/protagonist encounters more challenges and confronts and conquers enemies. Example: Dorothy has several encounters, including meeting the Wicked Witch of the West and surviving several assaults (angry trees and field of poppies).
7. Approach to the innermost cave	Stage 7: The hero/protagonist arrives in the *innermost* cave or the site of the central challenge. Example: Dorothy is captured by flying monkeys and is taken to the castle of the Wicked Witch. Her companions, while attempting to rescue her, are also captured.
8. Ordeal	Stage 8: The ordeal is the situation all of the challenges have been leading towards. This is when the hero/protagonist confronts the main antagonist or challenge. In most games, this is often termed the *Big Boss*. Example: Dorothy throws water on the Scarecrow and inadvertently kills the Wicked Witch.
9. Reward (seizing the sword)	Stage 9: The hero/protagonist is rewarded for defeating the main antagonist/challenge. Example: Dorothy is presented with the broomstick of the now deceased Wicked Witch.
10. The road back	Stage 10: Although the hero/protagonist has defeated the main antagonist/challenge, he or she may encounter problems on the return to ordinary life. Example: Dorothy realizes the Wizard is a man in a control booth. The balloon in which she is to travel home escapes.
11. Resurrection	Stage 11: The final conflicts and challenges are overcome and the hero/protagonist prevails. Example: Glinda the Good Witch tells Dorothy she can click her heels to return home.
12. Return with the elixir	Stage 12: Return to the ordinary world. Example: Dorothy awakens to find her adventure was a dream (or was it?)

Table 8.4   CHARACTER TYPES AND ROLES

Character type	Role
Protagonist or hero	The protagonist is typically the lead character in a game. Depending upon the genre, the player may play the game as this.
Mentor	The mentor provides guidance and insight and is typically an ally of the protagonist. Within a game, the mentor may provide the protagonist with aid, tools, insight or information throughout the game.
Threshold guardian	The threshold guardian provides obstacles or hurdles which help prepare the protagonist for future challenges.
Herald	The herald provides information to the protagonist. Within a game, the herald may not always be portrayed as a person or character but may be something that serves to inform the protagonist (a letter, newspaper, announcement, etc.).
Shape-shifter/trickster	The role of the shape-shifter is to provide an element of doubt. In games, the shape-shifter might take the form of an ally to the protagonist (who may not indeed be an ally).
Shadow	The shadow is the antagonist or central conflict for the protagonist. This type has informed the creation of characters such as Darth Vader, Voldemort and the Wicked Witch.

Attributes, Properties and Benefits

We are all confronted with difficult purchasing decisions at times. Sometimes the range of options can be so great, and the differences so complex, that it is almost impossible to identify which of the variations would best suit our needs or circumstances. As purchasers we are not always conscious of how we make choices.

In choosing one product rather than another at a similar price it is necessary to make value judgements. Such judgements are based on product *attributes* or characteristics, such as appearance, convenience or price. These characteristics arise from or are determined by the product's physical *properties* such as weight, size, shape, material, speed, power, surface finish, colour and range of functions. It is the embodiment of these properties in a particular product through its design

that gives rise to its attributes, which in turn influence its perceived *benefits* or value.

Our personal preferences and actual product purchase decisions are rarely rational. We make impulse buys, we are swayed by style and there are subtle pressures from advertising or from peer groups. Even the most rational of evaluation procedures cannot avoid questions of personal or social values, because the identification, selection and weighting of criteria are value-laden judgements. Sometimes, even quite radical shifts can occur in the values of large groups of people as a consequence of environmental, technological or political issues.

From: N. Cross, *Design and Designing* (T211), The Open University, Blk 2 (2010), p. 82.

narrative and game space

Within different game genres, the game environment or game setting plays an important role by defining the game space, supporting the narrative and providing a sense of immersion. The game space might be as simple as a checkered board

(for chess and checkers) or as complex as an immersive 3D environment. However, like narrative and character design, there are structures to help designers create and develop compelling game spaces that reinforce the narrative in providing a framework for interaction. Game designers Andrew Rollings and Ernest Adams outline five key dimensions of a game environment: the physical, temporal, environmental, emotional and ethical dimensions.[11] Table 8.5 provides an overview of each and how it relates to game design.

Frameworks such as this can help designers in determining the parameters of a game and the game play environment. They can also aid designers in meshing narrative and characters with game mechanics. Understanding the various dimensions of a game or interactive media environment is a vital first step in creating products that are plausible and which support the intended goals.

narrative and design

So far this chapter has limited the discussion to the importance of narrative in the design of games and related interactive media, but many of the issues raised are relevant to other fields of design. Clearly there is a profound role for narrative in design for film, dance and the theatre, but what about other domains? The world of product design is increasingly becoming the creation of interactions as artefacts become less important than the services they facilitate and support. Similarly with architecture, it's the experience and usability

Table 8.5 DIMENSIONS OF GAME ENVIRONMENT

Dimension	Purpose
Physical dimension	The physical dimension defines the physical space in which the player's character/avatar or game pieces move around. This dimension is comprised of scale and boundaries which define the size and edges of the playing environment. The physical dimensions are determined by the narrative, the scale and the scope of the game and are part of the physical game space.
Temporal dimension	The temporal dimension defines the role of time in the game. It describes not only temporal aspects, such as how much time a player has to complete an action, but also defines whether the game will include nightfall, seasons and time passage as well as delineating the impact that time passage will have on game play. The temporal dimensions are defined by the narrative.
Environmental dimension	The environmental dimension defines both the game setting appearance and atmosphere. It characterizes the game setting as fantasy or realism, the historical context, the geographical location and the overall mood and tone. The environmental dimension is manifested in the use of colour and lighting, the shape, size and placement of objects within the environment and the supporting materials, such as menus and documentation. The environmental dimensions are defined by the narrative and help reinforce the narrative.
Emotional dimension	The emotional dimension describes the emotions of both the characters in the game and the types of emotions that the design hopes to invoke within the game. The emotional dimensions are conveyed through the narrative, characters and physical design.
Ethical dimension	The ethical dimension defines the moral aspects of the game. It is by defining this aspect that character and roles logically follow rules that govern conventions within the context of the game. The ethical dimensions are conveyed through the narrative and characters and help reinforce the narrative.

Figure 8.4 Game over. (Shutterstock 64317307)

that increasingly characterizes the interface between organizations and people—not the physical materials in their buildings.

Designing today involves the creation of effective narratives that communicate what an artefact, system or environment can do. It is about providing engaging outputs where users or consumers want to take part in the story that design has created. The presentation and communication of design narratives can take place in many ways, but the visual world of images and forms offers exciting new possibilities for creating stories that don't rely on the written word and thus potentially they can be 'read' by global audiences.

CHAPTER SUMMARY

- Games in their many forms (entertainment, edutainment and serious) are becoming a pervasive force in contemporary culture.
- Good game design is challenging because it requires knowledge and balance of game genre, mechanics and narrative.
- Narrative is an important component in game design because it provides a framework for interaction.
- In the field of game design (and, more broadly, interaction design), a strong narrative storyline can enhance user engagement and immersion.
- Structures such as the quest and character archetypes can help designers develop narratives for use in many fields of design.
- Design fields such as product design and architecture are increasingly concerned with fostering engagement through successful interactions with an organization's systems and services. Narrative is increasingly important across the spectrum of design professions.

Background

Humans can be inspired by many things, such as a natural landscape, bird song or the actions of other people. But design can inspire us too. For example we might be inspired by a great building, a clever item of fashion design, a poster or a detail on an item of packaging.

The Project

This project invites you to create a portfolio of twenty-four images that visually illustrate what design inspiration means to you. These images can be photographs taken by you, images cut from magazines or found on Web pages, drawings or any other visual media. You can present your portfolio as a digital slide show or as collection on paper.

Guidelines

At the root of this project is a feeling for what it means to be inspired. It might manifest itself as stimulation or relaxation; it might bring about action or contemplation. Only *you* know what inspires you! It can come about from the smallest and the largest examples of design. The brief specifies that this portfolio will be visual. There will be no use of text to explain what you are trying to communicate, although text might form part of your collection of visual imagery.

Begin by exploring what it means to be inspired, and then reflect on what inspires you. Collect example images and edit your collection before deciding on the chosen ones. Ask yourself if you are trying to communicate one consistent message or if you intend many messages. Invite other people to offer comment on your portfolio. Do they read what you are trying to communicate? If not, consider modifying your collection.

part iii

designing for people

introduction to part iii

What is design for? There are many possible responses one might give: perhaps to resolve problems, to make beautiful things or to make profit for organizations or entrepreneurs. The authors in Part III seem to agree that design is for people. If a design doesn't match the needs or wants of those it is designed for, then it fails in the most fundamental way. This is no easy matter to address. People have different physical sizes; they have different levels of strength, hearing, mobility and hundreds of other distinctions. To compound the problem, we all have different moods, aspirations and sensitivities. We think differently. To design things which work for a market of people who differ in physical and psychological ways is very difficult. Nevertheless, it is so important that it is one of the main themes of design education across a variety of design fields.

In Chapter 9 Barbara Millet and Patrick Patterson introduce the term *user-centred design* to suggest that people are not merely one of the many factors to be taken into consideration when resolving design problems—people must be the *focus* for the whole sequence of designing activities. In fact, usability is the byword for Part III. How one develops a design to be usable is a theme touched on by all four chapters in this part. Partly it's shown to be a participatory approach involving potential users, consumers and buyers—in fact, anyone who might need to interact with the outcome. But it's also shown to be the application of sound investigative techniques that combine creative and analytical thinking. The purpose of such user-centred design is to create designs that match the needs of our bodies and the preferences of our minds.

For Bob Eves, user-centred design means understanding the meaning that can be read into design ideas and designed outputs. In Chapter 10 he reveals how design shape, form and colour prompt us to construct meaning, even where no meaning was intended. All designs, ranging from bridges to wallpaper patterns, convey messages which are picked up by our cultural antennae and interpreted. Whether you like it or not, you are a receiver and sender of semantic signals, and it can be a powerful capacity of the design practitioner.

In a similar vein, Randall Teal in Chapter 11 suggests that our subconscious feelings can play a significant role in creating or consuming design. He focuses on mood, particularly that form of socially constructed mood that occurs in public spaces. While he understandably illustrates his chapter with reference to built environments, it's possible to transfer the lessons to other design contexts where people might gather physically or virtually such as in multiplayer gaming. As with Bob Eve's chapter, we are let into a world of cues and suggestions that we absorb and rearrange to help us make sense of the world. If you can control and synthesize these cues, and combine them with your emerging understanding of the physical human factors of design, then you can possess a powerful design capability to create *delight*. Teal reminds us that the context for design is constantly changing and evolving, so we shouldn't seek to assemble some fixed toolbox of competences. Instead we need to be agile and flexible if we are to address future priorities such as contributing to social cohesion.

The final chapter in Part III takes us from the world of what designers *can* do, to the world of what they *should* do, because it focuses on ethics. Like semiotics, ethics and responsibility are constructed phenomena that are assembled from building blocks that are partly hard-wired into us and partly learned. Bryce T. J. Dyer confronts us with some difficult ethical questions, and these provide good preparation for aspiring designers who need to understand markets and understand themselves. As well as taking the reader into new ground of beliefs and values, Dyer brings the part full circle by revealing how ethics is central to inclusivity.

chapter 9

user-centred design

barbara millet and patrick patterson

ABOUT THIS CHAPTER

Products, whether in the home, at work or used on the go, have become increasingly complex. This complexity arises from significant advances in technological capabilities and from consumer demands for richer feature sets along with higher expectations about product performance and usability. Consumers no longer accept struggling to use a product. They protest, 'This product just does not feel right', 'I cannot remember all the steps needed to activate this function', 'The controls for this are awkward to use' or 'The newest update of my favourite software is confusing'. These types of statements suggest that design teams have failed to adequately consider the users during product development.

This chapter explores usability and the user-centred design (UCD) process, providing examples of the techniques, investigations and evaluations needed to ensure better products. Various UCD methods will be outlined along with discussion of how to integrate findings into product design and development.

---

usability

As researchers, we seek to gather information that will support the creation of successful products, such as vehicles, fonts, mobile devices, industrial equipment, games or buildings. Usability is widely recognized as a critical ingredient for product success. The benefits of developing usable products are increased user satisfaction, better performance and safety, fewer errors and training needs and, eventually, increased sales and corporate success. So what is usability?

Usability deals with maximizing user-product interaction by focusing on how well a product matches user needs and expectations. It is a quality that makes a product effective, efficient and satisfying to use. *Effectiveness* is the accuracy and completeness with which users achieve specific goals; *efficiency* is the conserving of resources needed to achieve those goals; and *satisfaction* is comfort in, and positive attitudes towards, the use of a product. The users of a product and their

> "The benefits of developing usable products are increased user satisfaction, better performance and safety, fewer errors and training needs and, eventually, increased sales and corporate success."

particular characteristics and the context of its use (that is, the set of circumstances in which the product is employed) affect these three primary elements. You may hear the term *user experience* applied to the development process. User experience frequently refers to the satisfaction component of usability, encompassing qualities such as aesthetics and pleasure. In this chapter, we take a wide view of usability, incorporating user experience as an important factor.

The idea of usability is loosely based on a valuable starting point for good design: the Principle of Least Astonishment. Computer programmers and interface developers have used this term for many years. This principle stresses that the most usable product is the one that surprises users least often—that is, the design that is most consistent with their expectations. However, it is interesting to consider that features which astonish users today might not astonish them in ten years, and those that do not astonish today may astonish in the future (one only has to use a product from the nineteenth century to see this at work).

the user-centred design process

Today, developing better products requires wide-ranging information from people who use, or might use, the product and understanding the contexts of use. UCD is a multidisciplinary approach requiring expertise in a wide variety of areas. For some types of products, it can involve interaction design, visual design, industrial design, human factors, hardware and software engineering, quality assurance and marketing. Only by understanding the user and the context of use do we ensure that characteristics of the product match the needs of the user. Achieving product usability necessarily requires a UCD approach.

The term *user-centred design* originated from seminal work by the leading cognitive scientist Donald Norman and human–computer interaction expert Stephen Draper in 1986.[1] UCD is also known as human-centred design, customer-centric design, and usability engineering. Regardless of its title, the approach always relies on user involvement during the design and development processes. More recently, experts have operationalized the definition to include approaches

Ergonomics and Anthropometrics

The field of *ergonomics* (also known as human factors engineering) is the systematic study of human capabilities, limitations and requirements and the application of such knowledge to design. The name comes from the Greek *ergon,* meaning work, and *nomos,* laws. So it means, literally, the laws of work. This title reflects the origins of the approach, which lay in attempts to improve the performance and efficiency of industrial workers and military personnel, through rational, scientific inquiry into human needs and behaviour.

There are two characteristics, therefore, that distinguish ergonomics both from other professional design approaches and from common sense. First, satisfaction of relevant user requirements is the overriding criterion, and, second, the approach is based on the application of scientific inquiry to the problem of ascertaining human performance, abilities and limitations.

A lot of ergonomics research is aimed at establishing guidelines, standards or rules that can be applied by designers in a variety of situations. Where this applies to the physical use of products, much of it is based on measurements of body sizes and abilities. The collection and application of such measurements is known as *anthropometrics*.

leading to a total user experience and which might incorporate anything the user interacts with. The proper use of this process involves multidisciplinary efforts. As Vredenburg, Isensee and Righi put it:

> [It is] an approach to designing ease of use into the total user experience with products and systems. It involves two fundamental elements—multidisciplinary teamwork and a set of specialized methods of getting user input and converting it into design.[2]

Many organizations now use UCD to create products that better meet user expectations. The UCD process describes design and development in which end users influence the product design. It ensures that design and development efforts result in usable products by focusing on usability goals, product functions and user and environmental characteristics.[3]

Traditional product design methods focus on technological capabilities, novel features and business goals. UCD focuses on satisfying user needs, overcoming the limits of traditional product design.[4] With UCD, users become central to product development, an involvement that has led to more effective, efficient and safer products, contributing to product acceptance and success. Table 9.1 highlights these differences between traditional and UCD product design approaches.

Figure 9.1 shows the UCD model offered by the International Organization for Standardization (ISO 13407).[5] The model consists of a five-stage, systematic approach. The first stage involves planning the process, stage two specifies the context of use, stage three specifies user requirements, stage four produces design solutions and the final stage comprises evaluation. The model encompasses the notion of iterative design. If the product does not meet stated requirements, the steps are repeated, starting at stage two. This enables designers and developers to incorporate user feedback, allowing them to incrementally refine the design until the product reaches an acceptable usability level. What is immediately clear from the model is the user and the context of product use are the major foci, ensuring delivery of usable products. Each stage in the UCD model depends on properly selecting methods to gather needed feedback from representative users.

Who Are the Users?

As modern products become more complex, with more functions available through their interface, many of them have become increasingly confusing to users. Consequently, a concern has grown to ensure that the design of products and systems becomes more user centred. But who are the users?

There are many different users for every design. The people who buy cars or computers, access services, interact with software or visit exhibitions differ enormously in their age, abilities and needs. Then there are the people who assemble and maintain designs—they are users too. Many elderly and disabled people cannot carry out—certainly with any ease or dignity—the range of everyday tasks that others take for granted. They are forced to choose products from a limited range that may suit them, and may have to adapt products themselves, to compensate for a product's inadequate design.

If we try to design for the 'average' user, we may only suit a small minority of the population. It is often more relevant to design for the extreme users—for example the smallest, tallest or weakest. Designing to include extreme users can also benefit the great majority of users; design should be *inclusive* where possible.

From: N. Cross, *Design and Designing* (T211), The Open University, Blk 2 (2010), Section 5.

Table 9.1 COMPARING UCD TO TRADITIONAL APPROACHES

Traditional design approach	User-centred design approach
Technology driven	User driven
Component focus	Solutions focus
Limited multidisciplinary cooperation	Multidisciplinary teamwork
Focus on internal architecture	Focus on external designs
No specialization in user experience	Specialization in user experience
Some competitive focus	Focus on competition
Development before user evaluation	Develop only user-validated designs
Product defect view of quality	User view of quality
Limited focus on user measurement	Prime focus on user measurement
Focus on current customers	Focus on current and future customers

From K. Vredenburg, S. Isensee, and C. Righi, *User-centered Design: An Integrated Approach* (Prentice Hall, 2002).

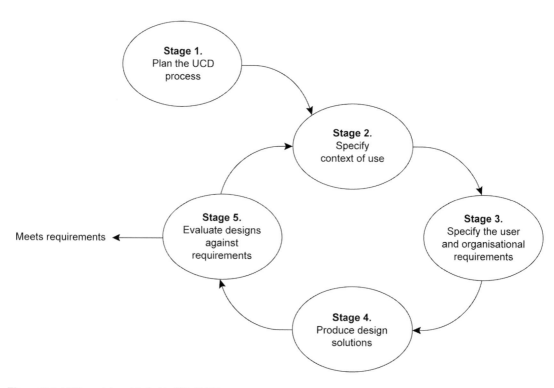

Figure 9.1 UCD model as detailed in ISO 13407.
(Copyright author)

user-centred design methods

Many different methods have proven useful in each stage of the UCD process. These methods can be divided into two categories: *design research* and *usability evaluation.* In the following sections, we examine these two categories and some of the UCD methods frequently used in academia and in practice. UCD methods are commonly used iteratively; they are not mutually exclusive and can be adapted to accommodate specific research goals. The methods presented in this chapter, and the development stages in which they are typically used, are presented in Table 9.2.

Design research methods

Design research is primarily a front-end analysis leading to concept exploration and ideation. The design research stages (stages 1 to 4 in Figure 9.1) lead to a better understanding of those who will be using a product and the context in which it will be used. Design research requires effective data collection and can employ traditional methods (e.g. focus groups and interviews), ethnographic research (e.g. video ethnography) and participatory design (e.g. Velcro modelling). The findings allow the identification of current and ideal behaviours which serve as inputs to the design. Ideation is fostered during this identification of ideal behaviours and the exploration of design alternatives.

Traditional design research methods

These focus on what people say and think, captured through techniques such as interviews, focus groups and questionnaires. These methods provide insight into the 'true user profile, user needs, and user preferences'.[6] Below we introduce three traditional methods.

1. *One-on-one user interviews* pose questions to an individual to find out what he or she thinks, feels, and expects. Interview sessions may be structured (tightly guided), semistructured or unstructured (loosely outlined). Sessions can range from fifteen minutes to an hour or more. Interviews are ideal for understanding

Table 9.2   METHODS MAPPED TO UCD STAGES AND ACTIVITIES

	Stages 1–3: Planning and requirements	Stage 4: Design solutions	Stage 5: Evaluation
Activities	Design research	Design research and usability evaluation	Usability evaluation
Interviews	✓	✓	
Focus groups	✓		
Questionnaires	✓		✓
Ethnography	✓		
Participatory	✓	✓	
User testing			✓
Inspection			✓

what an individual thinks about a topic without being influenced by others.

2. *Focus groups* are small groups of informed people who are gathered to address product research questions. This is similar to a group interview. Traditional focus groups are organized into sessions of up to twelve current or likely users in a structured discussion moderated by a trained practitioner. These sessions typically last one to two hours. Focus groups are helpful for gathering multiple points of view in a short period of time.[7]

3. *Questionnaires* are instruments for collecting data by asking representative users a set of questions in a specific order. Respondents usually answer the questions on their own, either online or by filling out a paper form. Questionnaires can provide useful self-reported data, demographics and information about opinions and preferences. The questions must be written in a way to increase the reliability and validity of the findings. There are two types of question formats: *open,* when respondents compose their own answers, and *closed,* when respondents select from available responses. Questionnaires are useful in collecting large amounts of data from a large population sample in a relatively short period of time.

Ethnographic research

This has its origins in anthropology but is now used extensively in product design initiatives. Ethnographic research, also known as observational research, is the systematic study of behaviour, focusing on what people do and how they behave in their natural environments such as at home or at work. Ethnographic research in design is exploratory; typically it is conducted to gain a better understanding of the users, tasks and environment. It is used to define requirements and inspire design ideas. Ethnographic research is valuable in situations where researchers cannot interact directly with end users—for example when researchers are attempting to understand the information needs of emergency-room doctors. In using this technique, the researcher directly or indirectly observes users in their environment but does not necessarily interact with them. While observing the users, researchers make careful, objective notes about what they see, recording all accounts and observations. Researchers continue to conduct observations until they have a good understanding of the focus areas.

There are many variations of ethnographic research. Three applied ethnographic approaches are outlined here.

1. *Field ethnography.* A person or group of people are observed by a researcher while they go about their normal lives. The duration can range from one hour to several days or even weeks. Traditional field ethnographies are ideal for use in the early exploratory stages, when researchers and designers need to learn more about the people for whom they are designing.

2. *Video ethnography* is the video recording of human behaviour. The video records can be used to supplement field notes or to record events without a researcher present.

3. *Self-reporting* techniques are used when direct observation is not practical because of cost, time or domain constraints. Many

self-reporting techniques exist, such as written dairies, visual storybooks and blogs.[8] In these approaches, the participant engages in self-guided reporting.

Participatory design

This actively involves end users in the design process to ensure the product designed meets their needs and is usable. In engaging in participatory design, designers and researchers value the involvement of users, viewing them as co-creators in the design process. Participatory design focuses on what people make.[9] Below we introduce three participatory design tools.

1. *Collage* is a tool that allows users to communicate experiences through sets of pictures and words. The researcher gives users the collage materials and a surface on which to arrange them. Collage is ideal for giving rise to feelings and memories.
2. *Card sorting* (Plate 12) is a technique used to understand how people organize information. It is conducted by presenting participants with written or pictorial cards conveying product characteristics and then asking them to sort the cards in a meaningful way. Card sorting allows researchers to understand how users think about products. It can provide clues to how users perceive product features, enabling designers to create better navigation and operation.
3. *Velcro modelling* (Figure 9.2) allows people to express their ideas through low-fidelity, three-dimensional constructions. Such modelling enables users to create actual forms with simple modelling

materials. This encourages creative expression solutions.

Time must always be taken to learn about the intended user group. This often requires a separate study to ensure your research design matches human abilities and limits. Box 9.1 provides an outline of how researchers set about discovering and comparing characteristics of particular user groups, in this case car drivers.

Reflection on design research methods

The data collected through design research methods are frequently qualitative. In fact, with the exception of questionnaires, all the data collection methods presented in this chapter are qualitative. But no matter what type of data you create, its value depends on appropriate analysis, interpretation and translation. Analysis of qualitative data usually entails examining, comparing and interpreting patterns or themes. Data can be analysed and synthesized from multiple angles, depending on the particular research objectives. Translation is the merging of user insights and interaction principles into practical requirements that aid design. Translation tools promote the conversion of user data into insights and design criteria. The variety of design research methods are matched to different types of data that might be needed. However, all share several common characteristics and phases of data analysis, such as data reduction, data display, conclusion drawing and

> **"No matter what type of data you create, its value depends on appropriate analysis, interpretation and translation."**

Figure 9.2 A user creating low-fidelity Velcro models.
(Copyright Steve Garner)

BOX 9.1. COMPARING DRIVERS

The purpose of this study was to examine visual attention and the useful field of view (UFoV) of older drivers in comparison to younger drivers. The study used a simulator with different driving scenarios. It examined eye movements, fixations and ranges in the UFoV with the purpose of understanding differences in visual attention strategies and the underlying cognitive processes.

Method

We recorded eye movement histories and fixation times while the subjects negotiated two different scenarios: urban and highway routes. A six-axis driving simulator created the scene images and closely simulated car dynamics and traffic scenarios. The visual images appeared on monitors located at the front and in the positions of left and right side-view mirrors and the rear-view mirror. An eye tracking system recorded participants' eye movements (Figure 9.3).

Results

There was a significant difference between groups of drivers. Older drivers used smaller ranges of UFoV throughout different traffic scenarios compared with younger drivers. Younger drivers had the largest UFoV range. Older drivers displayed a reduced functional field of view, inferred from their eye movement, points of fixation and time of fixations.

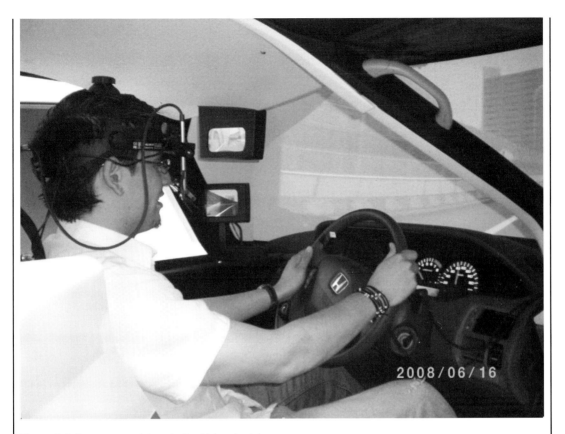

Figure 9.3 A younger participant in the driving simulator.
(Copyright author)

Recommendations

The shorter fixation times and longer eye movements determined the reduced ranges of UFoV for older drivers. Characteristics of the visual search strategies of older drivers are important for developing appropriate visual aid systems. Instead of having a search strategy of visual information scattered over different locations for the driver, an in-vehicle visual aid system could help drivers attend to specific, and fewer, locations where relevant events are more likely to occur in specific traffic scenarios.

Discussion

Knowing how much visual information older drivers acquire at a specific instant can be important in developing new technology for assisted driving. For instance, in-vehicle information system designers can take the theory behind UFoV measurement to develop technology that could aid drivers with restricted functional fields of view in real time and in situations where their UFoV may be reduced. For example the moments before merging into a highway may not be ideal for presenting information from in-vehicle systems. In addition, these measures can be useful in designing roads and highway information systems and in the positioning of road signs.

verification. Regardless of the method used, translating user data is a critical step that leads to design exploration.

A key principle of design research is that before designing a product it is critical to have a clear understanding of the target users. Design research methods reveal user needs and preferences through interviews, user observations and creative activities that encourage users to express their motivations, feelings and underlying concepts and beliefs about the steps involved in task procedures. The information gained with these methods then serves as input to the design. It is only with this understanding that products can be designed to support user behaviours in a way that will improve the user experience. Of course, not all design research methods are used in every design research initiative, but there are benefits from merging insights from multiple research methods.[10] The relative importance of which design research methods to use will depend on specific design and product objectives.

Usability evaluation methods

Once design concepts materialize, researchers then focus on evaluating usability. Usability evaluations assess the degree to which users can operate a product, the efficiency of the product and user satisfaction with the product. Usability evaluation methods (UEMs) are the means for such assessments, making an important contribution in developing usable products.

There are various UEMs available for evaluating product usability. Some methods make use of data gathered from users, while others rely on the judgements of usability experts. Different UEMs are applied, in an iterative fashion, throughout the product development process, ranging from the first low-fidelity design concepts through high-fidelity design prototypes. Testing throughout the product development life cycle ensures that development teams achieve easy-to-use, efficient, safe and effective products. Three types of usability evaluation methods are outlined here: inspection, inquiry and empirical testing.

Inspection methods

These are diagnostic techniques whereby usability specialists decide whether product design elements follow established usability standards and guidelines. In contrast to other UEMs, inspection methods rely only on expert judgement. Inspection methods are used mainly during the prototype design stage. The objective of inspections is to find usability problems that need to be eliminated through redesign. There are three key inspection methods.

1. *Guideline or standards reviews* are expert evaluations of products to assess conformance against a comprehensive list of usability guidelines. Many detailed usability guidelines exist in the literature.[11]

2. *Heuristic evaluation* is used for finding usability problems in a product so they can be addressed as part of an iterative design process. Heuristic evaluation involves having a small set of evaluators examine the user interface and judge its compliance with recognized usability principles (i.e. the heuristics). Heuristics have been established over many years of human–system interactive studies. For example leading Web usability consultant Jakob Nielsen's[12] main heuristics include:
   - using simple and natural presentation
   - speaking the user's language (rather than computer jargon)

- minimizing memory load on a user
- maintaining consistency within the design itself and with other similar applications
- providing feedback to users' actions
- providing clearly marked exits
- providing shortcuts for experienced users
- preventing errors
- providing good error messages
- providing adequate help and documentation.

3. *Expert review* is similar to a heuristic evaluation, except that experienced usability specialists conduct the review. These usability experts may rely on explicit rules or not, and may be provided with usage scenarios. In this technique, the experts usually work alone, although aggregating the problems identified across the evaluators usually leads to a higher proportion of usability problems detected.[13]

Inquiry methods

Researchers gather information about user likes, dislikes, needs and understanding of the product by talking to them, observing them using the product or having them answer questions in written form or verbally. Inquiry methods include focus groups, interviews, field observations and questionnaires. Because we have already introduced most of these methods in the preceding sections, here we focus on three representative questionnaires often used in product development to get qualitative and subjective feedback from users.

1. *NASA Task Load Index,* developed by Hart and Staveland,[14] is a subjective workload assessment tool using six dimensions to assess mental workload: mental demand, physical demand, temporal demand, performance, effort and frustration. The questionnaire uses twenty bipolar scales to obtain ratings for each dimension.

2. *Situational Awareness Rating Technique (SART),* developed by Taylor,[15] provides an assessment of the situational awareness provided by a product based on user opinion. The SART instrument has fourteen components.

3. *Post-Study System Usability Questionnaire (PSSUQ)* is a sixteen-item standardized usability instrument, comprised of three subscales (system usefulness, information quality and interface quality), used as a product evaluation tool.[16] The PSSUQ is typically used in combination with user testing and is administered at the end of the study.

Empirical methods

Empirical methods encompass observing and learning from users as they work with a product before, during and after the design and development process. In this section, we examine two empirical methods.

1. *User testing* is possibly the most important method for evaluating products and is considered by many as the gold standard to which all other UEMs are compared. It is a research tool that originates from well-established experimental methods, where the main objective in conducting a user test was to discover whether the product elicits the necessary human performance to meet the requirements established for it. When defects or problems are discovered,

Figure 9.4 Empirical user testing in a laboratory. (Copyright author)

opportunities arise to refine the design. User testing may be conducted in a laboratory or done remotely. In a typical lab-based user test (see Figure 9.4), an evaluator observes representative users perform a series of tasks using an application or prototype. The evaluator and one or more observers in the same or adjacent room record the time it takes the users to complete each task, whether the users were successful and any important comments or problems. This information is then used to develop a list of usability problems in the application or prototype. Remote user testing techniques are also available for extending user testing beyond the lab. Remote user testing techniques use the same basic methods as lab-based tests, but the test users are in geographically different locations.

The evaluator and observer(s) may or may not watch the tests in real time.

There are two types of user tests: formative and summative. In formative user tests, the goal is to reveal any potential usability problems (or defects) with the product before it gets released. These tests are conducted throughout the product development cycle to guide design. Summative tests focus on measuring and validating the usability of a product and are conducted at or near the end of product development. Summative tests can be used for hypothesis testing of a single design or competitive testing between similar products.

There are various types of user tests whose methods are similar. However, they each have different purposes and will vary on the emphasis of the measures (qualitative versus quantitative). Usability consultants Rubin and Chisnell, in their *Handbook of Usability Testing,*[17] identify four types of user tests within the individual phases of the product development cycle:

- *Exploratory tests* are conducted when the product is in the early design stages with the purpose of evaluating preliminary design concepts.
- *Assessment tests* (most usability tests) are conducted while the product is still under development with the purpose of uncovering the strengths and weaknesses of the usability of the product (see Box 9.2 for an example).
- *Validation tests* are conducted late in the development with the purpose of validating the usability of the product.
- *Comparison tests* compare two or more developed products against one another. A comparison usability test can also be conducted to compare the merits of two or more design alternatives during the earlier stages of the product development process.

2. *Field testing* is a procedure to collect usability data from either end users or beta testers. It is necessary to learn about changes in user long-term behaviour, because some new products have the potential for changing the way people work and interact. Changes in behaviour may only become obvious after an extended period of use. Field tests should be supplemented with heuristic evaluations and laboratory-based user testing so beta testers do not have to suffer from glaring usability problems that could have been detected earlier, when changes to the product are less costly.[18]

Box 9.2 reveals how research methods, results, comments and recommendations can be concisely presented to an audience.

BOX 9.2. USABILITY EVALUATION OF A MOBILE DEVICE USER INTERFACE

The purpose of this study was to explore the immediate usability of the user interface prototype of a mobile device. The mobile device solution offers voice-over-Internet protocol telephony and data application support. The focus of this evaluation was to conduct a user test on a subset of phone features.

Methods

Ten participants completed the following five tasks: (1) placing a call to a given local phone number, (2) retrieving a stored phone number, (3) answering an incoming call, (4) setting up a conference call and (5) answering multiple incoming calls and initiating a call transfer. After each task scenario, participants completed a three-part questionnaire measuring user satisfaction associated with (a) the ease of task completion, (b) the required time to complete the task and (c) the support information provided during the task.[19] On completion of all tasks, participants completed a poststudy survey containing sixteen items with seven subscales, which correspond to the general areas of (1) display readability/size, (2) learning/start-up effort, (3) intuitiveness, (4) mapping to mental model, (5) language, (6) error handling and (7) perception of ease of use.

Results

The mean completion times for tasks 1 to 3 were less than thirty seconds. The mean completion times for tasks 4 and 5 were much greater, but the scenarios for these tasks required a larger set of actions. However, most participants expressed dissatisfaction with the time needed to complete tasks 4 and 5. Participants completed tasks 1 and 3 with 100 per cent success. Task 5 had the lowest success rate (60 per cent) with failures mainly resulting because the call transfer function was not available from the main menu (the user interface design used a hidden menu to access the call transfer function). The satisfaction scores (5-point scales in which 5 is the best rating) for tasks 1 to 3 were good (4.5 out of 5). The ratings for tasks 4 (3.6 out of 5) and 5 (3.5 out 5) were slightly poorer given that some participants were unable to complete the task successfully and that recovering from errors took too long (more than two minutes on average).

The overall mean score for the poststudy survey was 3.6 ± 0.4 (with a 90 per cent confidence interval). The observed means for the poststudy scales were all well above the scale midpoint, and the lower limits of their 90 per cent confidence intervals were also above the scale midpoint, implying favourable usability.

Participant Comments

Each participant provided comments for the three most-liked and least-liked device attributes. The most frequently mentioned were:

Most liked: device physical characteristics (form, weight, size and materials), easy-to-use user interface and recognizable graphics.

Least liked: difficult to use the call transfer function, screen and font size were too small, having a phone keypad (instead of a mini QWERTY) and confusing user interface terms.

Recommendations Based on Participant Behaviour and Comments

Participants were positive about the product and its proposed functionality. They liked the design of the device, particularly its size and simplicity. Participants experienced the most difficulty when using the conference calling and call transfer functions. In fact, five of seven critical usability problems detected occurred when using the conference calling and call transfer functions. User interface modification for these functions was highly recommended. Specific recommendations were provided to the design team but are not included here.

Discussion

The primary focus of this usability study was on detecting and prioritizing problems in early designs of the user interface for a mobile device. This case study illustrates how user tests can be used to reveal potential usability problems with the product and/or interface before product release.

design success by understanding usability

Product success in today's marketplace depends on exceeding user expectations. The broad range of product types, uses, demands and expectations requires exploration during design to understand the mixture of human requirements and capacities. This mixture of human characteristics requires a holistic approach to product design and evaluation.

Product design and evaluation has recently broadened its scope to go beyond usability to creating user experiences. If designers and researchers are to adopt a truly UCD approach, they must embrace not only established methods such as lab-based user testing to measure user performance and satisfaction but also more recently developed methods such as desirability studies to measure aesthetic appeal.[20]

Because of the benefits of the usability approach, companies in various industries have already made usability engineering a key part of their product development processes. An unusable system can result in great cost to business, not only in lost sales but also in customer satisfaction, productivity and additional support required for an inadequately designed product. Poor usability designs, if found early in development, can be improved to reduce or eliminate serious problems rather than having to make costly changes after the fact. Addressing usability early in the design process is an advantage for all.

CHAPTER SUMMARY

- Good usability is now an expectation for all products.
- Usability is concerned with *effectiveness* (the accuracy and completeness with which users achieve specific goals), *efficiency* (the conserving of resources needed to achieve those goals) and *satisfaction* (comfort in, and positive attitudes towards, the use of a product).
- Even before beginning the design process, it is critical to have a clear understanding of the target users.
- The UCD approach relies on user involvement during the design and development processes.
- Many methods are available for performing appropriate requirements analysis, design and evaluation during the product life cycle.
- User-centred design methods are often combined within projects and can be adapted to the context of a project.

chapter 10

design semiotics

bob eves

ABOUT THIS CHAPTER

Like minds think alike. As a designer, hang around with a few creative people for a while, like painters, musicians, sculptors, poets, animators. Pretty soon you'll realize you have one particular thing in common—you all work with the concept of style, and because of this you have an appreciation for design semiotics. One of the things I aim to do in this chapter is introduce you to a few characters who have helped us define and apply semiotics.

Style is about distinction and difference. It's an identity that has individuality but can also belong to a collection. Think of styles of music—jazz, rock 'n' roll, hip-hop; or art movements—art deco, pop art, gothic; or films—*Star Wars,* James Bond; or car brands—Mercedes, Beetle, Porsche, Rolls Royce. They all have a specific character, like a personality, that is their style.

This chapter is about semiotics—that is, the meaning of signs and symbols we use to express style. Just as a language has words and grammar, so design and form have their own constituent parts. Going back to music, what particular sound would you associate with jazz; what sort of instrument? What image do you have in your mind for pop art, what type of colours, shapes or patterns? What form characteristics do you associate with a Rolls Royce car? What textures? And such characteristics are only part of the story. As well as what does gothic look like, what does it *mean* to be gothic?

> "Semiotics is embodied in every artefact or design created, be it deliberately or not."

Semiotics is embodied in every artefact or design created, be it deliberately or not. It is as much a design method as it is a study and academic discipline. So if you think you get it, or would really like to, read on and enjoy the world of semiotics. Play a few tunes, paint some lyrics, write some pictures and enjoy the jazz.

stylism and deconstruction

Look in an art or design history book for all the words you can find ending in *ism;* they are usually a term for a particular style, be it a periodic movement or fashion trend. Here's a few I can think of: futurism, brutalism, impressionism, expressionism, cubism, fauvism, surrealism, modernism, postmodernism, constructivism, dadaism, symbolism, classicism. Others don't end in *ism* but are

Figure 10.1 Semiotics—enjoy the jazz.
(Getty 97764489 RF)

significant art and design styles nonetheless. Different cultures and nations can have a particular aesthetic style, depicting their heritage or more recent influences. Music or films can fall into particular genres that have certain style characteristics. And styles can relate to distinctive brand identity. Here are some examples of styles. Look them up, consider what kind of styles they are and research their context. Think of some more; study them.

> Pop art, Memphis, new Romantic, art deco, art nouveau, Bauhaus, populuxe, googie, streamlining, De Stijl, new age, arts and crafts, gothic
> Rolls Royce, Chanel, Casio, Porsche, Atari, Mercedes, Apple, Dyson, Cadillac, Buick, Lambretta, Beetle, Pentagram, Archigram, Vespa
> Zen Buddhism, medieval, Oriental, Italian, Bolshevik, Tudor, African, Scandinavian, Islamic, Egyptian, Japanese, Victorian, royal, regal
> Sci-fi, James Bond, Star Wars, Quadrophenia, Robocop, Dr Who, Clockwork Orange, Barbarella, Thunderbirds, Joe 90, Stingray, Safari

> Jazz, punk, funk, hip-hop, psychedelic, soul, rock and roll, mod, acid house, garage, grunge, pop, electro, folk.

Box 10.1 presents a simple but practical exercise as an introduction to design semiotics. The method is one of deconstruction, the aim being to analyse a specific style to figure out what characteristics make it what it is.

Don't worry about how well you sketch or draw; I don't. Figure 10.2 is an example of what I started sketching for the style of Cadillac. See what I mean! I did all the sketches in this chapter, just to show you that if I can have a go and do it, then so can you. Design semiotics is not out of your reach; it is right there in your eye, mind, arm and pencil.

You might find it helpful to use a board onto which you can mount your images from the exercise. I call these 'mood boards'. Let the images communicate your chosen style without you saying what it is. Consider how colour, texture,

---

BOX 10.1. EXERCISE IN DESIGN SEMIOTICS

Choose a style—it can be an art or design movement or fashion trend, iconic brand, cultural identity, historic tradition, music or film genre or whatever. You could choose from those listed previously, but if you go beyond the list you are beginning to get it. Research into the style and collect images that depict the style. These can be of artefacts, graphical symbols, designs or images representative of a genre. Collect many to start with; then edit them down according to what moves you in a particular way. Include what you really like and what you dislike, but focus on what you feel are the iconic representations of the style.

Study the images and look for common features. Are there any recurring colours? What type of colour—bold, pastel? What are the textures—shiny, smooth? What shapes are used—angular, organic? What patterns—tessellated, spiral, symmetrical? What other images could be referred to—nostalgic, visionary? What is the emotional mood? What is the sensory feeling? Make notes, tracings and sketches by looking directly at the images and from memory; feel the style, tune in. Look at the whole and the detail, be obsessive and passionate, enjoy the enquiry.

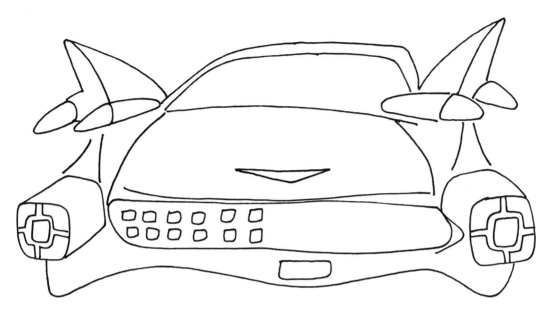

Figure 10.2 Cadillac sketch. (Copyright author)

shape, form and pattern can be made to work for you. Use drawn and found images. You might even include some descriptive words—perhaps by adding short phrases embodying the style. Be poetic. Do this as though someone had to guess or find out what the style is. Show your mood board to your tutors and fellow students and see if they can guess the style. Ask them to critique and comment on your work.

signs and signifiers

Semiotics is mind-blowing, because, as a designer, when you get it, you realize how important it is to design and that you always knew it but did not quite really know what it was. Although the theory can seem intellectual and academic, it's rooted in real-world practice. Semiotics is worth studying and applying because, in reference to the previous exercise, it can help us understand

design—and this understanding can bring a design to life.

The examination of semiotics presented here draws on the work of the linguist Ferdinand de Saussure (b. 1857). Importantly, he reveals how a sign is the consequence of the relationship between the *signifier* and what is *signified.* The signifiers are constructed through the media you select. You might create line or colour or descriptive words. It's not just how they are used in isolation but how they come together as a combined aesthetic composition. Sound familiar from the previous mood board exercise? But what is signified?

There are two types of signs: *natural* and *conventional.* Imagine lying beside a stream on a summer day, the soft babbling of the water, harmonious floral scents and colours, the occasional cool spray and gentle breeze. In this case, nature provides the natural signs. Compare this to a design for a bath shampoo container, where all the

Figure 10.3 Morphing from a flower to a container.
(Copyright author)

signs are constructed. I'll refer to these as 'conventional' signs. Can you translate that feeling of being by the stream, absorbing those natural signs, into a design for a container to be used by someone relaxing in a bath? Try it. What signs would you try to incorporate in the shampoo container to get the bather back to that stream? Think about the sensory experience of sounds, smells and touch. See it and visualize it. Taste it. Convert your imaginings into a design for a shampoo container. Consider the look and feel, how you interact with it through your eyes, mind, hands and body.

To develop your capacity to visualize natural signs, you need to practise. Think of a solid rock, exotic flamingo, fresh daisy, crisp cucumber, dry desert, delicate eggshell, luxury pearl. What signs appear? Could you translate these into the design of graphics, packaging, product, apparel, furniture, vehicle or architecture? Not in a literal or obvious way, but subtly, so that the natural sign-ness is almost in the DNA or genetic code of the object. If you did this, you would be applying symbolism, referring one sign to another. This is the designer's task with semiotics—to make it happen, to work

with signs and signification, to conceptualize. Try sketching a natural image that you want your shampoo container to embody. Then gradually transform the image through sketching. I call this 'morphing', and Figure 10.3 shows my example for morphing a flower into a shampoo container. The sequence looks a bit like a slowed-down animation.

In this very conceptual idea I intend that the container hangs on the bath taps and the bather can pick off the scented flower pods. These pods float in the bath, and to release the shampoo you pop them. To further exploit natural signs, I'd like the shampoo to smell of honey. What I've described here is a process of *reconstruction.* Use your sketches as a basis for generating ideas and concepts to reflect your original natural inspiration. Return to earlier images and examine them. Use them to inspire details for your designs. Approach the design like the resolution increasing on a screen, zooming in and panning out. Apply change and metamorphosis; try being subtle and extreme. Save all your iterations as material to reflect on.

Figure 10.4 A stone tablet is an example of conventional, constructed signs. (Getty 103023383 RM)

semiotics

Conventional signs are unnatural in that they are human-made, but they do offer a powerful constructed system.

In order to examine our constructions I need to refer to two phenomena at play in such systems: *difference* and *code*.

Orange is a colour; it is also a fruit, a different sign. So what is orange-ness? To try to define orange-ness we would need to know what sign we were dealing with. Are we talking about the *word* orange or the *colour* or *fruit*? It is also the name of a communications company, a *brand,* and this adds yet another dimension. To explore this distinction between a difference and a code, let's examine and combine two simple shape signs.

Figure 10.5 shows a small circle and an arc. They are both two-dimensional shapes, but the image might refer to a three-dimensional scene. What do you see when they are together? Perhaps a light in a cave? Can you think of ten different interpretations?

Now consider the same two shapes, but rearranged (Figure 10.5b).

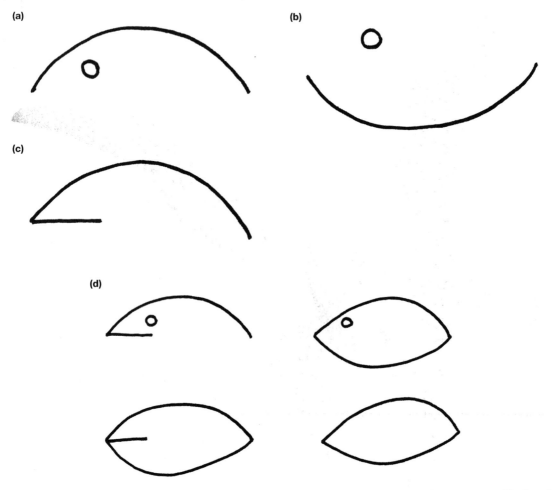

(a)

(b)

(c)

(d)

(Continued)

Figure 10.5a–e Interpreting drawings. (Copyright author)

(e)

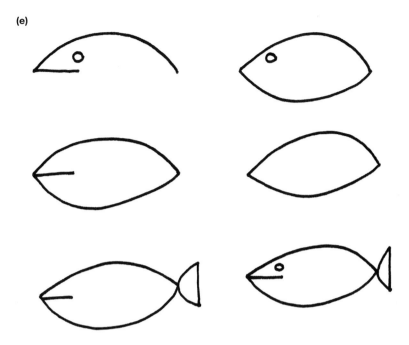

What do you see now? Is it different from before? If I replace the circle with a horizontal line, what do you see? (Figure 10.5c.)

The point is that of difference within difference. These shapes are individually different from each other and other shapes but form yet another difference when combined together. What do you see in these shape signs? They are all derivatives of those previous shape signs and are all different. How are they different? Is a sameness being revealed? Is a code emerging? (Figure 10.5d.)

Let's try adding a few more signs (Figure 10.5e).

Changing signs, developing codes

What created the fish-ness in the few lines of the drawings above? What has caused the signifier to give rise to the signified? At what point were you aware of code amongst difference? Of course some people might be more familiar with a fish sign or symbol. Now that the sequence has been revealed as fish, it's very difficult to see them as anything else. Convention is powerful. Look back at the previous images; they are now all unfinished fish! Nevertheless, these fish exhibit difference. Look at the difference in character of the fish brought about by subtly changing one sign at a time—a mouth, body, fin. How has that difference affected the character? What other codes are coming into play? (Figure 10.6.)

Look what happens when many signs change, many differences within the same code. How would you describe the character of each fish? Try it. What sort of descriptive words or language do you use? Which one do you think likes jazz? (Figure 10.7.)

So the signifiers in an image can contain difference and code. This brings us to two other forces at work in semiotics: *exchange* and *comparison*.

Figure 10.6 Small changes in sign change the character of a design. (Copyright author)

Figure 10.7 Changing signs to create difference within a code. (Copyright author)

Exchange tends to follow convention. Look at a vacuum cleaner, such as a Dyson (Figure 10.8). Taken literally, it could be exchanged for a carpet sweeper or a dustpan and brush. However, this image could be compared to a machine engine, diving apparatus, an astronaut's backpack or a James Bond gadget. Who'd have thought that cleaning could be so exciting?

Figure 10.8 Sketch of
a Dyson vacuum cleaner.
(Copyright author)

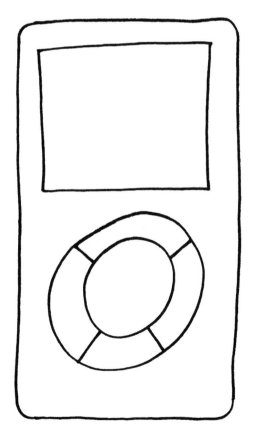

Similarly, look at a media player, such as an Apple iPod (Figure 10.9). Taken literally, it could be exchanged for, amongst other things, a record player, a stereo, a concert hall or an orchestra. However, this image could be compared to a tablet of stone (Figure 10.4), a luxury bar of soap or a doorway.

Table 10.1 is an example of exchanging and comparing for the Cadillac I sketched earlier.

Look at some designs around you. Pick some that appeal to you and some that don't. What exchanges and comparisons can you think of? What signifiers are at work? For the designer it can be the exchanges and comparisons that shape the intended or perceived style of a design. That is, they are influential in the effect.

Look back carefully at the style mood board, research and images you created for the earlier exercises. Ponder a while. What are the signifiers? What do they signify? Is there any reference to nature? Are there any sign conventions? Is there a code? What could the signs be exchanged for? Can you identify some comparisons, as I did for the Cadillac? Try to do this for

Figure 10.9 Sketch of an Apple iPod. (Copyright author)

Table 10.1   EXCHANGE AND COMPARISON FOR THE CADILLAC

Exchange	Motorcycle Scooter Bus
Comparison	Space rocket Cartoon car Jet thrusters

Status

Just as we might try to read meaning in what people say (or what they do not say) or in the expression on people's faces, so most of us try to read the signs that lie embedded in designs—even if this is largely undertaken subconsciously. One of the most powerful motivations to correctly interpret the signs embedded in designs is the attraction of status.

Take chairs for example. The status provided by the act of sitting is deeply ingrained in many cultures around the world, and it has a very long history. Even today, we might take part in ceremonial occasions where we stand while others, who are deemed more important, sit down. The seat as throne perhaps best epitomises the notion of seats as a symbol of power. Thrones were clearly in use in ancient Egypt. An example was excavated from the tomb of Tutankhamen, which would make it over 3,000 years old.

Of course, not everybody seeks status through the products they surround themselves with. Some people deliberately avoid certain products that promote ego or convey superiority. However, whether we seek or shun symbols of status, we are all, to a greater or lesser extent, using our ability to 'read' the symbols—to make sense of these indicators—which is what makes this phenomenon so powerful in the supply and demand of design.

---

individual signs as well as for the composition as a whole.

semiosis

The following theories on semiotics relate to the philosopher Charles Peirce (b. 1839). Peirce presents his definition of a sign as the consequence of the three-way relationship between *representamen, object* and *interpretant.* But don't stop reading! It's really quite simple. Let's take each one in turn before looking at how they work together.

R The *representamen* is an initial inferring of a sign. In design, this could be the sight of a colour or the feeling of a texture; in jazz, it might be the faint, shrill sound of a saxophone. It's more a sensation or a quality. Representamen in design are the aesthetic and sensory sign media such as colour, texture, shape, form and pattern, either in isolation or as combinations and compositions.

O The *object* connects the sign to the world. It defines relationships. Objects can be

Table 10.2   REPRESENTAMEN, OBJECT AND INTERPRETANT FOR THE CADILLAC

R Representamen	O Object	I Interpretant
Shine	Chrome	Flash
Glossy	Contrast	Luxury
Pointy	Wings	Rocket
Grid	Grill	Burn

Table 10.3   REPRESENTAMEN, OBJECT AND INTERPRETANT FOR THE VESPA SCOOTER

R Representamen	O Object	I Interpretant
	Wasp	Whizzing
	Body	Buzzing
	Aerofoil	Flying
	Graph	Zoom

anything that play a role in bringing about the representamen.

I   The *interpretant* is, quite simply, the effect of R plus O. Interpretants can be abstract entities such as ideas and concepts, within which are contained other representamen.

So the considered order in which signification of a sign takes place is R–O–I, and the process cycles like a continual daydream or a chain of images. It is a process termed *semiosis*. Let's examine this semiosis using the shampoo container referred to earlier and the natural signs that inspired it: the R (of the scent, the fluttering or the babbling) of the O (the flora, the butterflies, the water) creates an I (for example of falling asleep). In this case, it leads to a sign of relaxation or peace.

Who'd have thought a shampoo container could do this to someone taking a bath! The designer's role is to drive the sign semiotics of I by manipulating R and O. In this way, the semiotics become symbolic, and the intermediary links form a chain process through which semiosis takes place. This is continuous and ongoing throughout design. You can see this R–O–I in action in a couple of examples. First the Cadillac example (Table 10.2) followed by a new example (Table 10.3). This example for a Vespa scooter uses shapes, not words, as representamen.

myth

Another influential scholar of semiotics was Roland Barthes (b. 1915). Barthes constructed a signification system based on the connotations that signs possess. This is relevant to us as designers because all the various artefacts, systems and environments that result from design embody signs. In his book titled *Mythologies,* Barthes showed how straightforward connotations can embody very powerful myths. Barthes reveals how connotation can be constructed using *denotation,* and his elegant notion of semiotics is simply brilliant for design. Interpreting signs in the way Barthes proposes requires the designer to engage with the signifier–signified interface, first through denotation and then through connotation. The denotation becomes the signifier for the connotation, and the myth is embedded in the

connotation. I'll use a diagram to illustrate this (see Figure 10.10).

Putting it together, the diagram looks like Figure 10.11. Read from top left down to bottom right.

This semiotic process can help to illuminate myth, if we exchange form for denotation sign and concept for signified, as in the diagram in Figure 10.12.

Figure 10.13 is an example of denotation and connotation for the Cadillac style that I started earlier.

And Figure 10.14 is an example for a Vespa scooter, using shapes as signs.

As a designer you create myths through products. Work backwards. What are your intended

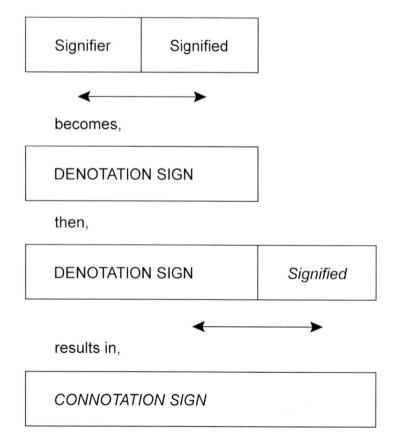

Figure 10.10 Illustrating the relationship between signifier, signified, denotation and connotation. (Copyright author)

Figure 10.11 The assembled signification system. (Copyright author)

Signifier	Signified	
DENOTATION SIGN		*Signified*
CONNOTATION SIGN		

Figure 10.12 Introducing form and myth. (Copyright author)

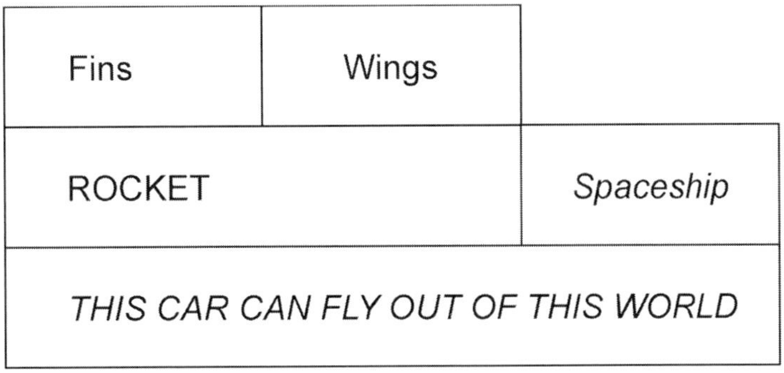

Signifier	Signified	
FORM		*Concept*
MYTH		

Figure 10.13 Applying the model to Cadillac style. (Copyright author)

Fins	Wings	
ROCKET		*Spaceship*
THIS CAR CAN FLY OUT OF THIS WORLD		

Figure 10.14 Applying the model to Vespa style. (Copyright author)

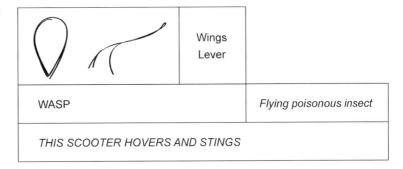

	Wings Lever	
WASP		*Flying poisonous insect*
THIS SCOOTER HOVERS AND STINGS		

Principles of Interaction Design

Many types of products require users to interact with them. At home, at work, while travelling and at play, we have to read screens, push buttons or operate controls. Because of this, interaction has become a major area for human factors research, and interaction design has become a normal part of the development process of a wide range of designs today.

Interaction design is concerned with the usability of products, machines and systems, particularly with respect to how they present information to users and respond to commands and inputs from the user. Designs have to be understandable if they are to be usable.

Human factors expert Donald Norman suggests that designs need to be *visible*, by which he means that it should be obvious how to perform basic operational tasks. A second important principle is providing *feedback* to the user to confirm a command has been received or action completed. A third interaction principle is to design for *affordance*—that is, to facilitate user understanding of function and potential. Donald Norman defines affordance as: 'Strong clues to the operation of things…When affordances are taken advantage of, the user knows what to do just by looking: no picture, label, or instruction is required.'[1]

---

[1] D. A. Norman (1998), *The Design of Everyday Things*, London, MIT Press.

and interpretants? What process of semiosis is happening? What are the myths, denotations and connotations?

design language

Have you ever been asked what a design is saying to you? What, you mean it can talk? What language? All design is saying something whether the designer meant it, liked it or not. The communication—in the form of an aesthetic, a style, the DNA—is translated through aesthetic media. The effect of the composition is greater than the individual parts. So what can design say to us? It can speak of romance, utility, luxury, fear, caring, energy and countless other concerns, but of course this is a process of translation—things get lost or distorted. So take care with semiotics, but don't let this put you off getting involved.

The next person I want to alert you to is the Bauhaus tutor Johannes Itten (b. 1888). Although he was largely referring to colour, his ideas help us progress our understanding of semiotics and language. Itten identified three categories of design language:

- Impression (visual)
- Expression (emotional)
- Construction (symbolic)

> "So what can design say to us? It can speak of romance, utility, luxury, fear, caring, energy and countless other concerns, but of course this is a process of translation—things get lost or distorted."

connotations and myths? What do you want to portray in a product? Do you see an iconic statement or concept? You can then direct and arrange the denotations through the signs and signifiers to create a form that communicates the required connotation or myth.

This is the semiotics of aesthetic design. Designers do this all the time. It is what makes people desire and love the products that they design, forming emotional attachments, sometimes for life. Look back at your style mood board once more. Ponder a while. What are the signs, objects

Itten offers a really effective and practical method of categorising words as part of a broader design language. By *impression,* Itten means the visual look or the physical appearance of a thing. Here are some examples of words that might define an impression:

Bold, shiny, pastel, fluorescent, translucent, matte, dark, muted, opaque, glossy, iridescent, smooth, glittery, blunt, angular, pointed, flat, curved, sleek, chunky, round, tapered, irregular, dull, bright, light, rough, slim, flashy, slimline, bulbous, cubic, conical, bold, sharp, streamline.

Expression is the emotion that may be evoked from a particular design arrangement, composition or style. It is the mood or feeling created. Here are some examples of words that can define an expression:

Happy, strong, dreamy, caring, nostalgic, naughty, angry, aloof, brash, powerful, melancholy, joy, safe, romantic, elegant, wistful, scary, sexy, chic, sympathy, luxury, frivolity, shy, earthy, coy, elation, sympathy, brutal, soft, sweet, cumbersome, cuddly, dynamic.

Construction is the symbolic reference to something that already exists. This could be a natural, cultural or commercial entity or even another style or genre. Here are some examples of words that can define construction:

Executive, aquatic, gothic, organic, ethnic, industrial, erotic, space-age, medical, futuristic, urban, exotic, regal, natural, sporty, civic, rural, aerodynamic, nautical, classical, modern, military, floral, majestic, psychedelic, postmodern, utilitarian, traditional.

Not all words have to fit one of these categories, and it does not matter if some overlap or don't fit at all. The point is that it is a good starting point to begin to develop your design language.

Study the words. Think of some more for each category. Look them up in a dictionary. Look through the dictionary and find descriptive adjectives, verbs or other words (it's easier than you think). Choose a letter a day to look up adjectives and descriptors. Write them down. Compile your own library. Use a thesaurus and look up what descriptors relate to other words and so on. Talk to your fellow students and tutors about different designs or styles, and use new words that you learn. Try to enrich your design language with many wonderful expressive descriptors. Use them in your design work to describe the aesthetic design intention, or to describe mood board images that inspire or influence you, or to critique fellow student designs.

Do any of these words relate to your style, mood board images or other designs that you have created? Which words would you use to describe the impression, expression and construction of your favourite designs? Consider the visual and sensory media; what signs or signifiers convey what words or descriptors? Is there a particularly dominant medium, such as a specific colour or shape, or is it the combination of aesthetic media that makes it successful?

Move on from the specific descriptors and try to be more poetic with design language; create your own words. Use metaphor and simile. For example a Wonka chocolate bar has 'Whipple-Scrumptious Fudgemallow Delight' on the wrapper. Create a poetic phrase for your latest design to describe the semiotics of your aesthetic design intension. Have fun, play with words, create new words and say them to fellow students and tutors.

Ask them what images the words evoke to them. Try creating aesthetic media and design compositions that express the semiotics of your creative design language. And, finally, what words would you use to describe jazz?

colour semiotics

Colour is an enigma of aesthetic design. Colour is not physically tangible—you cannot touch a colour—it's a result of visual perception through the eye and mind. However, it is a powerful semiotic medium. Choose a specific colour and consider how you would describe that particular colour to a person who had never seen colour before. What sort of words or other media would you use to communicate? How could you explain what it is to be colourful? Can you imagine a colour other than those that you have already seen before?

Physically colour has energy and frequency, from red (low energy and frequency) through the spectrum to violet (high energy and frequency). This is interesting from a design point of view as we designers might talk about 'fast' red, associating red with highly powerful designs for sports cars. But how can a colour be fast or powerful? Partly some colours have more impact than others, and partly it is a social construct. The enigma continues, as there are different, and in some cases conflicting, understandings of colour. For example, green is the colour of vegetation and as such it is used to depict qualities such as 'lush' or 'fresh'. However, it is also the colour of mould, so it could be used to represent rot or decay. Also, the semiotics of a single colour do not necessarily follow on when that colour is placed in combinations with other colours. For example,

red has a different character when placed with black compared to when placed with pink (see Plate 13). The effect changes again when the proportions change for the same colours in a colour combination.

The human eye can differentiate millions of different colours, so, as designers, we need an accurate system for specifying colours. We refer to *hue,* meaning its general place in the colour spectrum (green, red, etc.). We also refer to its *lightness* or darkness plus its tone or *saturation.* Look at standard colour charts such as those by Pantone or Munsell to see the variety of colours, varying in hue, saturation and lightness. Given the vast number of colours, the number of combinations and their combined semiotics gives the designer a huge variety of opportunities in design tasks. So what colours would you associate with jazz?

Colour concepts

Colour can produce powerful effects in design communication. It's an important tool in your semiotics toolbox. Try to build up a library of colours to inform your creative designing. For example collect colour images that you find interesting or potentially useful. The images can be natural, commercial, cultural or whatever. You might find it helpful to produce colour abstractions of an image in roughly the same colour proportions, describing the image and its perceived effects. Plate 13 shows some examples I have put together.

Use colour images for inspiration and to form part of your design language, along with textures, shapes and descriptors. Start by collecting many images and creating many colour concepts, then refine them until you have what you intend to be your semiotic palette. Colour can form the driving

Figure 10.15 Semiotics, the study of signs and sign processes, is central to designing today. (Getty 85102166 RM)

force and inspiration behind aesthetic design. It can become part of the front end of the design processes rather than a semiotic afterthought. Colour can embrace a conceptual ideal, it can impose a semiotic direction and it can provide an aesthetic foundation.

over to you

This chapter has offered suggestions for semiotic design approaches, and I have pointed out a number of significant people who have laid the foundations for our understanding of semiotics. A broad process has been identified consisting of three stages. The first stage involved deconstruction of a style using semiotic methods of analysis. The second stage concerned the formulation and compilation of a style grammar exploiting sensory and aesthetic design media such as colour,

texture, shape, form, patterns and words. The third stage concerned the reconstruction of new concepts, using semiotic methods of synthesis.

Your future education and practice will provide opportunities to develop your understanding and application of design semiotics. One objective underpinning this chapter has been to expose readers to an interrogation of aesthetic DNA in styles and images, and the task I charge you with is to use this knowledge to inform the generation of new design work, whether this be in graphic, product or any of the design domains.

Study semiotics in design. Try using semiotics in your day-to-day designing. Discuss it with your fellow students and tutors and other creative people that you know. Realize that you have one particular thing in common with them all. You all understand the concept of style, and in this way you have an appreciation for design semiotics. Like minds do think alike. Enjoy the jazz.

CHAPTER SUMMARY

- Aesthetic style can be a periodic trend, design movement, commercial brand, cultural style or a genre. The designer can identify aesthetic DNA, like a genetic, semiotic code that is inherent in all designs of the same style.

- Style grammar consists of the aesthetic media available to a designer: colour, texture, shape, form, patterns and words. Designers create combinations as part of their aesthetic design language.

- *Signs* and *signifiers* are present in all designs in the form of discreet features and the overall effect in the aesthetic composition. The designer can create and manipulate these throughout the design process.

- *Semiotic signs* have differences but can also be part of a particular code and, as such, can be associated with this or that specific genre. The designer can direct a particular design with an awareness of potential sign exchanges and comparisons.

- *Semiosis* of a design flows through stages of *representamen* relations to *objects,* leading to the *interpretant* of the design as a sign. Designers can reach out and communicate with users through the semiosis they create.

- *Myths* are connotations of signs based on the denotation of the aesthetic media.

- Design language descriptors have visual impression, emotional expression and symbolic construction as well as poetic metaphor and simile.
- Colour semiotics is powerful. The designer can structure and utilize colour with symbolic reference to natural, commercial and cultural images.
- Jazz is a music genre that presents structure and encourages improvisation. In this sense, it's a bit like design semiotics. Listen to more jazz.

chapter 11

designing for mood

randall teal

ABOUT THIS CHAPTER

We often view ourselves as intentional and rational beings, and it's easy to overlook the ongoing unconscious processes that aid our negotiations with the world. In particular, we easily dismiss the ways in which we attune to the *feel* of situations even before we have taken intellectual stock of their various elements and implications. German philosopher Martin Heidegger refers to this phenomenon as *stimmung* or mood; according to him, it constitutes one of the most fundamental aspects of our existence.

This chapter is about mood in design and how it is frequently overlooked. This seems to occur for two reasons. The first is that, although we experience mood readily and regularly in the changing situations of life, it frequently occurs so subtly that the shifts do not register consciously, and therefore we overlook mood's significance. The second reason is that, while familiar in our experience of life, mood often appears as some kind of ornament that we can add to a design later. This chapter focuses on mood in environmental design, but the observations apply to a wide range of other design fields.

---

what is mood?

In today's high-pressure design world, mood can seem a trivial concern when compared to the role that function plays in the creation of good design. However, mood is not trivial—it is, in fact, fundamental. Mood is fundamental to good design because it is the vehicle by which things announce their significance to us. It is the connection between nonrational aspects of ourselves such as feeling, sensation and intuition. Further, mood is closely connected to questions of the beautiful, the spectacular and the sublime, as well as less dramatic experiences such as comfort, satisfaction and well-being. In short, mood embraces

those experiences that any designer should aspire to bring to the work he or she creates and the people for whom it is created.

In using this term *mood,* I am taking up a technical term from the German philosopher Martin Heidegger. In describing mood, Heidegger was interested in the way that particular people and things we encounter in our day-to-day existence seem to touch us *first* on an unconscious level. Heidegger noted how humans are constantly adapting to new situations with very little reflection, simply through feeling and response. For example when encountering a building that we have never been to before, most of us can easily find the entrance with very little conscious thought

Figure 11.1 A public mood is created around a shared experience. (Getty 90798740 RF)

about where we should enter and what we need to do to operate the door hardware. In fact, the only times that we really notice these things is when they don't work; for instance if there is no apparent entrance, or if we try to walk through the door and find that it won't open. On these occasions, we are then forced to reflect on questions of why and what now.

The phenomenon of mood has two implications for design. First, since we are predisposed towards understanding certain cues and processes that come to us from our environments, we can use this to positive effect through design. That is, we can either design things to link up with this human capacity (say, by making buildings that suggest their entry sequence to the visitor, as shown in Figure 11.2),

or, conversely, one might recognize the habitual nature of patterns of behaviour and try to design in a way that is *unfamiliar* so as to alert users to specific things. Retail and advertising design frequently build on the latter strategy to grab attention. The second implication of mood arises from our ability to feel a certain way about encounters before we process them intellectually. In other words, design

> "Design can stimulate subconscious emotions and potentially create positive associations before more rational reasoning has taken place."

Figure 11.2 Buildings that communicate their points of entry. (Copyright author)

can stimulate subconscious emotions and potentially create positive associations before more rational reasoning has taken place. Designing for mood can help users and consumers make emotional connections to things and better relate to the built environment.

the shortcomings of the intellect

Junior designers frequently enter their design education at university with ingrained modes of thinking that are not well aligned with the working of mood. These modes of thinking are an inheritance received from a specific tradition of Western thought, one that is most often associated with the eighteenth-century thinkers of the Enlightenment and with modern science. This type of thinking is best suited to means–end problem solving and for regulating intentional action. I refer to this type of thinking as linear logic, and, although it is essential

to our everyday lives, it can also become a problem for designers, because important aspects of the process of design extend beyond logic.

Problems can arise in design, as they can in art, when logic becomes the predominant way of thinking, because questions related to mood tend to be ignored or misrepresented. In other words, when we create primarily from intellect, we tend to try to address mood through logic, which is a realm that is not mood's primary domain. For design disciplines in particular, such one-sided modes of thought are both dangerous and seductive. They are seductive because they are both familiar and safe, and they are dangerous because when we look at a problem only through the lens of logic, we tend to only see the functional, tangible and problem-based issues of design. Certainly, any design must function, but if it only functions in a utilitarian way, it neglects a critical aspect of its being, which is its potential to connect with us emotionally. Modernist city planning is perhaps the quintessential example of this shortcoming.

Figure 11.3 Modern redevelopment around the Pittsburgh Civic Arena. (Copyright author)

Here, form followed function, as modernists told us it should, but unfortunately in many cases, that is all it did—function in the most basic and utilitarian way. Perhaps one of the most extreme examples of this is Le Corbusier's *Plan Voisin,* where he proposed razing downtown Paris and replacing it with a grid of cruciform towers. In general, such rational approaches to cities around the world brought order and hygiene by creating expressways and demolishing decrepit buildings (and historic ones, too). It continues today, providing scales of construction previously unknown but frequently this 'progress' fails to acknowledge vital human factors (Figure 11.3).

We all need to learn from such examples of practice, but junior designers particularly need to use the failings of the past to bring about a better balance in their own work. For example, frequently design students will try to make their projects communicate impact and worth when design outputs have the capacity to project their own messages. They are imposing an intellectual construction on the work rather than bringing out latent qualities. Furthermore, the familiarity with traditional modes of thought tends to push

us towards solutions that rely on verbal clarification. Junior designers, particularly, will often make things that need an explanation added to them in order to work. For instance, in one project I sometimes set, junior design students are asked to photograph something they take to be beautiful and something they take to be ugly. They are then asked to render each as its opposite through drawing; to make the beautiful ugly and the ugly beautiful. It is interesting how infrequently students will attempt a solution that relies on mood alone. In most cases, students rely on intellectual transformation. The point is that this approach tends to miss creating the *experience* of beauty or ugliness.

It is also important to be clear that, by taking up and encouraging facilities outside of logic, I do not intend to deny logic and analysis. In fact, to swing to the other extreme of saying 'I just did this because I like it' or 'beauty is in the eye of the beholder' denies the physical presence of that which creates a mood. In reality one needs a blended approach. You will find that despite the tendencies towards more intellectualized approaches to making, with a little direction and encouragement, you can be amazingly good at picking up on the subtleties of mood and the ways it is being articulated. And so it is, too, with the greater problem of using design to engage with human emotion; despite initial unfamiliarity, its workings become very natural very quickly.

The fact that things live on in their own way after their creation is important for designers to be aware of. That is to say you will not be there to describe how, why or what something means. It is important that junior designers practise ways of thinking and making that recognize and engage the basic truths of how design is received and the significance of mood. Otherwise, it becomes easy to delude oneself into thinking that the only thing that matters is that a design functions in the most narrow sense of the word. Such a misconception only takes design further from human states of feeling.

mood is not only emotional

Feelings are a normal part of our encounters with the world, but it's rare that designs evoke big emotions such as joy, anger, sadness and so on. Responses are much more subtle. Designs modify emotions, they colour them. A single design can evoke different feelings at different times and in different situations. Mood works through subtle shifts in atmosphere and our ability to detect these shifts. For example coming into the classroom after having lunch, one can experience a discernibly different feeling from the same classroom at 8.00 a.m., but it's probably not a difference that we would call 'emotional'. In this difference, one's demeanour and behaviour shift to meet the demands of the new situation. Usually this occurs with little or no conscious intention. In this way, we find that mood is something that is all around us, something one is immersed in and swept up with.

Four Pleasures

Buying, using and displaying products has come to represent a certain type of pleasure. The pleasures of using a product are derived from the perceived benefits it offers to the user. The design psychologist Patrick Jordan[1] built on the work of Canadian anthropologist Lionel Tiger to construct and illustrate four types of pleasure outlined here:

Physio-pleasure: This is to do with the body and senses—pleasures connected with touch, taste and smell. In the context of products, physio-pleasure might arise from pressing the buttons on a mobile phone or feeling the texture of a fabric.

Socio-pleasure: This is the social bonding or shared identity characteristics stimulated by a given product. It might concern relationships with friends, colleagues or like-minded people, and the context can extend to the owner's status or image in society.

Psycho-pleasure: Psycho-pleasure refers to a product's ability to stimulate positive cognitive and emotional reactions. These might arise in use or in mere ownership. Sometimes these are rooted in functional qualities but they can also arise from more subjective emotional satisfaction.

Ideo-pleasure: This type of pleasure derives from the values associated with a particular product. These might be widely held social values or more personal constructs. Ideo-pleasure can manifest itself in physical characteristics such as the styling of form or in less tangible associations or beliefs.

[1] P. Jordan (2000), *Designing Pleasurable Products,* London, Taylor and Francis.

> **"A single design can evoke different feelings at different times and in different situations."**

Plate 1 Visual thinking externalized through digital tools. David Baldin's interlocking playground elements. (Copyright Michael Tovey/David Baldin) (see Chapter 1)

Plate 2 Embrace incubator, Linus Liang, Stanford University's Hasso Plattner Institute of Design. (Linus Liang/3StrandInnovation & Embrace 2009) (see Chapter 2)

PRODUCT EVOLUTION

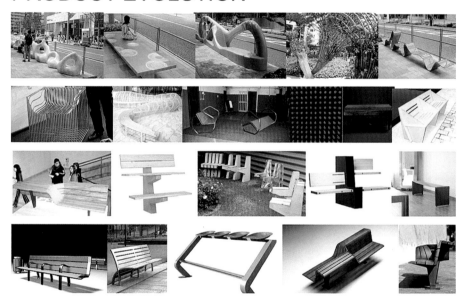

new materials, new assembly, new technology, new shapes, new configurations

Plate 3 Visually documenting design evolution. (Photo copyright Claudie Rousseau) (see Chapter 3)

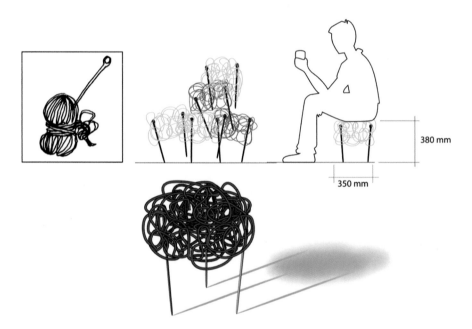

Plate 4 Quick doodles of observations and ideas using *Adobe Illustrator.*
(Photos copyright Anne Laliberté-Guitard) (see Chapter 3)

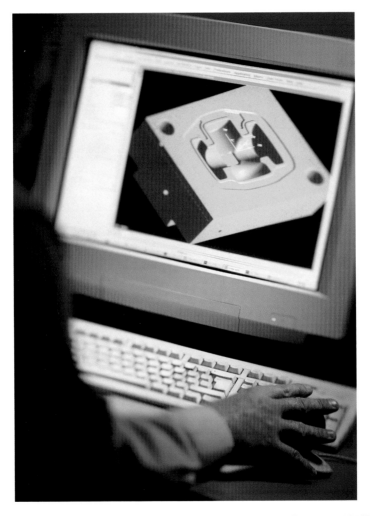

Plate 5 Rendered images can be an ideal tool for communication. (Getty dv634035 RF) (see Chapter 4)

Plate 6 Motorcycle design. Dimensions from full-sized mock-ups (a) used in a virtual model (b), leading to a digital montage (c). (Photos copyright Stephane Garreau) (see Chapter 5)

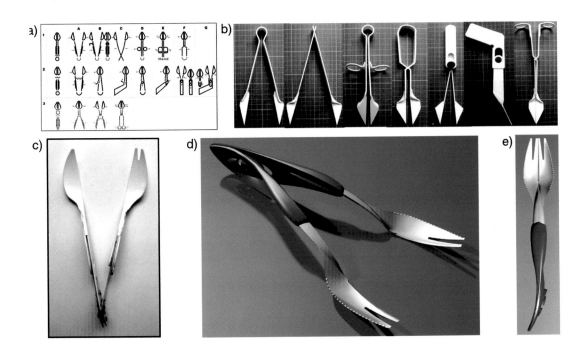

Plate 7 Eating utensil design. Diagrams (a), sketch concept models (b), proof-of-principle prototype (c) and virtual models (d) and (e) used in successive iterations of the design process. (Copyright Jack Ingram/Wei Li) (see Chapter 5)

Plate 8 A drawing of two Italian friends. Shellac on paper. (Copyright Mario Minichiello)
(see Chapter 6)

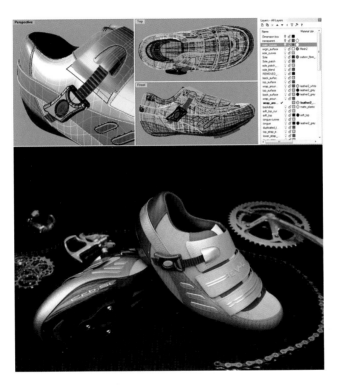

Plate 9 EV-L, 2009. Conceptual sneaker design by Shayne Reynolds, completed in his third year of studies of industrial design in a module that introduces students to the fundamentals of NURBS surface modelling for conceptual product design. (Copyright Shayne Reynolds) (see Chapter 7)

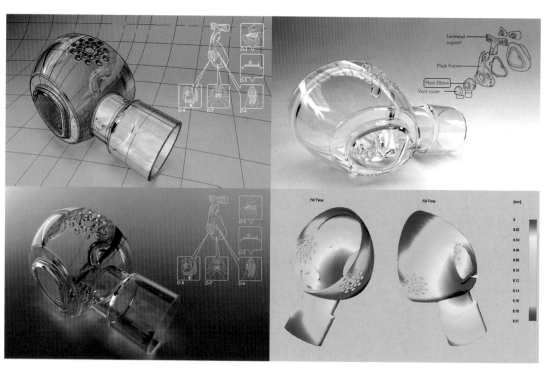

Plate 10 Nasal mask elbow component, 2008. NURBS surface model, high dynamic range imaging with caustics and design verification. (Photo copyright Paul Kouppas) (see Chapter 7)

Plate 11 Like game design, environment design seeks to enhance experience by engaging users in a narrative. (Getty 200492465–001 RM) (see Chapter 8)

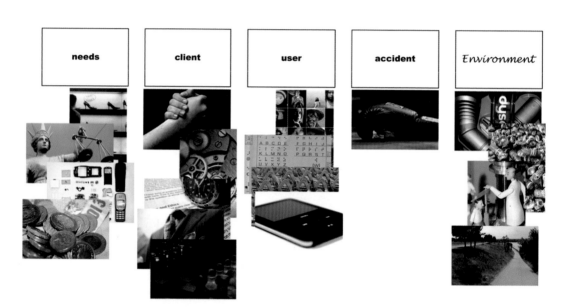

Plate 12 Example card sorting exercise in design research. (Copyright Stacey Birkett) (see Chapter 9)

LEAF, Lush, Fresh, Crisp, Clean

MOULDY, Rotten, Decay, Rancid, Putrid

MONA LISA, Classical, Traditional, Historical, Antique

PUNK, Anarchy, Chaos, Rebel, Blare

CEREAL, Nutrition, Vitamin, Wholesome, Energy

CADILLAC, Flash, Luxury, Streamline, Rocket

IMPERIAL, Empire, Power, Realm, Majesty

NEOPOLITAN, Sweet, Creamy, Dreamy, Yummy

NEON, Luminous, Electric, Lightning, Bright

OCEAN, Cool, Fresh, Deep, Aqua

WASP, Toxic, Poison, Hazard, Sting

ASTRONAUT, Cosmos, Astral, Space-age, Lunar

MOD, Stylish, Urban, Motor, Rebel

BLOOD, Life, Death, Action, Energy

SPIDERMAN, Dynamic, Action, Super, Hero

EXECUTIVE, City, Business, Commerce, Metro

SURGEON, Clinical, Sterile, Medical, Hygiene

COLA, Fizzy, Energy, Hyper, Drive

VOLCANO, Fire, Burning, Lava, Eruption

COAL, Mineral, Energy, Power, Pit

ROYAL, Luxury, Power, Regal, Majesty

MONEY, Power, Finance, Commerce, Luxury

ROCK, Hard, Rough, Tough, Stoic

CIGAR, Luxury, Business, Power, Boss

Plate 13 The semiotics of colour. (Copyright Bob Eves) (see Chapter 10)

Plate 14 Images applied to the stairwell at the University of Oregon. (Copyright Randall Teal)
(see Chapter 11)

Plate 15 Ethics in design decision making.
(Getty 94482451 RM) (see Chapter 12)

Plate 16 Rather than catering for disability, the focus of design has now shifted to the ethics of inclusivity—designing for all. (Getty BB1155-013 RM) (see Chapter 12)

Mood is like the weather on a rainy day, where the whole of one's involvements show up against the gloomy grey background.

There are two points to note here: (1) Mood is *in the world,* not in us; that is to say the things we do, people we encounter and the situations we become involved with have their own distinctive atmospheres. Think of being at a football game where when the home team scores, the crowd erupts in adulation. If we are rooting for the home team, their scoring and the crowds' response resonate for us, too, as adulation; but if we are rooting for the visiting team, not only are we disappointed by the home team scoring, but we probably feel doubly bad being in a such an atmosphere of adulation. The fact that mood comes to us from situations and resonates with us in particular ways brings us to the second important point about mood. (2) Heidegger's conception of mood draws upon a German word, *stimmung,* which refers to the tuning of a musical instrument. It suggests that our dealings with people and things can be compared to a musical instrument being tuned; that is, we are constantly coming into tune, *attuning,* with new situations and circumstances. The sports example is perhaps obvious, but what is sometimes more interesting and more difficult to grasp is the power of subtle changes in mood — these are the ones that designers need to be particularly aware of because they afford avenues towards sensitive solutions.

Such sensitivity can be difficult with the constant distractions of modern life, but humans certainly hold this capacity and have done for thousands of years. For example Greek consciousness appears to have been very sensitive to nuance in the environment. Sean Kelly describes this sensitivity as 'wonder', and he goes on to explain:

Homer's Greeks experienced a plurality of distinct kinds of wonder and the gratitude that goes along with them…I guess you'd have to say that the Greeks really could feel a wonder that indicates the presence of Athena as opposed to one that indicates the presence of Ares or Poseidon. You would have to say that these felt like wonders that share a family resemblance with one another, but that are recognizably distinct nevertheless.[1]

Further, Kelly writes with Hubert Dreyfus, this Greek awareness is:

importantly different from being *startled,* since when one is startled one's entire sense of the situation is destroyed — one finds oneself at least momentarily lost. In the experience of the sudden, one notices immediately a shift from one situation to another, without ever losing hold of the world.[2]

This description provides a helpful guide for what we might strive for in cultivating a greater sensitivity to mood. Like the Greeks, we too possess the ability to experience subtle changes in mood. For designers, hearing the call of mood might even be seen as our highest undertaking. In fact, for the Greeks, one's ability to rise up and respond to the demands of a situation was the greatest indication of one's character. Kelly and Dreyfus put it this way:

In the Homeric understanding the highest form of human life is to be open to, and be able to behave appropriately in, as many of the Homeric worlds as possible. Odysseus is the model of this highest form of life, and Zeus's main job is to protect strangers (people who go from world to world).[3]

Awareness of mood provides a reminder that our environments are constantly changing and that, in these changes, we are persistently asked to change with them. In short, as designers, it is our attuning to the moods of different situations that lets us develop appropriate responses to them.

the importance of mood in the built environment

Recognizing that mood is fundamental to the way we experience art, design—in fact all of life—helps focus the importance of learning to work with it. For example, in Lyon, France, the city parking authority decided that an effective strategy for revitalizing the downtown core would be to eliminate all street-level parking lots. In so doing, it felt that it could create greater cohesion in the urban fabric and have the downtown feel like it was a place primarily for pedestrians. To implement this change, it proposed moving all the parking underground. However, in this proposal, it quickly realized that, notwithstanding the technical challenges to underground parking, perhaps the greatest

challenge they faced was *to make people want to be underground.* This challenge was a challenge of mood. So, to have underground parking work, the designers figured that people must feel the parking to be safe, clean, easy to navigate and, if at all possible, an enjoyable experience. After having laid out the goals it felt were important to the success of this project, the Lyon parking authority was then able to proceed by developing a design strategy that addressed these challenges. In the end, this project ended up being a huge success. The design team dealt with the issues mentioned above through material treatments, well-crafted details, clear lines of sight, lighting, signage and graphics, and even classical music played throughout the day and night.[4] Such attention to detail creates more welcoming environments (see Figures 11.4 and 11.5).

However, such stories are not always the norm. A frequent detour around mood has been through the substitution of function and economics. One notable example of this comes in an adulteration of Roman architectural theorist Marcus Vitruvius Pollio's thought. Vitruvius claimed that a good building requires three things: 'commodity, firmness and *delight*' (my italics).[5] The eighteenth-century

Figure 11.4 Signage at a parking facility in Lyon, France. (Copyright author)

Figure 11.5 Parking facility in Lyon: safe, clean, well lit, well signed. (Copyright author)

French theorist J.N.L. Durand disagrees by saying that, as long as a building is economical, serves its function and remains standing, then it will certainly be beautiful.[6] In short, Durand suggests that we do not even need to think about delight, because it will take care of itself. Unfortunately (and many of us probably know this by experience), this is not the case. There are plenty of examples of dreary building projects that function (think Wal-Marts and strip malls), but this is the most limited notion of function. However, one might for a moment sympathize with Durand for making this statement, because taking on the idea of making something delightful is a daunting task. In other words, asking someone to make something beautiful is frequently the best possible way to ensure that they will create something horrendously ugly!

Here, mood provides a third alternative to either focusing on the questions of delight or beauty outright, or trying to eliminate them altogether. The notion of mood is helpful, because it acknowledges that designers are trying to make things that resonate with other humans but often have no means to approach or articulate this challenge. Mood offers a description of a multisensory experience of the world and allows designers to respond to something other than the problem of a universal (beauty) or a simple means–end relation (functionalism). For example, at the University of Oregon School of Architecture, one of the primary routes from the main floor to the design studios is a concrete fire stair—not the most pleasant of spaces. For many years, there would be a random mural here, some graffiti there, but not much else. These limited interventions may have helped with orientation to various floors but didn't do much for the human experience of the stairs. Eventually, someone finally decided to take an integrated look at the whole experience of this journey in an attempt to provide unity and diversity. He or she did this in a single, brilliant move. This move was to paint each landing wall, between floors, with an iconic image of a distinguished professor—each done as a black cutout on a single bold colour.

Figure 11.6 'Built drawings', Eugene, Oregon, and Moscow, Idaho. (Copyright author)

With that move, the stairwell instantly felt more unified, more interesting, more playful, and more pleasant to be in (Plate 14). This simple example provides a key point about design for the built environment—we do not merely look, we inhabit.

We can too easily forget that design's job is to *mediate* between the complexity of real environments and our ideas for them. In other words, real buildings quickly degrade into planned boxes with simplistic, two-dimensional, crudely detailed add-ons placed side by side when drawings and building are conflated. Here, certain details and materials that work in renderings take on an overblown existence as they become a real building. These types of construction, which are unfortunately found throughout our cities, are not so much buildings as 'built drawings' (Figure 11.6). That is to say instead of buildings that are designed to be multisensory frameworks for inhabitation, the built drawing reduces the experiential qualities of architecture into a mere object of vision. Built drawings in part are a product of designers' unawareness of the embodied subtleties of mood that are found in our three-dimensional, lived environments. In short, moves that are appropriate to drawings are often not appropriate to

actual buildings because they refuse integration into the whole of the experience.

Mood serves two purposes for us here. First, mood shifts focus away from the notion of the object that one looks at as the determination of good design, it opens the possibility to think more inclusively about what makes satisfying experiences. Mood is something that we are 'in'. So a building is not just something to look at, it is something we move through, engaging its materiality, feeling its spaces and understanding it through the relation of all its parts. In short, working with mood opens up the possibility for pursuing emotional connections in our design work, not through the look of a design or in its physical perfection but rather in that way a designed space, object or environment can structure, facilitate and contribute to significant experiences. Not only does this shift take the pressure off hitting such a momentous target as beauty, but it also opens up potential for a wide range of very specific 'beautiful' experiences. For example, it is beautiful to sit on the deck of a cabin looking out across a lake on a summer day, but is also beautiful to sit next to a fireplace on a cold winter day, and it is also beautiful to sit in a comfortable chair reading a book under a glowing floor lamp. Here, the stage is set to understand beauty as something that can be breathtaking as well as something that is simply unobtrusive; something awe inspiring as well as something that brings a momentary smile; something unparalleled as well as something completely mundane. In short, thinking about good design in terms of mood connects us to a bigger assemblage of elements and circumstances. When this occurs, designers can begin to incorporate a greater range of feelings, situations and people into the work they create.

mood and the future

There is great concern today with the issues and demands of developing a more sustainable society. In this context, mood also provides important perspective. Here, the technical definition of mood we have been working with is helpful. It is helpful, because mood acknowledges that our encounters with particular situations are always structured and facilitated by a multitude of factors coming together at any given instant. Such thinking is important in recognizing and working with ecological systems. Unfortunately, it seems that the problems of sustainability are even more susceptible to the seductions of pure intellectual problem solving than design generally. The issue with this approach to sustainability is twofold: First, the problem of addressing sustainability from a problem-solving perspective is that the real issues of sustainability—such as improved use of resources, conservation, efficiency and new technological fixes—tend to drive us into focusing on *only* these objects of design and their features. It neglects the heart of sustainability—the complex web of relations that is formed between a design and its environment. Here, rule systems for

sustainability such as LEED (Leadership in Energy and Environmental Design), despite the awareness and accountability they bring to sustainable issues, can also diminish one's sensitivity to specific situations. A rule-based approach to sustainability's advantage can be seen to be the same as its danger; that is to say developing rules for complicated issues can help to lay out a number of complicated interdependencies, but in doing so there is also the risk of erasing our awareness of their interdependency. Relational influence, such as the urban heat island effect—where the particular materials of multiple buildings in concert store and release heat and thus contribute to rises in urban temperature—is one example; another might be questions about the ways social equity, economic disparity and governmental institutions are factored into our thinking about what makes a system sustainable.

A second problem with treating sustainability as instrumental problem solving is that sustainable features frequently become conflated with good design. Although such things as photovoltaic panels contribute to sustainable environments, mood reminds us that good design speaks to the wholeness of a situation, not simple elements in isolation. It embraces beauty and challenges us to reflect on the role of designers in our move towards more sustainable communities. If mood is the emotional connection to things, how are we to factor this into our thinking on sustainability? It's clear that Vitruvius and Durand had differing views on what made a good building, but what might be our answer today? What are the specific challenges for sustainable design and designing? What skills do designers bring? Dutch landscape architect Adriaan Geuze provides one illuminating response when he suggests, 'architects and designers are in a

Comfort

Many examples of design seek to offer comfort to the user, but what is comfort? As a verb, it means something that affords physical ease and relaxation, and as a noun, it suggests a state of ease or well-being. In the first definition, the emphasis is on the *physical*; in the second definition, the emphasis seems to be on the *psychological*—the perception of comfort.

Physical comfort is partly determined by context. We can be relatively comfortable sitting in a cinema for two hours, sitting on a park bench during a lunch break or perching on a tree stump for a quick rest because, even though the seats and our posture vary considerably, they suit the need. Physical comfort is also partly determined by us as individuals because we all have different physical characteristics.

But there is a second group of factors at work here: psychological factors. We might judge some chairs to be comfortable simply because they look comfortable or because we like to sit in them. Physical comfort and psychological comfort are inextricably bound together. This relationship between physical and psychological factors lies at the heart of many of our purchasing decisions.

better position than anyone else to give a face to sustainability, to make the flag with which a broader movement can associate'.[7] Architects and designers must not forget that their skills for form-giving and identity-making are important to the sustainability movement; partly to promote awareness and buy-in, but also to augment the practices of daily life through the sense of well-being that can be provided by good design. As Geuze explains with reference to the palace in Amsterdam's Dam Square, we sustain those things we love. While skilled designers have begun to take seriously the ways our emotional connections help to vitalize long-term relations between people and the built environment, there

is much still to do. Environmentalist David Orr puts a fine point on the challenge:

> We are…becoming people accustomed to ugliness. The biochemist René Dubos once said that the worst thing we could do to our children would be to convince them that ugliness was normal. Much of what we've built in the post–World War II boom has been award-winningly ugly, or has caused ugliness somewhere else or at some later time. A full recounting of our sins in that regard could take on the flavor of a hellfire-and-brimstone sermon. But the only useful questions have to do with how and how long it will take to transform ugliness into something lovely and to improve our skill in dwelling.[8]

In other words, by focusing sustainability primarily on functionality, we end up forgetting the importance of the power of emotional ties to places we love. If we move progressively towards a world that is difficult to love, then will we move towards a world that will be difficult to sustain.

lessons for practice

Understanding mood in the context of design underscores the fact that every landscape, building, interior, object or product that is designed (or not) reaches us first at the most basic level of feeling. Every creation alters the resonances of a particular environment and people's interactions therein. Unfortunately the existential subtlety of the phenomenon of mood can be easily filtered out when one is sitting in a studio or behind a computer screen. In fact, the conventions of design representation often do not demand that we reconcile or respond to the complexities of any real context. Although such abstracted representation is necessary to the design process, the potential omissions that accompany design media suggest that designers must be ever vigilant so as to not create isolated things indifferent to the intricacies of the places in which they will ultimately exist. Here, the forgetting of mood (as our embodied interaction with the world) is ultimately forgetting the question of beauty. That is to say when one does not design in a way that recognizes the importance of the human capacity for feeling, then one is merely making machinery. In contrast to a purely functionalist outlook, the conditions for beauty arise when designers learn to create in a way that understands that, at our core, we are both thinking *and* feeling creatures.

We live in a world with much stimuli. Multitudes of different elements call for our attention daily and can easily cancel each other out. Often this cancellation causes us to stop listening, it causes us to be insensitive to the subtle messages of mood. When this occurs we begin to privilege clarity over depth, and with this change we come to accept strip malls, cheaply made items and environments that no longer make us feel good. If we are to become, like the Greeks, better attuned to mood, then we must learn to listen better and, in turn, to respond better. If we can achieve this, becoming more responsive to the nuances of mood, we give ourselves a basis for creating designs that exist with us in harmony. At the very least, designers who have learned to listen to mood can feel confident that the problems they are solving are the problems *as they exist,* and not as designers have made them to be.

CHAPTER SUMMARY

- Mood is a constant, if subtle, experience, but it is frequently overlooked in design.
- Mood is in the world, not in us.
- Humans adapt to new situations through feeling and response, and we need to take this into account when designing.
- While function is usually high on a list of design priorities, the function of mood as a connector between the rational and the intuitive is undervalued.
- Mood is not easily addressed through analysis and logic. Designers need to be able to adopt other thinking styles appropriate to the creation of emotion and experiences.
- Even for those not so skilled at 'reading' designs, our buildings, products and systems embody feeling, and they speak their truth without explanation from us.
- Mood works through subtle shifts in atmosphere and our ability to detect these shifts.
- Awareness of mood provides a reminder that our natural and designed environments are constantly changing, and we are prompted to change with them.
- Acknowledging mood assists us to design more inclusively and create more satisfying experiences.

chapter 12

ethics and design: I can but should I?

bryce t. j. dyer

ABOUT THIS CHAPTER

The appreciation of ethical considerations has a history extending back thousands of years, but only in recent centuries have we seen any recognition of the ethical accountability of those who create our human-made world. In the nineteenth century, social reformers such as John Ruskin and William Morris highlighted the ethical responsibilities of those who create the objects we surround ourselves with, embracing the conditions of those employed and the impact on the wider society. While the past fifty years or so has seen significant progress in defining the responsibilities of designers, the relationship of ethics and design is still only loosely understood. Those planning to enter any of the design professions would be well advised to examine the ethical dimension to their particular discipline.

Take a look at the packaging and labelling of various products around you. You can find wording that some items are, for example, 'recyclable', 'for age 6 and over' or 'for personal consumption only'. These are all statements grounded in ethical values and codes. As designers today, we are effectively communicators to a wider society and, as such, have a significant responsibility that comes with this role.

This chapter aims to raise your awareness of ethical considerations in your own design activity. It aims to increase your sensitivity to your decisions, your actions and the consequences. Clearly it can't address all the particular dilemmas of every reader, but what it can do is change the way you think when you engage in designing. It doesn't seek to give you answers, but it does seek to improve your ability to question. As the title confirms, this chapter is less about what you *can* do in design and more about your approach to what you *should* do.

---

beliefs and values

In simple terms, ethics can be described as being concerned with right and wrong. It concerns the moral, social and legal aspects of the actions we take. However, doing what is right, fair or proper in the process of design is not as easy as it may seem, because this frequently involves judgements that are subjective and relative. In essence, ethics is concerned with moral decision-making. It is commonly judged against both personal moral beliefs and those prevalent in society.

The practice of ethics can be traced back to ancient Greece, where scholars and philosophers such as Socrates, Plato and Aristotle would publicly debate human behaviour and

> "Our ethical or moral beliefs can differ widely; our interpretation of right and wrong can vary based on our culture, our experiences as individuals and the many influences around us."

decision-making, different ways of judging a dilemma and the values of different points of view in a given situation. This practice led to the adoption of philosophical systems such as *democracy* and new understandings of human nature, which in turn led to the creation of laws and codes of conduct. Today, designers converse with a wide range of people. These can be within their team and company but might also include their clients, customers, users, other companies, international organizations and perhaps even governments. A key problem for those who need to make ethical decisions is that our ethical or moral beliefs can differ widely; our interpretation of right and wrong can vary based on our culture, our experiences as individuals and the many influences around us. In design practice, there are numerous imperatives for ethical decisions—even if we don't immediately recognize them as ethical. These might include:

- Sourcing appropriate materials
- Presenting a product accurately
- Considering the impact of our designs on society or the environment from, say, manufacturing or distribution
- Our professional behaviour and the behaviour we encourage in others
- Our choices in dealing with clients, users and suppliers
- Our design decision-making process

Whilst a brand may set the tone for a given product—be it advertising, consumer items, video games and so forth—it is fundamentally the designer or design team who creates desire for a design and the messages that are delivered to the customer and wider society. In addition, many designs embody potential risk over misuse or other safety issues. Laws or legislation in the designer's chosen field may not cover the wide range of moral judgements that will need to be made. For example the imagery of a CD cover and the specification of material for a sofa both require moral judgements on the part of the designer. Unfortunately there are very few resources to assist the designer to become sensitive to ethics and to tread the difficult path of ethical decision-making in practice. More fundamentally, there are no books that can offer a firm answer on what you should believe or how you should act. By its very nature, ethics is subjective. The following task seeks to engage you in thinking about your own beliefs and values.

Examining your beliefs and values

Consider the following situation:

1. An architect has designed the building shown below. It is a low-cost housing development targeted at first-time buyers. The planners in a particular area have decided to allow a development of twenty apartments in this development. Should they be built?

   Do you feel this building project is ethically viable? You might argue that it depends on what the buildings are made from and how they are constructed. You may feel it is morally acceptable to build this because the new residents would

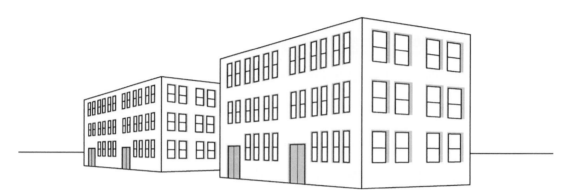

Figure 12.1 The basic housing development.
(Copyright author)

Figure 12.2 The development in a greenbelt site.
(Copyright author)

clearly benefit from it. Let's add some more information and consider the same situation again:

2. Now you are told the development will be built on greenbelt land and will require the felling of a wood of trees. Should it be built?

    Is this a good idea now? While you may have been willing to accept the original impact, you might have different feelings now. It gives rise to various lines of questioning: do the needs of the potential customers outweigh the loss of greenbelt land; who are the other stakeholders in this decision; does the land have

another important value already; are the anticipated residents vital to the community (e.g. nurses, teachers); can the people seek homes elsewhere; are the new buildings actually needed and on what basis was the decision made?

Let's evolve this situation one more time and consider again:

3. Now you are told the development must accommodate 200 apartments. It is to be built on greenbelt land and will require the felling of much of a forest of trees. Should it be built?

Figure 12.3 Multiple housing units requiring the felling of a forest. (Copyright author)

Here the number of people that stand to gain from this development is increased. Did your values change as the problem changed? Did you find yourself asking questions such as 'how many trees' or 'how great is the need'? Are your ecological concerns reduced if other benefits, such as number of people housed, are increased? Is a forest worth more than affordable homes? If you were involved in this project as a designer, how much responsibility would you comfortably shoulder? Thinking about this situation immerses you in ethically driven decision-making. It might be easy to judge and moralize with theoretical examples such as this, but it's incredibly hard to apply in practice—weighing up the different points of view, coming to a decision and converting this into actions. Designing is a process of anticipating the consequences of actions, and this includes anticipating the eventual perceptions of a design's target market.

belief systems and relativism

To increase awareness of ethics in design, this chapter now explores some different ethical approaches or *belief systems.* A belief system is a set of values or a way of thinking. For example vegetarians display ethical beliefs regarding the nonconsumption of animal products. Similarly that bedrock of many legal systems, the principle of 'innocent until proven guilty', or the medical profession's Hippocratic oath to 'do no harm' are ethically driven belief systems. They embrace concepts of what is deemed right or wrong for an individual and for a society.

This section focuses on two belief systems: *teleology* and *deontology*. These display distinctly different approaches. Teleologists would judge an action right or wrong based on its outcomes, whereas deontologists would judge an action right or wrong regardless of the outcomes. For example consider an engineer who has been offered employment as a member of a project team to create a new defensive weapon. This will be employed in various war zones. When determining whether it is right or wrong to design the weapon, the engineer could adopt either of these two standpoints:

Teleological (outcome-based): This is a defensive weapon to be used for the security of many. It is justifiable to take part in its design and development.

Deontological (action-based): This is a weapon that has the potential to kill. Any death caused by the designer's involvement is morally wrong no matter what the circumstances.

This example is an oversimplification, but it serves the purpose of characterising two alternative standpoints. In reality belief systems can overlap or be combined. An individual will often have to rationalize conflicting moral standpoints.

Consider some other types of belief systems:

- Utilitarianism: judgements are guided by the greatest good or amount of product for the greatest number.
- Egoism: driven by the greatest good for you, the individual.

- Hedonism: choosing on the basis of pleasure.
- Intuitionism: judgement based on instinct or experience.
- Environmental ethics: judgements about the relationship between humans and the natural world.

To demonstrate the application of ethical decision-making, consider the following design scenario:

A designer has been tasked to design a piece of clothing for active teenagers. This designer has opted to create a new snowboarding jacket, because she was very successful with a ski jacket design the previous year. The designer has decided to use polyester as the main material and red as the colour because she thought this was best suited to the target market (see Plate 15).

Which belief systems can you identify in this scenario? Perhaps the decision to design a jacket was an egoist decision? Do you think the choice of colour was an intuitionist choice, relying on instinct and experience? It's possible the knowledge that this type of jacket had previously been successful influenced the designer. Perhaps this is an example of utilitarianism in that the designed output (the jacket) would potentially satisfy the greatest number of purchasers.

Let's expand this scenario to include two designers and to introduce greater ethical conflict: Designer A believes that polyester is the best choice of material for the snowboarding jacket because it can be easily sourced, is extremely cost effective (meaning greater profit margin) and it has been a successful choice before. Designer B disagrees. He believes that the success of the previous jacket is not a consequence of material selection. Furthermore he thinks the polyester is supplied from an unethical source overseas. Designer B would rather use a more expensive, locally sourced material. Which designer do you have most sympathy with? At first glance, Designer B may seem to be the most ethical. He feels he is taking an environmental stance on a morally 'good' point of supply. Designer A is taking the stance of the financial profitability of the company. Which is morally superior, the financial well-being of the company or the well-being of the participants in the supply chain? It's these types of questions that increasingly occupy designers today, and it's not always possible to find a compromise that addresses the concerns of all. This scenario highlights the existence of *relativism.*

Relativism holds that ethical or moral standpoints are relative to an individual, group, culture or society. That is, they are not absolute and fixed. Increasingly today, designers need to be aware of cultural relativism and moral relativism when designing products because of the wide range of international markets our goods and services appear in. As designers we need to understand cultural relativism and appreciate that different cultures can have different beliefs than ours about rights and wrongs. Even when we feel we know a particular market well, we need to acknowledge that different demographics (men, women, children, French, American, disabled, etc.) might base their decision-making on widely differing belief systems. It means our designing must address different requirements and expectations, and this can give rise to new conflicts and tensions in the process of resolving a design brief. Whilst a designer will never be able to satisfy all parties or stakeholders, an awareness of all needs and expectations is prudent.

designers and behaviour

Designers need to be able to judge situations. They need to understand how people behave. But equally designers need to reflect on their own behaviour because this too sends out signals. An ethical design approach is founded on what a designer believes but it is also formed by the responses received from others. That is, the judgements of others contribute to who we are. The design professions, perhaps more so than many other professions, rely on systems of *professional ethics* and the acceptance of moral responsibility.

Writers on the subject of philosophy have defined the concept of the *golden rule* in their examination of virtuous conduct.[1] This is, in essence, 'doing unto others as they would do unto you' or 'to treat others as you would wish to be treated'. This concept is surprisingly consistent across cultures. The essence of the golden rule can be found in many of the world's religions in one guise or another. With this in mind, it offers a useful starting point for a designer's code of personal conduct. Let's start by assuming the golden rule should be applied to the design world. When evaluating one of our ideas, we might ask ourselves, 'would I use this myself?' Even such apparently simple questions can help us identify our subconscious beliefs that contribute to design decisions and compromises. If a particular design feature is confusing, dangerous or unattractive to us, then why should we assume it's acceptable to others? Such questioning can assist us to behave more ethically and more professionally.

Such awareness is vital in today's world, where many 'no win, no fee' law firms seek out potential avenues of litigation. For example we need to ask, 'can my design be obviously misused?' 'might my material choices be criticized on the grounds of health or safety?' and 'is there potential for injury?'

And it's not just the dramatic failings we need to be aware of. A designer acting morally and ethically will consider the lesser but still significant impact of opinions and perceptions of his or her work—from friends and relatives as well as direct users of the designed output. There are obvious limits to this, however. The majority of people are entirely sensible and only a small minority less so. The designer can only guard so far against potential claims. Much of this comes with experience, and the development of ethical judgement must be a conscious and ongoing process.

One notable example of negative ethical behaviour in design practice comes from the field of Formula 1 motor racing. This is an extremely competitive environment in which engineering excellence and race-winning success are the most prized commodities. In 2008 some designs for car components had been illegally obtained by one team copying another team's designs. Quite quickly the stolen designs were incorporated in the engineering of the other team's car. Despite the fact that society judges stealing as wrong (plus it's illegal within the sport's own rules), the individuals and team involved determined that the end result (increased opportunity for race success) justified the means.

A code of conduct cannot be defined by following the 'way it has always been' but instead has to proceed from first principles towards 'how it should be'. In many companies, there will be expected codes of practice regarding, for example, client relationships, schedules of payment, project deliverables and project liability. Today's commercial world has seen radically new approaches to ethical design practice embracing, for example, sustainability and employment policy. Some traditional values and old models of ethical practices have not survived. The designer today must question practice and policy and seek out ethical improvements.

We must respond to the ethical imperative of continually refining our professional ethical standpoint. This is not easy since ethics is a fluid, dynamic phenomenon which changes from place to place, decade to decade and generation to generation.

perception and deception

A key ethical dilemma that impacts on most forms of design is perception. The perception of a product—that is, what we think it gives us—is

Responsibility in Design

The word *responsibility* appears more frequently in design today than at any point in history. Partly this is driven by the culture of greater awareness of rights by users and consumers, partly by legislation and partly by wider awareness in all design disciplines of the implications of design decisions. One definition of responsibility is reproduced by Mark Bovens in his book *The Quest for Responsibility: Accountability and Citizenship in Complex Organisations*.[1] It's a frequently cited definition from Chester Barnard: 'Responsibility…is the power of a particular private code of morals to control the conduct of the individual in the presence of strong contrary desires or impulses.'

If we believe only in *passive* responsibility, where emphasis is given to responsibilities after an action or outcome, then a design failure might give rise to questions such as who was responsible, who was to blame or who is to be held accountable? However, if we believe in *active* responsibility, designers must anticipate design consequences. For example designers need to consider the potential for accidental misuse of their designs as well as normal use. As designers we need to understand the shifting boundaries of responsibility in our service.

[1] M. Bovens (1998), *The Quest for Responsibility: Accountability and Citizenship in Complex Organisations*, Cambridge: Cambridge University Press.

Figure 12.4 Bigger burger or smaller plate? Perception and deception in advertising. (Copyright author)

frequently just as important as its more tangible offerings. Whether we're talking about Web pages, jewellery, kitchen appliances or a new building, it's the perception of qualities and affordances that influence whether people like something or not. Perception lies at the root of many design briefs that seek to create desirability and generate sales. In the hands of skilled designers, the relationship between managing perception and ethical responsibility is symbiotic. But there is also the potential for design to be used towards deception rather than enhanced perception. I'm sure you can think of designs that embrace inaccurate communication, deception or misrepresentation. Consider a fast-food chain that wishes to increase sales of a range of burgers. How might the organization make the burgers seem more desirable in an advertisement? Here's a few of my ideas: You could advertise the burgers (and serve them) on smaller plates, thus making the burgers appear larger. You could place other items in the foreground or background to manipulate the sense

of scale (making consumers feel they are getting more for their money). You might associate the burgers with a personality or try to get consumers to buy into a lifestyle choice.

There are some ethical dilemmas here. It could be seen as wrong to attempt to fool consumers into thinking they are getting a larger product. This is deception. But how do you feel about constructing, perhaps falsely, some connotations or associations with status symbols or celebrities? Where does one draw the line? The designer needs to be mindful of thresholds in practice. One of the functions of professional design associations and organizations is to determine various acceptable thresholds of behaviour to assist the designer to formulate his or her own response to dilemmas.

key ethical issues in design

So far, this chapter has mapped out some of the domain of design that overlaps with ethics. This section turns to explore four key issues that define ethical designing today, and it ends with a warning about pseudo-ethics.

Ability and inclusivity

All areas of design now need to anticipate the needs of people who may be different than ourselves. The distinction between able and unable is increasingly blurred, and the term *disability* masks some real design issues concerning usability. The domain of architecture has particularly had to respond to new awareness of people's needs and wants. Building design has had to incorporate a wide demographic partly from new social pressures and partly from legislation. Accessibility to design for people from all walks of life and levels of ability has become especially important. Rather than catering for disability, the focus of design has now shifted to the ethics of inclusivity—designing for all.

Sustainability

Every design—be it a magazine, a shirt or a car— needs to stand up to audit regarding its use of resources and its impact on the environment. This not only covers such things as materials selection or the number of components in a product but also its wider implications. Manufacturers today seek to reduce the impact of outputs in areas such as distribution (both in terms of method and distance), the origin of materials used and the life

> "We can design in or design out waste, and it's frequently the designer who must make this ethical choice."

cycle of the design. Ethical designing prompts questions such as 'where does the resource come from?' 'what happens during its life?' and 'what happens when it is discarded by society?' Even graphic design must address the pressures of ethical interrogation. For example, the style and size of a font has a direct relationship with the amount of paper used in a publication. We can design in or design out waste, and it's frequently

Figure 12.5 Even graphic design must address the pressures of ethical interrogation. (Getty med242065 RF)

the designer who must make this ethical choice. Ethics have caused, and continue to cause, major changes to the way design problems are resolved and refined.

Intellectual property

The majority of designs are influenced by something else—quite frequently other designs—and designers must exercise ethical decisions on how much they should borrow from other sources. Of course, there are legal systems to guide decision-making, and many designs have received vigorous legal defence when intentionally copied by another party. Copyright, design right and patents can be expensive to defend but potentially much more expensive to infringe. It's the grey area outside of infringement that presents the designer or design team with difficult ethical decisions, because the pressures and opportunities are frequently unique to each situation.

Safety

It was discussed earlier how designers need to evaluate the potential misuse or misinterpretation of a design solution, and the consequences can be extremely serious. The capsize of the *Herald of Free Enterprise* ferry off the Belgian coast in 1987 with the loss of 193 lives was caused by human error compounded by a lack of a warning light indicating the bow doors were still open. The circumstances of this catastrophe could have been reduced with better design of the ship and its human systems. Similarly, road traffic accidents might be reduced if cars were fitted with speed limiters, but currently this is not deemed acceptable by the market. Design decisions, even those concerning product safety, are often significantly influenced by other stakeholders such as consumers.

Pseudo-ethics

Being 'green' has become a marketable commodity today. There has been a significant increase in market share for organic foods and products, fair trade and locally grown produce. However, these products also typically charge a premium for their purchase. It seems that ethics has a price. The market has also seen a growth in products that appear to address the ethical debates of sustainability without offering the consumer any real benefit. Some food products are sold as being healthy because they are low in fat yet are supplemented by an increase in salt or sugar—thereby trading one nutritional concern for another. Again design is intrinsically involved in such decisions, and the pressures on designers to bend to commercial priorities can be immense.

developing your ethical framework

Ethical design practice is not clearly defined. Individual designers need to work to develop their own ethical framework appropriate for their own discipline or profession. Some areas are more developed than others, and, in some places, new legislation or guidelines assist professional practice. This chapter concludes with a few strategies for student designers to develop their ethical framework for designing.

Engage in debate

Frequently overlooked is the value of simply discussing design decisions with colleagues, clients or other stakeholders. It's a strategy that has proved effective since the scholars of ancient Greece. Asking questions, listening to answers and creating counter-arguments allows points

Figure 12.6 Examine design ethics through discussion with colleagues. (Getty EA2736-001 RM)

of view to be tested and developed. Debate frequently tests evidence and reasoned argument. Of course, there will be subjectivity in all arguments as opinions, assumptions and interpretations of evidence will differ. Nevertheless, there is much to be learned from debate, and it provides an accessible means of developing your ethical framework.

Understand the law

All disciplines of design need to understand the legal context in which they operate. Whether it be a new seatbelt for a car, a new library building or an advertisement for soup, the design outputs are governed by law. In many ways, legislation and laws take away some of the ethical decisions that designers confront. Laws are a form of applied

ethics where legislation defines what is acceptable to individual consumers and society collectively. But even though our laws might determine what is right or wrong, there are still numerous requirements for designers to exercise their judgement about how the legislation might be applied in society. This is particularly the case in those design contexts where there are regular innovations, such as in biotechnology. While you may not agree with the increasing extent of legislation to which manufacturers and therefore designers must conform, the rules are there to protect you as well as consumers.

Seek evidence

The foundation of any useful opinion is evidence. Gathering evidence is a valuable skill for designers as well as for a wide range of other professions. At the root of evidence is usually data. On its own, such data has little value, but it provides the raw materials for analysis, which in turn facilitates interpretations and leads to the creation of knowledge through conclusions. Successfully generating meaningful data is vital to the creation of an evidence-based ethical approach to design. Data can be generated in many ways. It can be collected through questionnaires—perhaps sent by email, posted or given out. You might want to conduct one-to-one interviews or arrange focus group discussions. Alternatively, it might be relevant to collect secondary evidence—that is, evidence that others have generated, written about and made available through books or journals.

Key in all these techniques is how the research questions have been constructed—that is, what assumptions have been made and whether the respondents have been led in their answers in any way. For this reason, any survey needs to be pilot-tested first to make sure it is impartial and free from bias. Also make sure you have sufficient data on which to base your conclusions. Composing the wrong conclusions because your evidence came from too small a sample or an unrepresentative sample of people can result in poor design decisions. Make sure your research design is good. There's an important ethical dimension to designing and conducting research if the conclusions are to be applied in ethical design practice.

Multidimensional ethics scales

This technique for generating information was originally devised to evaluate marketing activities. It can vary in its design but typically involves participants making ethical judgements on eight characteristics derived from ethical belief systems.

Those taking part are given a specific context and are asked to rank each characteristic on a scale of one to five or one to seven (with one being positive and the high number being negative). A typical list of characteristics will include the following:

- fair/unfair
- just/unjust
- morally right/morally wrong
- acceptable to my family/unacceptable to my family
- traditionally acceptable/traditionally unacceptable
- culturally acceptable/culturally unacceptable
- violates an unspoken promise/doesn't violate an unspoken promise
- violates an unwritten contract/doesn't violate an unwritten contract

Multidimensional ethics scales have been used extensively in business, and this technique can be particularly revealing for design. At the end of a test, the scores are assessed to see how ethical the situation is perceived by adding, averaging or just reviewing the scores. This attempt to measure ethics relies on the ethical relativity of the person or persons completing the test.

Sooner or later, the designs you create will be questioned by other stakeholders. This could be a manager, lecturer, client or members of the wider society. They might not agree with your vision or the ways you have gone about realising your vision. Frequently these questions will concern the ethics of your process and products, and you need to call upon a developed framework to help you respond to questions and criticism. Increasingly, you will need to demonstrate that your actions and your outputs are ethical.

CHAPTER SUMMARY

- Ethics is about right and wrong. In essence, ethics is concerned with moral decision-making.

- The creation of products, systems and environments is increasingly grounded in ethical values and codes.

- Designing is increasingly a process of ethically driven decision-making. It's about weighing up different points of view, coming to a decision and converting this into actions.

- Designers need to understand cultural relativism. Different demographic segments base their decision-making on different belief systems. Designing must address various requirements and expectations, and this can give rise to conflicts and tensions.

- Designers today must question their own attitudes, approach and policy.

- The chapter identified four questions of ethical designing: are you practising inclusivity, are your designs sustainable, are you stealing other people's intellectual property and are your designs safe?

- Develop your ethical framework by engaging in debate, understanding the law and seeking good-quality data.

Background

Despite greater awareness of hygiene, hand cleanliness is still a major issue in both the developed and the developing world. A wide variety of illnesses continue to be spread by poor awareness of hygiene and poor practice. This is an issue affecting everyone. To address the issue, we have seen various campaigns, improvements to water supply, new types of products, the use of antiseptic gels or gloves and targeted education.

You have a single period of 24 hours for this project—that is, if you begin at 9.00 a.m. one day, you have until 9.00 a.m. the next day to complete the work. You are not permitted to spread your 24 hours over a longer period.

The Project

This project invites you to use your design skills to improve hand hygiene. You may interpret this as a communication project, a product design project or in any other way that leads to proposals that might potentially assist with hand hygiene. You can select the context you wish to work in—for example city streets, the workplace, a hospital, an airport, a public place where food is eaten and the home.

You have twenty-four hours to come up with a proposal that improves hand hygiene. Talk with people, find out about hand hygiene and the problems that people face. Generate some ideas and share these with people you know. Ask them to give you feedback on strengths and weaknesses of your ideas. Develop one or two of the most promising ideas. Anticipate people's questions about practicality, usability or cost. Create a presentation that communicates your proposal clearly.

Guidelines

This is a project about people: what people know, how they act and how design can both help and protect. It's about our bodies, but it's also about our minds and our propensity to gather in social groups. This is a project where you are designing for others, not yourself.

Don't settle on a context too quickly. Try to find real problems to address, even if this means working in an area that's unfamiliar to you. Remember that designing is about problem finding as much as problem solving. But don't spend too long investigating—balance investigation with creation and communication. Externalize your ideas using sketches and get others to comment on your ideas. Change, develop and improve your ideas—try not to get stuck in the rut of one idea which might block out other good ideas. When you have a proposal, switch from being a creator to being a communicator; put yourself in the shoes of other people and imagine what they need to understand and appreciate your idea.

part iv

business, markets and clients

introduction to part iv

The function of design as a primary driver in commercial and economic success is one of the most important themes in the whole collection. While some design can be personal or aimed at niche markets through one-off designs, the vast majority of the professional practice of design is shaped by pressures to create outputs in very large quantities and which offer value to a variety of consumers at the lowest possible production cost. Therefore, it's no coincidence that Part IV opens with a chapter titled 'The Business of Design'. But there's a double edge to this chapter by Stephen Peake. Partly it suggests that designing has commercial responsibilities, in contrast to, say, offering opportunities for expression. It also suggests that it's the business of designers to engage with the commercial world and to demonstrate corporate leadership that has for too long been dominated by professional managers.

This is a broad section that seeks to address four related topics that shape the commercial application of design skills and knowledge today. In some ways, Part IV represents the beginning of the design process, because Chapter 14 by Andrew Collier outlines the essential content of a successful design brief. Importantly, he reveals how a designer's capacity for creative inquiry can help formulate this vital commercial document that underpins all subsequent design activity. But there's a humble appeal at the core of this chapter that should resonate with all those who aspire to work in any of the design professions. This is the need to listen, and it fits well with the appeal in Part III for a user-centred approach to design. Through listening, we give respect to all stakeholders, and potentially we avoid those pitfalls that so many designs fall foul of.

In Chapter 15, Richard Woolley weaves together his expertise in business, markets and clients with reference to the car design industry. He reveals how a user-centred design process begins at the very start of a project and how designers need to engage with market research as a foundation to creative thinking. Importantly, this chapter emphasises the value of working with experts from other disciplines to co-create milestone documents such as the design brief. This is developed by other authors in later parts.

Concluding Part IV is a study of a Brazilian design consultancy that has developed an international reputation for packaging design. This chapter by Luiz Gomes and Ligia Medeiros offers a helpful synthesis of the commercial forces that designers must wrestle with. That is, they must find a way to make time for investigation, exploration and research whilst delivering detailed, practical innovation to the client.

Although the four chapters of Part IV draw on different branches of the design industry, we are given glimpses into an industry experiencing some common forces of transformation: the quantity of market information available necessitates that designers find ways to filter data; the design process and its downstream production processes are increasingly digital; the speed of designing is increasing and the commercial pressures not to fail are greater than ever before.

chapter 13

the business of design

stephen peake

ABOUT THIS CHAPTER

I have a warning for you. Out there, in many of the world's best business schools, leading academics have created courses that capture the essence of design thinking, and they are teaching business and management students how to apply this effectively in a variety of commercial organizations. This chapter seeks to redress the balance by inspiring designers to demonstrate leadership in business thinking. Designers are in an ideal position to combine design thinking with business thinking, but, for a variety of reasons, they have failed to do this through senior management and particularly at the boardroom level. If you have a vision for a fairer, more sustainable and satisfying economic system, then this chapter suggests some strategies that designers might apply in business leadership. The creation of our future world of artefacts, services and systems requires the application of new strategic thinking, and it's the business of designers to get involved. If the design professions don't lead from the front, this opportunity for creative strategic influence will surely be grasped by others in the business community.

---

two tribes

The worlds of design and business can seem very different. Commercial organizations have design groups as well as strategy units, and universities have design schools as well as business schools. But the relationship between these parts can differ widely, and in some cases an interface hardly exists. Crudely put, the worlds of design and business can all too often seem like two different tribes with their own cultures and languages. Some practitioners are sufficiently skilled to be able to travel back and forth between these organizational domains, while others have opened new gateways by challenging the boundaries between

the two. Enlightened designers, entrepreneurs and business leaders see the connections and parallels between the two cultures. Some have learned to speak the languages of these two domains, enhancing their easy movement across the interface and their ability to make convincing contributions when inside one domain or the other. Some are sufficiently skilled to be able to help others work across the divide by translating the necessary communication between the two cultures or acting as an ambassador in facilitating new relationships. The professional practice of design today requires all participants to move across boundaries into other specialist domains. This is as true for information designers and those

Figure 13.1 Cross the perceived boundary between
design and business. (Getty 99308107 RF)

at the art and craft end of the design spectrum as
it is for those who operate, or seek to operate, in
engineering or architecture.

The ability to work across boundaries has
become more urgent as design has become
liberated from artefact-centred purposes to
become a tool of service, system or interface
creation. In some ways, design and business
people share this enviable capacity to translate
and facilitate. They have more in common than
each might think.

Increasingly, all designers must work in a commercial environment, and they need a business

> **"In some ways, design and
> business people share an
> enviable capacity to translate
> and facilitate. They have more in
> common than each might think."**

head as much as a design head. Given the chance,
and some appropriate guidance and training, the
two heads can create a powerful synergy for intelligent commercial creativity. Business people are
incredibly creative, and, although they rarely refer

to themselves as designers, they increasingly apply a number of strategies of design thinking such as generating ideas in response to ill-defined problems, prototyping ideas to test them early on and visualising to assist communication. However, there are some design skills and knowledge that only become truly embedded with prolonged and sensitive application, which is why design thinking can be so powerful when exercised by those with a formal training in design. If you can combine this potential with the skills and knowledge of business thinking, you create for yourself a powerful passport and a marketable capacity to operate across these two worlds.

milestones in business and management

The skills of management are clearly one of humanity's ancient capacities, but the roots of a culture of management with its own corpus of knowledge is easier to date. In the English language, the term *management* emerges in the late sixteenth and early seventeenth centuries from the Latin origin *manus,* meaning hand. It probably refers to the exercising of a controlling hand in any of a variety of matters but particularly in the emerging commercial environments of that time. It may even be the root of the expression *hands-on*, referring to a practical involvement. Today management is sometimes synonymous with the term *business administration,* and management schools and business schools worldwide offer postgraduate qualifications titled master in business administration (MBA).

Theories of management and business administration developed with the burgeoning enterprise culture of manufacturing, trade and finance

that has come to dominate the world. The industrial revolution of the eighteenth century, with its demands to marshal resources on an unprecedented scale, provided the impetus to the formulation of what we now call management thinking. Business thinking was a much later development and can be considered as a twentieth-century phenomenon. Management today has become an essential strategic tool of organizations ranging in size from a one-person business to a multinational corporation. It finds application in public-sector services such as hospitals, in government at various levels, in private-sector companies and in organizations such as charities.

There are interesting historical roots to the development of management and business theory. Towards the end of the fifteenth century, Luca Pacioli, an Italian monk (and a colleague of Leonardo da Vinci), is thought to have been the first person to publish a detailed description of the double-entry bookkeeping system that had originated earlier within Islamic and European trading systems. The monasteries can also claim to have been influential in the creation of information systems that have come to underpin management today. In 1911, the mechanical engineer Frederick Taylor published his *Principles of Scientific Management* in the United States. This monograph provides a milestone in the establishment of the new science of workflow and productivity and is widely held to form the basis of modern organization and decision theory.

It marks the point where the complexity of logistical issues demanded the application of new scientific and mathematical methods, and their superiority was confirmed where organizational demands were immense, such as supplying food, fuel and munitions to troops in the Second World War. In fact, such was the superiority of the new

Figure 13.2 The twentieth century saw the establishment of the science of workflow and productivity. (Getty 81773060 RM)

science that it spawned new branches leading to new applied sciences. For example, systems engineering was practised in the Bell Telephone Laboratories in the 1940s, and this helped define project management as we would recognize it today.

dissecting management

Management isn't rocket science; it can be dissected to reveal some clear lessons, and this is precisely what happens in MBA courses. In this chapter, the dissection has the aim of helping designers integrate their design ability with the skills and knowledge of management. The following sections review some of the building blocks of management. Each gives rise to some important priorities for organizations today as well as lessons for designers.

People and performance

The culture of an organization is largely defined by those it employs. Essentially, business is about people—consumers, suppliers,

What Business Are We In?

In framing their commercial strategy, successful companies consider the question, 'what business are we in?' not in terms of the products they make but in terms of the market needs they satisfy. This is because the needs that users have tend to be more long-lasting than the products that temporarily satisfy those needs.

The idea applies quite generally, as can be seen in a comment from the Gillette company about the previous reliance on aerosol deodorants, after public concerns emerged about damage to the ozone layer from aerosol propellant gases. A Gillette executive said:

> We were a little like the railroads who didn't realize they were in the transportation business. We thought we were in the aerosol business because 80% of all users preferred aerosols and we were the leader in that segment. But when the ozone controversy broke, we found out we were really in the underarm business.[1]

In other words, the company had implicitly regarded itself as being in the aerosol deodorant market, but when it was forced to reconsider the manufacture of aerosol sprays, it reinterpreted its business mission as 'the underarm business', or personal hygiene products. The identification of the business it is 'really in' is a key part of how a company establishes its business mission and commercial strategy. It has obvious and vital implications for the scope and direction of new product development activity in a company.

[1] D. F Phillips, president of Gillette Toiletries Division, cited in 'After the diversification that failed', *Business Week* 28/2 (1977): p. 58.

From: N. Cross, *Design and Designing* (T211), The Open University, Blk 2 (2010), pp. 14–15.

Management is about the development of leadership, including how to develop a vision, how to align an organization behind that vision, how to motivate people to achieve the vision and how to assist them to develop in order to achieve improved performance. Since this area essentially concerns the human factors in the design of effective organizations, it should be apparent that design thinkers can make a significant contribution. Not only might they be able to offer creatively diverse ideas to organizational problems, but, as design consultant Jeanne-Marie Olson points out, designers can help organizations 'recognize which problem you are trying to solve so you aren't sowing the seeds of innovation on rocky soil', and to 'balance the ability to invent with the capability to help implement'.[1]

Business function and business process

In recent decades there has been a shift in management thinking away from organising by business *functions* towards organising by business *processes.* This is a movement away from the old order of marketing, sales, research and development, logistics, production, design, purchasing, finance and so on towards a new order based on processes such as strategy formulation, product development, customer relationship management, supplier relationship management, order fulfilment and returns management. In the new order, business functions are absorbed into business processes. Today organizations need to avoid seeing problems through narrow, departmental prisms. They need to apply integrated thinking if they are to achieve competitive advantage. Business schools place a lot of emphasis on the ability of managers to create systems where team members share a common understanding of business process.

employees and so forth—so managing the performance of individuals and groups is vital. Only through good management can a company establish the essential relationship-building practices that make for effective team working.

The shift from functions to processes may not seem particularly radical to you, but it has underpinned much new theory on business innovation. As a design thinker, you will recognize the power of a shift in mindset from problem-focused to solution-focused and action-oriented thinking. You may also already appreciate what the business schools have only recently begun to teach—that innovation can arise from iterative conversations at different stages of design and development. Former president of the Industrial Designers Society of America, Mark Dziersk, puts it this way:

'Designers need to be orchestra conductors. Design thinkers need to be able to mobilize cross-functional teams. That requires a skill set that includes effective leadership, the ability to inspire, respect of other competencies, and equal measures of charm and manic control.'[2] Teams that are created around business processes mix up people from different functions in an organization. This emphasis on process rather than function can be extremely useful when an organization is part of a supply chain having to interact with other organizations' business processes (Figure 13.3).

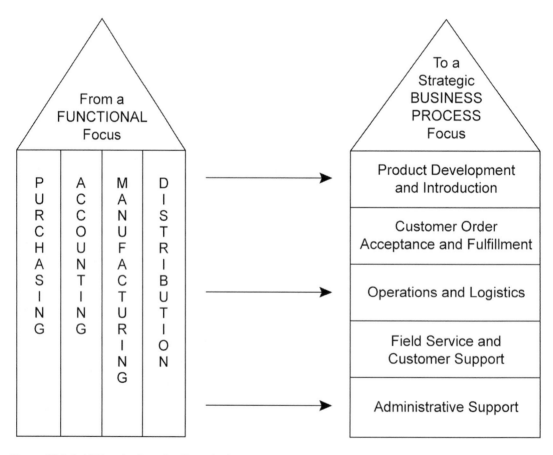

Figure 13.3 A shift from business function to business process. Image based on original published by Emerald Insight, www.emeraldinsight.com/content_images/fig/1570090606001.png (accessed 12 April 2011)

Strategic management

Strategic management is the analysis of how to be consistently better than competitors offering similar products or services. It involves understanding the core strengths of an organization. This might involve the resources that it commands or where the costs are in a product or service. Particularly a company needs to understand how and where it adds value. Greater value can come about through the delivery of the same benefits at lower cost and/or the delivery of new benefits which exceed those offered by competitors. Organizations rarely depend on one product. Usually they produce a mix of different products, and a key skill in strategic management is finding the optimum configuration between product mix and cross-functional capabilities within an organization. The challenge is to be able to do this over time as technology and markets evolve.

On the surface, strategic thinking and design thinking can appear to have little in common. As business strategist and innovation specialist Idris Mootee puts it, 'I am often asked the question of what "design thinking" has to do with business strategy. When talking about design thinking people refer to aesthetics (mainly high style design or usability) and generally they cannot relate this to strategy (strategy means spreadsheets).'[3] In fact, as we shall see later on, strategic innovation is in large measure frequently a result of design thinking. Roger Martin, dean of Rotman

Figure 13.4 Redraw the world of business. (Getty 73224060 RF)

School of Management, uses the concept of design thinking to 'explain how companies have to "go beyond pure analysis" to innovate, "crunching things other than numbers". Design thinking is about using a designer's palette to redraw the world of business'.[4]

Marketing management

The management of the marketing mix is perhaps the management domain most typically associated with creativity, graphic communication and design thinking. The marketing mix is the combination of product policy, branding, channels of distribution, communication and pricing. The origins of modern market-oriented thinking go back to the 1950s, when organizations challenged the common assumption that designing a better product would lead to more sales. This was a belief caricatured in the phrase 'build a better mousetrap and the world will beat a path to your door', but it had to give way to the gradual realization that products need to be *sold*. It was a hugely transformative period, and it saw organizations develop radically new approaches based on finding out what customers wanted and then producing a product or range of products to address the needs and wants. Today, marketing has become a vital bridge between the worlds of business and design. It provides information that steers the creation of a design brief and design specification through market and user studies. It also acts to channel information the other way—from organization to consumer—about the values and functions of products and services.

Financial management

While 'creative accounting' has negative connotations, there are certainly important synergies between creative thinking and the financial

foundation underpinning all successful innovation. Unfortunately, in some organizations design thinking has been limited in its application, for example to the creation of successful user experience, whereas it potentially can be used to deliver significant cost savings. In some consumer product industries, creative thinking early in the development process can lead to avoidance of waste, reduction in material usage, efficiencies in energy consumption and cheaper unit cost in manufacturing. But the possibilities for design thinking in financial management don't stop there. Elements of creativity might be seen to underlie expert accounting and certain tax avoidance practice. On a broader societal level, we are now engaged in the task of redesigning the international financial system in the wake of the 2008 credit crisis, and the financial modelling of ideas and the prototyping of new systems should be broadly observable. The language and formulae may not be so transparent to those whose specialism is design, but the purpose of modelling to understand, speculate and test ideas should be familiar. Also there are elements of design thinking involved in the investigative nature to some accounting processes, for example when there is some financial mystery to be solved. Design thinking never really got a foothold in the finance departments under the business function model. The new order of business processes provides more opportunity for design thinking to become embedded in strategy formulation, product development, customer satisfaction and supply chain logistics.

Information technology management

The distinction between technology and management systems for technology is an area which is rich in parallels with developments in design thinking. As organizations, both private and public,

> "The new order of business processes provides more opportunity for design thinking to become embedded in strategy formulation, product development, customer satisfaction and supply chain logistics."

have learned (sometimes to their great cost) about managing the design and implementation of new information systems, they have increasingly had to stand back and look at the bigger picture.

Today organizations cannot afford to simply adopt the latest technological innovations. They must consider interactions between information technology and individual and organizational behaviours and cultures. Information technology management—sometimes called knowledge management—is a potentially key source of competitive advantage or even outright innovation for organizations. This area depends on good collaborative working across the whole business process, and it calls for some sensitive understandings. Design thinkers can potentially make some powerful contributions by generating systems that mesh technological capacity with the preferences of those who will have to engage with the system. The field of health and social welfare is just one domain that has seen a wide range of innovations in services in recent years, and the co-working of design thinking and business thinking is evident.

innovation and strategy

In recent decades business education and practice have become obsessed with the word *innovation*—a word and a concept that also resonates strongly in the field of design. It therefore potentially provides a key bridge between the cultures of design and business, both in education and practice. Colloquially, innovation is often used to describe a new invention or the embodiment of an idea in a new design. In the business world, it is more usually used to describe the much larger *process* of change from original idea to successful adoption within markets. It can also mean a change in the way a business makes its money. Thus, the understanding of innovation within business is associated with 'downstream' design functions and with many other organizational functions, both internal- and external-facing.

Business leaders look to innovation as a source of *differentiation* and *competitive advantage.* It is core to strategy, that is, the plans to achieve goals. Typically, just as there are layers of management within an organization from the overall leader down, there are layers of strategic planning cascading downwards from the top. For large organizations consisting of different business units, the cascading strategy can be complex. Modern strategic planning is informed by some core concepts. Michael Porter, the well-known business author and management consultant, has usefully summarized these as the 'value chain' and the 'five forces'. I'll briefly introduce these before turning to three general strategies defined by Porter.

The value chain

The value chain examines a specific product or service delivery—for example a particular car from a manufacturer—to identify the chain of activities that take places and how each link adds value to the product or service. It is a customer-oriented view of what goes into to delivering the product at each stage (Figure 13.5).

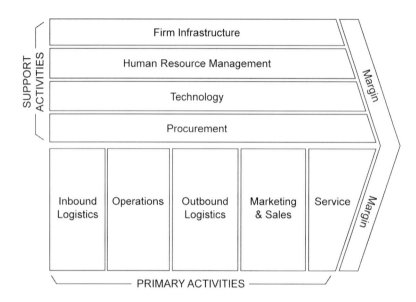

Figure 13.5 Michael Porter's popular depiction of the value chain. Primary value-adding activities (logistics, operations, marketing and sales) are supported by other activities (procurement, human resource management, technology) to create the final added value of a product or service. Image based on Dinesh Pratap Singh's visualization for Porter's value chain published at http://en.wikipedia.org/wiki/File:Porter_Value_Chain.png (accessed 12 April 2011).

The five forces

The five forces model attempts to explain why some industries are more profitable than others—and for the canny manager of a firm in a particular industry, how the firm might get ahead to rise above average profitability. The five forces are the threat of established rivals, the threat of substitute products, the threat of new entrants, the bargaining power of suppliers and the bargaining power of customers.

Industries where market share is concentrated in a handful of companies are less competitive than those where there are no dominant companies. The degree of rivalry between companies in a market depends on many factors. Economics is about choice—and the threat of substitute products recognizes that the demand for a particular product can be influenced by the demand for any potential substitutes (e.g. business-class airline travel versus video conferencing). Businesses in industries with few buyers (e.g. defence) behave very differently from those where there are many

potential customers (e.g. consumer goods). But if some industries are more profitable than others, why do less profitable ones survive? The answer to this lies in the barriers to entry into new markets and the barriers to exit for existing firms. In practice, firms are not free to jump around from one activity or industry to another without incurring significant entry costs into the new market or exit costs from the markets they are already in.

The three strategies

Porter also identifies three general strategies that a firm may follow.

1. *Cost leadership:* competing on cost by high asset turnover (e.g. an airline that uses its planes flat out or a restaurant that turns over its tables quickly), low operating costs (through high-volume, standardized products), bulk buying and general control over supply chains to squeeze prices down (the Wal-Mart story).

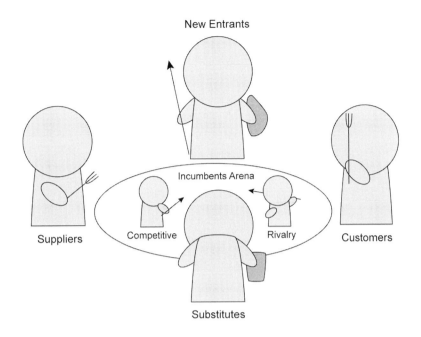

Figure 13.6 Porter's five forces depicted as four external players watching a competitive match between old rivals. Image based on original published by the Graduate School of Business, Pepperdine University, http://smehro.wordpress.com/chapter-5a/ (accessed 12 April 2011).

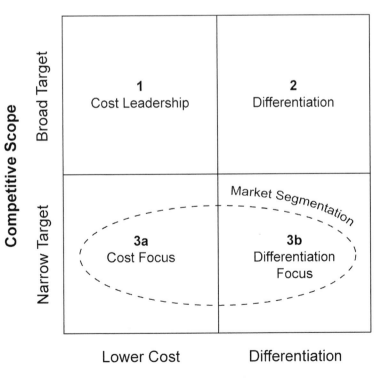

Figure 13.7 A two-by-two strategy matrix illustrating Porter's three generic strategies for competitive advantage: cost leadership, differentiation and segmentation. Figure based on original available at www.unconsultancy.com/10-strategy-tools-for-smaller-businesses/ (accessed 12 April 2011).

2. *Differentiation:* where target customers may not be price sensitive, there is opportunity for designs or innovations which deliver unique or greater benefits (e.g. Apple computers and some luxury brands).
3. *Market segmentation:* This strategy, often pursued by smaller firms, exploits either cost leadership and/or differentiation but in particular ways. It is subdivided into cost focus (e.g. niche cost) and differentiation focus (e.g. niche luxury brands).

For most organizations, the basis of competition will be defined by either cost leadership or differentiation. Most market segmentation tends to be narrow in scope, while both cost leadership and differentiation are strategies applied where markets are relatively broad.

business models

Businesses make money by a whole host of incremental innovations that affect their own and their industries' profitability as they surf ever-changing economic, social and technological landscapes. A recent fashion in which business leaders approach innovation is to think in terms of *business models.*[5] These are simplified representations of the way in which the organization or business goes about, well, its business—surviving or perhaps making money. A famous example of a business model is Gillette's razor and blades business model (also known as the 'bait and hook' business model), where the company has made far more money on replacement blades than it ever did getting new shaving products into the hands of consumers. Other more recent examples of this business model where consumers can be enticed

---

Heuristic and Systematic Designing

Some design problems are particularly suitable for a *systematic* approach to exploration and idea generation. Here I'm thinking of those problems where a finite number of technical principles might be applied to solve a particular problem. In this case, the design process involves systematically working through each in turn until the optimum principle is found.

In contrast, it is possible for designers to work from problem to solution in a much more intuitive way without overtly generating and evaluating alternative concepts. In this case, their *knowledge* and experience provide approaches and rules of thumb that enable them to home in on promising concepts. This is known as a *heuristic* design approach to problem solving.

A common heuristic approach is to break a complex problem into successively smaller problems until you are left with a set of problems that can be solved. Another powerful heuristic approach is that of successive approximation or iteration, that is, producing a rough draft solution and gradually improving it. Many experienced designers start with an idea for a solution and use it to explore the problem in hand, leading to new insights or modified ideas. This is the so-called solution-focused approach.

From: R. Roy, *Design and Designing* (T211), The Open University, Blk 3 (2010), p. 31.

---

into extended consuming include the marketing of printers and cartridges and mobile phones with call time.

According to Johnson et al., a business model consists of four elements.[6] Simply put, these are:

- A solution to a problem that a customer faces
- How profit is made (e.g. high volume, low margin)
- Key resources (e.g. people, technology, brand)

- Processes necessary to deliver the solution (e.g. training, development, manufacturing, budgeting, planning, sales, service and even culture).

Messing around with business models is not always a good idea—successful companies, by definition, have successful business models at their heart. However, there are certain strategic circumstances that can lead to, or require, business model innovation. Here I characterize five such circumstances:

1. The emergence of a disruptive innovation that has the potential to radically expand a market. For example the Tata Nano car inspired multiple design and outsourcing innovations, thus radically reducing the price of the vehicle.
2. Organizations offering technological innovation have opportunities to wrap a new business model around the product or service. For example Apple and other companies involved in digital music downloading are associated with innovative business models.
3. New or previously unrecognized customer needs can emerge. For example the entry of FedEx into the package delivery business was founded on a business model promoting reliability, distance and speed rather than competing on price or marketing.
4. The need to fend off low-end disrupters. For example if the Nano car is successful, it will threaten other automobile makers.
5. The need to respond to change brought about by the competition. For example Hilti, the quality power tools manufacturer,

changed its business model from one focusing on manufacturing to one of service in response to an increase in supply of cheaper products from other manufacturers.

Just over a third of companies born in the last twenty-five years in the United States and that grew their way into the Fortune 500 list in the past ten years did so through business model innovation. Though many managers are aware of the potential growth from genuine innovations in business models, it is not easy to achieve. Few organizations understand their existing business model well enough, and even when they do, and can see a route to innovation, change can appear risky and unattractive.

the business of design

Having briefly described some key elements that underpin business thinking, I'll now turn to the interface between business and design thinking and in doing so address the dual issues implied in the title—that is, that design is business, and it's the duty of designers to apply their skills in the planning, costing and marketing of today's products and services.

Tim Brown of IDEO, who has championed design thinking for many years, sees a vital synergy between design and business. He sees no conflict between business strategies of improving product quality or user experience and design innovation. He says, 'perhaps we should think of design thinking and Six Sigma [a business management strategy that seeks to improve the quality of process outputs by identifying and removing the causes of defects] as being part of a cycle, each feeding the other to create new and improved products, services and experiences.' He goes on to add an important rider: 'Of course the biggest challenge will be to build business cultures that are agile enough to incorporate both.'[7]

Writing in the *Harvard Business Review* in 2008, Brown suggested a number of steps for making design thinking part of wider business innovation in organizations. These can be paraphrased as:

- Involve design thinkers at the very start.
- Take a human-centred approach to capture unexpected insights.
- Prototype early.
- Co-create with experts, consumers, customers.
- Practise innovation across a range of projects from big to small.
- Innovation isn't linear—be prepared to adjust funding in reaction to discoveries.
- Bring on any relevant talents you can find, not just design thinkers.
- Stick with it so that your teams experience the full cycle from inspiration to implementation.[8]

The growth of interest in recent years in combining design thinking and business thinking has led to something of a backlash among purists from both communities. 'You can't teach design in 12 hours of an MBA', I overheard a designer remark in a business school seminar recently. There is an important point to this sentiment. The label

designer covers a multitude of roles and meanings across different sectors and industries, and there are many subcultures of design. Fashion creators, electronic engineers and software programmers might all engage in design, but they might present more differences than similarities.

A. G. Lafley, the recent CEO of corporate giant Procter & Gamble, offers an insightful reflection on the difficulties of bringing the worlds of design thinkers and business thinkers together. He says, 'Business schools tend to focus on inductive thinking [based on directly observable facts] and deductive thinking [logic and analysis, typically based on past evidence]. Design schools emphasize abductive thinking—imagining what could be possible.' However, Lafley sees clear advantages for the business community in applying more abductive approaches, because it helps 'challenge assumed constraints and adds to ideas [rather than] discouraging them.'[9]

This is a special moment in the evolution of our knowledge and understanding of the role of design and business thinking in organizations and the linkages between them. Within management, design is understood to be more than mere aesthetics. New types of career opportunities await those who can understand and speak the language of business as well as design, those who can confidently carve new channels across the design/business divide and those who can act as translators for others, facilitating their contribution across the divide.

CHAPTER SUMMARY

- As a student of design, you will enhance your career opportunities if you can work across the perceived divide between business and design—that is, across the two tribes. You need a business head as much as a design head.
- Management isn't rocket science; it can be dissected to reveal strategies and concerns vital to the success of any design.
- In recent decades there has been a shift in management thinking away from organising by business *functions* towards organising by business *processes.*
- Good design is as much about applying a viable business model as it is creative problem solving.
- Learn the vocabulary and concerns of business such as *differentiation* and *competitive advantage.* Combine your innovation practice with innovation strategy.
- Develop your knowledge of some of the concepts used in the business community to articulate (and innovate) around business strategy. It is an important step in understanding where there are opportunities for you as a designer to influence business thinking.

chapter 14

the design brief: are you listening?

andrew collier

ABOUT THIS CHAPTER

This chapter is about the design briefing. It is the foundation stone upon which is built all subsequent design work. If there are errors in the interpretation of what a client wants, no amount of creative idea generation will get the design team back on track. While the client must share some responsibility for effective communication, it is the designer's ability to listen and define the essential information that lies at the core of successful commercial design practice. This chapter draws on many years of commercial design practice at the consultancy SMC Design. It explores what a good written brief should contain, but it also examines the significance of listening in on the verbal exchanges between clients and designers. The context is the interior design of ships, but the lessons apply across a spectrum of design practice.

---

the importance of listening

Design is a commercial service. It begins when the client brings his or her enquiry to the design service provider. The enquiry might concern the supply of a new hat, a new piece of music or, as I will discuss here, a new interior for a ship. In some cases, the product may already exist and your job might be to improve it, enhance it or update it so as to make the client more competitive in his or her particular market. So a key duty of the designer—in fact the duty of all designers—is to listen to what the client says. No matter how much you think your role might be to interpret clients' requests, it must begin with you understanding the situation from their point of view, and this means learning to listen. In design today, too few people have developed their listening skills, and this reveals itself in lost work, poor customer experience, jobs going over budget, missed opportunities and dissatisfied clients. If design is about being sensitive to needs, creatively addressing limitations and synthesising complex situations, as I believe it is, then these must be founded on information, and some of the most important information is given by the client in the early meetings. This is not to say you have to take everything in a briefing literally, just that you have to listen, because listening is the first link in a chain that will lead to your design proposals and the eventual outputs. So far I have stressed the need to listen to clients, but, as you may have anticipated, a skill for listening will also find application in working with others in the design team, gathering data from potential users or customers and working with contractors. In fact, listening may be more important to your future career in design than your creativity! I've come away from business meetings attended by representatives of the client and been shocked by the impressions of design colleagues who also attended. To my mind they had completely misinterpreted what the client had said. In one meeting I had to go back to the client to check a particular instruction because I was the only one who had spotted it, wrapped up inside other more general discussion.

> "In design today, too few people have developed their listening skills, and this reveals itself in lost work, poor customer experience, jobs going over budget, missed opportunities and dissatisfied clients."

Perhaps one of the reasons why we are seeing a decline in listening skills is to do with the way design education has sought to build on design students' natural enthusiasm for creatively responding to opportunities. We need to take a step back, to place a little more emphasis on taking a brief before students employ their abilities for creatively responding to a brief. As designers we need to listen, document that output and really try to understand it before we even begin to formulate our research strategies, because our research will influence our creativity. If you don't listen, you follow the wrong lines of investigation and you come up with ideas that don't match the core needs, or they don't match as well as they could do. It can be surprising just how long this listening process can take, but it's time well spent because it can save a lot of wasted effort further down the line.

briefing and the gathering of information

SMC Design was established in 1993. It is a multidisciplinary practice, but the majority of its portfolio is in interior design, particularly the design of interiors for ferries, cruise ships and ocean liners. With over 40 new-builds and 40 refurbishment projects under its belt, SMC is one of the foremost design companies in this area of design. Plate 18 shows the sort of environment we commonly get involved in.

Recently I was involved in a project where the client invited SMC Design to tender for the interior design of a new series of ships. The brief suggested that the project was to improve the functionality of the on-board spaces and to provide an improved customer experience. With the original invitation to tender for the work, the client enclosed some clear briefing materials, including detailed information on the type of ships, passenger numbers, typical profiles, densities and statements about the owner's aspirations. It also included images that helped convey the problems as the client perceived them. The client confirmed that one of its current ships (one due to be replaced) was available for visits. I think of the six consultancies that were invited to tender for this particular work, we were the only one to make a site visit. This strategy didn't go unnoticed by the client, and I think it gained us a bit of credit; but it wasn't just a show of enthusiasm on our part. For us it was an opportunity to walk around the spaces, to take photos that weren't part of the official briefing, to hear more about the requirement firsthand and to talk with people who have daily experience of making these spaces function efficiently as, for example, restaurants, bars or children's rooms.

It's so important to observe how people use design if you want to improve the experience. In another project I took time out in such a visit just to sit with a cup of coffee and watch passengers join a ship at the beginning of a cruise. One learns a lot through the simple process of observation. You see how people group themselves. Just like birds, they 'nest', creating spaces between groups that feel comfortable. And different age groups display different preferences. For some ferry passengers finding the toilet may be the first priority; for others it's the restaurant or video games arcade, and these can have important consequences for efficient boarding, fast turnaround times and onboard passenger movement. It's these observations that are stored away for consideration when we begin the process of concept development. Without these insights it would be easy to make serious design errors, perhaps placing some fixed benching just where the passengers like to have flexibility for their nesting. This is an obvious danger if one works only from the ship's plans without really getting to understand the need.

I've mentioned a role for photography in recording observations, but drawing still has an important function when gathering data. I always carry a notebook with me, and many of my notes are supplemented with quick diagrams and images that capture the essence of, for example, a floor plan. I frequently use sketch images to help me communicate in a briefing meeting. I might use sketches to help me clarify what a client is saying or to make suggestions about possibilities. In both cases, the drawing is helping us achieve some sort of shared understanding, and this is essential if the client is to have confidence in what our firm might eventually come up with.

So far I've talked about some of the skills required in taking a brief, but there are also skills in giving a brief. As designers we can't assume that everyone who has the responsibility to give a brief has all the skills, so one of our jobs is to help people by facilitating discussion, asking open questions, and exploiting techniques that engage the brief-giver in revealing as much relevant information as necessary. Don't be scared to ask questions. It gives people the opportunity to confirm your interpretations or perhaps generate an illustration that might prove revealing. Answers to perceptive or insightful questions can also provide opportunities for creative ideas, and they might help you avoid developing concepts that lie outside of the scope for your project. We've been lucky in our work that most of the people providing a brief have been very skilled and very professional, but I have known situations where information has to be almost dragged out of a client.

points of reference

In my discussions with clients, I try to define points of reference, and to do this I ask a lot of who, where, what, why, when and how questions. For example if the subject is a restaurant, I need to know what type of food it will serve; if it's a steakhouse, do they have a style in mind? Many clients have conducted their own market research well before any design briefs are constructed, and it is important to know if there are some preferred or fixed points of reference. This is another situation where imagery has real value. We use mood boards not to impose an idea on a client but to help extract some of the client's feelings that may not have been embedded in the written or verbal briefings. We offer them imagery, textures, and colour combinations that seek to unlock hidden thoughts and preferences, and this supports gentle probing through discussion. An example of one mood board is shown in Plate 19.

It's quite natural for some clients to want to overspecify a brief. After all, it's their business and their ship. They have a huge emotional and financial investment in the project. They feel they understand the need, and they might have very clear ideas on what the final design should be. This is less of a problem with the major tour and ferry corporations, but it can still be a problem in some design situations. You have to be very careful not to undermine what a client brings to a project while demonstrating your own insights and knowledge through your own creative interpretations. Diplomacy is an important ability for designers to possess.

Since most large passenger ships offer extensive on-board shopping facilities, one of the points of reference in many of my design briefs is the land-based shopping mall. Increasingly, this is the case for other large public spaces such as airports. A company like Cunard may highlight a point of reference such as the Rainbow Room in New York as a way of communicating a particular style of art deco for an intended on-board environment. But it's important to realize that our job is not to copy these points of reference, nor construct a pastiche of them. Our job is to distil their essence through our own internal creative filters and combine this with limitations and practicalities dictated by the brief.

Points of reference are supported by marketing information on passenger profiles. Ships operating in the Australian cruise market must accommodate family groups of seven and above, whereas European operators arrange spaces to account for a family size of five. Cunard's market is more typically pairs of passengers, and statistically pairs spend more time on a cruise than their counterparts sailing with other companies. Sometimes the brief will contain demographic information on age, nationality and spending habits, but sometimes you may have to ask for it. Each of these market characteristics and expectations give rise to different interior design requirements. If you can create a profile of actual or potential passengers, then you are more likely to be able to accurately evaluate your design ideas later in the process.

creative researching

I like to think SMC is good at generating creative design solutions, but there is an equally important skill in applying creativity to the early stages of design—creatively establishing the brief, creatively researching a project, creative questioning. You need to draw information out of people, and you can't rely on a few set questions. Clients might need help to see how design can address their aspirations as well as their current requirements. You need to think on your feet. And you need to listen. I see it as my duty to challenge assumptions but to do this in a constructive and diplomatic way. I frequently find myself saying 'Have you thought about...' and the associated exchanges can lead to me understanding more about the brief or the client becoming aware of new opportunities and sometimes both. Clients are usually particularly receptive to new opportunities for revenue generation, and by knowing your passengers you put yourself in a better position for suggesting ideas for activities that will enhance their experience and be acceptable to the client.

The briefing is rarely a one-hit meeting. Where possible, I like to engage with various stakeholders over a period of time. Some information can be documented from the start, but other information emerges gradually. In today's commercial environment, you can't ignore any opportunities, and sometimes you only get the chance to attend one briefing meeting before pitching for a particular project. As noted above, most of the shipping lines are large corporations and they have clearly defined company systems and schedules for the refurbishment of existing ships and bringing new ships into commission. The procedures for briefing designers are clear, and most lines will have a department dedicated to refurbishment and development projects. The actual briefing might be undertaken by any of a number of individuals, but typically it would involve a marketing director or the director of operations or on-board services. Where the briefing is led by marketing, there would typically be an emphasis on future business and unique selling points; where a director of operations led a briefing, the emphasis might lean more towards resolving current problems such as improving throughput in a restaurant or increasing the number of tables for diners. Ideally these directors will know about current, emerging and predicted trends. They will be able to specify points of reference and will build these into the briefing, but some need more help than others.

the importance of looking

I try to be realistic about the limitations of design. When a customer books a holiday cruise, the list of criteria is unlikely to be headed by 'design of interior' no matter how much I believe in design. The most significant criteria for cruise customers are price followed by destination or itinerary. This is followed by star rating (e.g. luxury, budget), and lower down the list might appear the style of the ship (e.g. formal or informal, aimed at older passengers or families). While the brochures do present photographs of interiors, public spaces and cabins, these typically inform a decision-making process governed by price and geography. So, as far as the company is concerned, design is just one of the influential factors in operating a successful business, and it would be very difficult to approach a project without viewing it as such. In this respect, designing ship interiors is no different to the designing of many consumer products. Similarly, don't have too high an expectation for the appreciation of your design by the public who will use it. I might be thrilled with the way a ceiling resolves a particularly difficult design problem with levels, lights and ducting, but all this can go completely unnoticed by those who meet, chat, dance or eat in that area. Partly this is because people rarely look at the environment around them. Take shop fronts for example. The architecture in our towns and cities can be diverse and beautiful, but few people ever look up above the shop fronts to appreciate it.

Nothing frustrates me more than a designer who doesn't look. I think designers should have a hunger for the visual. They should absorb the visual world around them as a sponge absorbs water. Holding the visual world in our heads is difficult, hence the need to keep some form of visual diary—perhaps a sketchbook or an online blog of photographs—things seen every day. Design can be such a hectic profession that taking time to look, and really scrutinize the things around us, can often be sacrificed for more pressing demands. One of my old colleagues once said designers need to create themselves some 'playtime'—time for some unfocused looking as a way of assimilating the information we are constantly absorbing.

> "Designers should have a hunger for the visual. They should absorb the visual world around them as a sponge absorbs water."

problem finding

Certainly there is less time to complete jobs today than even a few years ago. Young design graduates today need to show they can hit the ground running if they are to impress potential employers. Having said that, I wouldn't expect a recent graduate to attend a project briefing in place of a more experienced designer. The skills and knowledge required to take a briefing come about through experience. I don't think they can be taught. I might sit with younger colleagues and engage them in the sort of dialogue that takes place in a briefing meeting, but it's hard to simulate the pressures, the exploratory dialogue and the diplomacy. I think this can only develop on the job. In design education, we place great emphasis on problem solving, but I think we should put more emphasis on defining design problems. It's the constraints and limitations in design that really stretch our ability to be creative, and we need to find ways to increase students' exposure to these.

I referred to sketching earlier as a way of teasing out from a client those thoughts and aspirations that may be buried deep down. Sometimes my sketches are no more than me trying to externalize what's going on in someone else's head. Partly I'm trying to help them visualize their thoughts—to help them bring an idea into being. I know this works with me when I'm sketching concept designs later in the process. Sometimes I have a clear idea in my mind of what I'm portraying, but sometimes the drawing process itself gives life to ideas. There seems to be a dialogue going on between my hand making the emerging drawing and my eyes and mind coming to understand the drawing being made. Sometimes it can be quite frustrating. A client might see something in a sketch that I didn't intend, and this can lead them to a new line of discussion. But I don't really mind if this helps unlock something important. Of course there are also times when a client changes his or her mind or reveals something new that is significant to the brief, and this is also frustrating, but it's part of the way humans operate so I've learnt to accept it and embrace it.

Like most other fields of design, at SMC we have moved to digital representations for most stages of activity, but, surprisingly, some clients still like to see hand-drawn images. There seems to be an expectation that detailed renderings will be 100 per cent accurate in their evocation of space and contents, whereas freehand sketches are permitted to have a lot of artistic licence. The film industry still uses freehand sketches in storyboarding for the same reason. Since sketches are relatively quick and inexpensive to produce, we tend to use them at various stages, particularly if we are trying to convey less tangible qualities such the created mood of a location. At other times we might go to the trouble and expense of a fly-through CAD presentation, but we need to be sure that the detail will not change significantly. CAD renderings are only as good as the information put into them, and to create photorealistic images, a great deal of time can be spent feeding information into the computer.

Tips on Writing a Brief

Writing a design brief is a creative activity that is critical to the whole design process. The following tips are based on some pointers published by Jens Bernsen of the Danish Design Centre.[1]

Identify the goal: Ask what the product should be if it did not exist but had to be thought out from the beginning. Seek to identify *The Big Idea* in the design brief.

Describe basic functions: What is essential and what is secondary to the functioning of the product?

Understand the users: See the product the way the user sees it. Speak with typical users and potential users. Examine complaints, because they can stimulate new ideas. Use scenarios and personas to build up understanding of users. Get under the skin of users' lifestyle and taste.

Understand product features and their value: A product is more than its visual form. Users experience a product through its sound, weight and perhaps smell. Value is increasingly dependent on effective and pleasurable interaction.

Build a narrative: Allow a new product to tell its story. Allow it to communicate its idea.

Revise the brief from time to time: Creating a brief is a dynamic process. The goals laid down by the brief at the beginning of the development project are not necessarily the final goals. A good brief describes a wish or a demand and never the solution itself.

[1] J. Bernsen, 'The Design Before the Design', *Danish Design Centre Magazine,* no. 2 (1996).

that determine what the design service will consist of. The design brief is the statement of the problem or, in more open tasks, the opportunity. It provides the intermediate stage between a specification of the requirements the product is expected to satisfy and the product idea that is generated in creative thinking. A good brief will provide information on the following four factors:

1. The goal: The overall aim of the project.
2. The context: This is the background to the project but might also specify who will use this product, where it will be used, why and so on.
3. The constraints: These are the guidelines and limitations to the project. Here a brief will specify any restrictions or particular requirements about, for example, the potential users, the environment, costs, strength, life span, assembly and so on.
4. The criteria: Broadly these are the desired attributes of the intended design output. They guide the designers as they work towards the goal. For example the criteria of an on-board restaurant might include providing an attractive dining experience for families, one that supports efficient self-service and presents surfaces that are easily cleaned.

the written brief

Listening and observing need to be converted into a written document at an early stage of the process. Such written documents usually form the basis of contracts and other legal documents

Box 14.1 is an edited brief from SMC's files. I like this one because it treads a difficult line between being too prescriptive, thus hindering creative designing, and being too vague, thus not allowing the design team to judge whether its ideas are relevant to the client's needs.

BOX 14.1. BRIEF FOR NEW CONCEPT OF GUEST STATEROOM

Goal: Creation of suitable on-board living accommodation

Context
Location: Ship will predominately be based in the Caribbean in the winter months (November to April); in the western Mediterranean in the summer months (May to October).
Age group: Families of up to eight people: four adults (generally comprising two grandparents and two parents/guardians) and up to four children up to age sixteen.
Passenger profile: Middle income with enough disposable income for perhaps two weeks summer holiday and a couple of extended long weekends or city breaks or party cruises. Fifty-five per cent American, 40 per cent British, 5 per cent European. Used to staying in three- to four-star hotel chains and shopping in premium retail malls.
Length of stay: Generally a two-week cruise. Some four-day cruises.

Constraints
Two standard cabin modules wide (2.8 metres by 2 metres) and 8.5 meters deep. Total 47.6 square metres
Enough clothing storage for up to eight people
Possible storage for folding pushchairs and luggage
At least two separate toilets and washbasins, one shower and/or bath
Two separate TV areas
One separate bedroom
Safe
Small fridge
Safety to be considered for younger children

Criteria (Design Notes)
Rooms to be light and airy and give an impression of space
Bright and cheerful colours to be used
All finishes to be durable for longevity of use
Versatile and multifunctional furniture, adaptable for different age groups and their needs

---

stakeholders and market research

A typical interior project for a major cruise or ferry operator will last thirty-six months. Occasionally we have the luxury of an additional two or three months before a project begins in which to define the brief. The real advantage of this preparatory time is that it gives many of the stakeholders—including the owners, the marketing department and the ship-building yard—time during which they can assume some ownership of the brief by assisting in its formulation. Some decisions will suit those responsible for building the design, while other decisions will suit those who have to make the ship work efficiently. The more time there is to resolve potential conflict, the more likely it is that the design and build stages will flow smoothly.

There has been a clear trend towards user-centred design, and where we feel we need information based on user studies or market research, this service would be purchased from expert specialist consultancies. It's not something that should be taken on without appropriate knowledge. The quality of information one gets from market research is entirely dependent on such things as the market sample chosen, the ways the participants engage with the research and the precise wording of any questions. Doing bad market research is worse than doing no research, because it leads you forward with false confidence. In my experience, it's not something that design consultancies are necessarily very good at, hence my preference to call in the experts as and when needed. Designers need to have an understanding of market research, but where big brands are concerned, the issues are so diverse and so vital to the success of the company that it's impossible to manage both market research and design.

Once the brief has been formulated, documented and agreed upon, we can begin the process of defining a range of creative concepts that meet the brief in different ways. Typically we might have four to six months to do this, but I have known the luxury of a year for this stage. The ship builders will need just over two years depending on the complexity of the project, but this includes some dialogue with the builders and any subcontractors involved. In some projects, we will work in close collaboration with a naval architect, as we did when we designed interiors for Cunard's flagship *Queen Mary 2*.

The contractual responsibilities receive close scrutiny, and we're very fortunate in our business

Figure 14.1 Cunard's flagship, *Queen Mary 2.*

that the shipyards hold ultimate responsibility for fixtures and fittings in new-build ships. It means we maintain a close dialogue with the shipyards, who inform us of any misgivings about design decisions. This might mean discussion about flooring surfaces that are both hard-wearing and nonslip, wall coverings that are effective and fireproof and furniture that won't impede evacuation in the case of an emergency. Occasionally we will ask the yard to construct full-size models. We have used full-size constructions of cabins, and these are particularly good to engage people who cannot read engineering drawings or who don't trust perspective drawings. We have also commissioned the making of full-size prototypes of furniture, but this is relatively easy to do compared with building environments. And of course we make a lot of scale models in the office during the design and development stages.

recent projects

To illustrate some of the points I made earlier, I want to turn to a few examples of recent work by SMC Design.

Pacific Jewel

In this project, the client was P&O Australia. This was what we call a 'conversion' project, which means that, alongside refurbishment, we changed the functionality of target areas of the ship. *Pacific Jewel* has British owners, and the ship went into dry dock in November 2009.

One of the areas we developed was a large restaurant towards the rear of the ship. Previously it was a self-service restaurant, and the client wanted this changed to a more formal dining experience with waiter service. This is now called

---

Specifications

A product design specification arises from the development of the brief into a comprehensive document. It includes not only the outline of the design goal and the major constraints and criteria but also the more precise limits set for the complete range of performance requirements.

A product design specification will contain a lot of technical information and requirements as well as user population information and marketing factors. In product design, it is quite common to distinguish between a technical specification and a marketing specification. The marketing specification puts more emphasis on the requirements of the user or purchaser, for example stipulating function, performance, price, product life and maintenance. The specification also details requirements of the producer company itself, such as design and production time scale, materials and manufacturing limitations.

The product design specification offers goals and guidelines to the designer, but the designer has to imagine and decide how to achieve the goals. The designer fixes the product properties in order to achieve the attributes and benefits desired by the user.

A product design specification documents attributes and properties in terms of the required product performance but without specifying a particular solution. In other words, it specifies what the product must do but not what it must be; it specifies *ends* but not *means*.

---

the Waterfront restaurant. Figure 14.2 shows how the space now looks, and Plate 20 shows the entrance. You might be able to identify some of the points of reference for the style. In its previous form, it offered an informal terrace environment using screens and rattan furniture. One of its distinctive features is the very high ceiling; this one is 3.7 metres high, which is very unusual in ships of this type, and it was written into the brief that we would not alter the structure of the walls or the ceiling.

Figure 14.2 The Waterfront
restaurant on *Pacific Jewel*.
(Copyright author)

The client was very clear on the functionality of this restaurant. The ship would cater for 2,000 people, and this restaurant would seat 1,600 people over two sittings. So we began by looking at how we might accommodate 800 people using arrangements of tables that seat two, four, six and eight people. The client supplied a lot of information on customer profiles and knew, for example, that 60 per cent of tables should seat six and eight for a typical Australian cruise. There are guidelines to help define acceptable densities in restaurants. A high density would be 1.8 seats per square metre, and in this project we were looking for about 1.5 seats per square metre. We combined this with looking at options for waiter stations and the different demands if the food was to be ready plated as opposed to silver service. We needed to understand the traffic flow of the waiters and the movement of the food being served. Even with clear instructions, we felt we had to express misgivings about the likely passenger experience at this density, and the client was happy to amend its demands. I think one of our jobs is to help the client see the practicalities and limitations in a situation. In our presentation, we took them through the practicalities of food distribution and the advantages of using raised platforms to maximize diners' opportunities to have clear sight of a window from the interior of the space.

Once we had a clear idea of seating arrangements, we were able to look at opportunities for dressing the interior. The client specified the desire for a contemporary feel, so we used examples of recent Australian interiors to devise a palette that contrasted light and bold colours against white and which could be used on hard and soft surfaces. We used these to construct a range of mood boards containing colour, fabric and product imagery and also generated some presentation boards that depicted the interior as we imagined it. In this design we accentuated the unusual height. The curtains can be pulled across or pushed back and thus used to inject drama and variety in conjunction with different lighting schemes. The chairs have been created to fit in with the contemporary theme, but even here there are practical features to make them easy to move, store and clean. Similarly with the carpet, the decoration is intended to hide marks caused by spills. But it's not all visual. We had to incorporate fire exits and routes so that the restaurant could be evacuated in the event of an emergency. There are a large number of regulations that guide safety, and we see part of our job as defining creative opportunities within regulatory constraints.

We took presentation and mood boards back to the client to show them our interpretation of their brief. Fortunately they liked it very much. How do I know to design like this? As I stressed above, it's partly through looking and listening to how other people have designed in the past.

Ocean Village Two

My second example is taken from a project to create a new outside bar area on *Ocean Village Two*. Figure 14.3 shows the space as it currently appears.

Different nationalities display different priorities when they board a ship. The British seem particularly keen to lie out in the sun as quickly as possible, perhaps because the weather is unpredictable at home. US and Australian customers

Figure 14.3 Exterior sun deck on the *Ocean Village Two*. (Copyright author)

display different preferences. This project required that we transform a rather plain sun deck into a bar facility for those who want to relax outside. Of course, the client hadn't overlooked the opportunity for increasing revenue through this new facility. The concept design is shown in Figure 14.4.

The space included rooms that could be used to service the bar but, as with the restaurant for *Pacific Jewel,* we had to look at the flow of items and people to define a practical layout. We placed a chilled bottle display cabinet on the passenger side of the bar. This freed up space behind the bar, reduced the need for customers to ask about what drinks are available and prompted impulse sales. It's nice when a design decision has three advantages and no disadvantages. As part of this scheme, we used stretched canvas in the ceiling area to break up the metal superstructure and create softer surfaces. We used soft, natural colours such as sandstone and introduced other natural materials in the bar surfaces, picking out details in contrasting colours. Overall we tried to create a space conveying quality using strong architectural lines and form with soft tones. I imagine this space will have a life span of seven to ten years, although upholstery may have a much shorter life span.

Figure 14.4 Concept design for the outside bar area.
(Copyright author)

CHAPTER SUMMARY

- Design is about problem finding as well as problem solving.
- Use all your senses in designing, particularly looking and listening. Don't neglect your other senses such as smell and touch.
- Use questions to help you define points of reference that guide your creative thinking.
- Carry a camera and a small sketchbook with you at all times to make quick visual notes of the things you see.
- Use drawing to help you unlock a design problem and to achieve a shared understanding with the client and other stakeholders such as users, cleaners, manufacturers and retailers.
- Build scrapbooks, notebooks or visual diaries. Not only will this provide you with a source of stimulation for future project work, but the act of making these visual notes will heighten your awareness of the world around you.
- Ask questions and probe the brief-giver, but be diplomatic.
- Watch people using designs. This might range in scale from watching people using Web pages to watching them using a city transport system. It can give you valuable insights to real problems in situations where people may not want to admit to their failings.
- Your written briefs should include the goal, the context, the constraints and the criteria.
- Remember that you are designing for all. In my design of ship interiors, I'm designing for the passengers, the ship's crew, the hotel staff and the owners, and resolving conflict between different demands is part of the designer's service.

---

chapter 15

designing for markets

richard woolley

ABOUT THIS CHAPTER

Land Rover is one of the world's premier automotive companies, and this chapter reveals the vital importance of market information to the innovation process at Land Rover. The chapter takes a close look at how market information informed the design of the new Range Rover Evoque, and in doing this it reveals some key trends for a wide range of design professionals about the relationship between information gathering and its implementation in design. It highlights the important synergy between marketing and design in industry today and challenges traditional perceptions of the sequential structure of the early design process. It suggests that market information can provide vital constraints to steer concept generation and development. This chapter highlights the importance today of good working relationships between design and marketing in organizations. It outlines a variety of techniques used at Land Rover to understand users and markets and how this information is applied in product planning and design.

---

land rover history

The first Land Rover made its appearance in 1948. While it took its design cues from military vehicles of the time, such as the American Jeep, it immediately gained a reputation for its ability, practicality, durability and strength. Over sixty years later, it is estimated that two-thirds of Land Rovers are still at work—many of them in some of the most extreme conditions and inhospitable places on earth.

In keeping with the forward-thinking philosophy that founded Land Rover, a radical, entirely new product was introduced in 1970 which created its very own vehicle category. This was the original Range Rover. It had the capability of a Land Rover with the comfort and performance of an on-road car. In the twenty-first century, the two brands of Land Rover and Range Rover are still part of the same company and encompass five models: Freelander 2, Discovery 4, Defender, Range Rover and Range Rover Sport.

At its launch at the Paris motor show in September 2010, the motoring press described the Range Rover Evoque as a major catalyst for change in the Range Rover brand (see Plate 21). Evoque not only brings a small, light and fuel-efficient coupé to the stable, it has revived the Range Rover brand, pointing the way towards more sustainable vehicles relevant to the global market. It brings Range Rover to a whole new range of consumers across the globe and starts the next chapter for the company.

Figure 15.1 Land Rover, Series 1, 1949. (Getty 90117206 RM)

Figure 15.2 Characteristic Land Rover lines in the Freelander 2. (Copyright Steve Garner)

This chapter takes a close look at the company's ability to innovate with products that are relevant to global markets and trends and that help develop the brand. It draws on the research and development process of the Evoque to illustrate how and why companies need to design for markets. In doing this, the chapter reveals the application of some important tools for market analysis. But even more important is the necessity for design and market research to work efficiently and effectively together. This chapter suggests that designers potentially have some unique skill sets that enable them to make vital contributions at the earliest stages of market research. Young designers need to develop their capacity for creative research, empathic analysis and concept creation as drivers of market investigations.

brand

In this chapter the word *brand* occurs regularly, and therefore I need to define this term before we move on. It originally referred to the marks burnt onto cattle as a way of distinguishing ownership, but the definition evolved a much broader use to include the identity of a specific product, service or business, typically exploiting a name, sign, symbol, colour combination or slogan.[1] Today brand encompasses the identity and personality of a product, company or service. As the famous advertising copywriter and advertising agency founder David Ogilvy put it, a brand is 'the intangible sum of a product's attributes: its name, packaging, and price, its history, its reputation, and the way it's advertised'.[2]

Many corporations with a leading presence in global markets will begin new projects with an examination of the health of their brand. You might find this at Burberry, Apple, Lloyds or Nike. Essentially a brand health audit explores how people view a brand and what values they attribute to it. It might involve sending out questionnaires or inviting people to attend focus groups or product clinics, gathering representative members of the public in one location to engage in discussions and activities. The Internet has also become a powerful way to gather market information.

Land Rover undertakes a major brand audit every five years. The most recent one, in 2008, explored vehicles in seven different countries and spoke to a broad range of drivers of various makes and models ranging from the Fiesta to the luxury Bentley. It sought the opinions of about 1,000 people for each distinct market group and

---

Product Evolution

The design of all product types is subject to change and adaptation over time. We might view this as some form of product evolution.

For example from their original tall, bulky mass, mechanical typewriters gradually became lower, smaller and lighter. They became electronic with new types of moving parts. Today we can type into handheld devices. Even the relatively bulky mass of a desktop computer offers a thin keyboard that is completely detached from the display and print functions and has even been reduced to a foldable, pocket item.

It is tempting to see such historical product developments as a form of natural improvement—a gradual process of change, something like evolution in nature. However, it is dangerous to draw too close an analogy between natural evolution and this human-induced or artificial evolution. The artificial evolution of products is influenced and determined by technological change, social priorities, marketing pressures, commercial power, consumer habits and, not least, the work of engineers and designers.

From: N. Cross, *Design and Designing* (T211), The Open University, Blk 2 (2010), p. 22.

Figure 15.3 Land Rover has some very distinctive brand
attributes. (Getty 89201137 RM)

engaged consumers in placing a wide range of car brands on linear scales for a variety of attributes. In this type of work it's vital not to reveal who is asking the questions, because this could easily influence people's decisions. It's for this reason that such studies are frequently undertaken by external market research agencies. Other information to support planning and decision-making is available through organizations such as IHS Global Insight, one of the world's leading economic, financial and political forecasting companies and used by a wide range of industries.[3] For Land Rover such information defines activity in current and future market segments. These are groups of consumers, or potential consumers, identified as having something in common that affects their buying decisions. Broadly, market segmentation makes reference to four types of consumer characteristics:

- Geographic—such as country, region, climate and whether urban or rural
- Demographic—such as age, gender, family size, income and occupation
- Psychographic—such as personality type, lifestyle, attitudes and hobbies
- Behaviouristic—such as purchase frequency, usage rate and brand loyalty

Companies such as Land Rover are not only interested in the global trends, they need to understand the various segments of local markets in the countries that they seek to design for. This means they need to understand a wide range of people, and the tools and techniques for achieving this understanding are vital. It probably comes as no surprise that the trend in motoring in recent years has been towards more fuel-efficient and smaller vehicles, ones that are more like cars than the sport utility

vehicles (SUVs) of the previous decade. Vehicles that exhibit the characteristics of two different categories—crossover vehicles—are becoming common. The brand audit identified this as a useful potential segment for Land Rover to move into, an area of white space, whilst the other sources mentioned confirmed this was an expanding area of the market. This became the starting point for the development of Range Rover Evoque.

creating the design brief

In today's commercial environment, any design brief needs to evolve in response to emerging

---

Brand

Brand is a characteristic of a product, or more usually a range of products, from a particular company. A brand typically includes a symbol or logotype but may make use of a portfolio of devices including names, colours, signs and slogans. Brand provides a visual identity allowing consumers and potential consumers to recognize the products of that company even when these are new additions to the range. It's for this reason that brand is at the core of an organization's advertising strategy.

But there's more to brand than mere recognition. A brand is a representation of values. In creating a brand, a company attempts to imbue this visual identity with values and characteristics that are both representative of the organization and attractive to the market. A brand might seek to make associations with reliability, modernity, tradition, quality, fun or any number of other characteristics that are deemed desirable by market segments. Brands such as Volvo or IKEA are about the lifestyle you are buying into as much as the individual products that are being sold. Brands can convey their values to purchasers, and, to a greater or lesser extent, the signs are interpreted by others, thus fuelling further consumption. Some brands, such as Coca-Cola and Apple, are globally recognized and have managed to establish shared values across disparate markets.

knowledge of markets and trends as well as in response to new opportunities and design ideas. This is in contrast to some precise briefs one might see documented in a design consultancy, because these form part of a contractual agreement between two organizations. At Land Rover the design brief usually evolves and grows organically as a consequence of the interchange between design and market analysis.

Armed with some potential hypotheses from the brand audit and Global Insight data, the company began to create structure around a loose set of attributes. At Land Rover we use documents to align people's understandings and to record shared understanding. These documented decisions allow the whole team to move forward. Consolidation might include a listing of product ingredients ranked in what we call a target pyramid, in which a wide variety of ingredients that

one hopes will be recognisable in the marketplace are ranked in order of priority. Some things are agreed as essential, while other things will only be desirable.

Creating target pyramids flushes out differences in understandings, perceptions and interpretations, and while at this point they are only hypotheses, they assist the team to feel comfortable going forward. Individual members or subteams can concentrate on specific tasks knowing they will mesh with the contributions of others later down the line.

research tools and techniques

There are many tools for market research. Some of these deliver quantitative data—for example a questionnaire might ask respondents to reply by

Figure 15.4 Example of a target pyramid. (Copyright Land Rover)

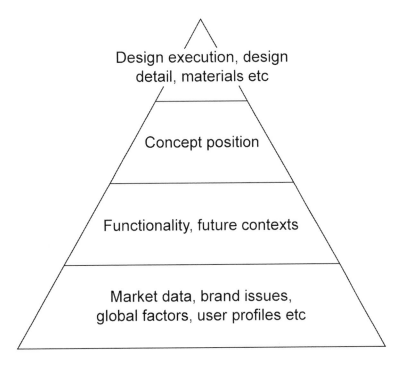

Design execution, design detail, materials etc

Concept position

Functionality, future contexts

Market data, brand issues, global factors, user profiles etc

ticking boxes and the findings could be represented as a pie chart. Alternatively, since absolute numbers of sales of particular vehicles is known, this can be accurately plotted as a graph. Other tools create qualitative data; they seek to generate findings about opinions, values and perceptions. Qualitative research is only as good as the questions you ask, but it is no less valuable than quantitative data and its rich depth can provide clearer insights where research is exploratory.

Focus groups and clinics

At Land Rover there is a preference for qualitative tools in market research. Questionnaires are used, but other approaches have proved more revealing. A focus group is a commonly used qualitative technique, where a group of people are gathered together to discuss a particular issue. They have been used in various situations requiring social and market research, including by political parties, where they inform policy-making.

Where participants are invited to engage in tasks as well as discussion, the meetings are usually referred to as clinics.

At Land Rover, groups of consumers—or potential consumers—are brought together to discuss feelings and attitudes towards a particular brand or model or towards competitor companies. Often consumers will be shown future concepts for new vehicles and asked to talk about how these make them feel—to personify them and associate words with them, to segment them into different types of concept. The participants might be a random selection of consumers, or, more typically, they would be screened to represent a particular geographic, demographic, psychographic or behaviouristic market segment. The intention of the researchers is to understand market opportunities for the brand that hit motivational hot buttons and to therefore lead the business to new concepts with market potential. Figure 15.5 presents an example of a quadrant

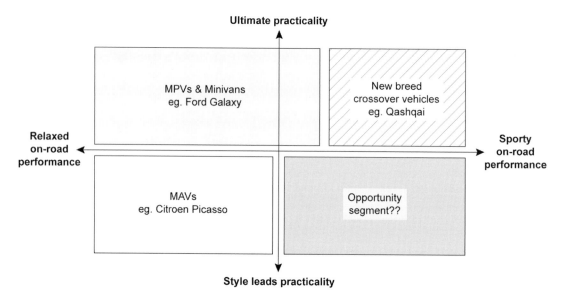

Figure 15.5 Example quadrant diagram. (Copyright Land Rover)

diagram mapping consumer perceptions of the small utility vehicle market. An opportunity segment is revealed bottom right.

Focus groups and clinics can take place anywhere—Shanghai, Sydney, Sheffield—and frequently will be held in multiple locations to gain a broad understanding of similarities and differences between markets. A focus group can vary in size, but it needs to be small enough to be managed by one researcher who acts as leader. Six to eight participants is typical. The moderator leads the discussion and will have a list of issues to guide the discussion (called a discussion guide), but importantly he or she will allow participants to develop their own topics of discussion. The most valuable insights are often revealed by allowing the discussion to go in those directions favoured by the participants, and the methodology of the research will often develop and be refined over the course of the fieldwork. The moderator seeks to facilitate the discussion, ensuring that all participants have the opportunity to voice their opinions, and to make sure that one or two participants don't dominate. Asking open questions is key, so a moderator would avoid leading respondents by saying for example 'do you agree this is a high-quality feature of this car?' and instead might ask 'when you use this particular feature, what are your impressions of the quality and why?'—*why* is the keyword used in qualitative research to understand not just the surface-level behaviour but the motivations *beneath* the surface.

Focus groups can include a wide range of graphics and props to assist the leader to steer the discussion. There might be pictures of cars or car details, and increasingly a focus group might employ computer-generated imagery and video. Occasionally a focus group might have a vehicle in the meeting room or, on rare occasions, a life-size clay model—although the logistics and costs of transporting such a model around the globe need to be weighed against the benefits.

In the Evoque project, focus groups had a function at both ends of the design process: they were used to gather data from a variety of market segments, and this informed the brief, specification and concept generation at the front of the process; and focus groups were used at the end of the process to test market perceptions of the final vehicle and to give the business confidence to proceed. In the initial stages, the market research helped the design team to understand reaction to a range of design concepts or caricatures. These are CAD (computer-aided design) or sketched images that are visual hypotheses for future vehicles. Twelve caricatures were created for Evoque, and each had its own distinct theme. They varied in their character, and were visualized in still and rotating form on a computer screen. Speaking to consumers about these led to clear feedback that enabled the team to see what people identified as positive and negative features and which concepts offered attractive white space within the market which Range Rover could credibly occupy. Importantly these concepts differed widely—you don't want twelve vehicle concepts that are very similar, because research subjects will focus on details such as headlamps rather than provide opinion on the overall character. Consumers were very easily able to map these concepts or caricatures against the existing market and importantly against the existing Land Rover and Range Rover models and to give each of them clear personalities. The most interesting concepts, which eventually led to the development of the Evoque, were described as having a personality that was modern, fun and inspired by the city.

Figure 15.6 Market research steered the concept of
Evoque. (Photo copyright Land Rover)

Profiles and personas

Creating a profile for a typical user in any given
market segment is key to creating a product—
but it is important that the profile is based on real
data. It's basically a summary of the characteristics of the user population in that particular market segment. The construction of user profiles
and personas—or 'pen portraits' as we call them
at Land Rover—formed a key technique in the
Evoque project. In his book *The Inmates Are Running the Asylum,* designer Alan Cooper proposes
that personas offer an important way of allowing
designers to create innovation in new and emerging markets. His key recommendation is:

> Develop a precise description of your user and
> what s/he wishes to accomplish...The actual

method that works sounds trivial, but it is tremendously powerful and effective...We make
up pretend users and design for *them.*[4]

Each persona is given a name, a face and a body.
Their history, needs, wishes and preferences are
concocted based on the findings from studies of
real people (see, for example, Figure 15.7).

Such personas might include the individual's
politics, values and motivations as well as more
tangible physical or lifestyle characteristics. Although personas are only caricatures, research
and design staff can become so familiar with
some personas that they acquire a personality.
They provide a vital function because the team
feel they are designing for a real person rather
than a faceless market segment.

MR. LUO – HANGZHOU PROSPECT

Aspirational but living a comfortable life, Mr. Luo is keen to show he is on trend by buying into the new City-SUV craze

Previous Vehicle
Honda Civic

Also Considered
Audi Q5 (locally built)

Household Fleet
Honda Fit

Age:	36
Gender:	Male
Family:	Married, 1 child (4)
Occupation:	Structural engineer in large privately owned company
Income:	Not disclosed
Lives:	Hangzhou
Hobbies:	Trips to the countryside, playing Majong, visiting teashops with friends
Heroes:	His father

Reasons For Buying This Model

Wanted more practicality over his old saloon – and very much bought into the aspirational style of trendy City-SUVs

Vehicle wants

Good fuel economy, high ride position and complete safety – all wrapped in a stylish design

Expects

Lots of standard equipment, great customer service

What's his story?

Grew up in the countryside and talks nostalgically about the days spent swimming in the cool clear waters of his homeland. Moved to the city for university and never left. Met his wife at university too. Works for a private company and, whilst he would like to work for himself, supporting his family is too important for him to take that risk. Wants his daughter to have a better life than him, may be educated in Europe.

Figure 15.7 Persona example. (Copyright Land Rover)

Sometimes the development of personas goes one stage further, and ethnographic films are created. Following the identification of key ethnographic similarities in a target segment, a camera crew and professional research team shadow real consumers throughout the activities of their normal daily life for a period of time. Land Rover was one of the first to use video to create such video pen portraits of real customers. This creates a fine-grained portrait, a mini documentary, on the target group. Clearly the resulting video only provides information on one particular family—perhaps only one particular driver—but with careful selection, the subjects being observed represent characteristics of the target market segment, and they provide insights to subtle needs, wants and preferences that would be very difficult to gather in any other way.

User trips

This technique is included in this chapter because it provides a simple means for designers to engage in user research. It offers a method for structuring an evaluation of a design, and it can be used with a prototype as well as a finished product. It is useful in areas of design where users must interact with your design, such as consumer products, Web pages and medical equipment as well as vehicles.

The essential idea of user trips is simple: you just take a 'trip' through the whole process of using a particular product or system. The key to the technique is to make yourself a critical, observant user. Once you have selected your target product, you need to decide who's viewpoint you will adopt; are you going to be a new consumer, an experienced consumer or perhaps a maintenance person? Perhaps you will adopt the persona of a disabled user. Then decide the limits and the variations to the user trip or trips you will take. It is usually a good idea to extend the trip into activities that come before and after the core activities of use, because these might inspire some innovative ways of improving the overall product experience. Similarly, you might seek to take your user trips in different conditions. For example if a designer took a particular car for a user trip, he or she might undertake the same sequence of tasks while driving on a motorway and in town, in dry and wet weather conditions, with passengers and without. The data you gather can include notes or a spoken recording. User trips in cars will frequently also use video evidence. The important thing is to capture all your actions, impressions, ideas and thoughts. This approach is particularly good for sensitising design staff to usability issues and failings. After trying this method a few times, you might find that you are adopting a more critical approach in your interaction with a wide range of items, and this is no bad thing for a designer. Being dissatisfied with accepted norms is often a prerequisite to making improvements. The clever skill is being able to turn dissatisfaction into constructive, creative criticism.

> "Being dissatisfied with accepted norms is often a prerequisite to making improvements. The clever skill is being able to turn dissatisfaction into constructive, creative criticism."

involving designers in market research

Market research does not stifle creativity; it can actually enhance it. Constraints provide challenges and stimulation, they provide something for creative people to work around. Of course, there are different types of constraints. There are functional constraints where the designer may have very limited room for manoeuvre, and there are softer constraints concerning, for example, interpretations of consumer values, where there might be more flexibility for the designer. The brand imposes certain types of constraints, but it can also be a source of inspiration.

Traditionally, getting to understand markets has been the sole responsibility of personnel in market research, but the new trend is to involve personnel from design in many of the activities— to become a consumer-centric company. In the Evoque project, designers visited many international markets and took part in focus group events, watching consumers react to their concept stimuli from behind a mirrored window. At other times, designers visited the homes of customers identified as highly representative of particular market segments. This can be a lively and fun way to increase understanding of market segments around the globe, and it leads to knowledge that other techniques can't deliver.

Another reason for involving designers in research is that frequently they see things differently; they might read research in new and novel ways, and they can extract different stories from research clinics. In contrast to more structured or analytical processes, designers can bring holistic interpretations or spot nuances in user feedback not picked up in transcripts or video evidence. It's not better than the work of market researchers; it's complementary to it. Perhaps designers have the potential to make valuable contributions to market research because they simply care about people and the interface between people and things.

Since Evoque was to be a prestige brand, design figured strongly in the various discussions and activities with members of the public. It was

> "Another reason for involving designers in research is that frequently they see things differently; they might read research in new and novel ways, and they can extract different stories from research clinics."

clear that those who would be buying Evoque could be defined as 'design progressives', and people were chosen dependent upon their reaction to contrasted pairs of related products, such as a Mont Blanc pen with a Bic biro. In these studies, participants were asked questions that

Figure 15.8 Evoque interior. Effective design requires excellence in detail as well as concept. (Photo copyright Land Rover)

revealed their perceptions of design characteristics such as functionality, value, status and brand. As a designer involved in market research, one needs to be thick-skinned and not easily upset by feedback. Listen carefully to what users or potential customers are saying, and then share with the research team what you think you heard. This allows others to confirm your perceptions as well as assists the process of transforming understandings into ideas. It's a very iterative process, but the harder you listen, the fewer iterations are required to have confidence in an idea.

The picture being painted is one of interplay between market analysis and creative thinking. That's not to say that designers are always constrained. There are frequently opportunities for blue-sky thinking, and the creation of caricatures referred to earlier is an example of loose, conceptual creativity. As well as concept creation, there are numerous opportunities for creative thinking to resolve issues around embodiment or detail design.

ongoing creative research

Once a clear proposal for Evoque had been developed, further market research was undertaken to assess the perceptions and opinions of selected market segments. Much confidence was gained by the broad consistency of positive feedback from clinics in several different world markets. Since Range Rover is a global brand, it was vital that people across continents bought into the Evoque concept. Of course, the decision to develop a concept requires some bravery, particularly where a market is new. When a concept car was created and shown at international motor shows (the LRX concept), it was also reviewed at a large-scale clinic in Europe. Reaction was

overwhelming, and the development team felt particularly proud of the Evoque and confident in its success.

There's an important lesson here for the creative research process in a variety of industries. If you are going to use design to ask questions, you need to understand the sorts of answers you might receive and how you might apply the resulting information. It's being able to communicate design intent through research that is so vital and yet potentially difficult. Understanding people is key to this, so no matter whether you have a background in market research or design, you need to be able to empathize with research subjects, to pay attention and to communicate effectively.

Nearly all of the research discussed in this chapter was qualitative, with only a minority of soft quantitative data. For a manufacturer such as Land Rover, working in numerous markets, it would be very difficult and costly to engage in large-scale quantitative studies. And even if a company conducted such studies, would they inform the design process any more successfully? Probably not. Companies like Land Rover need to have sufficient confidence in a concept in order to justify the resources of development, and the various clinics make a big contribution to this. The Evoque project was driven by words such as *modernity, fun* and *premium,* which emerged from the research clinics. It wasn't driven by findings that could be expressed in percentage terms. We save this type of research for when we have a more developed vehicle design where we need to construct a detailed business plan.

Establishing a concept for development from amongst a variety of caricatures requires a particular ability to cope with ambiguity—that is, imprecise or conflicting information. It's something that designers are usually very good at: homing in on what is desirable whilst working with incomplete information. This ability is more traditionally valued in concept creation, but its importance in areas such as market research and exploration is increasingly recognized.

Market research today is not a rubber-stamping exercise for design. It cannot be used to merely justify new ideas. Market research is part of the creative process. Companies need to genuinely want to listen to what people have to say and to learn from them. Getting new product development right demands that companies can synthesize vision with analysis and reflection, and they must achieve this within short time frames. While market research must continue to occupy a location at the front end of the product creation process, this chapter has revealed the vital role that creative thinking can play in defining markets and interpreting feedback from potential customers. The design of the Range Rover Evoque reveals how the company has challenged traditional lines of demarcation. Designers have moved outside their traditional roles and responsibilities; they have become key personnel in the 'design before the design'. Today designers increasingly use their ability to generate concepts in order to seed the research process. It's a completely different strategy from the traditional model, where the function of design was to clothe the skeletal need defined by market research. The new model is much more likely to identify subtle but important customer perceptions and market trends and to give rise to product innovation. It's a more holistic process.

Clearly it's not just designers who can bring creative thinking to commercial teams, but designers do have the ability to stimulate research through the concepts they visualize, and they can capture distinct, holistic interpretations in research clinics. Their contributions can help shape as well as respond to research activities. Their participation blurs the boundary between what has traditionally been two distinct phases—one analytical and one creative. Even when a project is well into development, there is value in engaging designers in the various clinics to test market acceptance and customer opinions. Modern commercial pressures demand a fast and efficient design process, and many companies have sought to better integrate their research and development and to improve the necessary iterations. At Land Rover, the Evoque project stands as testimony to the success of their vision and processes. You can find a video of the Evoque development process on the Range Rover Web site.[5]

CHAPTER SUMMARY

- Designing for markets requires personnel from market research and design to work together efficiently and effectively.
- There is an important relationship, in a wide range of industries, between gathering information on markets and the application of such information in design.
- Market analysis requires creativity as well as systematic rigour.
- Concept generation, in the form of product caricatures, can guide and enrich market research, especially if such caricatures cover a broad spectrum of possibilities.

- Young designers should develop their capacity for creative research, empathic analysis and concept creation in market investigations.
- Market research seeks to reveal the characteristics of the various markets in which a company operates. Market segmentation is a process of defining groups that exhibit particular characteristics.
- The tools for market research can be divided broadly into two groups: quantitative (e.g. questionnaires) and qualitative (e.g. profiles, personas, focus groups). User trips can sensitize a designer to usability issues.
- Market research does not stifle creativity. Knowledge of consumer values and needs provides vital constraints that can enhance innovation through challenge and stimulation.

chapter 16

creative analysis in packaging design

luiz vidal gomes and ligia medeiros

ABOUT THIS CHAPTER

Creativity is central to design and designing. While most people probably believe that the purpose of creativity is to solve problems, this chapter makes the case that it's actually creative analysis and problem formulation that provide the essential foundation to successful design practice today from architecture to fashion design. This chapter introduces a selection of packaging and graphic design projects undertaken by a small but influential design consultancy in Brazil, a major and still developing economy on the world's stage. The examples of recent work at Usina Escritório de Desenho illustrate the application of a set of investigative design tools that the Usina team considers vital to creative practice.[1]

problems and solutions

As humans we intervene in situations. We try to convert unsuitable situations into suitable ones. As a species we are good at collecting information through our senses, processing it in our brains and interpreting it. Typically, we try to bring prior experience and intuition to problems. But even this seemingly careful process can lead to incomplete understandings and only partially successful ideas. The professional practice of design demands something both methodical and flexible. It requires an ability to gather valid information but to hold it in a state of creative flux. It requires designers to take great care when making decisions or fixing on answers, because with a bit more creative thinking, it might be possible to generate more important questions, which in turn lead to better solutions. However, clients want to pay for results, not process, so there are understandable pressures to reduce the question-asking activity in order to get on with the generation and detailing of a design proposal.

Many younger designers feel they don't have the skills to undertake problem-finding activities. Unlike other fields, such as the human sciences, the focus of design education has traditionally been on creativity rather than the skills of data gathering and analysis. This is unfortunate, because the design community is ideally placed to create innovative research through the combining of creative thinking with sound investigative processes. There's a huge potential here for designers who can deal with today's speed and volume of information, who can creatively assemble and decompose questions, who can structure problems as they structure their ideas—using temporary, sketch models of perceptions and

Figure 16.1 Creative problem finding is a key service of design teams today. (Copyright author)

understandings—and who can harness all this to an ability to create and communicate clear design proposals that address the emerging problems.

Designers are perceptive people. They have valuable abilities to closely scrutinize the world around them. Some designers are particularly good at detecting functional, aesthetic, informational or technical problems and formulating the questions they embody, while others excel in the transformational skills of converting understanding to new solutions, objects or products. Some are good at imagining new uses for existing designs. Developing skills such as drawing frequently has the added bonus of heightening the ability to visually examine the world. Whatever an individual's preference or emphasis, it seems clear that good designing is the harnessing of creative problem finding with creative problem solving. One of the challenges for designers today has become how to develop a rich and personal style whilst combining this with rigorous and proven methodologies— marrying the subjective and the objective.

Expert designers seem to revel in difficult questions; they seem to feed off issues for which there is no immediate explanation or resolution.

> **"Good designing is the harnessing of creative problem finding with creative problem solving."**

Complexity and controversy fuel rather than hinder design discussions and the process of intervention. Since the designer is always an intermediary, there are bound to be conflicts, perhaps involving matters of taste, values or costs, but the core skill here is embracing such difficulty. It's not an easy skill to master, but it is, perhaps, the most vital for a designer today.

towards subject-specific design methods

Hopefully, you can already see the human dimension of this chapter. Successful designing is not just the harnessing of technology. Neither is it the imposition of a straitjacket of procedures or approaches. It is the creation of a working space that is informed and supported by the abilities of individuals and groups of design participants.

There's not one ideal process; there are many, each tailored to suit the particular context in which it will be applied. At the core of this is the co-working of creative strategies for problem and solution formulation. It's not that problem finding is analytical and solution generation is creative. One needs to be creative in research, concept generation, detail design and pitching the proposal to the client. Similarly, one needs to be analytical and methodical in all stages of design, including those traditionally viewed as exclusively creative, such as concept generation.

Each organization involved in design will have evolved approaches, methods, strategies and techniques to suit its particular requirements, context or markets. But all are under pressure to achieve economies whilst improving performance. From the early definition of design methods observed by John Christopher Jones[2] and his contemporaries in the early 1960s, it's possible to discern a trend towards specific methods generated to address the particular needs of various design fields. The writings of Bonsiepe, for example, chart the definition of methods appropriate and necessary to industrial design as distinct from, say, architecture or engineering.[3] Embedded in this hierarchy is the journey towards methods that embrace divergence and convergence, synthesis and analysis, the subjective with the objective. As the engineering scholar Bucciarelli observed, 'in each new project, old structures of work division are challenged ... creating a new vocabulary and a new discourse'.[4]

The second half of the twentieth century saw industrial design fragment into separate specialisms, but it was only in the latter years of the twentieth century that distinct methods and approaches were formulated for these specialisms based on the particularities of the respective knowledge base, working approaches, client demands and technological opportunities. Packaging design, for example, emerged as a significant branch of industrial design, displaying a symbiotic relationship with graphic communication and displaying features of methods and approaches from both parent domains. Even in these apparently specialist domains, new submethods continue to emerge. This chapter continues with a close examination of one consultancy where its context— in this case, commercial graphic design practice in Brazil—has played a significant role in the generation of methods and approaches that might usefully inform the global design community.

creating design knowledge at usina

Brazil is the largest country in South America. As the world's fifth largest country and the eighth largest economy by nominal gross domestic product, Brazil commands a place as one of the four major emerging economies collectively referred to as the BRIC countries (Brazil, Russia, India and China). Brazil also has a rich wildlife and huge reserves of natural resources.

The largest metropolitan areas in Brazil are São Paulo, Rio de Janeiro and Belo Horizonte—all in the southeastern region. São Paulo is the largest and richest city in Brazil and is the capital of the state of São Paulo, the most populous Brazilian state. The city exerts strong regional influence in commerce and finance as well as arts and entertainment.

Usina was established as a company in 1998 in São Paulo—renowned as a demanding market in Brazil—by two newly graduated designers from the University of Santa Maria. The word

Figure 16.2 São Paulo, the largest and richest city in Brazil, provides the base for Usina Escritório de Desenho. (Getty 95481373 RF)

usina in Portuguese means a plant consisting of buildings with facilities for manufacturing. Also, in adopting the Portuguese word *desenho* instead of the international expression *design* in the company name, the founders made a clear step to differentiate themselves in the competitive market of São Paulo.

A large proportion of Usina's business focuses on packaging design for food and beverage companies, but it also works for manufacturers of various consumer goods such as cosmetics and hygiene products. Its in-house designers work on a wide range of graphic and physical packaging for product lines, visual identities and manuals. During the last decade, around 3,000 projects were undertaken for more than forty brands in twelve Latin American countries. Usina has developed strong loyalties inside the industry, and about 80 per cent of its work is with clients who have been partners with the consultancy for over five years.

Usina's work embraces market analysis, studies of artefacts, technological innovation, identity creation and messaging. Much of its work involves raising efficiency in existing product lines and services, generating innovations in processes and improving service quality. Projects can lead to tangible outputs, such as product prototypes, marketing schemes or new environments, and they can lead to less-tangible outputs, such as increased understanding of product positioning or greater market awareness. Beyond design outputs, its creation of new knowledge has influenced the intellectual standards of the markets in which the company operates. In line with other leading design organizations, one might consider Usina to be in the knowledge business rather than the product business.[5] This may explain Usina's success in markets saturated with computer-aided design visualizations and where agencies seek to compete through a downward spiral of service price. The conceptualization of design as knowledge is liberating. In this sense, design might assist a client to achieve new perceptions of markets or selected users, it might underpin technical innovation or production engineering or it might take the form of discovery, diagnosis or improvement. If design is knowledge, or at least the search for knowledge, then as designers we have a duty to understand and apply the processes expected of professionals today.

In the late 1990s, when Usina was founded, a typical Brazilian company in the food sector had only six or seven product lines. Today a product line can exceed fifty variations differentiated by, for example, flavours, sizes, or special editions. This increase has been mirrored by an explosive growth in packaging. There are significant pressures for such packaging to be tailored to suit local markets, so there has been a co-evolution of globalization and a movement to adapt packaging to reflect local market characteristics. In Latin America, it is common for design consultancies to be asked to merely restyle mainstream packaging products even though innovation could increase market share or profitability. Usina recognizes and works with these conservative pressures whilst promoting innovation where possible.

towards a taxonomy of creative problem finding

Typically, a packaging design project begins with an approach from an advertising agency or an industrial product manager. Sometimes the enquiry includes a range of background information and a clear idea of the brief, but there are other times when a client is looking for guidance. The design brief and an attribute list are both tools commonly used in this design stage, where the goal is to define the problem situation plus any major instructions and guidelines. At Usina, the briefing will be taken by a senior member of staff, and it's his or her role to assess whether the information received is sufficient for starting the project or if more is required. It's quite normal, at the early stages of a project, for the problem to be poorly outlined. Even the client may not understand the whole problem. So one of the values of using the services of creative design people is that they can bring creativity to the interpretation of problems. They can, for example, look beyond the superficial to deeper underlying problems resulting in the generation of clearer and more relevant instructions or guidelines in the brief and the accompanying contract. Creative problem formulation helps avoid wasted research, it saves time and can lead to real innovation in a marketplace.

In order to analyse this problem situation, it's helpful to identify four influential components, which we label IS, FS, WD and ID. The design stage concerned with the definition of the brief can be divided into initial situation (IS) and final situation (FS). IS includes the initial approach from a potential client and any early discussions. FS doesn't refer to the deliverables of the project, perhaps an advertising campaign or a design for packaging. Instead it refers to the finalization of problem formulation on which subsequent concept design and development will be founded. In the same way, a problem can vary from well-defined (WD) to ill-defined (ID).

After receiving any written or verbal briefing, and as they formulate the problem to be worked on, the design team must characterize the design problem situation to scope out key factors. These might include the finances of the project, the final users or consumers, the market, the potential materials and manufacturing processes, the channels of distribution and sales. The design problem is categorized according to its degree of identification with the four components IS, FS, WD and ID. There follow some short examples of design

situations that illustrate this basic taxonomy. Each example includes an illustration of the guidelines generated by Usina to assist conceptual design.

Case study 1: ice pop

This example displayed a well-defined initial situation (WDIS) and a well-defined final situation (WDFS). The initial situation specified that the design should present individual packaging of four distinct ice cream products (see Figure 16.3). It would be aimed at the young adult market. The work formed part of the manufacturer's strategy to unify the visual language of various products in its portfolio. Indicators of a well-defined final situation include the specification of materials, colour,

Figure 16.3 The resulting ice pop product range.
(Copyright author)

process and the channels of distribution and sale. The brief specified that the ice pop packaging should be manufactured in an opaque but flexible polymer, printed using rotogravure, printed in five colours and distributed to supermarkets, bakeries and cake shops.

Guidelines for the ice pop project

It was specified that the ice pops themselves should be unaltered because they are classic products of this manufacturer. The different identities, flavours and textures should continue to be recognized visually by the purchaser. The corporate visual identity should be strengthened in the process of package unification. The opaque material does not allow the consumer to see the ice pop, thus increasing the importance of graphic communication on the packaging. Realistic illustrations were suggested to indicate texture and taste. There should be little variation in the composition of the graphic elements. Visual imagery should emphasize the creamy attributes of the product. The name and logo should occupy prominent space on the packaging.

Case study 2: labels for cleaning liquids

This example displayed a well-defined initial situation (WDIS) and an ill-defined final situation (IDFS). The task was to design a system of labels for fifty types of flasks for retailing cleaning liquids. (see Plate 22) The primary purchasers were women whose families had medium to high purchasing power. While some key variables were fixed—for example the packaging for transportation and distribution channels and sales could not be altered—the containers were not defined. Thus it was not possible to define the materials and

processes for printing the labels, and this created an ill-defined final situation.

Guidelines for the labelling project

It was specified that the cleaning liquid would be unaltered. The visual identity of the product and brand should be redesigned because it was the key element in the unification of the label system. Flask units should be organized and grouped consistent with the characteristics of the contents (for example by function, fragrance or concentration). The redesign of the visual identity of the brand should translate the functionality of the product line through graphics that reinforce the emotional ties that consumers have with the brand name. The label system should use white to suggest cleanliness and colour to highlight the brand name on a dark background for contrast.

Case study 3: new alcoholic drinks

In contrast to the previous two examples, this one displayed an ill-defined initial situation (IDIS) and an ill-defined final situation (IDFS). The project concerned the design of a flask, label and visual identity for a new sparkling vodka drink. The target market was adult consumers in Brazilian cities, in the medium to high economic category. The client allowed the design team to define the key characteristics of the three component parts: bottle, label and the product visual identity. Because the product was new to the market, nothing was specified regarding materials, production processes, shelf display, packaging for transportation, distribution or marketing strategies.

Guidelines for the vodka packaging project

Traditionally, distilled drinks are sold in glass bottles, so the concept designs (see Figure 16.4)

Figure 16.4 Concept designs for vodka packaging.
(Copyright author)

attempted to combine this tradition with modern forms. A key characteristic was the transparency of the beverage and the bottle, plus the unique sparking character of the drink. The guidelines defined opportunities for coherence between the two-dimensional graphic label and the three-dimensional bottle form. Also, inspirational key-words were created deriving from the physical characteristics of the beverage (bubbles, effer-vescence), desired attributes (vigour, energy) and consumer experience (pleasure, entertainment). These assisted in the creation of identity.

Rotation, Reflection and Translation

Design displays repetition. Our urban landscapes reveal re-peated forms of houses or office blocks, graphic designers use repetition of motifs for visual effect and emphasis and fabric designers create pattern through various forms of rep-etition. Three common systems for creating patterns through repetition use rotation, reflection and translation.

In rotation, a motif is repeated by turning it about a cen-tre, which might lie outside the motif. Here pattern can be built up by a sequence of repetitive steps. This technique can be used to create, for example, decoration around the rim of a plate or the plan for houses around a curved street.

In reflection, the motif is mirrored about a line. This can frequently be seen in clothing, where each half of a garment, around a centre line, is a reflection of the other half. In this case, the outcome is symmetrical.

Motifs can also be reoriented or translated to add va-riety to a pattern. They might be moved through 90 or 180 degrees or any other angle, but they must be translated consistently for the pattern to work.

Rotation, reflection and translation can be combined to create intricate patterns and arrangements.

From: C. F. Earl, *Design and Designing* (T211), The Open University, Blk 4 (2010), pp. 46–50.

Follow-on work

Following on from the successful project to pack-age the sparkling vodka beverage, the client asked the company to take on the redesign of the container and label for the client's traditional vodka. The purpose of this redesign was to de-velop new markets for this traditional drink and to increase overall market share. The project dis-played yet another situational profile. It had char-acteristics of an ill-defined initial situation (IDIS) and a well-defined final situation (WDFS). There were opportunities to apply outcomes from the sparkling vodka packaging project to this project in terms of materials, fabrication processes and distribution systems.

creative analysis in design teams

During the initial stages of a project, the client and designers must communicate effectively, and sometimes frequently, to reduce misunder-standings and develop a working relationship. All subsequent design actions rest on the founda-tion created here. For the designers, this stage is characterized by immersion in the problem. In large projects, tasks are frequently distributed across several members of the team, increasing the complexity of analysis and communication. A distinguishing characteristic of successful design teams is their ability to combine their creative skills with analytical techniques; this ability ensures that any subsequent design and development is point-ing in the best possible direction for success.

The process of analysis is a dismantling pro-cess, a taking apart to reveal the components that make up the whole. Analysis is a process of identifying relationships between parts. It seeks to understand organization, define hierarchies and identify inconsistencies. Analysis lies at the core of design thinking, but it is at its strongest when it is combined with a designer's ability to create, to assemble knowledge to bring about new and innovative constructions.

> "Analysis lies at the core of design thinking, but it is at its strongest when it is combined with a designer's ability to create, to assemble knowledge to bring about new and innovative constructions."

At Usina there is a strong belief that the creative process begins at the analytical stage of a design project, and in all work the creative team engages in research and analysis. Decisions made about direction and approach to analysis will create information which, in turn, will have a significant influence on the designed outputs. Collecting information is very important in design, but it represents only part of investigative work.

Just as significant is the way a designer chooses to interrogate data. For the packaging designer, there are decisions to be made about how to gather data on, for example, consumer needs, wants, preferences or values and how to apply this data in design and development. It can be very tricky investigating design characteristics such as form and shape or contrasting aesthetics of competing manufacturers. In some ways the designer operates like a biologist exploring and probing a creature's morphology or shape evolution as well as its physiology. But a designer also creates meaning through his or her outputs, so design analysis must also include semiology, the

construction of meaning. An alternative comparison would be with a volleyball coach who studies videotapes of games, collecting data on the moves and positioning of players. The key dual message here is that (1) engaging in investigations can lead to valuable discoveries and insights that can be transferred to concept or detail design, and (2) involving designers creates ideas, models or prototypes of possible futures, and these provide opportunities for applying a number of analytical tools to provide new insights to markets and users.

The final section outlines six types of analysis exploited at Usina. They are presented as six tools that can help in design practice. Each offers opportunities for designers to engage in creative investigations that can find application in both problem finding and problem solving.

six analytical tools

Semiotic analysis

Semiotic analysis explores the messages communicated through designs and the meanings constructed by those who come into contact with those designs. It might apply any of a number of individual techniques to make valuable contributions to packaging design and the designer's task of converting written briefs into visual design proposals. Such analysis might exploit focus group interaction or more traditional questionnaire-type documents to explore how features of particular designs symbolize qualities and values for consumers. It might seek to examine how a design signifies a quality directly or literally. We call this 'denotation'. An example of denotation is the use of the clear glass bottle in Figure 16.5 used to denote the purity of the vodka contained within it. Alternatively, research might explore how designs hold 'connotations' for people. These are qualities or values implied indirectly. An example of connotation can be seen in Figure 16.5 again. Here the drawing of the eagle in the background of the image suggests positive connotations with eastern European military power and the roots of vodka making and vodka drinking.

There can be many types of output from semiotic analysis such as diagrams and mind maps. They might identify keywords and suggestive schemes, complemented by information linked to situations and cultures. The techniques of semiotic analysis enlarge a designer's visual vocabulary and increase the awareness of signs and symbols at play in various cultures.

Diachronic analysis

Diachronic analysis is the study of development over time. In design it refers to research which seeks to increase understanding of the evolutionary progress of a product type, such as glass bottles. Diachronic analysis embraces aesthetic and technological change and particularly seeks to identify big leaps in progress. It looks for innovations in, for example, materials, new uses and impacts. It draws on various sources of data, including books on history, library catalogues, journals, collections, and testimonials from users.

A helpful way to represent the data created by diachronic analysis is through the use of pictorial sequences or flow charts. These allow viewers

Figure 16.5 A graphic of one particular packaging concept. (Copyright author)

to make quick comparisons, see progressive changes and to identify key events such as points of radical change.

In 2000, during the redesign of the chocolate drink Toddynho, diachronic analysis revealed some interesting transformations of the shape of the letters *T* and *Y* over the life of the product. The original logo used letter forms that were styled and rippled, suggesting motion and smoothness— entirely in keeping with the desired modern image of careful production and quality of chocolate. In the 2000 project, the designers incorporated this traditional typography with new characters in the labelling of the new packs (Figure 16.6). More recently still, new printing technology has enabled the Toddynho character to achieve three-dimensional effects.

Synchronic analysis

This is the analysis of similar or competing products. Research might focus on any of a variety of characteristics of a rival's products, including technical, functional or aesthetic attributes. Essentially this suite of tools seeks to assist comparisons of designs. Techniques of synchronic analysis might reveal shared qualities such as adverts that appeal to particular segments of a market or marketing campaigns that identify with contemporary products or personalities. Synchronic analysis uses product attributes such as shape, form and function in order to make comparisons and to reveal where designs possess distinctive or unique qualities. It would refer to product catalogues, company reports and industrial publications as well as research investigating the views and opinions of representative users. It can lead to a variety of reporting devices, including tables of visual source material, documentation of assessment criteria and written reports.

Selected synchronic analysis was undertaken as part of the development of the visual identity for Vitarella, a brand of biscuits. The graphic design of competitor companies was analysed to understand their use of visual elements such as symbol, logo, typography and chromatic patterns and to contrast attributes (Figure 16.7).

In the development of Vitarella's noodle product Vitarella Lamen, six components of recent advertising campaigns by competitor companies were selected for evaluation: logo, verbal and

previously   1st redesign - 2000   2nd redesign - 2003

Figure 16.6 The Toddynho package design over a number of years facilitates diachronic analysis. (Copyright author)

Brands that use secondary elements in a packaging visual identity   Brands that use just the logo on the packaging

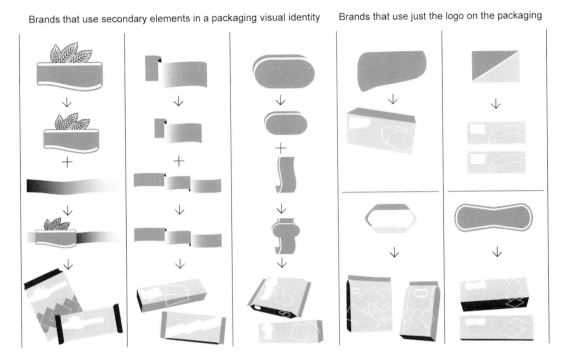

Figure 16.7 Synchronic analysis of biscuit brands.
(Copyright author)

visual communication of flavours, photographic illustration of the product, communication of the nutritional benefits and materials used in manufacture. Each component was allocated a quality score between one (reasonable) and five (excellent). This type of research can collect answers from a variety of stakeholders ranging from the design team to large numbers of actual and potential consumers. The subsequent analysis can help designers understand the product category and help to develop a marketing strategy.

Consumer profile analysis

This type of investigation links research to design with the definition of clear customer groupings based on demographics and behavioural profiles. It consists of the collection and evaluation of data related to expectations, preferences and requirements of consumers. It seeks to understand why consumers made certain purchasing decisions. One technique uses photographic and written surveys to capture age, gender, interests, spending habits and other activities. It leads to outputs in the form of textual descriptions accompanied by pictures of real people using and consuming the product under study, not just those anticipated as being 'perfect and ideal customers'.

Analysis of determinants

In the field of packaging design, this type of investigation typically displays a focus on materials, manufacturing processes and costs. Great attention is given to limits or constraints—that is, what cannot be changed and what has to be. As well as written reports, the outputs of determinants

Packaging Brand Design Scoring from 0–5	Brand Visibility/ Sub Brand	Flavor Recognition	Flavor Pictures/Icons	Pictures Bowl and fork	Benefits Front panel	Material Metalized
Competitor 1	**5** Yellow used as visual identity on the shelves; There is no sub brand	**5** Easy identifcation (big font sizes)	**5** The picture illustrates product's flavour	**5** Bowl, fork: clear identification of elements	**4** Pointing out the cooking time; Does not communicate microwave use or free of trans fat	**5** Metalized, but the layout does not explore this feature
Competitor 2	**3** The color background changes according to flavor. It has two sub brands	**5** Clear recognition of the products' flavor though the background color	**3** The 'flavour picture' is use as a side dish	**3** Hard to identify the elements	**3** Pointing out the cooking time; Does not communicate microwave use or free of trans fat	**3** Plastic
Competitor 3	**2** The color background changes according to flavor. It has one sub brand	**5** Clear recognition of the products' flavor though the background color	**1** The 'flavor picture' is use as an side dish	**2** Hard to identify the elements	**3** Pointing out the cooking time; Does not communicate microwave use or free of trans fat	**2** Plastic
Competitor 4	**2** The color background changes according to flavor. It has one sub brand	**5** Easy identifcation (big font sizes)	**4** The picture illustrates product's flavour	**3** Bowl, fork: clear identification of elements	**3** Pointing out the cooking time; Does not communicate microwave use or free of trans fat	**4** Metalized, however it is explored in exagerate way suggesting that the product is artificial
Packaging Design Strategy						
VITARELLA	Keep the Vitarella yellow wave; Do not use sub-brand	Use a different color background for each flavor	Represent flavor through Iconic pictures	Take picture of the product within a bowl with cutlery	Explore graphically the benefits of the product	Explore the metalized finishing packaging in detail

Figure 16.8 Synchronic analysis scoring product characteristics used in packaging. (Copyright author)

analysis can take the form of cause-and-effect diagrams.

Tangential analysis

The sixth type of investigative tool is tangential analysis. This is the use of real and virtual environments to elicit deep-rooted responses to designs from current or anticipated consumers. The research subjects are placed in highly realistic environments and, depending on the context, are allowed to interact with two-dimensional and/or three-dimensional representations. It can be a revealing technique for packaging design and development. Research questions might focus on various attributes of the design or they might seek to capture relevant memories, reveal associations or uncover hidden meanings. Tangential analysis can incorporate the study of other products, even those from different sectors or industries, where similar problems or characteristics are apparent. Tangential analysis is particularly revealing when used in conjunction with other tools described here.

Brazil is clearly set to be a major world market, and traditional design practices are being given innovative emphases in a new generation of consultancies such as Usina Escritório de Desenho. This group has attracted a significant portfolio of clients through the application of creativity in problem finding as well as problem solving. The tools and approaches discussed here are particularly well suited to packaging design, but they can be used to good effect in all fields of design.

A Short Interview with Darryl McDonald, Senior Art Director, EuroRSCG Life, London

Q: What are the most important things to know for a student who wishes to be an art director?

A: 1. Learn the rules (and apply them) before breaking them.

2. Don't replicate a style you admire. Create your own style so you stand out from your colleagues.

3. Don't be precious about your ideas. There's always another solution in case your teacher, boss or the client rejects it.

4. Don't fall in love with your work; it won't love you back.

Q: What do you wish you'd been told when you were training as a student designer?

A: I think this question invites cynicism and regrets, neither of which I have. I've worked with great talents, won numerous industry awards and travelled to exotic places through my work. That being said, I wish I'd been told that advertising (and any media-oriented career) involves a lot of hours that take away any chance of having a life outside of work! Creating the best work involves intense periods, late nights and weekend work. So you'd better love—really love—what you're doing before pursuing a career in advertising and design. Because if you love your job, it won't feel like a job.

Q: What's your top tip to readers?

A: Have a portfolio with ideas and that isn't afraid to take chances. Design without an idea is just wallpaper and pretty pictures. A design with a strong idea, however, will get you the job.

CHAPTER SUMMARY

- This chapter has been about creative analysis in design, the application of creativity to problem finding. Apply your creativity to research and analysis.
- Successful problem finding is a vital prerequisite for creative problem solving. Use your design skills to ensure you are solving the right problem(s).
- Design today demands approaches that are methodical, flexible and creative. Develop an understanding of analytical methods. Learn how to conduct sound investigative studies and how to analyse data.
- Ask insightful questions. Expert designers find difficult questions stimulating.
- Use creative design thinking to generate material, such as drawings and models, that you can incorporate into research studies.
- Designers act as intermediaries between various stakeholders. Being a skilful intermediary is a vital professional skill.
- This chapter has taken its examples from packaging and graphic design, but the lessons apply to a wide range of professional practice today.

Background

This project invites you to design for a market which is currently unknown to you! The first part of the project asks you to use a random generation technique to find a market. If you have a world atlas, think of a number and then look up that page number; if you have access to the Internet, try using a tool such as Google Earth (www.google.com) and entering two or three letters in the search box. This should generate a list of places. There are two rules in this project. Rule 1 is you must pick the first place you identify that isn't in your country of birth or residence. When I did this, I entered 'mu' in the Google Earth search box, and Mauritius was first in the list.

Once you have randomly generated the name of a city, region or country, you can begin the project.

The Project

Your task is to generate a design that potentially has value and meaning for your target market. To do this, you will need to investigate this place: what is the climate, what is the economy based on, what might the people there need or want? Your investigations might lead you to think of clothing, information systems, transport, media, children's needs, medical products, food packaging, tools, domestic items and a host of other contexts. Rule 2 sets a ceiling for the unit cost of your design: your proposal for a design must cost less than twenty-four dollars (US) to manufacture or produce.

Guidelines

This is a project about getting to know a market. It's about being creative in your investigations as well as being creative in generating ideas. How might you find out about a market that is unknown to you? You might try to contact someone from that area, look it up on the Internet or use a library. What can you deduce from its location, its climate? Try to define five characteristics of your market, because these can inspire design ideas. Your ideas can be for new designs or improvements of existing designs.

Your design ideas don't need to be detailed. If you have a few ideas, pick one and create a presentation of that idea. It's important that others can understand your proposal, so use images and some words to explain it. Assessing unit cost can be difficult, so an estimate is satisfactory. Comparing your idea with similar designs might help you judge prices and costs.

part v

sustainable design and designing

introduction to part v

Sustainability has become one of the most frequently used words today along with *eco-design, green design* and *design for the environment.* We increasingly find the word sustainable in marketing and sales literature, in appeals for reduced consumption or lifestyle changes and in descriptions of designs as diverse as public transport systems and packaging for soap powder. Its appropriation for so many different purposes illustrates both the imperatives and the contradictions in the term *sustainable design.*

This part presents four different perspectives on sustainability. It opens with a reflection on what is one of the biggest design projects illustrated in the collection—the transformation of Berlin into a sustainable city. In Chapter 17 David Heathcote and Dorothea Strube reveal how modern initiatives for sustainable living are founded on far older approaches and attitudes.

In Chapter 18 Philip Davies reveals how the energy consumed over a product's lifetime of use can be far more significant in an assessment of sustainability than other factors such as what materials it is made from. Davies introduces life cycle assessment as a practical tool that can assist those involved in design and development to make judgements and to foresee the implications of decisions. He reminds us of the simple fact that 'what goes in must come out', and as designers we need to acknowledge this principle of mass balance. What emerges is a picture of sustainability as a system of interrelated forces. As designers we are encouraged to apply our creativity at the systems level and to embrace both the hard forces such as energy efficiency and soft forces such as consumer

preferences. The notion of design responsibility within a global community is developed by Tom Greenwood, who unpacks the potential contradictions for a design profession frequently required to both stimulate and moderate consumption. He reveals a type of design intelligence whereby innovation can improve the well-being of individuals and society whilst reducing overall impact—particularly on the environment. There are lessons here not only for sustainable design but how we might achieve sustainable designing through new processes for creation, development and evaluation.

This part paints a picture of sustainable design as mainstream and established. Gone are the days when it was a small, alternative community of interest. Today sustainable design is big business, and many of the examples in this part reveal commercially successful products and systems that help large populations to consume ethically and sustainably. But that's not to say that the pioneering spirit that defined the early eco-design community has disappeared. Emma Dewberry reminds us in her chapter that there is still a vital role for people to protest and to intervene directly in a world characterized by disadvantage. Significant populations in the developed and the developing worlds are still largely disenfranchised from the services of designers. Dewberry appeals for us to look at our world afresh and to engage with fundamental issues such as health care, housing and industrialization.

This is a part that builds on the chapters of earlier parts. You will read important reinforcement about the design process, the value of representations, designing for users and markets and the commercial context of design.

chapter 17

berlin: a sustained city

david heathcote and dorothea strube

ABOUT THIS CHAPTER

Sustainable design is not attractive in itself; it isn't an aesthetic; it doesn't appeal only to ideas of perfection of form or material. It has to felt to be a good thing—a thing expected, not noticed. When ubiquitous sustainable design is available to a society that has embraced the ethic of sustainability, then there are the beginnings of a sustainable culture.

In Berlin, Europe's second largest city, graphic designers produce a whole range of products to help Berliners understand which of five waste bins to put their rubbish into. Berliners in turn expect those five bins to be there in the first place. Berlin is a city where a tram is not a loser cruiser and riding a bicycle is so normal it has become a nuisance. All Berlin expects sustainability to be part of its normal transactions. To understand why sustainability is now an integral part of Berlin's culture, it is necessary to understand the historical conditions that made Berlin and Berliners what they are.

---

history

Berlin is a modern city. Although it existed in the Middle Ages and has Baroque palaces, it was only after the unification of Germany in 1871, when it became the capital, that the population approached 1 million. It reached this landmark in 1880. After 1880 the city both boomed and busted, racked by sequential political and economic misfortunes: the First World War, hyperinflation in the 1920s, the Second World War, the division of Germany in 1947 and the Berlin Wall 1961–1989. At its peak early in 1942 the population was 4.5 million; in 2010, it was 3.4 million.

Since 1990 Berlin has become the capital of a reunited Germany but has nonetheless suffered economically again because it is no longer the showcase for the competing ideologies of capitalism and communism—the funding of superpowers has been withdrawn. Yet as a city with a future, it has no equal in Europe, being the capital of its most powerful economy. Events have combined to create a city of great significance that has grown fast in short spurts and equally at times stagnated, been destroyed and then reconstructed. As a result, different periods of growth, decay and regrowth are clearly geographically defined. Moreover, the last period of regrowth, dating from 1989, has come in a period when sustainability was already recognized as an issue in city design and governance. In the period after the building of the Berlin Wall in 1961, Berlin became a place of both contesting Cold War ideologies but, more significantly for this chapter, a place of cultural opposition to the Cold War that found common cause in the rejection of communist and capitalist ideas of material progress. The effect of this culture on the subsequent development of Berlin has been instrumental in making it a place where sustainability is taken as a given in consideration of the future of the city.

The periods of growth followed by dramatic halts had a remarkable effect on the built environment of Berlin, almost freezing it at two points: the first, immediately before the First World War and then again before the Second World War. Following this there was a period when, under competing ideologies, Berlin was reconstructed as a showcase for different visions of the Modern City. Berlin is a case study for three recent periods of urban design. The designer with an eye for history will find in Berlin a city where the best tendencies in urban design of the nineteenth and twentieth centuries are preserved and clearly bordered, as if they were in typological jars, leaving them to be analysed for their merits rather than their failures: the bustling, fast growing, expedient nineteenth-century industrial city; the suburbanized, leisurized city of the early twentieth century and the reforming, experimentally Modern City of the second half of the twentieth century. Berlin has had the advantage for designers of all stamps that the various haltings and destructions that Berlin suffered in the twentieth century repeatedly made space for the new within the pre-automotive borders of the late-nineteenth-century city. Berlin still expresses perfectly the design ideology of the new German state of the nineteenth century. This sought to invent a new physicality for itself through rational analysis of problems, standardization and the self-conscious emulation of foreign exemplars to create 'types'—pragmatic yet ideal solutions for any given problem, simple or complex. This idea of the design of ideal types, which are created through the assemblage of standards (often types in themselves) in innovative, rational sequences was both utilitarian and efficient, values that in themselves underpin modern ideas of sustainability.

the feel of berlin

Until 2008 it was still normal to fly to Berlin Tempelhof, a pioneering airport, part Grand Central Station and part ocean liner terminal. Built between 1927 and 1941, it has been described by leading architect Norman Foster as 'the mother of all airports' and is emblematic of the unique urban experience of Berlin. The first airport with an underground railway connection, the site is close to the centre of the city, and arriving there had the feeling that the aircraft was like a train, the disembarking passengers immediately entering the grand hall of a terminus that lay on the edge of the inner city. The feeling that Berlin is somehow less spread out than other cities would already be set by the slow run-in over the city, which from the air has a compact appearance with the outer suburbs lying right up against the inner city and the flat, forested and lake-filled Land Brandenburg that surrounds Berlin. Equally visible were the nineteenth-century city blocks that make up much of Berlin's inner suburbs surrounding Alexanderplatz in the former East and Kurfurstendamm in the West.

Comparing Maraun's 1896 Pferdebahn Plan of Berlin to the 1923 Pharus Plan of Gross Berlin, one can see that Tempelhof Airport was built at the edge of the 1896 city on the Exerzier Platz der Berliner Garnison in the southwest of the city just within the Berliner Ring railway that defined the edge of the city. This sense of compression of

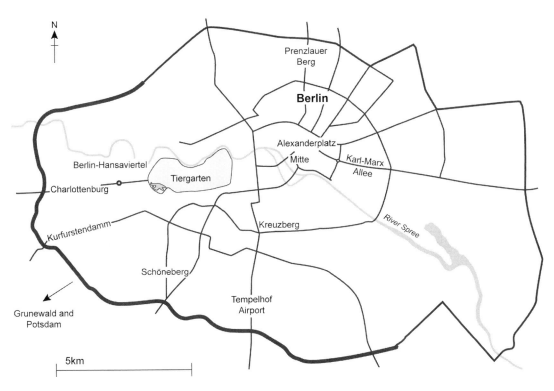

N

Figure 17.1 Some of the regions and places of Berlin referred to in this chapter. (Copyright Ryan Cox)

time and space, of an airport inside the limits of a Wilhelmine Berlin, gives the immediate sensation of the intense modernity of air travel and at the same time the feeling of a nineteenth-century capital on the edge of the new century.

On the opposite side of the city is the inner-city suburb of Prenzlauer Berg, which even in 1896, was only just touching the outer railway ring. Prenzlauer Berg today is one of the quarters of old East Berlin that has become fashionable for the new Berlin residents, including affluent residents from the United States, Britain, France and Italy. In 1896 Prenzlauer Berg, like all of the newly developed suburbs, was based on a grid system. This and indeed the entire character of Berlin's inner city suburbs was defined by James Hobrecht's

'Binding Land-Use Plan for the Environs of Berlin' of 1862. Hobrecht, an employee of the Royal Prussian Planning Police, was given the job of planning for Berlin's expansion over the coming fifty years. His plan was based on his experiences visiting Paris, London and Hamburg and combines the grid system favoured in Paris with an accommodation of existing settlements and infrastructures of the more laissez-faire London. Hobrecht's plan did not prescribe the architecture of the suburbs, and the design of the buildings was left to the local building profession. The critical examination of other countries' approach to design problems became a normal feature of the Prussian government's approach to built-environment design. At the heart of the earliest areas of the new Prenzlauer

Figure 17.2 Mietskasernen, the typical apartment blocks of Berlin. (Copyright David Heathcote)

Berg suburb lay Wörther Platz, now Kollwitzplatz, laid out as a public garden in 1885 to 1887. It lay on the north side of a Jewish cemetery; to the east lay a water cistern and water tower and to the west two large breweries. A tram passed down one side of the Platz, taking people south to Alexanderplatz and north to the ring railway. Each street around the Kollwitzplatz area was lined with ranks of five-story terraces of apartments, known by the visceral term *Mietskasernen,* and, at street level, shops.

the inner city suburb typology

Typically the straight streets of *areas* like Prenzlauer Berg had a hierarchy. An area like Kollwitzplatz was defined by larger *allees* that surrounded it. These are wide arterial thoroughfares that were used to navigate the city as a whole. Leading at right angles off these were smaller streets of two sizes: cross streets that bisected an area defined by the allees and less significant streets that were slightly narrower. Within these areas were usually several small squares. These areas are experienced as self-contained districts with quiet centres and the main arteries of the city at their perimeters. Within an old borough like Prenzlauer Berg, there are a number of smaller subdistricts, the older and more salubrious toward the centre of the city and those less so out toward the perimeter of the city. Buried in the heart of these residential streets were local institutions such as

Figure 17.3 Synagogue on Rykestrasse, Prenzlauer Berg.
(Copyright David Heathcote)

schools, churches, synagogues, hospitals and industrial works. Often these were incorporated into the terraces that lined each street—like Germany's largest synagogue, still on Rykestrasse, Prenzlauer Berg.

These terraces, which still dominate most of Berlin's inner suburbs, were laid out with a practical and decorative uniformity that expresses the rapidity and confident growth of the nineteenth-century city. The most striking feature of the terraces that line the streets of Prenzlauer Berg is that along each of them are many high, vehicle-sized entrances that lead to the interstices between the grid plan of the streets. These entrances were also part of the Hobrecht Plan and were intended to give access to fire engines.

Beyond these entrances, leading back from individual terraced blocks, are more tenements, the *hinterhofs,* normally three deep, each smaller and darker than the last. In one instance, there were thirty hinterhofs in one block in Prenzlauer Berg. These were sequentially cheaper accommodations than the apartment blocks facing the main streets. Sometimes the inner areas contained small works or stables and in a few were even large factories. A whole universe of hinterhofs lay through these gated entrances that were tiny districts in themselves, Dickensian rookeries.

Each district and its hinterland were home to many different classes. The richest lived on the first-floor *belle etage* apartments, facing the street. These apartments were often as wide as the whole terrace building, and the smallest might have only two rooms with a shared toilet on the landings of the communal stairs. The essential layout of these nineteenth-century Berlin apartments did not differ from area to area, and the difference between wealthy and not so wealthy might only be a few details such as balconies and bays and decorated ceilings.

Berlin life in the nineteenth century was for most defined by the idea of the block; living on the

---

Grids

The grid has been one of the most important guiding concepts in design, and its influence can be seen in all fields of design ranging from town planning to graphic design. You can see the powerful influence of the grid in the layouts of today's magazines, newspapers and Web pages, but the formative landmarks were established in the early decades of the twentieth century.

Bau und Wohnung (Building and Home), published in 1927, was designed by Willi Baumeister, a pioneer of the 'new typography' in prewar Europe. It described a famous experimental housing development called Weissenhof in Frankfurt, where leading modern architects built demonstration projects. Both the book and the architecture it presents reveal the use of grids to organize space and design elements. This new typography was rigorously promoted in the famous German design school, the Bauhaus. Baumeister ranked words by size according to their importance in the message. He saw typography as rooted in the movement of the eye and hence necessarily asymmetrical, unlike the old typography of axially symmetrical layouts. Hence, elements move around the cover to activate your interest to open the book, but the calm act of reading down an inside page is disturbed only to signpost its themes or to embrace a visual text. Baumeister's grid is simple, and diversity is created by the ranking of letters and their dynamic placing.

From: C. Cooke, *Design and Designing* (T211), The Open University, Workbook 2 (2010), pp. 36–37.

---

block was akin to being in an urban village, divided from others not by countryside but by wide, busy allees that were uninviting to cross. Communities were forged fast in these environments in a city full of immigrants. Block by quickly erected block, the city housed millions. Places like Prenzlauer Berg were the first stage of the new industrial Berlin that swamped the old Baroque provincial capital of Prussia. However, compared to London, the city remained physically small because of its very practical, high-density, standardized design.

These districts were repeated almost identically across the city between 1870 and 1914 and are the typology of nineteenth-century inner-city Berlin. In time this type, or group of types, proved very flexible, and, necessarily, a second tenet of German design emerged to adjust them to new innovations. To the idea of the type was added the notion that the job of the designer was to incrementally evolve the type until an exterior force, like the mass availability of electricity, enabled the type to make an evolutionary leap to a new type.

suburbs and leisure

By the early 1900s, the wealth generated during the *Grunderzeit*—or foundation period after unification—had generated a familiar reaction: a flight to the suburbs. The wealthy and health conscious sought refuge from the city residential quarters, initially in the nine-kilometre-long area of wood and lakes between Berlin Charlottenburg and Imperial Potsdam known as the Grunewald Forest and Zehlendorf. By the end of the nineteenth century, these suburbs were heavily influenced by the arts and crafts movement. Hermann Muthesius, whose 1905 book *Das Englische Haus* celebrated the style, built several houses in the Grunewald/

Figure 17.4 Zehlendorf housing in Alpine style.
(Copyright David Heathcote)

Zehlendorf, and even the emperor had an English-style house, the Cecilienhof (1912–1917 by Paul Schultze-Naumberg) looking across the water from Potsdam to Zehlendorf. *Das Englische Haus* and its influence is typical of German design. Muthesius was paid by the Prussian government to study new English houses with a view to designing a new form of housing evolved from what it perceived to be an innovative foreign type. Today the Grunewald/Zehlendorf suburbs display houses of several types, many of which show a Germanization of ideas, such as the use of vernacular styles that underpinned arts and crafts architecture.

With these suburbs came a railway branch line with new stations between Berlin Charlottenburg and Potsdam that were linked into Berlin's mass transport system—in this case, the S-Bahn in 1913. Some stations were integrated into suburban shopping villages, such as the development at Mexikoplatz built in 1904–05 by Gustav Hart and Alfred Lesser, which displays characteristics of Jugendstil (art nouveau) as well as arts and crafts. A new more surprising development was a motor car test track and later race track, the Avus (1907–21) built by the Automobil Club von Deutschland between Charlottenburg and the Potsdam end of the Grunewald/Zehlendorf. The Avus became an early example of recycling when, in the late 1930s, it was integrated into the Reichsautobahn road system.

As the Grunewald/Zehlendorf developed from being a riding park for the rich into a residential

Figure 17.5 The Strandbad Wannsee, Europe's largest inland lido. (Copyright David Heathcote)

area for a wider spectrum of the affluent, it also became a focus for the new cult of healthy leisure that swept Europe. The Grunewald/Zehlendorf became a place of exercise, of walking, cycling, picnics and swimming in the small lakes and riverine landscape. By the late nineteenth century, many Berliners used the Grunewald/Zehlendorf as a nearby holiday location. Swimming became popular, beginning with informal places where people could change and swim and that after 1918 were formalized into great lidos like the Strandbad Wannsee (1929–30, Martin Wagner, Richard Ermisch). City bathing resorts were as susceptible to type design as the Villa-Kolonie or the Mietskasernen, and by 1945 there were many similar bathing resorts in Berlin.

Even with the suburbanization that followed the First World War, and more than a million new residents, Berlin didn't grow as radically as cities like London. One reason for this was that post-war residential growth was achieved through the development of a modern rationalization of the dense terraces of inner Berlin; that is, through the evolutionary modernization of the Mietskaserne type. The new Wohnsiedlungen terrace blocks were built with green space and public health in mind. Built containing a smaller range of apartments than Mietkasernen and dispensing with the hinterhofs, which became green space, they retained a compact footprint. In addition they benefited after the mid 1920s from the addition of rationalized kitchens derived from designs for the

Figure 17.6 Frankfurt Kitchen
of 1927.

Frankfurt kitchen designed in 1926 by Austrian architect Margarete Schutte-Lihotzky. This kitchen
type, based on compact ships accommodation,
is an example of the German ability to take one
type and apply it to a new environment, thus creating a new type—in this case, the fitted kitchen.

DDR and GDR

With the Second World War came destruction
and eventual physical partition by the Berlin Wall
in 1961, ushering in a new phase of the city's
development, a period of reconstruction but still
largely within the long-established borders. In East
Germany, the new German Democratic Republic
(GDR) of 1949 made the Russian sector of Berlin into its capital. Thereafter East Berlin became
an advertisement for the virtues of East German
communism. The communist capital included
the Unter den Linden, the old centre, Mitte, and
the great museums of old Berlin around the Muse-
umsinsel (Museum Island). The old buildings were
maintained and restored, though they remain
blackened and pockmarked by war. However, the
Baroque City Castle of Berlin was demolished to
be later replaced by the Palace of the Republic
(1973–76), which, as well as being the parliament,

had a disco, bowling alley, theatre and thirteen restaurants. (This in turn is now demolished and there is a proposal to re-erect a replica of the old City Castle.) More significantly for the GDR regime, it built Karl Marx Allee (1952–60), a kilometre of apartments for workers and professors alike that embodied a vision of future communist affluence, and redeveloped the Alexanderplatz as a showy modernist commercial centre. The futureological Fernsehturm (TV tower, 1965–69) trumped West Berlin's prewar Funkturm (radio tower) at Charlottenburg. The ordinary East Berliners received new housing estates, well designed and idealistic, and the authorities maintained the old transport system, including the trams. They did not develop the automotive infrastructure, leaving the autobahns pretty much as they had been prewar, with the exception of the transit autobahn to West Germany, which was subsidized by West Germany.

In West Berlin the city became not the capital of West Germany but a showpiece of the affluence of the Western world. The United States and West Germany poured money into this little island of capitalism in a sea of communism. While the Kurfurstendamm became its shopping centre, the central area, called the Kulturforum, near the border with the Potsdamer Platz in the East was developed into a showcase of free modern architecture housing various well-endowed cultural institutions such as Scharoun's Berlin Philharmonie (1956–63). Its open interiors were emblematic of the West's architecture war against the East. Where the East had the totalitarian and Stalinesque Karl Marx Allee, in the West, a competition, Interbau, was held in the late 1950s to redevelop a quarter symbolising liberal affluence. The Hansaviertel (1957–61) included buildings by many of the world's leading modern architects, such as Niemeyer and Le Corbusier, who built a

version of his Unité d'Habitation there. In the late 1960s, the West Berlin authorities had a New National Art Gallery built within sight of the East with its old museums, a great glass box by Mies van der Rohe—his last work (1968). Later there was even briefly a magnetic monorail, the M-Bahn (1983–91), leading into the Tiergarten, the largest park in Berlin. Both sides endeavoured to forget the past through modernism. This was the Berlin of the spy movies—the austere ideologue East and the glittering cocktail party of the West.

Berlin would be interesting as a museum of nineteenth- and twentieth-century architecture and planning if there was no 1970s and 1980s. It was what happened in the city in those decades that makes the city the individual place it is today.

counterculture

While both cities, Berlin East and West, developed new architecture to show off the merits of their respective politics, the societies of the two Berlins changed too. In fact the population of Berlin shrank, particularly in the West, as power ebbed away to other, richer parts of West Germany. In the East, reconstruction and general development slowed as the East German and other communist economic systems stagnated. In both parts of Berlin were areas where the old nineteenth-century inner-city suburbs survived in a damaged state. Here accommodation was cheap, unregulated and still in many ways being cobbled back together in a process of ad hoc reconstruction. In the East, Prenzlauer Berg, around the newly named, politically correct, Kollwitzplatz, was an area of big, interesting neglected old apartments, 80 per cent of which dated from before 1945. In the West lies Kreuzberg, another old borough, larger and more diverse than the Kollwitzplatz district of Prenzlauer Berg. Both areas in their own way became the heart of what was to become a new Berlin and for reasons that were unintended by either side.

Kreuzberg, to the southeast of the city centre, developed as an industrialized working-class area in the late nineteenth century, but it was not until it was one of the poorest areas of West Berlin, surrounded on three sides by the Berlin Wall, that it became famous. By the late 1960s, as well as being an area of Turkish *gastarbeiter* immigration, it had begun to attract young people: students, artists and musicians escaping from the affluent conformity of the so-called economic miracle in the rest of West Germany. Rents were low, the buildings were interesting run-down nineteenth-century tenements; many could be, and were, squatted. Kreuzberg became a nonconformist island within the larger island of West Berlin. West Berlin was a place where you could live the countercultural life, exempted from military or government national service simply by living there. Like lower Manhattan in the late 1940s, it became an area of clubs, bars and experimental lifestyles. By the early 1980s, it was a sister to the New York of CBGB's frequented by Iggy Pop and David Bowie (who lived in Schoneberg). More importantly it was a concentration of young West Germans who were in the vanguard of new lifestyles. With all the rock and roll and sexual freedom was a world of alternative schooling, organic food, macrobiotic diets and general greenness. In many ways Kreuzberg defined Berlin in the 1980s. Today Kreuzberg has a population 200 per cent larger than in 1989, it has returned a green minister of parliament to the Bundestag and has the youngest population of any city district in Europe.

Prenzlauer Berg played a similar role for the East Germans. After 1945 it was a neglected area of run-down nineteenth-century buildings that, although damaged, survived the war. In the 1950s, the area was known as Schonhauser Ecke after the area beneath the raised U-Bahn station (Eberswalder Strasse) where East Berlin's Beatniks used to meet. By the 1980s, it was the centre of East Germany's countercultural opposition; writers, intellectuals and political activists liked its neglected gentility close to the Alexanderplatz. Unlike Kreuzberg, Prenzlauer Berg was a place where people were concerned to live progressively but, for obvious reasons, under the radar, and therefore it was an alternative middle-class enclave hidden in a poor, rather neglected, area of inner Berlin. Before unification, Berlin's most progressive populations were young and led alternative lifestyles and were not well-off. They embraced many hippy values: a lack of concern for material things, organicism and the reuse and recycling of material culture. In short, on both sides of the wall the most progressive Berliners believed in sustainability.

gentrification

The fall of the Wall in 1989 unified a city where 100,000 flats lay unoccupied. It was an empty city where property and rents were cheap. In the rest of the developed world, the phenomenon of gentrification, the colonization of neglected areas of cheap but interesting buildings by the children of affluent parents, had existed since the 1960s. This process was usually led by the tastemakers of contemporary culture, typically nonconformist graduates, musicians, designers and artists. In Berlin, while few radicals in Prenzlauer Berg could

Figure 17.7 Gentrification in Prenzlauer Berg. (Copyright David Heathcote)

move West, the ageing Kreuzbergers, kidults who wanted a new place, maybe a bit less noisy than Kreuzberg moved to Mitte and to the Kollwitzplatz area of Prenzlauer Berg. There they had their first children, discovered interior design, had the park made into a playground and developed the local schools. Now it is known as an area of young families, long Sunday breakfasts in genteel cafes and shops for yummy mummies. There is an artisan market in Kollwitzplatz twice weekly.

Though this gentrification is regarded as a disaster by many in Berlin, it perhaps represents the future of sustainable living, not only in Berlin but in Europe. It is the aspirational culture of tomorrow. In gentrified Prenzlauer Berg lives a mature society of all ages who have green habits developed through three generations in many cases. It is a culture ingrained with the habits of reuse learned either by choice in Kreuzberg or by necessity in the old GDR Prenzlauer Berg. As Prenzlauer Berg and Kreuzberg became expensive, the young, culture-rich but money-poor have moved on to other undiscovered districts, and following close behind are the speculators to buy up and restore old dinosaurs like the yuppy-friendly, Stalinist, Karl Marx Allee. But it has its upside. The politicians of the counterculture now have positions of power in the city government, the eco-activist parents pressure the schools and local services to improve. Because of the new green politics of Berlin, the old infrastructures that survived in the East have been restored and rejoined to those in the West. Should it wish to, the city's legislature can act against the gentrifying speculators.

The austerity habits of the East and the island nature of West Berlin have coalesced to form a robust and sustainable urban culture that builds on its past. In the East, the tram system survived long enough to be restored. On both sides, East and West, the old allotments or Schrebergarten have survived long enough to be revived and become the object of eco-gentrification. The old leisure habits of Berlin have likewise survived through a combination of poverty, lack of development and the freezing of expansion caused by Cold War politics. The lakes are still there to be swum in, and the walking and cycling culture of the austere East and countercultural West can flourish in a reunited city and its restored countryside. Recently, the new Prenzlauer Bergers have begun to move back into the suburbs like Grunewald/Zehlendorf attracted by the charms of peace, greenness, gardens and good schools that have lain dormant while the inner city was rediscovered. But with them they bring inner-city habits; dividing too-large, too-expensive villas into apartments and applying the lifestyle of the inner city to the neglected Villa Kolonies.

In the city centre there is still room for new ideas. Booming consumerism has led to new designs which, though fashionable, are founded on the ingrained Berlin love of reuse and remodel sustainability. Alongside Berlin's river, the Spree, abandoned industrial yards have been redeveloped as beach clubs, tiny bits of Ibiza relocated from the Mediterranean. However, this aspect of Berlin culture, which has been so important in developing the modern image of Berlin, is under threat. In 1989, it was not only flats that lay empty; there was a great deal of empty space and many deserted commercial buildings, and these were reused by youthful entrepreneurs as clubs, exhibition spaces and bars and shops. But as Berlin has redeveloped in the past decades, commercial forces have taken over these spaces and redeveloped them so that in formerly exciting areas like Mitte, experimental building and space use has been replaced with international chain stores. The ad hoc and low-rent use of derelict buildings and

Figure 17.8 Biomarkt, Kollwitzplatz. (Copyright David
Heathcote)

spaces was not only a sustainable use of the city,
it was part of Berlin's new identity and its future
sustainability as a creative city. The collusion of
the Berlin City Authority in the commercial development of Berlin's centre has all but stopped the
very sustainable availability of cheap space for
young cultural and commercial entrepreneurs, un-
dermining a unique creative resource for the city.

In Prenzlauer Berg, as well as all the organic
food and biodynamic vinotheques are shops selling remade furniture—old furniture deconstructed
and rebuilt as a kind of eco-modernism. This consumerism can seem glib, but it too represents
a radical change in the design world, because
the equivalence of new, used and reused in the

aspirant consumer's mind represents an unconscious acceptance of many of the precepts of
sustainability.

Berlin's late emergence into the modern, con-
sumer-driven world took place in a culture where
necessity demanded reuse and recycling. This
culture, existing in both East Berlin and countercultural parts of the West, provided a powerful
underpinning to a broad public acceptance of sustainability and sustainable design—certainly more
so than the current sustainability of easily obtain-
able organic food and funky furniture. Because of
Berlin's unique recent history, it finds itself a city
that has not grown much beyond its horse and
pedal boundary and where much of what was

good about the premotorized city still survives. It's a city where a disproportionately large number of sustainability-minded people of many generations and of all political views coexist. This is a population who now influence the direction of the city, a city which is now the capital of the largest economy in Europe. It would be natural to assume that circumstances like these would create a climate of preservation, but in Berlin there is a taste for the new. Modernization is seen as culturally progressive, so the trams are not dispensed with but are modernized. This taste for revival, not preservation, is most evident at the basic level of the most common form of accommodation in Berlin: the apartment. It also reveals the important legacy of type on design.

incremental development of the type

In many parts of the developed world, the idea of a design system based on types, almost platonic forms, might be anathema, but in Germany it is regarded as a norm. If, in a civilized society, the civic realm is the interface between the people and the city, in design the type might be its equivalent. But the search for ideal types has its complications because of the need to embrace development, adaptation and evolution. The idea that types must be continually modified through incremental innovation until a new type emerges has been a key principal in postwar German design. A good example of this design principle is the 1.9-litre Volkswagon diesel engine that began life in the 1970s and in its current computer chip and turbo form is an engine that dominates the world—it has become an ubertype through modification. In the less-elevated world of sustainable Berlin, the

> "Design forms a backdrop to human life, not a disguise for what it lacks."

new Berliner has made the Mietskaserne apartment of the late nineteenth century a type reborn as a sustainable type through retrofitting.

Apartments in Berlin share a great number of similarities. Almost all Berlin flats come in white, and, though good original fittings exist, it is more usual to find the retrofitting of modern floors and doors. Bathrooms are uniformly fitted and tiled in white. Kitchens too tend toward the contemporary and utilitarian—there is very little theatre of cooking. Generally apartments are accessed by common stairs and landings. Thus, except for size, aspect and location, there is little to distinguish one apartment from another or even one district from another. This ubiquity represents not monotony but an approach to design which gives character to the whole city, much as people used to say of the eighteenth-century city. Though this cannot be described as anything more than plain and comfortable, it is cool somehow. Berlin design at every level is based on the idea of standards— standards that deliver a reliable service and quality of life. Design forms a backdrop to human life, not a disguise for what it lacks. It is this combination of ubiquitous comfort and vibrant city life, where excess is balanced by dependability, that makes Berlin cool. Life there is still *gemütlich*—that is, convivial, not just stylish.

sustainability

In Berlin sustainability translates as maintaining standards of affluence while progressively trying to minimize the ecological impact of the city. While type design and incremental retrofitting new technology can make any flat liveable, this idea can only function because its inhabitants— collectively the city population—expect themselves to live in that way. In other words, the civic society of Berlin sees no contradiction between affluence and sustainability, and this is expressed through a new social contract where the citizens try to engage with sustainability in return for the city, its public and private sector, providing an infrastructure that will support sustainability. For design this means that its products must act as a mediator and facilitator between the individual and society, whether it be the design for waste disposal graphics, new products for the retrofitting of old housing, packaging for food products or infrastructures like public transport. Though

> ### "Counter-intuitively, the definition of sustainability lies in the culture of the city, not the rainforest."

this may sound like a recipe for a uniform society, in reality there is as much insubstantial design for the bored consumer in Berlin as anywhere else. But in Berlin transient fashions and a never-ending series of new bars, restaurants and clubs are all underwritten by a recognition that sustainability means a substrata of material standards (designs) that are to be expected and maintained, enabling the surface to be whatever you like. This attitude owes a lot to its unusual history, which has repeatedly had to make necessity the mother of invention to use and reuse the city. In Berlin, East and West, this has come from what would be described elsewhere as counterculture, which in Berlin has always recognized the need for a social contract between the individual and the city—a contract between living things, material things and ideas—each must care for the others. In this equation, sustainability seems a prerequisite for every activity pertaining to the city. Counter-intuitively, the definition of sustainability lies in the culture of the city, not the rainforest.

Designing Milton Keynes

Is it possible to design a city in the same way as one might design a consumer product, an advertising campaign or other types of design output? Consider the following characteristics of the development process of Milton Keynes, the largest of the United Kingdom's 'new towns' that celebrated its fortieth anniversary recently. Today Milton Keynes is home to a quarter of a million people with plans to double in size. It has been the biggest public sector-designed urbanization project in the United Kingdom.

Milton Keynes is located forty miles north of London. It began with framework planning which led, in the late 1960s, to the layout of its grid structure embracing several ancient villages within its greenfield site. The planners learned from the urban regeneration mistakes of older cities such as Glasgow and took time to listen to a wide range of stakeholders, gaining insights to the priorities of different groups. The planning and design was driven by a mission to be people-centred—an early film on the project was titled *A City Begins with People*—and there was a particular focus on facilitating 'meeting, markets and mobility'.

The integration of housing, industry, recreation and transport was modelled in various ways, including using modelling clay built up over a scale plan. Modelling helped define densities, journeys, green spaces and ongoing growth, and it was essential in converting the concept into something buildable and affordable. The designing has continued to the present day as Milton Keynes adapts to becoming a sustainable city.

CHAPTER SUMMARY

- Berlin reveals that key principles of sustainability—such as efficient housing types and mixed urban communities—have been embedded in the city planning and development since the nineteenth century,
- In Berlin sustainability translates as maintaining standards of affluence while progressively trying to minimize the ecological impact of the city.
- The notions of standardization and type bring a rationality to designs ranging from architecture to graphic communication. Types are associated with efficiency, value and the reduction of waste.
- Berlin's progressive populations before unification were young and not well-off. They led alternative lifestyles. In short, the progressives on both sides of the Berlin wall shared an agenda for sustainability.
- The inner city has seen much gentrification. Today it provides a hub for the booming German economy.
- Berlin's modern consumer culture is rooted in the reuse and recycle culture of its past.
- Counter-intuitively, the definition of sustainability lies in the culture of the city, not the rainforest.

---

chapter 18

designing for life cycles

philip a. davies

ABOUT THIS CHAPTER

The abilities that designers display can be astounding. However, the recent priority of sustainability confronts them with new challenges that cannot always be met using old approaches. I believe that sustainability is the most important issue facing the design profession today. Is this belief just a personal opinion, or is it supported by hard scientific evidence? Are there any universal principles and tools to be applied in this area? What are the needs and opportunities for collaborating with other professionals with similar goals? Is sustainable design to be achieved through technological improvement alone, or are there softer, human issues to take into account? This chapter addresses these questions. Sustainable design is a relatively new field; it is not an area of consensus. Therefore, only tentative answers can be provided in some cases. This chapter emphasizes the importance of product life cycles and life cycle assessment (LCA) as a tool for designers. It also discusses some of the limitations of LCA and introduces ideas about systems-level design and emotional factors relevant to sustainable design. First we will look at underpinning facts about mass balance and climate change.

what goes in must come out

Matter is neither created nor destroyed. This basic law of physics is the basis for an important principle known as *mass balance*. Applied to a system, the principle of mass balance tells us that whatever mass of substance enters a system, minus whatever leaves, equals the mass of substance accumulating inside the system (see Figure 18.1). If, over a period of time, the accumulation is zero or negligible, the principle reduces to: *what goes in must come out.*

My local water company applies the principle of mass balance to work out the monthly bill for my house. This bill consists of two charges: one for the amount of clean water entering and another for the waste water leaving the premises. The first is measured by a meter, but there is no meter for the waste water. Nonetheless, the water company uses the principle of mass balance to estimate that the quantity of waste water (not counting rainwater runoff) will equal that of clean water, which is a good approximation. In the case of the house, where the boundaries are physically identifiable in the form of a floor, walls and ceiling, the mass balance principle seems obvious—almost trivial. Much more interesting results come when we apply this principle to abstract systems such as a person's lifestyle, a manufacturing system or the economy of a whole country. For

Figure 18.1 The mass-balance principle applied to a system having a boundary. (Copyright author)

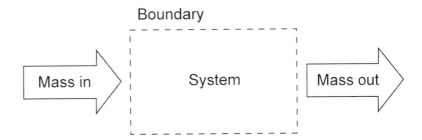

Boundary

Mass in

System

Mass out

instance, a mass-balance study of the manufacturing economy of the United States has revealed that, for every 100 kilograms of raw material input, just 6 kilograms of manufactured output results. The principle of mass balance suggests therefore that 94 kilograms of waste is generated in the process.[1] The 94 kilograms is rarely perceived by most people, because it may be flowing out of the chimneys of factories, into rivers and into the waste bins behind factories. These numbers draw attention to the very large flows of material that are used by industry to sustain the relatively small flows that we encounter in everyday life. Imagine a simple operation such as pouring out a glass of orange juice. To make this possible, amounts of materials many times larger than would fit in the glass had to occur to process the oranges, make the orange juice carton, transport the orange juice and provide services for all the numerous staff involved in manufacturing orange juice.

> "A mass-balance study of the manufacturing economy of the United States has revealed that, for every 100 kilograms of raw material input, just 6 kilograms of manufactured output results."

a closer look at waste

Any material flow must have a source and a destination. If we trace any given flow through its various processes, then both the source and the ultimate destination will be found in the natural environment. Sustainable design is concerned with minimising or controlling such flows so as to minimize harmful effects, particularly on the environment. Clearly wastefulness is not a uniquely US problem; rather it is a feature of industrial economies and systems in general. To get an idea of how much waste is produced in the United Kingdom, for example, try to picture the 20.7 million metric tons of commercial and industrial rubbish consigned to landfill each year.[2] It is enough to fill about 500,000 large lorries. This is such a large amount that the United Kingdom is running short of space to bury it. Improvements in recycling are part of the answer, but we need some creative thinking if we are to reduce our waste mountains such as the 717,000 tons of packaging waste that the United Kingdom exported in 2008.[3]

In general, waste may come in solid, liquid or gaseous forms. Solid waste, such as rubbish in landfills, catches our attention because it is visibly ugly; but the invisible liquid and gaseous waste streams often turn out to be even more noxious in the long term. These may flow into the oceans

Figure 18.2 Bales of crushed aluminium cans ready for recycling. (Getty 108910765 RM)

and atmosphere, eventually spreading over the whole globe, in which case it is very difficult to recover or remove them.

As an example of liquid waste, take phosphorous, which tends to travel through water. This chemical element is present in every cell of every plant and animal, including humans. It is literally part of our DNA. Therefore there is no substitute for phosphorous. We obtain it from our food, which is grown with the help of fertilisers containing phosphorous, mostly in the form of phosphates, which are mined from deposits found in some countries, notably the United States and Morocco.

Phosphorous leaves our bodies in excreta and enters the waste water treatment system. From there, it passes through streams, lakes and rivers before reaching its final destination—the sea. Now if all known reserves of phosphates were dissolved uniformly in the oceans, each ton of seawater would contain just 0.065 grams of phosphorous, which is hardly any greater than the current concentration of phosphorous in seawater.[4] Since there is currently no viable process for extracting phosphorous at such tiny concentrations, this mass-balance calculation highlights that there is a need to restrict carefully the flows of this water-borne substance

Figure 18.3 Ugly solid waste and invisible gaseous waste. Which is worse? (Getty 56529911 RF)

before it becomes diluted to the point where we can no longer recover it. Technical solutions to this problem are being developed. Recovery of phosphorous from waste water is already practiced in some countries. Measures are being introduced in Europe to restrict the dosage of phosphate fertilisers so that none runs off directly into rivers. On the whole, however, much more needs to be done to safeguard our reserves of this precious substance and thus avert future food shortages.

As an example of a waste in gaseous form, consider chlorofluorocarbons or CFCs. Until the early 1990s, CFCs were extensively used as working fluids in refrigerators. However, during the 1980s, scientists became aware that the ozone of the atmosphere was becoming depleted, especially above the Antarctic, where a growing hole in the ozone layer was observed. This caused concern, because the ozone layer is important in filtering out ultraviolet radiation from the sun, which has harmful effects on living organisms, including skin cancer in humans. This depletion of ozone was linked to the CFCs escaping from refrigerators. To reverse this problem, it was agreed by means of the Montreal Protocol (which came into force in 1989) to phase out the use of CFCs. Refrigerators were redesigned to use alternative fluids, and as a result the ozone layer is now recovering.

waste and climate change

Possibly the most publicized type of air-borne waste is carbon dioxide and the other greenhouse gases responsible for global warming and climate change. This topic is so frequently mentioned that there is a danger that we become weary of hearing about it. In case we forget its importance, here are some key facts about climate change:

- Since the end of the eighteenth century, concentrations of greenhouse gases have increased due to burning of fossil fuels, population growth and changing agricultural practices.

- There is evidence that temperatures are rising, rainfall patterns are changing and supplies of food and water are being disrupted, with serious impacts on human well-being, health and survival.
- Those most severely affected are the world's poorest, most of whom live in developing countries which bear some nine-tenths of the burden from these impacts.[5]
- The world's poor are the least responsible for climate change, since they contribute only a small amount to the emission of greenhouse gases. Per capita emissions from developed countries are typically many times higher.

These facts point to an extremely unjust situation. A recent report by the Global Humanitarian Forum brings home the magnitude of this crisis. It estimates that 'every year climate change leaves over 300,000 people dead, 325 million people seriously affected, and economic losses of US$125 billion'.[6] It also points out that the number of people seriously affected (meaning that they need immediate help as a result of climate change) is thirteen times greater than the number injured in traffic accidents. This report makes sobering

Figure 18.4 Reducing greenhouse gases is a global priority. (Getty 84390937 RM)

reading; we *must* face up to the challenge posed by climate change. Because the source of the greenhouse gases lies largely in the products and technologies that we use, designers are very much at the forefront of this challenge. They must devise ways of reducing, removing or reversing the emissions of greenhouse gases, just as they removed ozone-depleting substances from refrigerators in the 1990s.

The changes needed are large. A recent report by the United Kingdom's Committee on Climate Change has concluded that the world needs to halve its emissions of greenhouse gases by 2050.[7] Because emissions by the United Kingdom are large in proportion to its population, and because the world population is growing, the United Kingdom needs to reduce emissions by a factor of five. For other industrialized nations, a similarly large factor applies. This cannot be achieved just by tweaking the technologies we have. To illustrate this, let us suppose that we were to restyle all the cars on our roads to make them slightly more aerodynamic, thus improving the fuel economy. This kind of fine-tuning, though important and worth doing, would not by itself give the level of reduction sought. Much more innovative approaches are needed, such as different engine technologies and fuels, different modes of transport or indeed inventions or lifestyle changes that cut down on travel. Whichever technology area we look at, and whichever environmental issue we consider, we tend to reach similar conclusions: radical changes are necessary, not just slight improvements. So we are talking about redesigning things in a big way. Before we embark on this process, we need some tool of analysis and measurement to help scrutinize product designs and assess our starting point. This tool is called life cycle assessment.

Life Cycles of Designs

Today designers must understand the impacts of their products on the environment throughout their entire life cycles, from planning to disposal. Not only must companies consider the environmental implications of their manufacturing, they need to develop products that are environmentally sound in their use of materials, in their consumption of fossil fuels and which incorporate better reuse, recycling and safer disposal.

The life cycle is a sequence of stages that can be seen in many fields of design. Typically it ranges from raw materials extraction (e.g. mining) and processing (into workable materials), to manufacture and assembly (of these materials into the product), to transport and distribution (of the product), to its use and maintenance (by purchasers and end users) and finally to its disposal, recycling or reuse. This cycle is often referred to as the stages from 'cradle to grave'.

Design teams may exploit distinctly different strategies in their assessments. There are quantitative methods such as life cycle analysis, and various computer-based tools that allow us to see the implications of design actions, such as using an alternative material for a product casing. These can be mixed with strategies that generate qualitative information.

life cycle assessment

Designers tend to focus their efforts on individual products: for example a bottle of lemonade, a motorcycle, a pair of underpants or a digestive biscuit. Therefore it is interesting to apply the principle of mass balance to these simple product units. This is what happens in life cycle assessment (LCA). In LCA we consider all the different stages of a product's life and calculate the mass balance associated with each one. The first stage to consider is the *manufacturing* stage.[8] Most products rely on several factories or processes to manufacture their constituent parts. These factories may in turn receive supplies from several processing plants, mines, forests or other sources of raw material. In LCA, we need to examine all these operations and tot up the mass flows associated with each one. We then need to look at the mass flows associated with the *use stage* of the product, which occurs after it has left the factory. For example a fountain pen uses ink. A car uses petrol. Many products require energy in some form, resulting in mass flows of fuels and materials. Electricity is among the most common forms of energy. Even though there is no mass flow through the mains cable of an electrical product, frequently a power station far away receives coal and emits carbon dioxide in order to provide the electricity. If the electricity comes from a wind turbine, the mass flows will be much less, but still not zero because materials and energy were needed to build the wind turbine and these need to be taken into account. Finally, we need to look at what happens when the product reaches the end of its life. It could be recycled, reducing the raw material requirement for subsequent products, or it could be discarded and release substances to the ground or atmosphere. This is the *disposal stage.*

The entire balance sheet of material inputs and outputs associated with the life cycle of the product is referred to as the *inventory.* Often there are so many items in the inventory that it becomes convenient to use software packages to assist with LCA. These packages use a database of information about the mass flows associated with the manufacture of common materials, such as aluminium or steel, in specific countries where the product might be used. They save the designer the effort of repeating the whole inventory calculation every time such materials are used. The software packages also store information about

> "The reason for doing LCA is so that we can gain information about the environmental and social impacts of products and make decisions about their design or operation so as to reduce these impacts."

all manner of common processes, such as shipping and electricity generation. To give an idea of how extensive product inventories can become, consider a product such as a chain saw. The LCA package *SimaPro* lists some seventy substances involved in the life cycle of a chain saw, though some of them only feature in very small amounts.[9]

The reason for doing LCA is so that we can gain information about the environmental and social impacts of products and make decisions about their design or operation so as to reduce these impacts. The inventory is the basis for calculating these impacts, which—in order to allow meaningful comparisons—must be categorized in some way. For example, *SimaPro* records impacts in three broad categories, according to whether they affect human health, ecosystem quality or resource.[10] Inevitably, these impact calculations rely on scientific models that make assumptions and may be subject to some inaccuracy and debate. Nevertheless they are necessary, as the inventory information alone tells us nothing about the significance of the mass flows associated with the product.

applying life cycle assessment

Sometimes it is possible to do crude LCAs on the back of an envelope, and this is often a good place to start. For example, in my place of work, some washrooms have electric hand dryers whereas others have disposable towels. Which requires less energy throughout its life cycle? The hand dryers use electricity, whereas the disposable towels use paper. It is not too difficult to estimate the energy requirement in each case and compare. The electric dryer comes on for thirty seconds each time and draws an electrical power of 1.4 kilowatts, thus amounting to about 0.012 kilowatt hours (kWh) of electrical energy. The paper towels weigh two grams each and the manufacture of paper requires energy of about 10 kWh per kilogram.[11] Thus 0.02 kWh is required per paper towel, significantly more than the electric dryer uses. In addition, there are other factors such as the transport of the towels to the washroom and removal of the waste towels. These will add to the overall energy requirement of the paper towels. So, here, a manual LCA has straightaway suggested that the electric dryer is the solution requiring less energy, and more sophisticated analysis using software tends to confirm this conclusion.

However, LCA is not always so straightforward. One difficulty arises from processes with several inputs and outputs. A sawmill, for example, uses the same process of sawing to convert logs into both planks and sawdust. So should we count the electricity used by the sawmill as belonging to the planks or to the sawdust? We could choose the planks on the basis that it is the main product while the sawdust is by-product. However, it turns out that sawdust has many uses (e.g. it can be made into fibreboards or burnt to produce energy), so this solution hardly seems satisfactory. Other approaches include allocating in proportion to the mass of the two products or on the basis of their economic values.[12] In the end, there is no right answer. This is a quandary for LCA but an opportunity for those designing the process. If the efficiency of a whole process (of which sawing logs is just a simple example) is improved, then gains will accrue for all the products downstream. There are many potential advantages to collaborative working between, for example, the process engineer and the product designer, because this brings to light an overall picture of the product life cycle and the significance of the different processes within it.

Another kind of difficulty arises when it comes to interpreting the results of an LCA to determine which design options are better or worse. Value judgements that are not purely scientific enter the picture. This is especially true if the impacts are in different categories or if they affect different people in different ways or over different time scales. How can we compare pollution of a lake to climate change? The first is a local issue, whereas the second is global. Or how would we judge the construction of a hydroelectric dam? It may provide a source of renewable energy and help slow climate change in the long term. But the immediate consequence is that people are evicted from their villages and wildlife habitats are destroyed as valleys are flooded. So in this case there is a conflict of time scales. If we look deeply into any LCA, we are likely to find similar dilemmas.

A further type of uncertainty arises with products where the user behaviour has a big influence. Here is an example from the United Kingdom, where a controversy has arisen over disposable versus reusable nappies (US: diapers). In response to the controversy, the UK Environment Agency has overseen a detailed LCA comparing the two options.[13] There are many factors to consider, such as the energy efficiency of the washing machine used to launder the nappies, its water consumption, the temperature of the wash, the

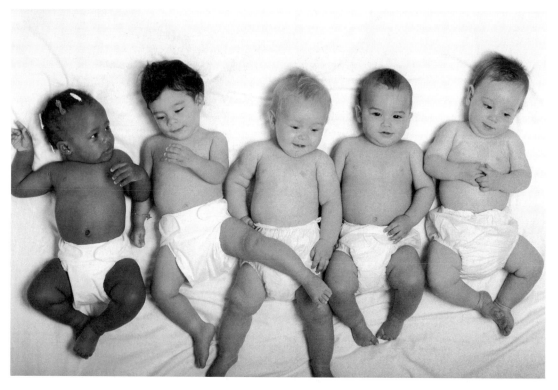

Figure 18.5 Which type of nappy (diaper) is better for the environment: disposable or washable? (Getty 78468481 RF)

size of the load, whether the nappies are tumble-dried or dried outdoors on a line, etc. Thus the study was unable to reach a verdict about which type of nappy is better for the environment, concluding: 'it is consumers' behaviour after purchase that determines most of the impacts from reusable nappies'.

Rather than try to deal head-on with the dilemmas and controversies raised by LCA, the role of the designer is to invent new alternatives that overcome the disadvantages of the current options and thus reframe the debate altogether. For example, biodegradable disposable nappies are now becoming available. And new washing machines using ultrasonic transducers may reduce the need for energy and chemicals in laundering

reusable nappies. This illustrates how LCA is not the end point of sustainable product design; instead it is frequently the starting point. All designers should have it in their toolkit.

efficiency

An important outcome of LCA is that it shows the relative impact of the different stages of the life cycle: manufacture, use and disposal. If one stage has a much higher impact than the others, then this is a good place to start making improvements. Now it turns out that for many (but not all) products, the biggest impact comes from the use stage. This is likely to be true, for example,

Figure 18.6 The biggest impact of many types of product occurs during the use stage. (Getty 83120284 RF)

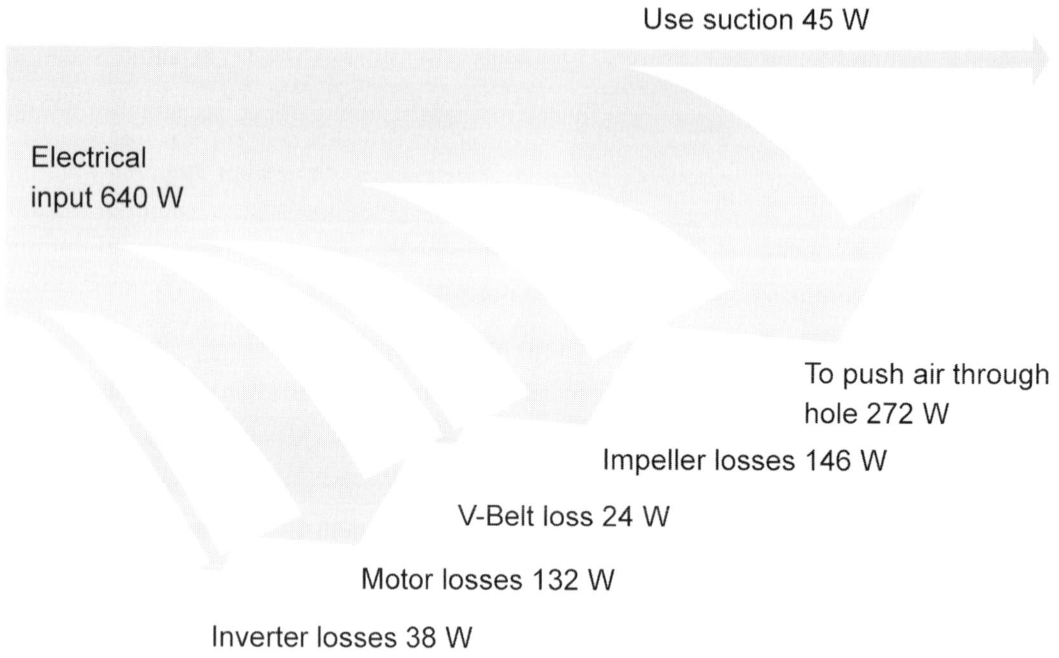

Use suction 45 W

Electrical
input 640 W

To push air through
hole 272 W

Impeller losses 146 W

V-Belt loss 24 W

Motor losses 132 W

Inverter losses 38 W

Figure 18.7 Sankey diagram for the greenhouse cooling
fan. (Copyright author)

of a hairdryer, a mobile phone, a car or a building. Further, within the use stage, it is often energy
usage that is the key issue. Therefore it is very
important to improve the efficiency of products so
that they use less energy during their lives.

Energy is a very well defined quantity in physics and subject to exact laws of thermodynamics.
Like mass, it cannot be created or destroyed, and
there are precise constraints regarding conversion
of energy from one form to another. Thus it is possible to write mathematical equations quantifying
energy conversion for many types of physical process. Examples include flows of fluids (e.g. in a
pump or around an aeroplane wing), processes
using electricity and magnetism (e.g. electric
motors and generators) and those involving mechanics of solid bodies (e.g. gears, axles, screw
threads and levers). This means that we can often

do calculations to pinpoint inefficiencies in products containing this kind of stuff and predict how
changes to the design may improve the situation.

Efficiency is about getting products to do more
per unit of energy used. So to improve efficiency,
it is first necessary to have a clear idea about the
function of the product. Here is an example, from
my own experience, about redesigning a fan used
to ventilate a large greenhouse. In this case, the
function is to move air. To do so, the fan has to
overcome some resistance to the airflow. In this
example, the resistance occurred where the air
passed through some large porous cooling pads.
Based on the appropriate mathematical equations for this situation, I was able to work out
that the minimum energy needed to move the air
would be 45 joules per second, in other words a
power input of 45 watts (W). Therefore it would

be impossible for the fan motor to require less than 45 W. However, the amount of power actually used was 640 W, suggesting that the fan was operating with an efficiency of only 45/640 = 7 per cent. Where was the remaining 595 W getting wasted?

To visualize this kind of situation, it is convenient to draw a Sankey diagram, as in Figure 18.7. This shows the various energy inputs and outputs to the system using arrows of proportionate size. It can be seen that losses occur in various components: 132 W in the electric motor, 24 W in the drive belt, etc. The largest loss is associated with the fan aperture (i.e. hole), since air has to be accelerated at this point in the system, requiring 272 W of energy. Once this bottleneck was identified, the efficiency was readily improved by increasing the diameter of the aperture for a given airflow or by using the same aperture with a smaller airflow. This done, however, other sources of inefficiency gained importance. The inefficiency of the motor and belt became more significant at the lower speeds of rotation used to achieve this smaller airflow. Consequently, these components had to be swapped for more suitable types. As a result of such a series of changes, the power input for a given amount of air moved was reduced by nearly 70 per cent; in other words, the efficiency was improved some threefold. A further benefit was that, with the smaller energy consumption, it became economic to connect the fan to a solar panel and dispense with the mains electricity supply.

systems thinking

To make improvements in efficiency, frequently it is important to view products not in isolation but as part of a system. This was the case with the greenhouse fan, where I optimized the new fan specifically for the type of ventilation system of which it was part. Why hadn't the professional fan designers beaten me to it? Not because they lacked scientific knowledge about fans, but because they could not see each application where the fans were used. So they designed their fan to cope with the situations where resistance to airflow was highest. Even if this meant consuming more electricity than needed for most applications, no customer would complain about that; whereas some might complain if ever the fan failed to move enough air. The fan was like a forty-ton lorry carrying a one-ton load—it works but it's not efficient. The term *systems thinking* is often used to describe design improvements achieved through analysing systems at various levels. It is one of the most important routes to sustainable design. Often it requires not only new technical solutions but changes in how design activities are managed and shared among designers dealing with different parts of the system.

On the topic of energy efficiency, consider another example: the purification of drinking water from seawater. As a resource, water is even more important than oil, as no one can survive more than a few days without water. However, in many arid regions, fresh water is in short supply and the only option is to extract it from the sea by separating the salt—a process called desalination. Due to the large quantities of water needed, however, energy usage is a matter of concern in desalination. To reduce the energy input of desalination has required a concerted team effort, as a desalination plant consists of several components each designed by specialists. Pumps pressurize the seawater, which is fed to membranes that allow the water to pass while retaining the salt. At the outlet of the system, there is an ingenious device that recovers energy from the outgoing water and uses it to boost the pump at the inlet. Systems for control and monitoring and for adding small quantities of chemicals are also needed. Over the last decade or so, hundreds of specialists with varying expertise have worked to refine the design of these different components of the whole desalination system. As a result of this Herculean effort, the

amount of energy to desalinate one cubic metre of seawater using state-of-the-art equipment has gone down from about 4 kWh to 3 kWh.

As in the example about nappies given earlier, the efficiency of products should not be considered in isolation from the behaviour of people that use them. Otherwise there is a danger that user behaviour may thwart attempts by designers to reduce environmental impact through technical improvements. Think about electric cars. Compared to conventional vehicles running on petrol or diesel, overall these are more energy efficient and can use energy from renewable sources such as wind turbines or solar panels. Even if the batteries of the cars are charged using electricity coming from conventional power stations using coal, oil or gas, these large power stations are usually more efficient than a conventional car engine. As a result, electric cars generally have less impact on the environment and cost less to run, per kilometre, than standard cars. However, if electric vehicles become popular, there is a danger that people will drive more kilometres per year, because they can afford to and because they feel that the environmental impact per kilometre is lower. As a result, the environmental benefits from the introduction of electric vehicles may not be fully realized, and we may be back to square one.

emotion and behaviour

The phenomenon outlined above, of not making expected efficiency gains, is called rebound, and it has been observed in relation to a number of products such as low-energy light bulbs and high-efficiency boilers for heating houses. Low-energy bulbs are cheaper to run, so people install more of them and leave them on for longer.

Why Don't People Recycle More?

There are many reasons why people don't embrace recycling. Some consumers still aren't aware of how important recycling is. Others base their purchasing decisions on product use rather than product disposal. People are rarely prepared to bear the costs of recycling where there is no immediate benefit to themselves. These barriers to recycling are being addressed by legislation, particularly in developed nations.

The environmental drivers of recycling are complex. For example increased recycling is not always accompanied by reduced energy consumption. In Europe, cars are required to satisfy increasingly strict regulations on recycling and efficiency. However, the number of cars and their engine sizes continue to rise through market demand created by user preferences.

Design can have particular consequences for disposal and recycling. Being able to separate components made from different materials allows separate recycling. The way parts are joined together will determine how easily they can be separated, and the number of parts will affect the costs of disassembly. For example, the front of a microwave may use many different materials: glass for the window, coated metal for the door, a plastic handle, a liquid crystal display, plastic buttons and so on. For effective recycling, all these have to be disassembled. The decisions taken in the conversion of a concept design to a detailed design have a considerable influence on the environmental impacts of the final product.

From: C. F. Earl, *Design and Designing* (T211), The Open University, Blk 4 (2010), pp. 34–35.

Heating becomes cheaper, so people live in warmer homes. However, rebound does not mean that designing for energy efficiency is a waste of time. Rather it highlights the need for designers to interact with makers of energy policy to ensure that it is part of an overall strategy to reduce energy usage. Policy measures to control fossil energy usage can include, for example, carbon taxes, carbon quotas or regulations concerning specific product categories.[14] Rebound happens when consumers reason: 'It's gotten cheaper, so I'll use more of it'. Though frustrating for sustainable designers, this is at least rational behaviour. In contrast, some products elicit responses of a more emotional kind.

A salient example is bottled water. Most supermarkets offer several brands of still mineral water, with prices ranging from cheap to very expensive. In comparison, tap water in the United Kingdom costs only about 0.1 pence per litre. You can easily carry out your own blind test, in which you ask a friend to say which type of water tastes better without having seen the label. In such tests people usually cannot distinguish among brands of bottled water, or even between bottled water and good-quality tap water. Given that the activities of bottling, shipping and disposal result in bottled water consuming vastly greater quantities of energy and resources than tap water, consumer preference for bottled water appears to

Figure 18.8 Fair-trade coffee farmer, Uganda.
(Getty 90423635 RM)

be in direct contradiction to the efforts to improve the efficiency of fresh water production through desalination as mentioned above. Why should people be ready to pay a hundred times more for water that does not really taste any different? The explanation lies in the emotional lure of the attractive bottle and the desirable and trustworthy brand shown on its label. Though this example of bottled water is useful for showing the role of emotions in design, it would be simplistic to imply that we are usually rational beings who occasionally let emotions get the better of us. In fact the distinction between rational and emotional behaviour is often quite hazy. Think of something you bought recently—were you being emotional or rational on that occasion? Typically, it is not so easy to unravel. Almost all decisions about products involve emotions at some level. This is simply because emotions reflect what we value in a product. The outcome of this emotional involvement may be negative sometimes, but it can equally well be positive. For example at the moment there is a huge market in fair-trade products because people feel angry about exploitation of workers in factories and farms where some other products originate—they value knowing that their purchase supports fair working conditions and investment in social projects.

Similarly, there is no reason why emotions cannot drive consumers towards positive decisions in reaction to the unsustainable use of resources, pollution or the effects climate change—if they have the choice. Designers can and should make such choices available. To do so, they need to be ready to engage with both the hard science of energy efficiency and the softer aspects of human behaviour that determine the success or failure of products in the real world.

CHAPTER SUMMARY

- Global warming, caused by increases in carbon dioxide, is currently resulting in much human suffering, damage to ecosystems and economic loss.

- The need for sustainable design follows from the obvious but frequently neglected principle of mass balance—what goes in must come out.

- Mass balance applies to movements of solids, liquids and gases. Liquids and gases, though invisible, can pose the greatest threat because they are difficult to remove or recover once dispersed in the environment.

- Life cycle assessment (LCA) is central to sustainable design, as it links specific mass flows and their impacts on the environment with features of products over which designers have control. LCA can assist with design choices and identify where to focus design activity.

- Energy efficiency is key to reducing the environmental impact of many products. The greatest energy consumption often occurs during the product use stage, as opposed to the manufacture and disposal stages.

- The scientific approach of making products more efficient is not always enough. The designer must also engage with the emotional responses of consumers towards products.

- Life cycle assessment frequently suggests that whole systems, not just individual products, need to be considered. We need better collaboration by designers of different parts of systems. Equally important is collaboration with engineers that design manufacturing processes and with those people who make policies regulating how products are deployed and used.
- Sustainable design requires radical, rather than incremental, improvements to existing products and systems. This calls for unprecedented levels of creativity and innovation.

chapter 19

is sustainable design viable?

tom greenwood

ABOUT THIS CHAPTER

The twentieth century saw huge changes in consumer culture and design, with mass production and globalization delivering cheap goods to the general public and causing a significant shift in the way we consume. Products that were once accessible only by the rich were made available to almost everyone—at least in developed countries. Items that used to last a lifetime could be used once and thrown away, and we were introduced to a huge array of so-called life enhancing products that we never knew we needed. Material standards of living had never been so high, but towards the end of the century, concerns were raised about the rate at which we were consuming our resources and about the true environmental and social cost of our industrialized economy. This chapter is about this journey of realization. If consumption has to change, then surely there are major implications for design and designing in the years ahead.

---

the cost of consumption

Concerns about the social and environmental costs of mass consumption are not new. In the 1960s and 1970s, pioneers such as Victor Papanek and Rachel Carson spoke out about the dangers of mass consumption, adding concepts such as 'design for the environment' and 'design for society' to the design debate. Now in the early part of the twenty-first century, it is clear that many of their fears were well founded. As Figures 19.1 and 19.2 reveal, increasing greenhouse gas emissions such as carbon dioxide, methane and nitrous oxide are mirrored by significant increases in global temperatures, threatening the stability of the ecosystems that we rely on for food and water. It's hardly a surprise that we have seen an increase in hurricanes, droughts, and wildfires as well as rising sea levels.

Our consumption of natural resources continues to accelerate, causing finite supplies of materials such as oil, coal and natural gas to deplete, threatening our future ability to produce energy, material goods and food. Almost every aspect of our lives—from the plastics in products, the fibres in our clothes and detergents with which we wash to the energy we consume and the fertilizers used to grow our food—is derived from oil.

As supplies reduce, prices rise, and we have no clear alternatives. Species are being lost from the global ecosystem at a rate of around 27,000 species per year[1] as we cut down more forests and hedgerows for industrial farming, not just to feed our growing population but increasingly to

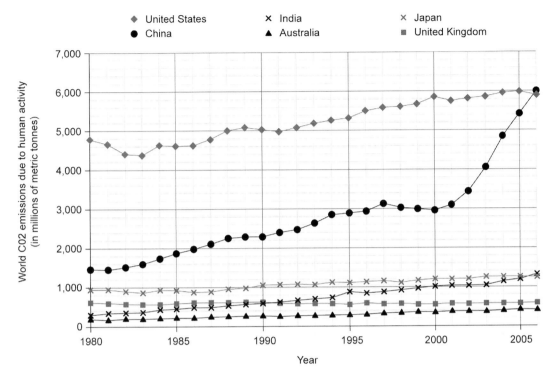

Figure 19.1 Selected global carbon dioxide emissions (1980–2006).
From: U.S. Energy Information Administration, Dec 2008.
http://www.eia.gov/iea/carbon.html.

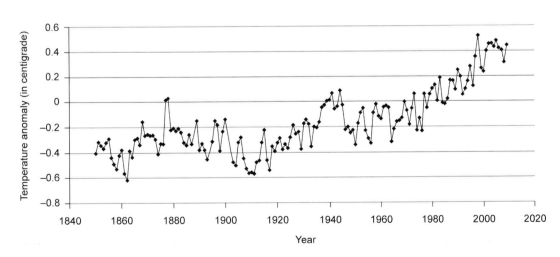

Figure 19.2 Selected global surface temperatures (1850–2009).
From: U.S. Energy Information Administration. See also
http://en.wikipedia.org/wiki/File:Instrumental_Temperature_
Record_(NASA).svg.

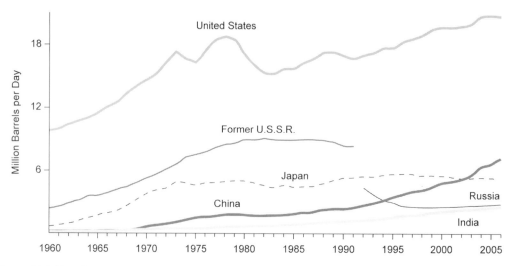

Figure 19.3 Top oil-consuming countries (1960–2006).
From: U.S. Energy Information Administration, *Annual Energy Review 2009,* http://www.eia.gov/FTPROOT/other/perspectives_2009.pdf (accessed 23 April 2011), Fig. 63, p. XXXIV.

produce biofuels and plastics. And as our consumption continues, we also continue to generate huge volumes of waste, with the United Kingdom producing around 20 million metric tons of landfill waste per year[2] and the United States producing over 130 million tons.[3]

We exist in a global community, and many of the issues we face, such as climate change, pollution of the oceans and depleting resources, affect all nations. Weather patterns are likely to become more extreme and unpredictable while both fuel and food become more expensive, causing many to struggle to keep themselves warm and fed. We've already seen examples of extreme weather, such as France's heat wave in the summer of 2003, which killed more than 11,000 people; the cold winter of 2007 in which more than 22,000 UK pensioners died; and, of course, Hurricane Katrina in New Orleans, which killed almost 1,500 people in 2005 despite 90 per cent of southeast Louisiana being successfully evacuated. Within

our lifetimes, the problems that we've created will cause major social unrest. We cannot insulate ourselves from these problems; our global systems tie us into dependencies. For example, Russia and the Middle East increasingly supply Europe's energy, the West depends on China for many products and India for clothes. Increasingly some countries depend on South America and Africa to produce selected food items. It would be very naive to believe that we will not be affected by problems in other parts of the world and to believe that our society and economy can survive without them. Our continued commitment to unsustainable consumption is fuelled by our ignorance of the issues. Many have a blind belief that we will find a technological fix to any problems if and when they occur, and assert that taking action now is simply too expensive. Yet the cost of inaction is even higher. The 2006 Stern Review on the economics of climate change, commissioned by the UK government, estimated the global financial

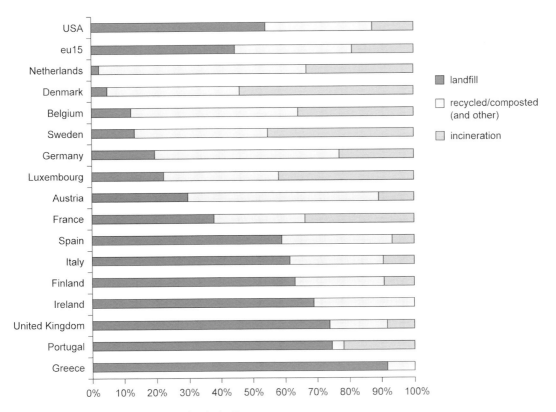

Figure 19.4 Comparison of how countries deal with waste: landfill, recycling and incineration.
From: Based on European Commission, Eurostat.
http://epp.eurostat.ec.europa.eu/statistics_explained/index.php/Municipal_waste_statistics.

cost of climate change at £3.68 trillion unless it is tackled within a decade.[4] On a social level, the United Nations has predicted that, by 2050, more than one billion people could be forced to leave their homes due to drought, famine and rising sea levels.[5] We have reached a critical stage in history that requires us to take immediate and radical action or face irreversible consequences that threaten our entire way of life.

what's design got to do with it?

The issues that we are facing are both near and real. Partly they are cultural and political issues. It could be argued that the changes that took place over the past century were complex socioeconomic issues in which designers, like everybody else, were just professionals doing their jobs. However, in a world facing problems insurmountable by any individual or organization, we must all ask what we can do as professionals. We as designers clearly do have the opportunity to improve the health of society and the natural environment. We are trained to find creative solutions to problems, constantly ask questions and always strive for perfection. It is largely this ingenuity and determination that we have to thank for the developments in material quality of life over the past century, such as improved health care, improved transportation, better facilities for the disabled and greatly improved telecommunications. Designers, more so than many, play a critical role in shaping our world. In a world of mass production, virtually everything—including packaging, clothes, buildings, vehicles, computer systems and even food—are professionally designed. Business managers and marketing departments may well in many cases provide the design briefs, but they are integral members of the design team. From conception of the idea through to the final design that transforms the brief into something viable and tangible, it is designers that shape our world. Designers are experts in the aesthetic, functional and commercial benefits of good design. Now, in the same way we need to be informed about the potential social and environmental impacts of our work. Only as informed professionals can we design for the new context we find ourselves in; to create products and services that are not just commercially but also environmentally and socially beneficial. With information now so easily available, designers at all levels—from students to senior designers in large corporations—have the opportunity to take issues of sustainability seriously. We now need to recognize that good design is sustainable design.

design in context

A large part of the problem of industrial design is that practitioners are often trained and employed to design artefacts. A typical design brief might state something like:

Design a free-standing bread toaster with two vertical slots large enough to hold thick slices of bread, a high-lift mechanism to make it easy to remove the toasted bread, a removable crumb tray, browning adjustment knob and a removable croissant warming rack. The toaster should be no larger than 300 millimetres wide, 180 millimetres in height and 200 millimetres in depth. It should have a brushed stainless steel finish to match other kitchen appliances.

Briefs that specify the end product so clearly deny the designer the opportunity to investigate and therefore solve the real problem. In this case, the problem is not that the consumer needs a toaster with two toast slots, a croissant warming rack and a stainless steel finish but that the consumer needs a convenient and effective method of toasting bread, warming croissants, and so on in a product that looks attractive within the kitchen environment. If the design brief provides all the answers, then the designer has little scope to demonstrate his or her abilities and produce truly innovative solutions. Even more significantly, though, the brief describes no real social, environmental or even business context in which the product will operate. Even with the best of intentions, a product or service designed in isolation is unlikely to provide any great benefits to its users or the wider society.

Sustainability in a literal sense is quite simply the ability of a system to be sustained. Obvious as this may sound, it highlights the fact that sustainability is about systems rather than artefacts. There is no such thing as a sustainable product, only sustainable businesses, lifestyles and ecosystems. Designing for sustainability therefore requires us to take a much broader and more informed perspective, recognising that all products and services are integral parts of social, environmental and financial systems. Products designed in context can be specifically tailored to deliver positive results, not just for the balance sheet of the manufacturer but also to society and the natural world.

design for the environment

Design for the environment and *eco-design* are terms commonly used in reference to sustainable design. While these terms do not represent sustainability in its full sense, they do highlight that design has a major impact on the natural environment. The products that we design are responsible for the destruction of natural habitats, consumption of finite resources, emission of air and water pollutants and the dumping of waste materials. As designers we need an understanding of how good design can be used to minimize these impacts.

The concept proposed by Edwin Datchefski that all products should be 'cyclic, solar, safe and efficient' provides a simple but reliable starting point.[6]

Cyclic recognizes that all materials are finite and will eventually run out if they are not returned into the material system to be used again. The life of a product is usually considered like human life, from cradle to grave. Sustainability however, requires us to think of materials as living from cradle to cradle, constantly being reincarnated at the end of their useful life, sometimes by people who reuse or recycle them to create another product or by nature, which absorbs them as nutrients back into the biosphere.[7]

Solar refers to the use of renewable energy throughout a product's life—in production, transportation, use and disposal. This could come in any form from solar heat to wind-generated electricity to human power. A product designed for sustainability will aim to eliminate the use of finite energy supplies such as oil, gas and even nuclear-generated energy during its life cycle.

Safe simply means that the product should not pose a physical threat to the environment, whether it be in a literal sense such as plastic bags choking marine life or through the emission of harmful chemicals into water, air and soil.

Efficient recognizes that even renewable and recyclable resources are limited in quantity and that we cannot afford to waste them if we are going to meet the needs of a growing global population.

Sustainable Design in 1870

The Austrian, Michael Thonet (1796–1871), and his brothers developed the first chairs to be produced in very large quantities to standardized designs. Their designs were based on techniques of steam bending locally sourced beech wood that were invented and patented by Michael Thonet in the mid nineteenth century.

The cross-section of the wood used was round and of small diameter (typically twenty to thirty millimetres), and steaming gave a range of long curved shapes. The bentwood components were then screwed, bolted and glued together using batch production techniques. Thonet chairs were utilitarian, unpretentious and cheap. They became the standard furniture for Viennese cafés and later for French and German interiors. They were perceived as outside the culture of artistic taste, yet they became commonplace throughout Europe and remain so today. Some of Thonet's designs, with only small variations, continue to be produced.

As well as producing sustainable chairs, Thonet's process advanced thinking about mass manufacture. He simplified production with preprocessing of materials, standardization, use of interchangeable parts, division of labour and the packaging of furniture in parts for local assembly. All these elements are now thought of as essential to modern mass production.

The basic principles of design for the environment are very simple, but applying them in reality is a far more intricate and skilled job. A product's life cycle can be extremely complicated, and many aspects of it will be out of the designer's control. However, designers can use their influence to enable more positive solutions to be developed, even when critical factors are not within their scope of influence. For example, the designer is unlikely to have any significant control over the method of transport used to distribute the product for sale, but he or she can deploy other strategies such as specifying a manufacturing technique that is available close to the point of sale, minimising product weight and designing for efficient stacking so that the maximum number of product units can be fitted into a shipping container. Well-conceived and well-executed design strategies can reap significant environmental rewards.

design for society

A product or service also has a wide array of social impacts throughout its life cycle that are just as important as environmental issues. Good design can have many positive impacts, such as improving safety, encouraging healthy lifestyles, providing education, strengthening communities, creating employment, fighting crime, saving time and, of course, giving people joy, fun and excitement. It is these positive social aspects that are often the key selling features of a product or service, providing both physical and emotional benefits to consumers that they're willing to pay for. These benefits are also often the motivation that draws creative individuals to pursue careers in design, excited by the opportunity to enrich people's lives. In contrast to these benefits, though, many products and services also have unintended negative consequences for society. This can include sweatshop labour in production, risk of injury during production and transportation, damage to the user's health, encouraging antisocial behaviour, excluding those with disabilities, increasing dependence on technology, reducing choice and reducing freedom.

When designing for social benefit, we should aim to ensure that our product or service is fit, fair and safe.

Fit refers to fit for purpose, meaning that the products we create perform their function. This could be something very practical such as drilling holes or something softer and more emotional

Figure 19.6 Do you know who made your clothes, where and in what conditions? (Getty 99277676 RF)

such as providing joy and entertainment. Whatever the intended purpose of the product, the first step of good social design is to meet the functional needs of the user.

Fair acknowledges that products and services have a wider role in society than simply providing a function to the people who purchase them. For

---

Eight Eco-design Guidelines

The following list of qualitative design guidelines is based on recommendations published by PRé Consultants in the Netherlands (www.pre.nl/ecodesign/ecodesign.htm).

1. Understand the whole life cycle: Consider the whole process from the beginning of one product life cycle to the beginning of another (cradle to cradle).
2. Natural materials are not always better: There may be hidden energy and environmental costs with natural materials.
3. Think 'energy': Energy consumed in use will often be far greater than energy consumed in manufacture. In design, think 'energy' rather than 'materials'.
4. Increase product life span: There are clear environmental benefits if a design can be made more durable, upgradable and attractive for long-term use.
5. Design services rather than products: Sometimes a service can offer a better solution to real-life problems—for example car-sharing schemes are becoming popular in Europe.
6. Use a minimum of material: Exploit design thinking rather than simply adding material. Do more with less. Reducing weight will reduce transport costs.
7. Use recycled materials: There are a lot of recycled materials available, but few companies are using them. Use design to improve the status of recycled materials.
8. Make your product recyclable: Many products *can* be recycled, but very few *will* be. Design for disassembly and easy recognition.

---

example, factory workers should not be exposed to hazards, the public should not be subjected to air and noise pollution and people with disabilities should not be excluded from activities such as travelling by bus or train.

Safe to some extent overlaps with *fair,* but it emphasises the specific risk to personal health and safety that can be caused by products, not just through accidents but also in terms of less-visible risks such as repetitive strain injuries, toxic chemicals and radiation.

Designers cannot control all of the social impacts of their designs, particularly when it comes to issues such as fair trade in production and distribution, which are often issues of company policy rather than design. However, designers do have a big opportunity to reduce the social burden of their designs and create products that truly enhance peoples' lives. A great deal can be achieved for example by using only nontoxic materials, applying the principles of good ergonomics and inclusive design and using intuitive design to make it simple and pleasurable to use products and services responsibly. With careful consideration of people's physical and emotional needs, everyone can benefit from good design.

the techno-fix

The designer must consider a broad range of issues when designing for social and environmental sustainability. Sustainable design is typically seen as a technical challenge that, through good engineering and the application of new technologies, will improve efficiency, improve performance and increase safety. However, technological fixes rarely provide a perfect solution. For example, ozone-depleting gases such as chlorofluorocarbons have been replaced as refrigerants and blowing agents by hydrogen-based gases, but these are still greenhouse gases contributing to climate change. Similarly, energy-efficient compact fluorescent light (CFL) bulbs use significantly less energy than standard incandescent bulbs but also contain mercury and, in some cases, printed circuit boards, which can be difficult to dispose of safely. We certainly should not play down the benefits of technology, but we do need to recognize that it is not the answer in itself.

It is the soft, emotional side of design that can reap the greatest rewards by influencing behaviour and culture. Human-centred design can encourage more sustainable lifestyles and behaviour in the truest sense. For example, a state-of-the-art hybrid or electric car can provide incremental reductions in energy consumption and reduce inner-city emissions, yet a city cycle hire scheme like the one in Brisbane, Australia, or the Vélib scheme in Paris can produce much greater emission reductions, as well as reduce noise pollution and congestion, reduce the danger posed by cars to pedestrians and provide a healthy, affordable and convenient mode of transport to the general public.

Such benefits can be greatly enhanced when combined with a well-designed, comprehensive network of cycle lanes and emotive branding and marketing that make it socially desirable to travel by bike. Of course, cycle schemes do not offer a direct alternative to the car commercially, but they do highlight the social and environmental benefits that are possible by focusing on lifestyles rather than technology. In fact, the limits of technology are demonstrated by basic physics. Any technological improvement will have a maximum possible efficiency. The laws of physics dictate

Figure 19.7 Cycles at a docking station in Brisbane. (Copyright author)

the amount of energy required to boil a litre of water, cook a chicken or light a room at night and therefore provide us with a theoretical maximum efficiency for any given scenario. These theoretical limits are often far better than current actual best practice, with much of the energy, water and material we consume literally being wasted. However, with current predictions stating that we need somewhere between 60 per cent and 80 per cent reduction of carbon dioxide emissions by 2050[8] to avoid the worst effects of climate change, it is clear that technological efficiency alone cannot provide the answer. For example, if a high-efficiency twenty-watt CFL bulb has an efficiency of approximately 20 per cent in terms of converting electricity to visible light, then this means that only four watts are actually required to provide the same level of light, and the remaining sixteen watts are wasted. If a bulb could be developed that was 100 per cent efficient, then it would just achieve the 80 per cent reduction in energy consumption that we are aiming for. However, if we consider that 100 per cent efficiency is an unachievable ideal and the fact that if light bulbs are more efficient, people will be less vigilant about switching them off when leaving the room, then we will still be some way off our target. If we want to make big steps forward, then we need to adopt a more human approach to design, not just improving technical efficiency but helping people live more sustainable lifestyles.

the business dilemma

The need for fast, radical and genuine action to develop more sustainable products and services is well recognized by society, government and business leaders. Many businesses now have in-depth sustainability and corporate social responsibility policies highlighting their commitment to building a sustainable future. However, the reality is that virtually all of these policies are not genuine sustainability plans but rather damage limitation plans, totally incapable of delivering real sustainability. It's easy to condemn businesses for their lack of commitment, but we need to recognize that businesses and the designers employed by them face a serious dilemma. Each business has developed its own formula for success that it is understandably reluctant to change. If a car manufacturer or a book publisher that has been trading successfully for several years or decades is told that it needs to radically redesign its business model for sustainability, then it is being told to take a step into the unknown, and it is only natural that it would see this as a big risk. And it's not just businesses that are resistant to change. Consumers have deeply ingrained cultural and habitual behaviour patterns. They won't change their lifestyles without good reason, and, as behaviour is largely emotional rather than rational, even good reason will, in many cases, be insufficient.

Marketing sustainable products is therefore a particularly difficult challenge. Companies that do take the plunge and develop more sustainable products and services naturally want to show off their good work. Yet despite the majority of consumers saying that they would like to purchase more ethical goods and services, when it comes to actually forking out hard-earned cash, there is a widespread scepticism towards green and ethical products.[9] Consumers' doubts may, to some extent, be irrational, but they cannot be ignored. A sustainable product or service that nobody wants to buy has no benefit to anyone. So, if we are going to make radical changes towards sustainability that are commercially viable, we need to

> "It may sound like a contradiction that radically different products and services should appear familiar, but that is part of the design challenge that we face."

ensure two things. First, that consumer fears are unfounded, because sustainable products and services are just as good or better than conventional equivalents and, second, that they appear at least as familiar and attractive as conventional products. It may sound like a contradiction that radically different products and services should appear familiar, but that is part of the design challenge that we face. As designers we need to understand consumers' emotional relationships with products and present new ideas to them in ways that they can relate to, that do not appear alien and that excite a sense of progress and improvement. It's a challenge that requires an integrated approach to product innovation, service design, branding and marketing.

design for profit

There is much debate over whether business can ever be truly responsible and play an active role in developing a sustainable future, but in a capitalist society there is no hope of sustainability without the active participation of commerce. It is unrealistic to expect any profit-driven business to pursue sustainable goals purely out of goodwill. It must be able to see clear potential to profit from doing the right thing. So where is the profit in sustainable design? Well, at its most basic level, sustainability is about eliminating waste. If you can

reduce the amount of material used in a product, the amount of packaging, the level of refrigeration or the energy in production, then you can save the business money. Resources cost money, so it is inherently profitable to use resources efficiently. For example, research by the Waste & Resources Action Programme (WRAP), the UK organization for waste reduction, has shown that there is potential to reduce the weight of 500-millilitre plastic drink bottles from 25 grams to 20 grams and 2-litre bottles from 42 grams to 40 grams.[10] If these lighter plastic bottles were adopted around the globe by the carbonated soft drinks industry, there would be huge savings in materials and energy. The United Kingdom alone could save 3,400 tons of plastic per year, saving the industry £2.7 million.[11] Similarly, designing products in a way that makes high-value materials easy to reclaim at end of their life has clear commercial benefits.

What isn't so clear is the commercial advantage of reducing a product or service's waste during use, since consumers pay for the energy to power their products and for any consumables such as print cartridges, batteries and washing powder. In fact, such consumables are extremely lucrative for manufacturers. For example, the US inkjet cartridge market is worth more than $10 billion per year.[12] There is no simple answer to this problem, though replacing physical consumables with service contracts and making consumable components efficient and reusable offer some scope. Overall, though, simple waste reduction can never deliver the massive reductions in resource consumption that we need. A different approach is required. Rather than trying to make inherently unsustainable product and service concepts more efficient and less toxic, we should be looking to make sustainable product and service concepts commercially viable. The concept of 'product design' needs to be replaced by a more integrated approach to 'business design'. The challenge for design is to develop truly effective, sustainable ways of meeting people's needs that people are prepared to pay for. Designers need to be tuned in to the commercial potential of their ideas. As a general rule, an idea has commercial potential if it can do one or more of the following for its target customers: make them money, save them money, save them time or make them feel good. If your design concept has great social and environmental benefits but does not score well on any of these factors, then it needs a major rethink. If, on the other hand, it does show strong potential, then you may have the foundation of a business case that could motivate management or investors to help make it a reality.

But can you really develop new business concepts that encourage more sustainable behaviour and make money? Normally, when people give examples of sustainable design, we see things such as furniture made from recycled materials, biodegradable packaging and appliances with improved energy efficiency. Rarely do we see examples of fundamentally new product and service concepts that change the way people live, work and think. We need to broaden our view, to see that many of the great examples of sustainable design will not necessarily be found where we expect.

> **"Rather than trying to make inherently unsustainable product and service concepts more efficient and less toxic, we should be looking to make sustainable product and service concepts commercially viable."**

One concept that has been much talked about in sustainable design circles is the 'product service system'. The idea is that a company provides products for consumers' use through a service rather than selling them the physical product. For example rather than selling a home heating system, the company sells the service of keeping the customer's home warm. The theory is that, because the business is selling end results rather than physical products, it is paying all the direct costs and so has a vested interest in maximizing efficiency and reliability. Also, by providing a service, it has a strong incentive to ensure ongoing customer satisfaction. Theoretically, it could deliver huge benefits to consumers and the environment as well as being highly profitable. However, some major practical and cultural barriers have prevented the concept from catching on. In some instances, new ideas have been out of tune with culture and behaviour. For example trials by Electrolux to provide residents with pay-per-wash washing machines in their own homes were conducted with great promise but revealed that, while significant water and energy savings could be made, consumers were not comfortable with the idea of paying for each individual wash and preferred the feeling of owning their washing machine outright.[13] However, new versions of this concept are beginning to emerge that are more in tune with consumers' needs and desires. For example the online file storage and backup service DropBox provides customers with a virtual server where they can store their data and coordinate files with team members, just like a traditional office server. However, unlike the washing machine example, the service does not provide the customer with a physical product but substitutes it entirely with a service that has clear consumer benefits. The service is significantly cheaper than installing and maintaining on-site servers, automatically synchronizes files with off-site staff via the Internet and provides reliable and effortless data backup. These benefits provide a clear selling point for the consumer, but there are environmental benefits too. Because the supplier is paying all the direct costs of operating the system, it has a vested interest in ensuring that it is as reliable and energy efficient as possible.

When we open our minds to see sustainable design as being about encouraging more socially and environmentally positive behaviour rather than creating sustainable products, we find many more examples. The online auction Web site eBay is not what you might normally think of as a great example of sustainable design. However, by creating an online marketplace where individuals can trade directly with one another, it has changed consumers' attitudes about secondhand goods and created a huge market around the world for goods that would previously have remained idle in people's homes or been thrown away. eBay does not produce any physical products of its own but earns commission and fees from its 84 million active users who trade around US$60 billion worth of products every year.[14]

As we look to the future, we will increasingly need to consider the possibility of replacing physical products with service systems such as the examples above. Not all of our needs, however, can be met by services alone, and products will always play an important role in our lives. For

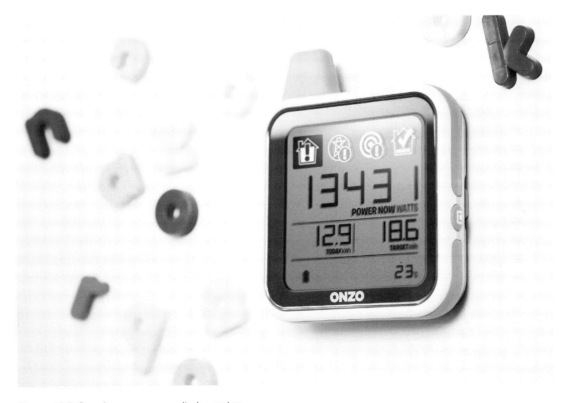

Figure 19.8 Onzo home energy monitoring system. (Copyright Onzo Ltd.)

example the Eglu chicken house by Omlet has encouraged a new generation of town and city dwellers to get involved in producing their own food for the first time (see Plate 23).

Over 30,000 Eglus have been sold since their launch in 2004, and a strong community of owners has developed, many of whom have gone on to grow their own vegetables, keep bees or even teach others how to keep chickens. The key to the Eglu's success is that its design not only makes it simple to keep chickens, but its modern styling has made it appeal to a younger, urban demographic. And it's not just the product's form that's great; it's backed up by a well-conceived service model that includes the delivery of chickens to the customer's home.

Another product designed to encourage more sustainable lifestyles is the Onzo smart energy kit. It is a home energy monitoring system that uses great product and interactive design to make saving energy at home both easy and fun.

The stylish unit can be free-standing, hung from a wall or stuck to a fridge, clearly displaying key data about the user's energy consumption and linking with a Web service that allows users to interact and learn how to reduce their energy consumption. A key part of its success is its unique approach of combining utility companies' need to attract and retain customers with the consumer's desire to save money. By approaching design from a consumer perspective, it is able to add value to the service offered by utility companies, resulting in an initial order from a UK energy company worth over £7 million.

There is huge potential to develop highly profitable businesses that deliver massive social and environmental benefits by providing people with more attractive, efficient ways of living. The examples above are by no means perfect and in some cases were not even intended as examples of sustainable design, but by applying the principles of good design they have succeeded in creating profitable businesses with real social and environmental benefits. Sustainable design should not be viewed by designers as a constraint or burden but as a catalyst for innovation that drives them to think about problems from a new perspective and develop truly ground-breaking solutions.

CHAPTER SUMMARY

- As designers, we must now recognize that good design is sustainable design.
- Resistance to change is the greatest barrier to sustainable design. The challenge is to make new ideas seem familiar and attractive.
- Designers can often achieve more by influencing behaviour than by implementing new technology.
- Products cannot be designed in isolation. They must be designed in context with social, environmental and financial systems.
- We must aim to make socially and environmentally responsible products and services commercially viable.
- Product design must be replaced by a more integrated approach to business design.
- Sustainable design should be considered as a driver for innovation and progress rather than a constraint.

chapter 20

eco-intelligence: designing for the real world

emma dewberry

ABOUT THIS CHAPTER

What is design about? Partly it's about stuff, the things we buy and own, but it's also about questions and decisions. In designing it's easy to pander to the consumption of design without seeing these questions and decisions. This chapter is about challenging our assumptions and habits. It's about a new type of intelligence that has ecology at its core. The chapter suggests we are well overdue a new model of designing that focuses on questions and decisions, particularly those that promote quality of life for all and which build resilience in human–ecology relationships. We need to shift design thinking to respond to the problems of our time.

If you've ever tried to play a new game, you'll know how important it is to understand the rules. Well, the rules of design and designing are changing, and you need to understand these changes if you're going to play design professionally. Partly the changing game is created by a new emphasis on ecological and social goods. It demands new creative strategies, new thinking even. We need to foster new behaviours, bring about new ideas and actions and demonstrate what design can do for society today and in the future. Design is in transition, and this process of change is illustrated through five short stories.

---

looking forward from the past

Some time ago I won a prize at school; I can't remember exactly what for, but I do remember the visit to the bookstore to choose the book. At the time I was engaged in a bit of a battle persuading my school of the usefulness of combining arts and sciences as a preparation for university and a career. In pursuing this argument, I'd come across the discipline of industrial design. So, browsing through that bookstore in the design section, I came across the book *Design for the Real World:* *Human Ecology and Social Change* by Victor Papanek.[1] This book challenged my view on the scope of industrial design. In effect it steered me towards my life mission to explore the purposefulness of design and to build an understanding of the ecological and social constructs of design and designing. I encourage everyone to read this book, but particularly students of design. There have been other, more recent, authors who have built on Papanek's foundation to reveal the role that design has played in positively benefiting society— for example Nigel Whitely and Bruce Mau.[2] Forty years on, Papanek's message is no less powerful. In fact, the context in which we now live further emphasizes the importance of his core appeal to consider the purpose of design and to take seriously the responsibility and consequences of design decisions and outputs. Of course some of his ideas and language are no longer fashionable, but broadly speaking there is still much currency in Papanek's demonstrations of how design can

---

Victor Papanek (1927–1998)

In this age when we take seriously the appeals for sustainable living and ecologically aware consuming, it's easy to think we have created our own green agenda. But we owe a debt of gratitude to Victor Papanek, who, with a few like-minded radicals in the 1960s, laid the foundation for today's broad acceptance of sustainability among professionals and the public alike. He has written several books but is perhaps best know for his seminal text of 1971 *Design for the Real World*, which is still one of the world's most widely read books on design.

Victor Papanek was a designer and educator who championed socially and ecologically responsible design. He foresaw today's concerns about diminishing energy and resources and appealed for the design professions to exercise leadership in a system of production and consumption that was fatally flawed. He was particularly critical of designers who fed the hunger for wasteful, showy or unsafe products. He is quoted as saying 'by creating whole species of permanent garbage to clutter up the landscape, and by choosing materials and processes that pollute the air we breath, designers have become a dangerous breed.'

Papanek's own portfolio of design reveals a concern for engaging people in developing countries with the development of food supply, sanitation and heath care. He worked on reforestation projects, human-powered vehicles, furniture and a transistor radio powered without batteries or mains electricity. Amongst his radical suggestions is that professional designers need to devote 10 per cent of their time to assisting the developing world.

---

help address a range of world problems such as inefficiency, lack of subsistence, pollution and market-led obsolescence to name only a few. His work embodied the revolutionary spirit of the 1960s. It stimulated and informed radical new networks that helped shape the ethical underpinnings of the professions of design practice and design education. He provided a critical discourse on the industrialized path that design embraced; a path he saw as largely devoid of morality, driven solely by commerciality. Unsurprisingly, at the time of publication, his work was derided by many sections of the design establishment who saw it as utopian, unrealistic and an attack on industrialization and the burgeoning consumer culture. The label of 'unrealistic' is one that has persisted, and for many people, Papanek's ideas are still seen as naive in the real world—ironic given the title of his book. It is this notion of 'real world' that forms a thread through this chapter.

what is the real world?

The underlying narrative of much design education in our universities, and one that is often unspoken, is the effectiveness of design to create profit. While there is attention to needs, these are primarily framed as opportunities for furthering profit. There has been too little real questioning of consumption, too little time devoted to a serious contrast of the needs of various stakeholder groups in any given design opportunity. If design education is about questioning, we could at least question the necessity for perpetual economic growth and the role that design plays in sustaining this. What's needed is a strategy that embraces design's creative thinking but which also displays a willingness to situate design

> "Our criteria for economic success can often exclude other quality-of-life measures such as ecological well-being and social cohesion, which may provide better indicators of whether a society is flourishing and whether it is doing so sustainably."

within a bigger picture. We need to reanimate that capacity of design to critically review, question and perhaps disrupt the status quo. We need to provide new lenses through which world problems can be revisualized and responded to through design.

Industrialized societies are increasingly preoccupied by quantifying progress and development in terms of material flow through the economy. Designed outputs make up a significant part of this. Our criteria for economic success can often

exclude other quality-of-life measures such as ecological well-being and social cohesion, which may provide better indicators of whether a society is flourishing and whether it is doing so sustainably. However, at present we mostly fail to incorporate such measures into real-world design work, and where they are part of the mix, their influence is diluted to the extent that they are not key drivers in decision-making processes.

So what exactly do I mean by the term *real world*? Real-world problems include poverty, poor health, water shortages, food insecurities, fuel poverty, diminishing oil supplies, deforestation, soil erosion, inequitable resource distribution and conflicting belief systems. They are not problems that happen to somebody else; they are *our* problems. Design, and particularly design thinking, can help partly through strategies of reframing problems, creativity, and technological innovation but perhaps more importantly by a bold willingness to consider solutions that don't conform to the economic-driven paradigm of design.

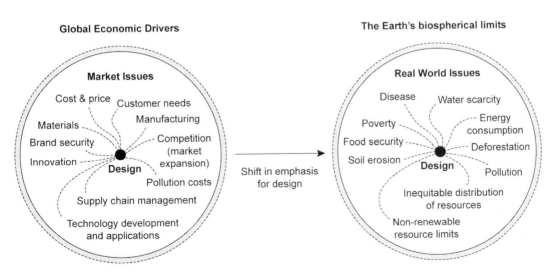

Figure 20.1 The changing emphasis for design thinking and practice. (Copyright author)

A real-world picture needs to reflect the biospherical limits of the earth. These are the limits to sustaining life and are ones that societies, globally, need to understand and work within. Thus the ecological dimension for design thinking is a critical one but is too often dismissed, in both education and practice, as being too complex, too abstract and too difficult to translate into design terms. The reality is that human health and well-being are codependent on the health and well-being of the ecological systems of which we are an integral part. Without water, food, energy and resources, we would be unable to survive. The second half of the twentieth century revealed the interdependency of living and nonliving systems. We began to question our dependency on increasingly distant sources of energy and the impact of reduced food security, food miles, genetic modification, water shortages and water quality. Sustainability has become an issue in our daily lives as we learn about dramatically decreasing biodiversity, increasing levels of environmental pollution, ecosystem devastation and human health scares. We have begun to question just what development means. Within the next decade, we will see a new agenda that forces the design professions to confront issues of global inequities in wealth and well-being while simultaneously playing a role

> "Within the next decade, we will see a new agenda that forces the design professions to confront issues of global inequities in wealth and well-being while simultaneously playing a role in protecting the very resources that development depends on."

in protecting the very resources that development depends on.

towards the personal

A real-world emphasis shifts the parameters and focus for designing. Designers now need to employ their skills for creativity and innovation in new ways if the results are to be sustainable. They need to be able to integrate new moral and ethical imperatives with proven strategies for problem solving. But shifting design practice to respond to the complex problems of our time isn't easy. We are left wondering what this new type of design looks like, how it works and what its purpose is. Industrial ecologist John Ehrenfeld describes sustainability as a complex set of relationships that need to function correctly. He suggests that a successful transition to sustainability will require a focus on domains currently forgotten in the modern world:

- our sense of ourselves as human beings: *the human domain.*
- our sense of our place in the natural world: *the natural domain.*
- our sense of doing the right thing: *the ethical domain.*[3]

The essence of Ehrenfeld's message is one of personal accountability. It is a concept which has been almost lost in commercial systems where those who bring products into existence are very remote from those who use them. It is compounded by the sheer diversity of designed stuff in our world, the diversity of the people who use this stuff and the various possibilities for use, misuse and disposal. The notion of personal responsibility potentially represents a fundamental shift for design; a shift that reconnects design to the changing physical, social and economic landscape of our world. It is no longer relevant to consider design as simply a means of producing stuff, be that consumer products, adverts, houses or transport systems. Decisions geared to promoting limitless growth are unreal in the situation we now face, and, whilst improvement in well-being is important, it cannot be founded on an increasing transit of nonrenewable resources through the economy. Design thinking and practice has great potential to be a central force in the redesign of our ways of living and working (the human domain) and in producing systems that are both equitable (the ethical domain) and ecological (the natural domain). It is through its flexibility and creativity that design can offer alternative lifestyles that are attractive, rewarding and sustainable. For this potential to be realized, though, it is important for us all—designers and those who seek to utilize design—to let go of existing norms that dominate thinking in this subject. We need a new participatory approach to building systems for sustainable consumption.

other pressures shifting design

Peter Senge and his coauthors examine this process of profound change in people, organizations and society.[4] They challenge the idea that what we learn from the past is always a good guide to the future. After all, the future may be very different from the past, requiring different knowledge and perhaps even different systems for creating knowledge. The sustainability debate is a good example of this. It confronts us with new circumstances that involve difficult issues in complex settings. Such change requires us to evolve new

learning processes. Senge calls one new learning process 'presencing', and it has its own particular characteristics including a distinctive U shape to its process (see Figure 20.2). This visualizes an emergent relationship between sensing and realising in a three-step process:

1. *sensing:* to deeply observe the world around us
2. *presencing:* to reflect and develop a depth of inner knowledge and understanding to support sustainable change
3. *realising:* to collaborate between the individual, the community and the wider world to produce new activities

The U process shifts our focus from decisions based on past experiences, views and assumptions to a state of seeing the reality of what is required for a present situation. Such shifts in thinking allow new ideas, thoughts and experiences to develop, which in turn feed new knowledge and skills for interpreting the present and creating new futures. What this model describes is a deep level of learning; one rooted in personal experience and which underpins potentially powerful transformative thinking.

Stuart Walker, professor of sustainable design, discusses the limits of current design in his book *Sustainable by Design.*[5] He calls for designers to reframe their thinking about the creation of functional objects in the context of sustainable development. He sees creativity and innovation as essential for developing new sustainable directions but also recognizes that 'the development of fresh perspectives can be hindered by the terms, conventions and expectations of established practices'.[6] Walker draws out some characteristics of design reframed in the context

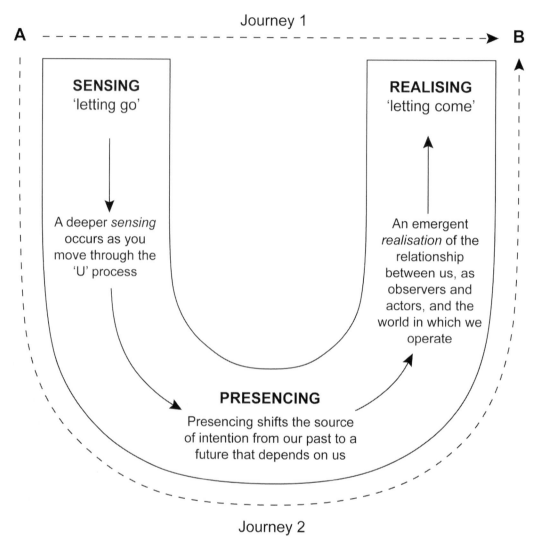

Journey 1

A

SENSING
'letting go'

A deeper *sensing*
occurs as you
move through the
'U' process

REALISING
'letting come'

An emergent
realisation of the
relationship
between us, as
observers and
actors, and the
world in which we
operate

B

PRESENCING

Presencing shifts the source
of intention from our past to a
future that depends on us

Journey 2

Figure 20.2 Presencing and its U process (after Senge
et al.)

of sustainability and contrasts these with conventional design. For example he contrasts the focus on the artefact in conventional product design with a new, more holistic perception of creating material culture. In this he identifies a move away from a solutions focus to a strategy where the focus is on possibilities. Walker calls for the design professions to reject strict boundary definitions and the demarcations evident in the current professional creation of material culture to a context where the creation of products results from peoples' love of the activity and a love of the environment and the world. Some may see here a reflection of the nineteenth-century writings of William Morris and John Ruskin. But this is an entirely new call based on the realities of the twenty-first century.

Behind this call is a commentary on the values of, and reasons for, design and the industrialized nature it has assumed over time. Shifting the game rules for design so that it addresses ecological and social objectives alongside traditional economic ones requires a pulling apart of its modern habits and assumptions and a reconstruction, a putting together of design, so that it effectively responds to deeply connected issues embedded in today's social and ecological context.

Challenging current behaviours and assumptions isn't easy to do. Our decision-making preferences are deeply rooted in existing ways of thinking and doing. That said, some creative thinkers have found opportunities to demonstrate practical alternatives, and this chapter continues with a brief reflection on five examples of design practice.

five stories of design for today's real world

This half of the chapter highlights how design thinking can deliver outcomes that benefit society and our wider ecological system. It does this through five mini studies or stories. In their own way, each offers something radical in its approach. Each demonstrates a letting go of some aspect of traditional thinking. The examples have been selected to offer variety; some are situated in the commercial world, others arise from personal innovation and a commitment to change. These are not deep case studies, they are small vignettes, and so the detail of thinking, design process, ownership, power and influence cannot be drawn out here. However, each highlights design thinkers with their sights on today's real world.

1. Lunar resonant lighting

Streetlights are helpful products. They light our cities, towns and villages in the hours of darkness. But there is a vast waste of light with a huge environmental impact. Every year, around the globe, millions of tons of carbon dioxide (CO_2) is pumped into the atmosphere due to inefficiencies in street lights. Around 30 per cent of the light emitted from a streetlight is directed vertically upwards or dispersed to areas it is not needed. This wasted light equates to about 120 kilograms of CO_2 per year for every streetlight. Multiply this by the 7.5 million streetlights in the United Kingdom alone, and this wasted energy creates 830,000 tons of CO_2 per year—the equivalent of that produced by half a power station.[7] Streetlights are the largest factor in light pollution and account for about 8 per cent of all electricity used for lighting in the United States. Images of city lights as seen from space have been captured by NASA as part of the 'Visible Earth' project.[8]

In response to this widespread problem, a design collective in San Francisco, Civil Twilight, created a new streetlight that would work alongside ambient moonlight. Its Lunescent streetlights present an ecologically responsive approach to urban lighting.[9] They respond to ambient moonlight, dimming and brightening each month as the moon waxes and wanes through its phases.

Lunescent streetlights also respond to changing weather conditions such as cloudy skies. This means that the need for artificial lighting is dramatically reduced as the luminosity of the moon is taken into account when determining nocturnal illumination in a particular location. Utilizing available moonlight, rather than overwhelming it, saves energy and mitigates light pollution, while intensifying the urban experience of one of the most fundamental and beautiful cycles of

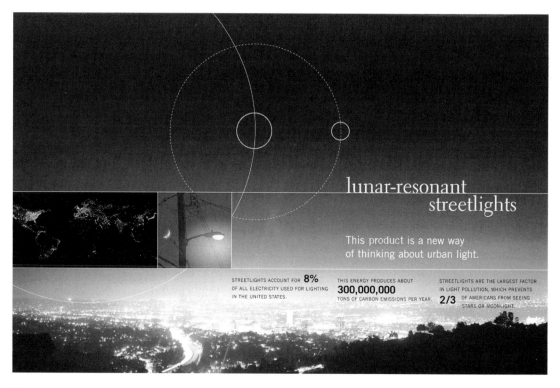

Figure 20.3 Lunar-resonant urban lighting reduces light pollution and carbon emissions. (Copyright Lunescent.com/ civiltwilightcollective.com)

nature. This solution significantly helps challenge our assumptions about the need for large energy infrastructures, particularly those based on non-renewables, through a much lower energy intensive lighting solution. The Lunescent fixture uses high-efficiency white light-emitting diodes and recycled aluminium and offers energy savings of almost 90 per cent; it uses only 16 watts of electricity, compared to 150 watts for a standard metal halide fixture.

Lunescent streetlights represent an ecological intelligence much needed in design thinking and practice, they return the beauty of moonlight to areas where it has typically been drowned out by artificial lighting, they facilitate new interactions and relationships to nature and they reduce overall

light pollution at night where current light levels are responsible for declining numbers of insects and other nocturnal species. These streetlights form a dynamic, responsive, intelligent urban infrastructure. They are just one way that cities can be not only more efficient and sustainable, but also be more connected to local environment and culture. The concept for Lunescent was awarded the Metropolis Next Generation Prize in 2007.

2. Personal urban mobility

This is again a story of resource efficiency, but this time it originates from within the structures that dominate economic thinking and practice. The car company General Motors teamed up with Segway, the company that launched the first self-balancing, zero-emissions personal transportation vehicle, the Segway® Personal Transporter.

The partnership with General Motors has resulted in the 2030 concept vehicle EN-V, unveiled at Expo 2010, Shanghai (see Plate 24). The EN-V, short for electric networked-vehicle, is a two-person city car aimed at contributing to a 'better city, better life' by easing urban congestion and reducing carbon emissions. It is a car one-sixth the size and price and about five times as energy efficient as a conventional passenger car.[10] One may argue that this is solely an efficiency project aimed at positioning both General Motors and Segway as innovation leaders. Cynics might suggest the project ensures investment and visibility in future technologies that help increase market share and profit margins as we see increases in urban population this century. This may be so, but this project also reflects an agenda about reconfiguring resources to create lifestyles that work in environments that will become increasingly densely populated. If we challenge traditional technologies that currently deliver personal mobility and freedom, we also instigate a debate concerning the environments in which effective mobility operates and how such environments can be fostered. The EN-V is built on a low-carbon platform; it demonstrates a

much-reduced physical and ecological footprint for a car; it helps us create a vision of what our future urban mobility needs may be and suggests ways in which they can be met.

3. Auto-disposable syringe

How can the design of a syringe be a social innovation? Well, here's the story. Every year 1.3 million people die from blood-borne infections such as hepatitis B and C and HIV-AIDS, transmitted through the reusing of syringes; that's more than those who die from malaria. On average, syringes are reused four times in the developing world, even though new syringes cost very little (less than a cup of tea from a roadside vendor).[11] Back in the 1980s, Marc Koska read a newspaper article that predicted multiple syringe use would become the main cause of the spread of the HIV-AIDS virus. In response, Koska designed the K1 auto-disposable syringe, a single-use needle whose simple design locks and disables the plunger of the syringe once it has been used.

Alongside this technical innovation, Koska realized how essential it was to shift established mindsets about the importance of using sterile medical equipment. Nonsterile and unsafe practices still continue in many parts of the world,

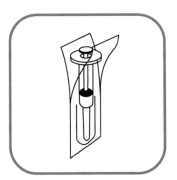  

Figure 20.4 Visual communication of safe syringe use.
(Copyright SafePoint Trust)

including in those institutions considered to be part of the mainstream health services in the developing world. In addition to his product innovation, Koska's mission was to deliver accurate information to people in the regions most affected by infection as a result of widespread needle sharing. He established the educational charity SafePoint, which works with local community networks to foster an understanding of local contexts and cultures, to devise appropriate and effective message delivery systems concerning safe needle use. Although there is a relationship between the success of the charity's message and the sales of K1 syringes, Koska argues that both are about improving quality of life, and to do this the syringe company needs to be profitable.[12] The design message here is that as well as developing a sound, functional and much-needed technical solution to a widespread social problem, innovative thinking was also applied to the problem of how to persuade people to change their behaviour—not just the recipients of injections but also those responsible for giving injections and those responsible for developing local policy and providing funding to support safer medical practices. All of these people are stakeholders in the success of this system of design thinking aimed at improving the lives of millions of people.

4. The afterlife of PIG 05049

This is an intriguing case of a communication designer who was inspired to investigate the afterlife of one particular pig in an attempt to portray its story in the complex and disconnected world of food production. The project seeks to open consumers' eyes to the reality surrounding the systems of raising and processing livestock today. Christien Meindertsma documented all the products produced from one real pig, PIG 05049, raised on a commercial farm in the Netherlands.

The study does not aim to be a commentary on large-scale farming and modern food production methods; rather, it offers a much broader perspective. It seeks instead to raise awareness of the reliance we have on such animals and, particularly, the impact of this on our material world. She discovered 185 food and nonfood products that Pig 05049 contributed to, from familiar pork products to less-expected ones such as an aluminium mould, a train brake, a bullet (part of the pig is used to help disperse the gunpowder), a bone china cup, a heart valve and extra-calcium yogurt. Meindertsma's aim was to reconnect the storyline about where manufactured products come from. As she points out, 'There are very many steps between the raw material and the end product in modern commercial production...so knowledge gets lost. [Even] the pig farmers...don't know all the end-products that are made from their pigs.'[13]

There are many examples of life-cycle thinking in books on design for environment, but these are often generic; for example they might select their examples across a broad product field. Often, their discussions are limited to particular stages of product life such as manufacture, use and reuse or disposal. What is unique and useful about Meindertsma's project is the way the information is made transparent to nonexpert audiences. It's easy to relate to because it focuses on something that is familiar to very many people: a pig. This is a very effective piece of communication design and lightly leads people to explore issues of ecological well-being and their relationship to the constructs of modern commercial farming and global manufacturing. Pig 05049 won the Play category in

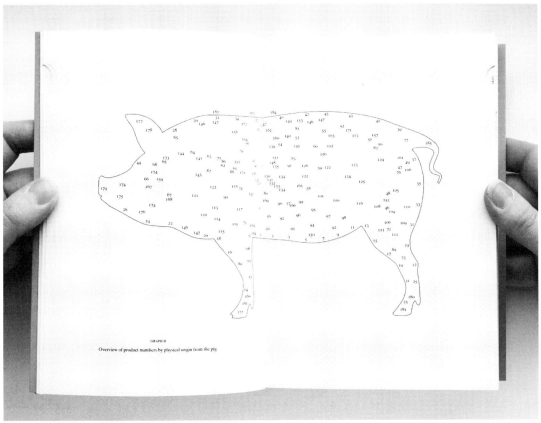

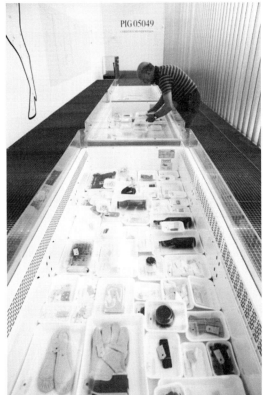

Figure 20.5 PIG 05049: book and products exhibited at the Kunsthal in Rotterdam, 2008. (Copyright Christien Meindertsma; pictures by Kenji Masunaga)

the 2009 award of Danish nonprofit organization, INDEX, whose strap line is 'design to improve life'.

5. Object Orange

Object Orange is a small group of artists who do things differently. They create visual responses to the problem of neglected spaces and buildings within their communities. Their aim is to transform these communities by changing perceptions of what care and neglect mean today. Based in Detroit, Object Orange began by painting abandoned buildings in a bold orange colour so that they stood out distinctively (see Plate 25).

This evolved into a social crusade to bring attention to the spread of urban decay in parts of the city. This not only raised the profile of disowned and neglected architecture, but it also raised awareness of how such buildings were being used, for example as bases for drug distribution. Neglected buildings were shown to have a significant influence on social well-being and particularly on the lives of young people growing up in urban environments. The group of artists sought to highlight the problem and in this way initiate conversations that enabled new types of action to emerge. In a city where some of the richest neighbourhoods in the United States function alongside some of the poorest, Object Orange aimed to puncture apathy towards derelict space and help foster new awareness and action to create better and safer communities.

In predawn expeditions, they target dilapidated buildings and unlawfully paint the properties in Disney's 'Tiggerific' orange paint. Four of the group's first eleven houses were immediately demolished and the land cleared. Object Orange suggests this aids the regeneration of green spaces and a more optimistic community outlook, particularly where levels of crime have also been reduced—perhaps

---

Design Thinking Is Not Enough

There is frequent reference in this collection to 'design thinking', but perhaps the time is right for the definition of a new type of thinking—a reconfiguration of our cognitive abilities that better addresses the priorities of sustainability. Design thinking is characterized by a willingness to engage in solution speculation even before a problem is fully defined, it is a style of thinking that is fed by the making of representations and it's comfortable with uncertainty. The notion of design thinking has, in some ways, liberated and democratized design, but the new applications for design thinking in, say, business or politics have revealed shortcomings. The roots of design thinking in the service of product innovation, mass production and consumption hold it back from more radical application in design theory and applied philosophy.

The priorities of sustainability require all of us—and particularly those in the design professions—to operate under a different paradigm. The required change is revolutionary, not evolutionary. Today's design thinkers must have a grasp of the political and ethical context of designing at a time when the social context of design is in transformation—a move from the material to the immaterial and from method to methodology. Whereas design activism was once served by an ability to reimagine alternative futures, the priorities for the new design activism concern the very building blocks of futures and the systems and interdependencies that link them. To be a design thinker is not enough.

---

as a direct consequence of Object Orange's intervention.[14] This is a project that combines awareness raising, social protest and direct action. Whether we term this project activism or not, it reflects an interesting shift in the scope of what artists and designers can do in response to social and ecological issues they feel uncomfortable about. Promoting unlawful activities is not the headline here. Object Orange is constructive rather than destructive. It is about building understanding of the idea of challenge—of questioning social norms and perhaps our blindness to things that have become familiar. The responses are not always comfortable and readily acceptable, and this is where creative and sensitive thinking can be so vital.

towards eco-intelligence

The priority for design in the twenty-first century is to raise awareness, challenge and empower. To inspire others we need to look differently and deeply at the problems and contexts of design. We need to apply creativity to evolve new solutions that are relevant to both society and the environment. We have the potential, but today that potential is being realized only in small isolated pockets of practice. Influencing the vastly bigger proportion of design production and design consumption that goes on under the banner of industrial growth and development is the challenge for design professionals today. This isn't an antigrowth thesis; growth is important in bringing quality of life to the billions of people whose basic needs are currently not being met. Growth and development are part of the answer, but not the total answer.

Designers have always been in the business of creating alternatives; visualising how things might be and how we might live, exploiting technologies that bring about deeper understandings and more sustainable behaviours. This chapter stands as a call to action to generate a new understanding and awareness of our material culture. At its core is the vital message that the resilience of humankind is dependent on the ecological systems that support it. It is in deeply knowing and understanding today's real world that designers, as a collective, can continue to create wonderful things, spaces and ideas that help all to flourish into the future.

CHAPTER SUMMARY

- Designing for the real world challenges accepted norms and questions our collective blindness to ecologically unsustainable practices and social injustice.

- Today's real-world problems include poverty, poor health, water shortages, food insecurities, fuel poverty, diminishing oil supplies, deforestation, soil erosion, inequitable resource distribution and conflicting belief systems. They are not problems that happen to somebody else; they are our problems.

- Measuring progress, development and success requires new indicators based on new priorities today. We need eco-intelligence.

- Design thinking allows us to respond to real-world needs through strategies of reframing problems, creativity and technological innovation. Designers must review, question and disrupt. They must bring a bold willingness to consider solutions that don't conform to current paradigms.

- Designers are accountable for their work. Reconnect with your social and ecological landscape through experience, reflection and interpretation.

- Read *Design for the Real World* by Victor Papanek.

Background

There are numerous examples of transfer from the so-called developed world to the developing world: technologies, political systems, economic structures and finance are a few of the exports. This project is about potential transfer the other way. It's about how people in the developed world might learn from people in the developing world.

The Project

Find one way that people in countries in the developing world might inspire more sustainable living in the developed world. Communicate your proposal using images and words. The long-term aim of this project is to demonstrate a portfolio of successful designs by the year 2024.

Guidelines

This project aims to stretch your skills in challenging assumptions. You might want to begin by challenging assumptions about the division between the developed and the developing world, or about consumption and economic growth. This project focuses on sustainability, but it also encourages you to see new outlets for your design skills and knowledge.

There are many alternative starting points to this project. You might want to investigate various approaches to good stewardship of the earth's resources such as water; you might want to focus on one type of resource such as energy or materials; you might explore sustainable living, the production of food, the uses of waste (e.g. bio-fermenting), manufacturing or communication. Alternatively, you might take a social perspective and explore the maintenance of the family unit, cultural bonding, inclusivity or addressing disability. You might use a problem in the developed world as a starting point for investigation of the developing world. Or you might begin by investigating emerging nations and transferring your findings to a developed world context.

part vi

the professional practice of design

introduction to part vi

In some respects the whole collection is about the professional practice of design. All the chapters have provided insight to traditional and emerging roles and responsibilities for those who want to earn a living by designing. But there are some pointers that suggest we need to look further than new practices—we need to anticipate completely different professional design roles. In some ways Part V sought to provide a wake-up call to the various design professions to place sustainability at the core of their missions, but a new professionalism must go even further. Today designers are called to work across disciplines and to find a way around outdated lines of demarcation.

Terence Kavanagh provides an ideal introduction to Part VI because his reflection on materials bridges the sustainability concerns of Part V and wider concerns of professional practice. His chapter does not reiterate warning messages—instead it seeks to liberate designers by revealing how innovation in materials can improve usability and performance as well as addressing the sustainability debate. Interestingly, Kavanagh suggests that some of our most important lessons for future design might be found in some of our most traditional materials.

In Chapter 22 Sharon Poggenpohl examines the vital characteristics of professionalism in graphic communication at a time when low-cost powerful computers have opened up creativity for the masses. She appeals for designers to recognize the urgency for building bridges between previously distinct professional services—in particular between graphic design and product design. Her own bridging work is founded on the pillars of sound research, and she appeals for designers to apply their design skills in innovative ways so as to provide unique insights to the needs and wants of new communities of users. Poggenpohl charts both the attributes of those skilled in design and the challenges for them in future models of collaborative working. In doing so, her chapter anticipates the final section of the book, which seeks to support the reader in designing a future career in design.

Clyde Millard illustrates some important competences for designers with reference to the development of an electronic thermometer in Chapter 23. He suggests that resolving detail is frequently more important than concept creation, and he uses his own practice to illustrate how multidisciplinary working, involving engineering, material science and design, manifests itself in reality.

Part VI concludes with a chapter on intellectual property (IP). For too long, IP has been seen as a consequence of design and innovation rather than a driver. Claire Howell lays out the various forms of protection an individual or organization might consider, but most importantly she appeals for designers to embrace the strategic opportunity presented by intellectual property rights. Of all the tools presented in this book, the IP tools might well be the most valuable over the span of your career.

chapter 21

old materials, new materials

terence kavanagh

ABOUT THIS CHAPTER

This chapter reveals how materials can impart the most fundamental characteristics on a product, including performance and personality. Since customer experience and satisfaction are vital to design, then designers need to consider more than a material's utilitarian functionality. New materials are constantly being developed, offering new possibilities for creating user experiences. There now exists the ability to specify new hybrid materials offering revolutionary characteristics. Never has the designer had such choice, and never has the designer had to think so much about the appropriate use and processing of materials.

This chapter examines the interface between creative design and materials science with reference to both modern and traditional materials and product innovation. It embraces a range of materials and design contexts but it focuses on fabrics because these underpin some of the most creative and commercially successful designs today. Examples are drawn from fashion, sports equipment and engineering. This chapter reveals how informed selection and use of new materials can enhance product longevity, assist recycling and reduce landfill. The lessons for sustainable global design lie in materials old and new.

---

an historical perspective

For the archaeologist, the term *material culture* is used to describe the artefacts of past cultures. In Lyall Watson's book, *Lightning Bird: The Story of One Man's Journey into Africa's Past*, he describes human ingenuity with materials some thirty thousand years ago. An early group of hunters took shelter in the Terra Amata cave in what is now southern France.

> Among their garbage are sixty pencil-shaped pieces of ochre ranging in color from yellow to purple, a variation that can only be produced by heating or firing the natural red ore. Most of the pieces still show signs of abrasion, which suggests that they were made and used as colored crayons, as a source of pigment.[1]

Watson suggests these early people had the ability to recognize and select appropriate minerals, ones which might have needed excavation or carrying considerable distances. Furthermore he suggests it displays:

> foresight and creativity in the discovery and use of techniques, such as heating or firing, which induce color changes. It includes the complex

procedures involved in abrading and pounding the ore, collecting it in suitable receptacles, and mixing with water, urine, plant juices or blood. It also presupposes some powerful motive for going to all this trouble in the first place.[2]

This powerful motive undoubtedly derived from a need to create visual representations, which manifested themselves in some of the earliest examples of cave painting. To this day, similar pigments are still used in the making of art.

The tools to create art and images in general have evolved significantly, but the pens and brushes used today would be recognisable to people who lived thousands of years ago. For example, the design of the calligraphy brush, which originated in China in the Qin dynasty around 221–207 BCE, is still in use.

The calligraphy brush is a masterpiece of elegant design, totally fit for the purpose in hand. Its performance as a writing or painting tool is not only dependent on the skills of the painter, it is also dependent on the appropriate selection of materials by the maker of the brush. Although a wide variety of materials can be used for calligraphy brushes, including vegetable and synthetic fibres, the material of preference over centuries has been animal hairs or bristles. The selection of the type of hair to be used is based on an understanding of the expectations of the user. These expectations can be articulated as a series of performance criteria that inform the design decision process.

Figure 21.1 Peacock feather calligraphy brushes, China. (Copyright author)

Users will have individual preferences for different sizes of brush or for a specific firmness or softness. These affect the ability of the brush to absorb a particular quantity of ink and its responsiveness to application of pressure. This is by no means a full set of performance criteria for a calligraphy brush but it illustrates the kind of user expectations that a producer needs to respond to. Developing descriptors of required characteristics is a complex matter. Many of the sensations we experience with materials are a mixture of the objective and subjective.

> **"Many of the sensations we experience with materials are a mixture of the objective and subjective."**

The selection of appropriate materials are some of the most pivotal decisions in the design process. For the designer of the brush, this requires a comprehensive knowledge of animal hairs and their potential to meet user expectation. Each type of hair will respond in a particular way. By testing materials—in this case the animal hair—the maker can achieve the right combination of characteristics to arrive at a brush that will be capable of making the required range of marks.

Material Matters

Without a material form, a design is only a plan or idea. The specification of materials and the making of decisions about processing, forming or assembling materials are vital aspects of the designing process. Often the materials chosen will significantly influence a design. Four factors guide material selection:

1. *Materials have behavioural properties.* These include strength, stiffness, density, durability and so on. With a good understanding of material properties, it's possible not only to use materials in appropriate ways but also to turn disadvantages to your favour with innovative ideas or new applications.
2. *Materials have processing properties.* By understanding how materials are variously worked, designers can identify appropriate techniques for manufacture, fabrication, joining, assembly and finishing.
3. *Materials have psychological connotations or associations.* All materials have qualities that can be sensed through our hands, eyes and perhaps our nose. Additionally, we give materials attributes. We might view one plastic as unattractive and another as warm and welcoming. Designers need to understand these connotations and associations, which are constantly evolving in the marketplace.
4. *Materials have costs.* These might be direct financial costs, for example specifying a high-quality fabric in fashion clothing, but there are other costs, too. There might be indirect environmental or social costs to design decisions, through manufacture, use and disposal of materials.

the classification of materials

Familiarity with a basic classification or taxonomy of materials is essential for any designer engaging in the material world. In the case of materials, the taxonomy is multilayered and increasingly becomes more complex as new materials innovations emerge. Familiarity with the system of classification is important, because it underpins the material comparisons and therefore material selection.

Materials will normally be grouped into classes displaying similar structures or properties. However,

Figure 21.2 Ceramic raku vessel with tin glaze (David Scott). (Copyright author)

as a result of the great variety, and with new materials being produced on an almost daily basis, any classification will have its limitations. As a starting point, there are some general descriptors of families of materials. These include ceramics, metals, polymers and vegetable matter such as woods. Each material group is classified by its specific traits and contains its numerous variants.

As an example, one richly diverse group of materials is ceramics. They are formed primarily by the combining of various materials found in the earth. There are numerous subgroups of ceramics, including rough earthenware clays that can be used almost straight out of the ground and which are porous; stoneware that is nonporous and opaque; porcelain which is nonporous but translucent; zirconium dioxide that is so tough it can be used to make ceramic knife blades or silicon carbide, which is used in many composites because of its hardness and durability. Another subgroup includes the diverse materials largely made from silica that include various forms of glass. An important influence in defining a taxonomy is the commonality in methods by which a material can be processed or combined with others. Establishing classifications of materials also involves the mapping of performance characterizations. These can provide the designer with valuable insights to the technical and aesthetic qualities of specific examples of materials.

Plate 17 Stand back and take in the bigger picture.
(Getty AA024330 RF) (see Chapter 13)

Plate 18 Concept visualization of a ship interior. (Copyright Andrew Collier) (see Chapter 14)

Plate 19 Mood board created as part of concept exploration for a restaurant.
(Copyright Andrew Collier) (see Chapter 14)

Plate 20 *Pacific Jewel,* entrance to the Waterfront restaurant. (Copyright Andrew Collier)
(see Chapter 14)

Plate 21 Range Rover Evoque. (Photo copyright Land Rover) (see Chapter 15)

Plate 22 Part of the Veja product range showing new labelling. (Copyright Luiz Vidal Gomes/Ligia Medeiros) (see Chapter 16)

Plate 23 Eglu, innovation in products and services. (Copyright Omlet) (see Chapter 19)

Plate 24 General Motors' Miao (Magic) EN-V concept car. (Copyright General Motors) (see Chapter 20)

Plate 25 Object Orange. (Copyright Object Orange) (see Chapter 20)

Plate 26 Fabrican© nonwoven spray-on dress.
(Photo copyright: Fabrican, Manel Torres; photo by Ian Cole) (see Chapter 21)

Plate 27 Innovation in fabrics can lead to improved performance and new types of product. (Getty 109724970 RF)
(see Chapter 21)

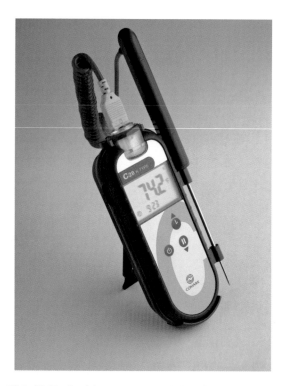

Plate 28 The food thermometer consisting of a handheld unit,
stand and interchangeable probe. (Copyright Clyde Millard) (see Chapter 23)

Plate 29 Interior of DZ Bank in Berlin, by Frank Gehry. (Photo copyright Theodore Zamenopoulos/Katerina Alexiou) (see Chapter 26)

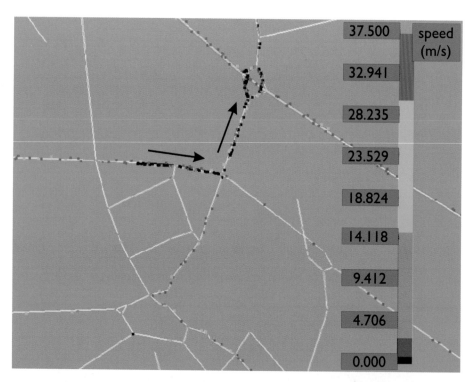

Plate 30 A snapshot from a TRANSIMS simulation of traffic in the city of Milton Keynes, United Kingdom, showing congestion at a roundabout. (Copyright Joan Serras)
From J. Serras, 'Multidimensional Multilevel Representation for Microscopic Traffic Simulation Models', PhD thesis, Open University, Milton Keynes (2007). (see Chapter 26)

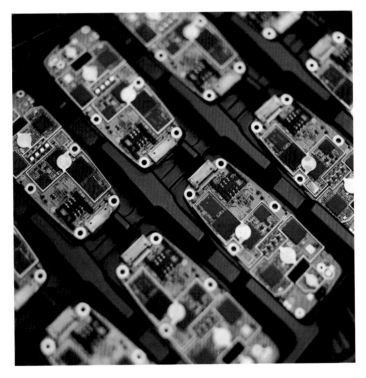

Plate 31 Designers need to manage the big picture, understanding the trade-offs when taking a concept into reality. (Getty 200122867-001 RM) (see Chapter 27)

Plate 32 Some brands have an international reputation
for high value. (Getty 72797188) (see Chapter 27)

the characterization of materials

Material science has established a robust taxonomy of materials. The materials scientist today is still concerned with defining a material's characteristics, its capabilities and, in economic terms, the consequences of its selection. A number of resources exist to help the designer tap into this expertise,[3] but the reader would be well advised to possess a basic command of materials terminology if such resources are to assist in materials selection in design today. Assessing the potential of any material for a given design job involves an understanding of a material's attributes. These include physical attributes such as weight and density, mechanical attributes such as strength and elasticity, thermal responsiveness such as conductivity, electrical properties such as resistance and other characteristics, including those that relate to optical and acoustic properties. An understanding of these attributes is a critical factor in ensuring that the designer achieves the functional and performance requirements of a product.

Physical attributes are only part of the story. Materials also give rise to sensory perceptions, and these too can be documented as attributes. There are descriptors associated with the way materials are perceived through the five senses—attributes that are experienced through touch such as hard or soft or rough or smooth, visual attributes such as colour, opacity or translucency and acoustic qualities such as sound absorption or resonance. An understanding of these attributes helps inform the creation of the aesthetics of a product.

Similarly, materials can convey cultural associations. This includes the perceived value or merit of a material. These attributes might be described through a series of dyads such as expensive/

cheap, modern/traditional, commonplace/exclusive or lasting/disposable. They are particularly useful to situate a material in the marketplace. Take textiles for example. Silk, viscose, linen, cotton and polyester offer different but, in some cases, very similar physical attributes depending on how they are processed so that, in theory, they could be used to produce quite similar fabrics. However, consumers may have specific preferences based on judgements and associations revealed through the dyads described above. This can be difficult to quantify, but equally it can be key to commercial success. An understanding of these cultural associations is important in making the right selections to meet customer expectations.

It is relevant to frame the attributes of materials according to their abilities to be processed. The designer needs to know, for example, whether a material can be formed by casting or moulding, whether it can be polished, abraded or coated or is capable of bonding through welding, gluing or sewing to other materials. How a material can be processed will largely dictate the manufacturing and construction process, and therefore it has a major influence on the product that results.

Since economics is so vital to design success, there is a need to evaluate materials by their cost, including potential impact on the environment. Materials need to be sourced and transported to the point of processing. There are costs associated with that processing, including energy and the management of pollutants and waste. Finally, there are the costs of disposal at the end of a product's useful life. These might be comparatively easy financial calculations, but there is a less easily quantifiable impact that is associated with increasing consumer demand and the impact this has on the finite resources at our disposal. An understanding of the cost of a material and

Figure 21.3 Tea whisk, bamboo, Japan.
(Copyright author)

its processing must inform the design decision-making process.

The characterization of materials may seem rather dry, but it provides knowledge vital to innovation. Understanding material attributes helps the designer make better choices, but there are many different perspectives one might adopt.

> "The characterization of materials may seem rather dry, but it provides knowledge vital to innovation. Understanding material attributes helps the designer make better choices."

discovery and experimentation

Bamboo is a grass, an exceptional material that lends itself to literally thousands of applications. In the Far East, it has been used over many centuries for shipbuilding and architecture, bridges and scaffolding, furniture and fabrics and for the production of simple domestic implements such as the traditional tea whisk (Figure 21.3).

Bamboo has some very distinctive characteristics, which in the context of this chapter make it a good subject for examination. With regard to its sourcing, it is a natural renewable material that grows prolifically and quickly and is the ultimate sustainable resource because it requires little or no fertilizer. It is easily harvested and requires little processing. With regard to physical attributes, it is a hollow tube, exceptionally strong and light, with a hard surface and fibrous interior. It is a composite material comprising cellulose fibres in a lignin matrix not dissimilar to a composite of carbon fibre and resin. The fibres are aligned along the length of the bamboo, and this produces significant tensile strength and rigidity.

The many uses for bamboo and our understanding of its performance have been garnered over many centuries. Its characteristics have been studied and harnessed—often involving much trying and testing—and this experimentation continues in modern times.[4] The area of textiles has seen some of the most recent bamboo innovations. It is highly probable that bamboo fabrics will in the future surpass cotton manufacture, because it has now been established as one of the best-performing natural fabrics of its kind. It is both silky and cool in summer and warm in winter and has the ability to wick moisture from the body and facilitate fast evaporation. It is naturally antibacterial, hypoallergenic, antistatic and biodegradable, and it offers natural ultraviolet protection. Early understanding of bamboo and its uses came from artisans' familiarity with the material. Contemporary understanding is now more likely to come from science and technology.

An important way that designers can acquire knowledge of materials and their performance is by experimentation. It is only by testing and analysing performance and the making of prototypes that the designer can recognize what will be required from a material in a given situation. Although much can be obtained by an examination of technical literature and by computer simulation (and in some cases, that will be the only route available), a physical engagement with materials provides the greatest opportunity to develop a proper intuition of a material's capability for processing and manufacture. Such a hands-on approach allows for serendipity, the production of happy accidents and unexpected discoveries. In the same way as the child learns from play, the designer must, in a more disciplined way, experiment with materials to learn about them. As David Pye notes, 'One might even differentiate invention and discovery by confining the term "discovery" to intentions arising from chance occurrences not deliberately courted.'[5] However, such is the technical nature of many of the materials being created today that they do not necessarily lend themselves to experiment or play in the way that, for example, wood and metal did in the past.

As a result of their complexity or novelty, many of today's new materials demand a level of technological expertise beyond most designers. Their specification in design projects is often best facilitated by collaboration with others in materials science or engineering. However, it is equally important, when trying to understand a new or complex material or process to make the effort to develop an understanding of the science and engineering principles that underpin the technology. This can be alien territory for the design-trained practitioner, but without this grounding the dialogue between the scientist or engineer and the designer is likely to be ineffective. No question need be considered naive in the context of this dialogue, only the way it is expressed. Endeavour to make this move toward the materials world, because the rewards are great. There is much scope for work at the interface of the studio and the laboratory. While designers need to continue to use their tried and tested approaches to practice, this can be supplemented with hybrid or quasi-scientific techniques of experimentation and testing to inform designing which is both creative and practical.

innovation in fabrics

Design visionaries of the twentieth century such as Issey Miyake, Paco Rabanne, Pierre Cardin and Raymond Lowey have all envisaged worlds where fabrics played novel new roles. For some, fabrics could have air-conditioning properties, they might monitor our health or even help the healing process. Other visions include textiles that could be sprayed straight onto the body to create clothing. In the twenty-first century, the development of new materials and processes has allowed all these visions to be realized.

Collaborative research between Imperial College and the Royal College of Art, London undertaken by Manel Torres has led to the creation of Fabrican©, a spray-on fabric. The act of spraying, using a spray gun or an aerosol can, creates a cross-linking of fibres that adhere to each other to create an instant, nonwoven material (see Plate 26). The fabric and its performance can be tailored to meet various needs, and by using different types of fibres (natural or synthetic) and incorporating scents and colours, it is possible to provide great flexibility for a wide range of uses, including medical applications.

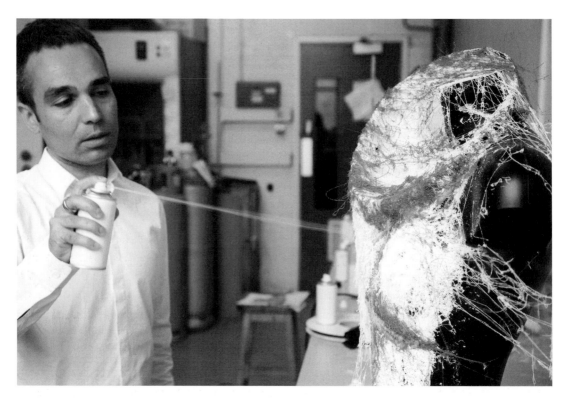

Figure 21.4 Building Fabrican fashion using a mannequin. (Photo copyright: Fabrican, Manel Torres; photo by Miquel Sobreira)

This is an example of materials innovation that was developed through interdisciplinary research, linking the subjects of engineering, material science and design. It is hard to imagine it could be achieved by any other means.

Fibres are the fundamental form of materials used in textile production. The process of spinning can combine fibres to produce yarn, and yarn can then be processed through different types of machinery to produce textiles. The diversity of fibres now available has resulted in a fabulous array of possibilities as textile technology consultants Sarah Braddock Clarke and Marie O'Mahony point out:

> Textiles have ceased to be regarded as a flexible, permeable, decorative material best suited to clothing and soft furnishing…In the past few years there has been tremendous growth in diverse applications…It seems that no area of design activity has been unaffected, from the automotive industry to medicine, architecture, sport, product design, aerospace and fashion.[6]

As an example of new ways of using textiles, consider an ocean racing yacht. A fast yacht requires high levels of performance in some of the most challenging environmental conditions. There is a great tension between producing a craft strong enough to survive the huge forces produced by wind and waves while at the same time being light enough to move quickly through the water. The challenge of the trade-offs necessary between lightness and strength is also of paramount importance in automotive and aerospace industries. Of course failure to get the combination right has potentially catastrophic consequences. Nearly every material on a racing yacht today is made of, or will include, some form of textile. For example the hull will be made of carbon or glass textiles and resin bonded together into a composite matrix. The different materials retain their identities — that is, they do not dissolve or merge entirely into one another, although they act in such a way that the performance of the composite is greater and different from the individual component materials. The spars, deck hardware, sails and ropes will also contain textiles in one form or another. Carbon and aramid textiles have great strength and most significantly lightness.

In the automotive industries, similar challenges exist. The use of carbon fibre reinforced ceramic composites in brake disk applications is now commonplace in high-performance automobiles because it brings a combination of thermal and mechanical properties. It is possible to produce a disk one-third of the weight of a traditional cast iron version. The carbon fibre provides strength, while silicon carbide ceramic provides the matrix that is extremely durable. In many respects, this is not dissimilar to the molecular structure of bamboo.

solving problems through materials

A number of common problems face designers today, and frequently materials can play a significant role in their solution, as Chris Lefteri's book *Materials for Inspirational Design* reveals.[7] For example the issue of environmental pollution, and more generally the demands of sustainability, mean we need to find alternative materials for a range of components and products. Also there are new demands for improved performance, plus there are pressures for rationalizations that contribute to cost savings or efficiencies. Add to

Figure 21.5 Nearly every material on a racing
yacht today includes some form of textile. (Getty
sb10066425ad-002 RM)

this the increasing demand for many commodities such as minerals that were once regarded as commonplace but which are now increasingly costly or diminishing at such a rate that their replenishment cannot meet future demand. Seen collectively, these pressures indicate a perilous situation. Never before has innovation through new or replacement materials been so urgent.

Innovation through materials is the mission of Cool Acoustics™, which originated as a postgraduate research project at Loughborough University. The company creates instrument designs and specifications using polymers in place of traditional woods. Not only does this conserve depleting stocks of tone-woods, but it offers new opportunities for innovation.

Figure 21.6 shows the Secret Valentine guitar, a collaborative project between Cool Acoustics and master guitar maker Rob Armstrong, working to the exacting specification of musician Gordon Giltrap. As in all acoustic guitars, the soundboard—the flat panel on the front of the guitar—shapes the sound and is connected to the strings via the bridge and saddle. Soundboards are traditionally made of spruce or cedar softwoods, but these materials have two major quality concerns. First, they are vulnerable to tonal and structural changes caused by fluctuations in temperature and humidity—cracking and warping are not uncommon. Second, since no two pieces of wood are the same, there can be variations in the tonal quality of guitars that are mass produced to a standard construction. The soundboards manufactured to the designs of Cool Acoustics are made from foamed polycarbonate that doesn't have the shortcomings of softwood; plus it provides outstanding tonal quality. Furthermore, the polycarbonate is cheaper than high-grade tone-wood.

Figure 21.6 A recent addition to the Cool Acoustics™ guitar range with musician Gordon Giltrap. (Copyright Eddie Norman/Cool Acoustics)

Improved performance—the achievement of a better combination of desired qualities such as strength, lightness, visual appeal and reasonable cost in manufacture—continues to pose a significant challenge for designers in a wide range of disciplines. But this is particularly the case with contemporary sports equipment and sportswear. The training shoe or 'trainer' is one of the most ubiquitous products of the twenty-first century, and it has bridged the worlds of fashion and sport by combining aesthetic appeal and high-performance functionality. Consider one component of the typical trainer, the sole. Much research and development has been devoted to achieving a sole that absorbs the shocks that can be generated by running or jumping. Some early developments of sports shoes used ethylene vinyl acetate, a semirigid foam, for the sole. Although this foam was initially effective in distributing shock loads, its performance diminished over time as a result of the inevitable deformation of the air cells embedded in the foam. With the advent of more resilient polymers, such as thermoformed polyurethane, it is now possible to provide shock absorption in a totally different way with virtually no deterioration in performance over time. By applying computer models that simulate the physical movement of users, manufacturers today can create soles that offer high-quality shock absorption characteristics.

In addition, because the material can be coloured and finished in a variety of styles, it meets market demands for variety and aesthetic appeal.

A common challenge for the designer is the maintenance of performance while reducing manufacturing costs. This can be seen in recent developments in protective equipment used in sports. It is paramount that any design must guarantee, as far as possible, the safety of the sports performer. In the case of the leg protection pad for cricket players (Figure 21.8), the design has to be able to protect the legs from the potential damage that can be caused by a high-speed projectile—in this case, a hard leather-covered cricket ball, weighing 160 grams and travelling at

Figure 21.7 The challenge to achieve aesthetic appeal and improve performance, adidas®. (Copyright T. Kavanagh and A. Duncan)

up to 150 kilometres per hour. The traditional pad was an elaborate and heavy construction of fabric padding reinforced by bamboo rods. Today lighter and stronger materials are available that not only provide greater protection but which also overcome the need for labour-intensive manufacture and assembly. The modern one-piece moulded pad has reduced the cost of manufacture and brought about improvements in performance.

the future

A number of recent developments will have a major impact on how designers will work with materials in the future but I highlight two here. First, are the staggering recent developments in materials and advanced manufacturing through materials science research. Second, but of equal importance, are the social and economic impacts that spring from significant growth in global demand set against a pattern of diminishing resources. Clearly these need to be considered in the context of climate change and other issues associated with the future sustainability of the planet. In many respects, the first must mitigate against the immediate threats of the second. In considering new areas of exploration in materials and manufacture, two developments are of particular note: the creation of materials at a

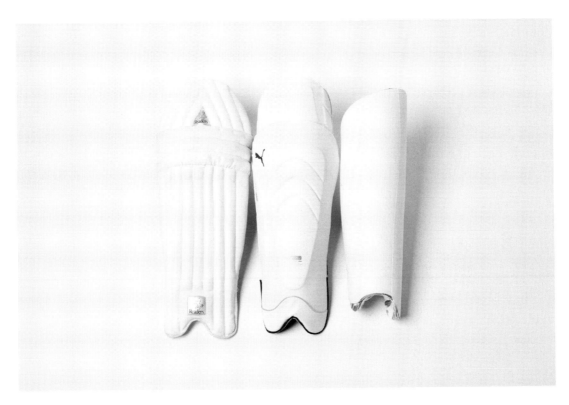

Figure 21.8 The evolution of the cricket leg pad, reducing manufacturing costs and improving performance. (Copyright T. Kavanagh and A. Duncan)

molecular level—*nanotechnology*—and technology's attempts to discover new paradigms and models that will facilitate innovation in material science and its applications inspired by a study of nature—*biomimicry*.

Nanotechnological processes have the potential to revolutionize the manufacture of products in two distinct ways. They change our perception of top-down processes such as reforming bulk materials into something smaller, and they inspire a rethinking of bottom-up processes such as assembling structures from tiny component units. Fashion researcher Suzanne Lee points out: 'The former has resulted in the nano-surface textures now appearing in clothing. The latter, potentially more exciting but still only just nascent, is referred to as *molecular manufacturing* or *molecular nanotechnology*. Using this technology, atoms can be individually positioned or, ultimately, made to self-assemble. This area of science imagines universal assemblers able to build structures, molecule by molecule, according to a set of instructions.'[8]

The consequences of nanotechnology processes are already having a significant effect on materials and their performance in daily life such as the nanoparticles used in coatings that protect surfaces such as waterproof fabrics, scratch-resistant paints, self-cleaning glass and in protective medical products.

A significant new paradigm in the creation of new materials arises from our growing understanding of how problems have been solved in nature. The phenomenon of biomimicry is now well established and has given rise to numerous innovations. The aim of biomimicry is not to copy nature but rather to understand the science behind natural phenomena. In the world of material science, biomimicry can inform the development of smart

materials or hybrids that offer unprecedented performance safely, economically and sustainably. As science writer Janine M. Benyus points out in her book *Biomimicry: Innovation Inspired by Nature*, these materials, although wonderfully strong, are manufactured by petroleum-derived materials that are processed using large quantities of energy to create great heat and pressure and employ toxic chemicals. By contrast, the spider can produce an equally strong fibre at a normal temperature without the need for such heat, pressure or toxicity. Benyus captures the essence of the ambition of biomimicry when she says:

> If we could learn what the spider does, we could take a soluble raw material that is infinitely renewable and make a super-strong water-insoluble fiber with negligible energy inputs and no toxic outputs. We could apply that processing strategy to any number of fibre precursors. Imagine what it would do for our fiber industry, which is now so heavily dependant on petroleum, both for raw material and processing![9]

There is little doubt that many new materials will come from our closer understanding of nature. More importantly, such understanding might well stimulate new thinking for a sustainable future.

Never has it been more important for designers to take an ethical stance about the materials that are used in the production of their designs. It is not just about the commodity but also about how it is processed. As Benyus points out, there is a need to question the approach of 'heat, beat and treat', where large amounts of energy and chemicals are used in bringing a material to market. It is now vital to think 'reduce, reuse, recycle' and to reduce the impact of industrial production. Globally we need to reduce energy used and resources needed while ensuring biological and chemical stability and safety. Above all, it is vital to identify renewable or sustainable sources of materials.

Observing nature and the way it works to sustain its ecology may be seen as a metaphor for a sustainable industrial ecology. What will be critical is the thoughtful management of resources, energy efficient methods of manufacture, responsible attitudes to consumption and the effective disposal of products at the end of their useful lives through recycling. This has to happen if this planet is to be sustained for future generations and to improve the quality of their lives. The designer has a major part to play in this endeavour.

CHAPTER SUMMARY

- Materials can impart the most fundamental characteristics on a product, including performance and personality.
- Informed selection and use of new materials can enhance product longevity, assist recycling and reduce landfill.
- The characterization of a material involves the definition of its attributes. These concern its physical qualities, its ability to be perceived through the senses, its ability to convey cultural associations, its processing characteristics and its cost factors.
- Engage with materials to develop your knowledge. Explore and investigate them though studio practice, experimentation and reading technical literature. Seek to learn from materials scientists.
- Both human history and nature have much to tell us about the creation and use of materials in the future.
- Nanotechnology has the potential to revolutionize the manufacture of products through both a top-down and a bottom-up influence.
- Never has the designer had such choice in materials, but never has it been more important for the designer to take an ethical stance about the materials that are used in the production of their designs.

chapter 22

user-centred collaboration in graphic design

sharon helmer poggenpohl

ABOUT THIS CHAPTER

The craft of graphic design has been democratized in the digital realm with software packages and templates making the appearance of graphic design easier to simulate. Information is increasingly passed through electronic means, yet many educational programs hang on to print as their foundation. If the craft of graphic design is available to all—and aesthetic sensibility remains elusive for most ordinary or casual amateurs—is aesthetic skill a sufficient platform on which to base a career? I would answer no; it is an entry to the profession qualification. What, then, does a graphic designer need to know and perform today?

This chapter appeals for closer collaboration between graphic designers and product designers. Both groups will benefit, but there are particular values for the graphic design community. These values concern an improved ability to meet the needs and wants of users, a better ability to create and apply prototypes to test and develop ideas and professional skills of sensitive leadership in collaborative team working. But there are challenges too. Design is still a young profession, and this chapter concludes with an appeal to bring maturity through stronger design research. Understanding and applying these pointers can enhance employability and help junior designers make an impact in an organization.

an interface between graphic design and product design

All designers, but particularly graphic designers, need broad knowledge of cultural, social and technological change, and this is dynamic; they must keep abreast of new developments and continue learning within the condition of continuous change. They need true intellect and understanding with which to participate in teams that address difficult social problems relating to information and its use. If anything, the world of information has become both more accessible and more complex. Of course, someone can decide to become a boutique designer working with small businesses on small projects over which he or she and the client have tight control, but my interest here is in young designers who want to change the world through smart participation on significant projects that necessarily cross disciplinary lines. Such problems are not static or simple but exhibit a changeable and complex character.

For too long the various subdisciplines of design have been isolated from each other. Design is a discipline that encompasses urban and regional

Table 22.1 OVERLAPS BETWEEN DESIGN SUBDISCIPLINES

Urban / Regional Planning	Architecture	Environment	Product	Communication
Aesthetics	*Aesthetics*	*Aesthetics*	*Aesthetics*	*Aesthetics*
Commercial use	Building materials			
	Building types			
	Business investment			
	Climate	Climate		
	Construction	Construction	Distribution	Distribution
Energy	***Energy Engineering***	***Energy Engineering***	***Energy Engineering***	***Engineering***
		Flora / Fauna		
	Function Human Factors	***Function Human Factors***	***Function Human Factors***	***Function Human Factors***
Industrial use		Interpretation	Interaction	Interaction
			Manufacture	Information
	Material science		Material science	
Meaning	***Meaning***	***Meaning***	***Meaning***	***Meaning***
Parks		Parks		Media
Patterns of Use	***Patterns of Use***	***Patterns of Use***	***Patterns of Use***	***Patterns of Use***
		Public services		
Recreation		Recreation		
Residential use	Structure	Shelter	Shelter	
	Style	***Style***	***Style***	***Style***
Tax investment		Tax investment		
Transportation				
Waste disposal				
Water supply				
Zoning plan	Zoning compliance			

Aspects shared by four or all sub-disciplines are presented as bold italic.

Reproduced with permission from S. H. Poggenpohl and Keiichi Sato, eds, *Design Integrations, Research and Collaboration* (Intellect Books, 2009), p. 11; graphic from author.

planning, architecture, environment, product and graphic design for example. Yes, they all operate in somewhat different realms relating to their physical result, yet their issues and processes overlap. To understand just how they overlap, I developed Table 22.1.

Revealingly, all the subdisciplines appearing in this table share some common concerns, including aesthetics, meaning and patterns of use. It would be useful to step back from this bigger view to examine one particular interface: the one between product and graphic design.

Historically, product and graphic design have shared interests and practices in, for example, signage, packaging and exhibit design. The digital realm has increased shared practice to include that of interface and interaction design. Communication and product design subdisciplines bring different perspectives to these shared practices, but both are essential to the success of many projects. One key topic of shared interest is semantics.

A number of design theorists have examined the semantic or meaning dimension of products. Klaus Krippendorff, professor of communication at the University of Pennsylvania, states that meaning is the focus of design.[1] Buildings, parks, objects, words and images mean something, and it is the meaning of these designed artefacts that people consider and interact with. Back in 1973, the psychologist J. J. Gibson coined the term 'affordance'.[2] Artefacts speak to people through their apparent affordance—that is, they suggest what actions can be performed. In some situations, design can be misleading—door handles that say 'pull' with their form but require a physical push to open or misaligned type entries in voting ballots that cause voters to select against their intention. In these cases, the artefact has failed to communicate effectively; its meaning was confusing, giving rise to a wrong action. We need to remember that product designs communicate and graphic designs function. Graphic design has been slow to recognize its functional characteristics—its attention has too often focused on being artful. If design is beautiful and unique but fails to be understandable and useful

(function), people's interaction with it is frustrating. More than anything, design for interaction on Web sites has brought home to graphic and communication designers the importance of function to users of electronic communication. While product designers have a long history of considering function, they can learn something about communication from graphic designers. Likewise, graphic designers can learn something about function from product designers. Interestingly, when I look at how the Library of Congress in the United States categorises these two subdisciplines, I find product design under Technology and graphic design under Art. One would hope that products and communications can be both technologically smart and functional, and also artful in affordance and communication.

towards user-centred design

Another shared interest across product and graphic design is design process as it relates to understanding users. *User-centred design* (also called human-centred design) takes the end user into consideration in the design process. The designer is not an isolated genius, expressing and creating his or her own reality to an eager but passive audience, but instead is a mediator for people and their way of life.

In 1986, the French sociologist Abraham Moles expressed the role of graphic design in an article titled 'The Legibility of the World: A Project of Graphic Design'. He framed legibility within everyday life and the projects people want to accomplish. Moles understood design as a support to an individual's life—for example to find an airport, change a colour, follow instructions, compare alternatives or any of the many searches, procedures or comparisons that advance action in daily life. Design's measure of success is found in supporting user action. He writes:

> Wanting a legible world, design seeks to transform *visibility* into *legibility*, that is, into that operation of the mind that arranges things in the form of signs into an intelligible whole in order to prepare a strategy for action.[3]

He goes on to suggest that poorly conceived and developed design robs people of time and that we need to find methods with which to study everyday life. One candidate approach is *micropsychology*, which uses as a guide the concepts of micro-scenario and of generalized costs to permit the analysis of micro-anxieties, micro-pleasures, micro-structures, micro-events, or micro-decisions—the entire web of life. Successful user-centred design finds ways to study the micro-events of people's lives as they relate to design, and this may happen in various ways throughout the design process. In the early design stages, examples include observing users perform tasks such as searching a database for specific information and noting how their search strategy changes or their frustration or level of satisfaction changes. Napawan Sawasdichai, a PhD student with whom I worked, studied how people searched various Web sites.[4] She set a task on a Web site and videotaped ten individuals from two positions as they worked on the task. One camera observed the screen, and the other camera observed the participants' faces. Figure 22.1 illustrates Sawasdichai's coding scheme—adapted from one called 'Chernoff faces', in which each facial feature represents a certain dimension of the search, the time spent or the participant's state of mind. For example eyebrows (angle and weight)

indicate a struggling state, the size of the face indicates the amount of information collected, the hair indicates decision-making (no hair—no decision) and the mouth indicates satisfaction. Each face is a composite of the participant's search activity. By scanning the ten faces, the researcher can see the commonalities of participant experience. In scenario two, only one participant was dissatisfied with the result (facial frown); in scenario one, seven participants were satisfied and three were dissatisfied.

With a user-centred approach, the designer is no longer centre-stage, but has been replaced by the people to be served by design.

Universal and participatory design

How people actually accomplish tasks has an interesting history. A significant milestone in the early twentieth century was the work of F. W. Taylor in the United States. His time and motion studies brought a new international focus on efficiency, but the broader movement can be seen to include the disability rights movement of the 1970s (with roots in the 1960s civil rights movement) that culminated in the Americans with Disabilities Act.[5] This revealed that fundamental work was needed to understand what disabled people required to access buildings, public transit and the streetscape. New awareness confirmed that designers needed to design for someone who was not him- or herself; they should not merely project their own body or mind onto a situation, but rather they needed to observe users and be empathic. This approach to considering the users of designed objects led to a more general concern for people, now referred to as *universal design*.

The Scandinavian participatory design movement of the past thirty years that sought to respect and collaborate with the people who would

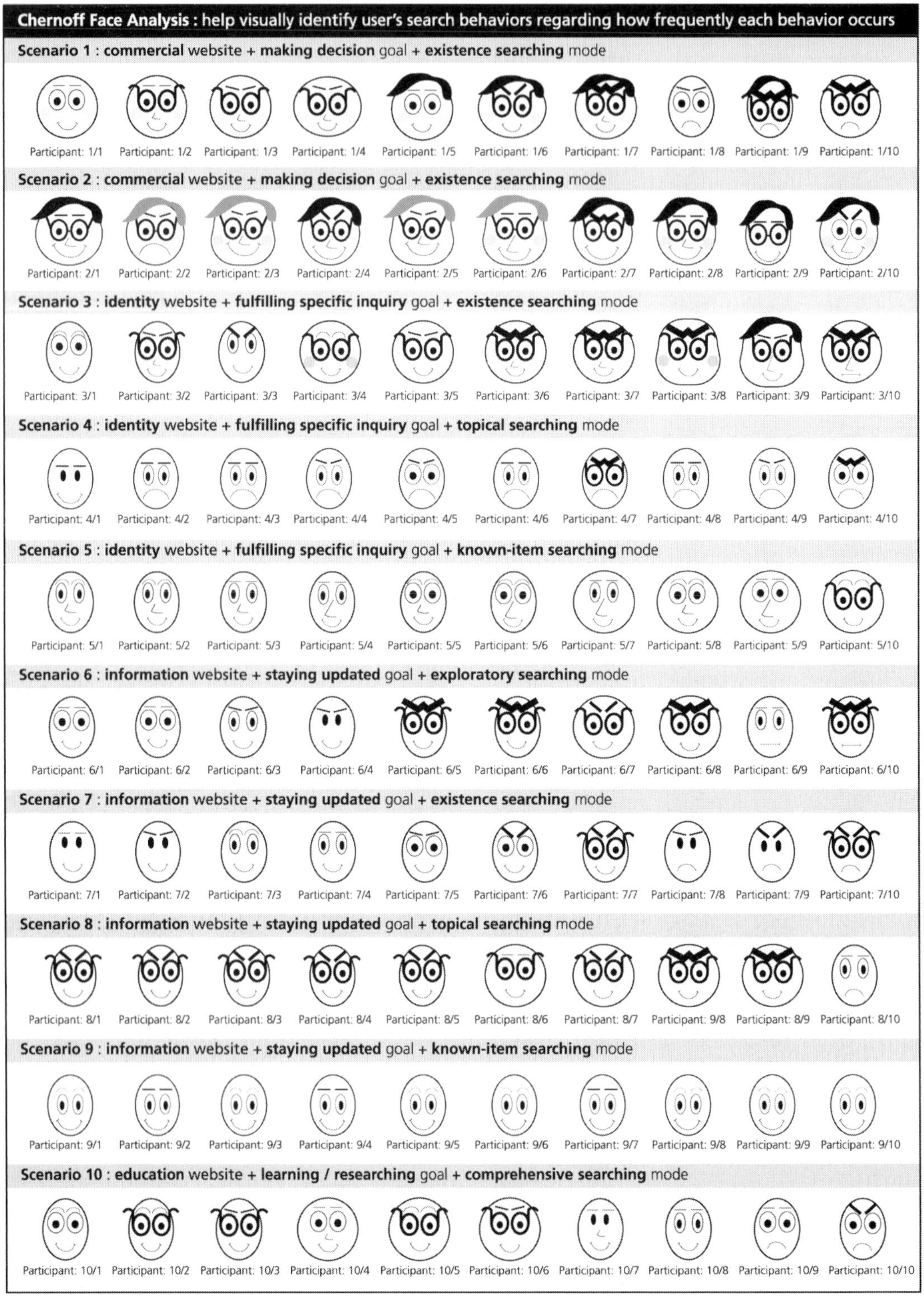

Figure 22.1 An illustration from Napawan Sawasdichai's research using Chernoff faces to summarize Web site search scenario results. (Copyright Napawan Sawasdichai)

ultimately use a design also embraced this emerging tradition. To these forerunners, we should add digital technology that has become increasingly refined and robust during the past decade or so. Where previously it was difficult to achieve technological goals, today's more reliable and adaptable technologies make it possible to probe how people actually conceive of a task and what their mental model of tasks and goals might be. In the redesign of a city park in the small Colorado mountain community where I live, the elicitation of feedback from residents and others was vital. The planners and designers for the park took public comment seriously, but such processes are not without difficulty, as I will discuss later.

In later design stages, asking people to interact with prototypes while being observed helps designers to see weaknesses in their own thinking, enabling them to make adjustments to improve a design before significant money is spent on its final development and release. Designers are good at creating prototypes. In the past, prototypes were largely of the appearance variety—their look and feel was vital. Today designers create prototypes that support the questioning processes of design. The following sequence of images shows a

Figure 22.2 A designer observes children playing a prototype game. (Copyright author)

Figure 22.3 Testing ideas using prototypes can provide unique insights to user perceptions, strategies and preferences. (Copyright author)

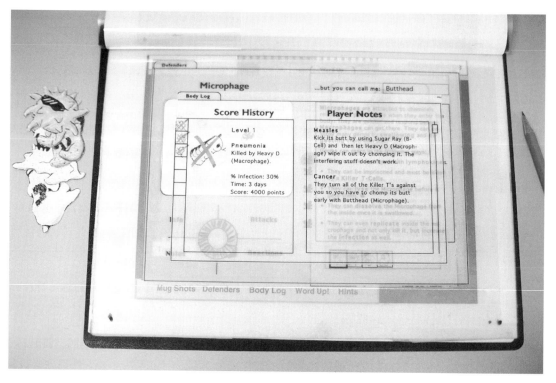

Figure 22.4 The prototype game simulates the screen messages, characters and playing environment. (Copyright author)

designer using prototypes to engage users (in this case, children) to better understand whether a design is working. The project concerns the design of a computer game that aims to help students learn about blood and how it attacks germs. The characters in this disease drama include macrophages, T-cells and red blood cells. I think we will see more and more learning tools taking the form of games.

teamwork

Increasingly, both product designers and graphic designers are concerned with developing information products. Developing information products invariably requires a team of people, because few individuals have the necessary breadth and depth of knowledge and skills. One essential ingredient is the creative skill of thinking about something that doesn't yet exist but which could be useful. Working with others who contribute ideas and skills enriches one's experience through informal learning. Outcomes and processes inherent in such work broaden one's perspective and provide preparation for future learning and work. Teamwork can be both frustrating and rewarding. Many university design programs have teamwork built into their curriculum. The problem with this is often that teams are composed of individuals with the same background—all product or all graphic designers for example. This sets the

Being Creative with Colleagues

Most designing is a team effort. Teams can help to clarify a problem and generate some initial ideas through formal meetings or informal discussion. Many design teams use a loose form of brainstorming to toss ideas around at the early stages of a project. When some initial ideas have been produced, meetings, discussion and further brainstorming are a very good way of generating more ideas and developing the initial ones.

Engage a few of your colleagues by circulating preliminary ideas to get their comments. Perhaps meet to discuss and develop your initial ideas. Further versions can then be circulated for comment and improvement until the work is finalised. This is essentially employing the powerful heuristic of successive approximation or iteration.

By involving other people, you can usually work more creatively than by keeping the problem to yourself. A danger is that you might expose your ideas to criticism at a stage when they are only partially formed and vulnerable. One way of guarding against this is to resolve to treat criticisms as opportunities for improving your ideas rather than as discouragement. Try to work with people who are not inclined to be overcritical.

From: R. Roy, *Design and Designing* (T211), The Open University, Blk 3 (2010), p. 98.

stage for intense competition to control the project and provides little opportunity to learn new perspectives on an idea or observe different skills brought into play. Teams with mixed backgrounds provide a richer and more realistic foundation for collaboration.

The Illinois Institute of Technology, where I formerly taught, has had for the past fifteen years, inter-professional projects that engage both undergraduate and graduate students across many disciplines.[6] Projects are posted by teachers to solicit students to join based on their interest and the list of disciplines the project will need. This

experience is important preparation for participation in commercial design projects. Today design success relies on a combination of leadership and well-developed interpersonal skills. Information products are developed by teams that include interface and interaction designers, software designers and content experts. More and more projects require the ability for combining skills of planning and team working with international and intercultural collaboration.[7] Breakdowns in communication require remedy. To effectively work with others, designers need to be clear about what knowledge and skills they can contribute; have empathy, understanding and respect for those from other disciplines; understand the foundational differences among disciplines and be willing to find common ground for action. People need preparation for teamwork, they must have opportunities to reflect on collaboration and the social and intellectual dynamics of this work that can be rewarding and frustrating. Collaboration is not always easy, but it is the future of design.

what do designers bring to a collaborative process?

Designers bring many attributes to collaborative design projects, but here I focus on some key skills that seem vital for professional practice today.

Being communication savvy from multiple viewpoints

Designers who work in collaborative situations become good listeners. They foster the commonalities, approach conflict with an open mind and are willing to see problems from different viewpoints. Human chemistry of a team is not inconsequential. Designers need to get on with different personality types. This attention and flexibility of mind support the second attribute.

Conceiving and constructing representations to support creative synthesis of multiple points of view

Designers are adept at representing relationships through a variety of models, including images, constructions and diagrams. The more forms of representation the designer understands and can use, the better. Abstract diagrams particularly can help collaborators to sort out relationships, set boundaries and see priorities and emerging patterns of agreement. This skill is rooted in a co-working of communication and representation. It is less about making pretty diagrams (certainly at the early stage in a project) and more about constructively and interactively thinking together.

Creating prototypes that reveal emerging ideas and unresolved problems

As a project begins to take shape, the prototypes that the designer creates synthesize and make physical the emerging design. Some prototypes may not look anything like the artefact to be designed. They may be developed to answer conceptual, behavioural or procedural questions, eliciting interaction from potential user groups. It is often important to use simple materials and actions that signal the tentative character of the design at the early stage. Even seemingly crude prototypes can foster genuine interaction from users, as they are not intimidated into acquiescence by a polished representation. Pop-up books provide a useful example of applying interactive prototyping. With these one can select sequentially, pull, flip, unfold, etc. Such simple actions can reveal user thinking: what attracts, what

is selected, any desires, confusion or other mental state important to understanding how a developing design might work. Prototypes advance design thinking through user feedback and signal to the collaborative team how their thinking is developing and where unresolved problems or unrealized opportunities exist.

Applying appropriate processes

There is a real skill in applying design processes that respect users and glean information from them through observation and interaction at various stages of a project. Skilled designers bring thoughtful and creative design processes to their collaborations. These can change fluidly based on the dynamics of information acquisition, whether from other team members with different disciplinary perspectives on the project or from users or other stakeholders engaged with prototypes or planning.

But alongside the application of skills come a number of challenges.

challenges for designers in collaborative processes

The difficulty of organizing design knowledge

Where are the theories that support our design performance discussed, challenged or demonstrated? Where can serious criticism of design process or achievement be found? We need to see more discussion of design failures.[8] In 2007, this author undertook a review of design literature going back five decades and found twenty-nine journals covering a range of design subdisciplines (excluding architecture, which has a more developed knowledge base). Many new journals failed to thrive and quietly died. Some were notable in their time, such as *Design Quarterly* or the *Information Design Journal*, both of which surprised many in the design community with their unexpected demise. From the list compiled, the trend is clear: only two journals have survived from the 1960s, no survivors from the 1970s, four from the 1980s, eleven in the 1990s, and twelve in the first decade of the twenty-first century.[9] This demonstrates changing interests among the design community—a growing appetite for better-documented ideas and claims, a growing interest in research backed up with evidence and thoughtful, well-researched criticism. This has implications for masters courses and beyond, and we have seen growth in PhD design programs worldwide—there are now nearly 100 doctoral programs distributed around the globe.[10] Faculty and students engaged in these programs generate research, reviews and critical commentary. To do so, they must read, consider and sometimes challenge new information or knowledge. This is how design knowledge advances.

> "Where can serious criticism of design process or achievement be found? We need to see more discussion of design failures."

Creating a culture of applying design information

Another crucial dimension to the above discussion cannot be overlooked: design practitioners need to take research results and well-founded criticism seriously. Embedding information into practice is a major challenge for the design professions. We need a model of practice that seeks out new knowledge and integrates it into the

creative and analytical processes of commercial working. This is nothing more than normal professional attention to continuous change.

Dealing with conflict

Design is a subject that naturally gives rise to conflict. The questioning of accepted norms, the creative reconfiguring of ideas, the challenging of design requirements and the potential diversity of participants will all, potentially, create frictions and conflict in design projects. Such conflict means that designers need to pay particular attention to justifying their decisions or positions. However, for a number of reasons, designers are increasingly relying on superficial research to underpin their design outputs. Commercial pressures combined with a lack of research training mean that information about, for example, users and markets can be quite weak. In the profession generally, there is little recognition of theories that might back up design positions. How much stronger design could be if we could apply theories and results from deeper investigations from sociology, anthropology, business or marketing, with their proven theoretical and methodological grounding.

Building on tacit knowledge

Too often designers' performance is predicated on what Michael Polanyi called 'tacit knowledge'—knowledge that is developed through experience.[11] Such knowledge is difficult to describe in words; you might know this as that feeling of 'rightness' when a designed layout is satisfying, but it can arise in many different situations. The educational practice of the critique is an attempt to overcome this difficulty; it requires intellectual engagement with design that goes beyond making something, aesthetic flair or one's personal charm and sales ability. Critiques engage the participants in the context for which something is being designed. It embraces both the perceptions of the problem and the proposals for solution. It embraces a proposal's competitive advantage, its creative form and aesthetic resolution, its functional characteristics and other criteria specific to a project.

> **"Such knowledge is difficult to describe in words; you might know this as that feeling of 'rightness' when a designed layout is satisfying, but it can arise in many different situations."**

towards an agenda for research in design practice

It is unfortunate that education and practice are so disconnected. Design practice has little time to engage in unfunded research. However, it can identify important research needs that the university sector can supply if only a new symbiotic relationship could be fostered. Currently the research done by corporations is proprietary; it reaches a broader audience only when it is too old to competitively matter. On the other hand, in general, universities are mandated to openly publish their research findings as they serve the public good. The following research issues go some way towards a new agenda. They should particularly strike a chord with those who see their future at this interface between design research and design practice. They are in no particular order.

Design needs its own research identity
For the past half century, design research has been using methods from other disciplines.

Perhaps we need to develop methods that are more fitting for the research questions that interest design. Fundamental issues such as how robust research findings need to be, how immediately results are needed and whether the research is exploratory or in-depth will guide methodological approaches. New research methods need to be tested for their usefulness to design and their acceptance by other disciplines regarding their legitimacy. Some individuals are addressing these issues. For example, Karel van der Waarde, a design practitioner and teacher, is using rhetorical theory to analyse medical information for patients.[12] Rhetorical theory was able to make visible some otherwise invisible problems concerning how particular information was constructed and disseminated. He used existing theory in a new way to help understand an ongoing practical problem.

There's a need to develop design strategies and approaches
Theories that are useful to design performance such as gestalt or action theory, or theories of feedback or rhetoric, need to be identified and demonstrated as models and further demonstrated through practice in actual design projects.

We should sell research like we sell design
Research findings are often reported in a dry, standardized form that turns off practitioners. Not only do we fail to reveal how research findings might be applied in specific and immediate design needs, we fail to engage the practitioner community. We have the skills to interpret and communicate, but we don't apply them. It would also be useful to get feedback. We need to know how things worked out and what new questions

or problems arose. In a sense, performance cases are needed as a proof of concept for the research and its findings.

We need to improve collaboration in design

We need to find better ways of negotiating a common process, including an understanding of how different disciplines can fit together and contribute to a project. We need better decision-making processes that engage important stakeholders, and we need to understand design complexity in the form of interactions between information, changing priorities, design interventions and creative insights. Reporting on how conflicting decisions are addressed and the power of visual methods could allow designers to make powerful contributions to knowledge.

A need for documented case studies

Design theory and practice would be better informed if we generated thorough case studies or stories that could be searched and accessed. Too often designers finish a project and never unpack the knowledge gained—whether through research or application. Other disciplines such as business, health care and the law have a substantial and searchable repository of cases. The technology for these things exist—the real need for work is in relation to the intellectual foundation for the cases; understanding how design practitioners or researchers might use them, what information is needed and what can be filtered or tagged for access.

Leadership within a user-centred process

Design will always operate within a context of imperfect and dynamic information. Despite a growing awareness of user-centred design, we need strategies for acquiring knowledge of users' needs, habits, understandings and lifestyle. We need to be able to judge that we have sufficient information for our goals at different stages in a design process and when we need to synthesize this through design leadership. That is, at what point should user investigation stop and the designer or team take professional responsibility for making decisions about users in a project? User-centred approaches can become a crutch and a time-sink with diminishing rewards.

skills for a life in design

As long ago as the 1970s, Skidmore, Owings and Merrill, a large and notable US architecture firm, had a chart of the changing responsibilities of designers within the firm. Because architecture is a well-developed subdiscipline of design, it is no surprise that very early on the firm thought of how a life in architecture might unfold. A life in design can follow many paths. It seems that we are, by nature, either drawn to specialist or generalist activity, and within either of these, to particular interests or skills that we want to develop and whose rewards (creative, intellectual, monetary) bring us to further development. For too long our focus has been on developing designers for their earliest position, believing that their further development would occur on the job. Of course this happens, but it may be too slow, too limited or incomplete for some. The diagram presented in Figure 22.5 shows various paths in design that are typically available. The critical decision points are flagged: deciding to take a first degree in design, to join a consultancy or a corporation, to take a graduate degree, to follow a professional degree or a research degree program, to become a teacher or researcher. One may also return to corporate or consultant work or embrace the high-risk possibility of opening one's own design practice or becoming an entrepreneur.

None of the many decision points are trivial— because they are *your* life in design. The figure cannot show all possible transitions one might consider, such as when to move from a consultancy

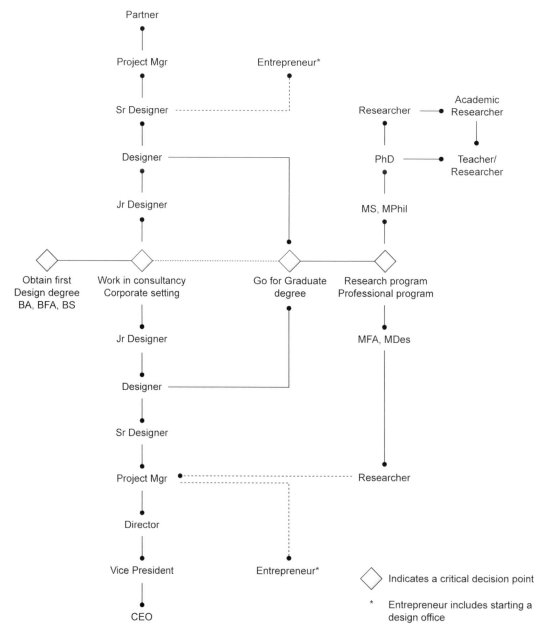

Figure 22.5 Career paths for designers, revealing critical decision points. (Copyright author)

to a corporation or vice versa, or when to take an advanced degree in design or another discipline, or when to create one's own design practice, or become an entrepreneur. Figure 22.5 does show what is beyond a first degree and a first design position, because designers need to think strategically about their interests, skills, knowledge and future. Design evolves based on changing social, cultural and technological developments; thus, to be an effective designer, you too must pay attention and evolve.

There are many perspectives on design, but those that isolate the subdisciplines are short-changing the true value of design and the collaborative contribution to be made. More than ever, design now exists in a social context—one that reflects many dimensions of change: cultural, economic, social, political, ecological and even philosophical and spiritual. Solving technical problems and resolving aesthetic character are no longer sufficient, so the designer is called upon to be observant of change and engage in continuous learning and reflection as a condition of his or her role as a designer. Using and doing research are ways to improve design performance; they can also be instrumental to understanding problems and opportunities in new ways.

Designers cannot know everything a project might depend on; yet they cannot be naive and ignore what escapes their knowledge or skill. Collaboration or teamwork remedies such shortcomings and provides informal learning that extends knowledge and experience. For example projects that involve a synthesis of development needs and ecological sensitivity or that include sensitively crossing cultural boundaries will test designers and their teammates. These can foster new ideas and new ways of working that enrich the designing process.

Converting a Concept into a Proposal

Your design might be very creative, but can your idea be manufactured? Will your proposal be usable, safe and a good value? To answer these questions, you need to turn your concept into a well-defined design proposal. It's something that all designers, from graphic artists to architects, need to do. It's a stage that requires the definition of components and the arranging of these components in the most effective way. It is a complex phase of the design process. Not only do designers and design teams have to address difficult problems, they have to do this in ways that allow creative development of the concept. Practical constraints must be integrated with innovative ideas.

For many design disciplines, the process can be broken down into four stages:

1. identifying the components of a design
2. arranging or configuring those components
3. assembling or connecting those components
4. defining the characteristics of all components (e.g. appearance, material, size)

To be able to test a design—which might be a page layout, a medical product or a new garment—a designer needs to understand the components of his or her design, the designer needs to have a clear proposal for arranging and connecting these components and each component needs to have sufficient detail to be made. Another name for this transition is *embodiment*, because a concept is embodied in a defined proposal.

During a life in design, many paths open up, and those selected will provide challenges that reinvigorate design and personal growth. No longer tied to an industry that may disappear or an instrument or technique, design is tied to human purpose and meaning in the sense presented by Abraham Moles—to help people fulfil their own life projects. It is open-ended in its contribution to a humane and life-sustaining future.

CHAPTER SUMMARY

- All designers need to be highly tuned to cultural, social and technological changes. This is particularly important for those working at the interface between product design and graphic communication.

- Design is a complex negotiation because of its divergent stakeholder needs.

- Some characteristics of design, such as the creation of meaning and being user-centred, are found across the spectrum of design disciplines.

- Multidisciplinary understanding is vital, but it makes demands on our systems for collaboration. Achieving good understanding within multidisciplinary teams leads to an improved ability to meet the needs and wants of users and a better ability to create and apply prototypes to test and develop ideas.

- Designers need to bring intellect and understanding to design problems. They need to apply research strategies that are innovative, revealing and thorough, because research increasingly provides the foundation to advanced, innovative design.

- There is an emerging new agenda for design research—one aimed at informing both education and practice. It concerns the development of new strategies and approaches, the documenting of data that has proved revealing and the fostering of leadership in the creation and application of new knowledge.

chapter 23

the importance of detail design

clyde millard

ABOUT THIS CHAPTER

For many designers, the most exciting part of a design project is the initial concept stage, producing those creative and good-looking sketch proposals, models or computer-aided design (CAD) images. But the real satisfaction in design comes from seeing your product finished, manufactured and being used. This chapter looks at the less glamorous but essential post-concept design activities that help convert a design idea into something usable and makeable. It's a stage that all designs have to pass through, and it requires a combination of creative and analytical skills.

This chapter looks at how concepts are translated into layouts for practical and well-defined products and how these layouts are then developed into detail design proposals. It is a complex phase of the design process. Not only do designers and design teams have to address difficult problems, they have to do this in ways that allow the creative development of the concept. Practical constraints must be integrated with innovative ideas. This chapter looks at the building blocks of all designed outputs: the components. It suggests that understanding how components might be configured and detailed is just as important and creative as coming up with the initial concept.

from concept to layout

Earlier chapters in this collection have made strong cases for the importance of various skills and knowledge in the design process. Some have outlined the vital need for well-defined user requirements, others have highlighted the importance of creative thinking or sustainability awareness. This chapter seeks to convince you that the really important skill of being a designer in the twenty-first century is being able to convert a concept design into a detailed design in your own specialist field. In a crowded jobs market, it is

dangerous to overly rely on creative ability alone. Those designers who can guide a product towards manufacture, distribution and retail are in a position to take advantage of a much wider range of employment opportunities.

Concept design is concerned with presentation of ideas rather than precise or finished forms, but it is as well to bear in mind, even before presentation, that you will need to translate the concept, or concepts, into reality. Too much use of artist's licence can lead to credibility problems later on. This chapter is interested in all those activities that take place *after* concept generation that lead to the establishment of well-defined products. To achieve this level of completion, many and various decisions have to be made about how the parts or components of a particular product will be arranged, how functions will be implemented and how components will be sized, made, shaped and finished. The result is the definition of the design as a whole. We can call this whole the *layout*. Although the design is not finished when it reaches the end of the layout stage, all the major design decisions have been made. Changes to the design after this stage can be very costly. Another name for this phase of the design process is *embodiment*, because a concept is embodied in a particular form. Essentially the concept is embodied in the layout. Most designs require further work after embodiment. For example components usually need to be precisely specified in their dimensions and manufacturing processes need to be defined. This stage of *detail design* frequently overlaps embodiment and like embodiment, it's a stage in which the designer will, ideally, remain actively engaged even if other specialists, such as production engineers, become involved. Only the designer can ensure that essential, but perhaps intangible, qualities of the concept are carried through. Also it provides vital feedback to inform future concept design; many a designer has said, further down the development process, 'if I'd known that, I would have designed it differently in the first place!' There may be many satisfactory layouts of a concept that meet the demands of the various stakeholders in a design project. Some may more successfully suit user needs; others may suit the manufacturer better. And of course, there will be some layouts that are not practical or desirable. Layout is usually achieved through iterations—that is, cycles of development—with the design becoming clearer at each stage. This can be a complex process

in which the details of a design are progressively defined.

Different design disciplines and situations will have differing norms or conventions for presenting design concepts, and the amount and depth of design thinking will vary between concept and layout and between layout and detail design. For instance a fashion designer might present concepts as freehand sketches and a product designer might present photorealistic CAD images but both will require some layout work. Whatever the situation and however the concepts are presented, they will need to be resolved into layouts that lead to detail design. Suppose you have some ideas for a new product and have made some sketched proposals or drawings. Your sketches would probably seek to convey the main ideas, what goes where and what it will look like. Identifying these parts is the first stage along the journey to the final product. The principle would also apply to an item of clothing, a graphical user interface and many other design situations.

four stages in creating a layout

Taking a design from a concept to a layout can be complex, and it demands a more systematic approach than is usually adequate in concept generation. To reveal this systematic approach, I have presented the process of concept to layout as four stages:

1. define the main parts
2. define arrangement
3. define connections
4. define shape, material and appearance.

These are not fixed in practice, and there will be differences from one design discipline to another. Nevertheless, the four stages provide a useful guide.

Stage 1: define the main parts

In the first stage, the main parts or components are defined, and some of these will be apparent from the concept designs. These are the main, functional parts that must be present if the concept is to be realized and stakeholder requirements satisfied. Concept proposals will have provided approximate shapes and sizes and will have given an indication of the relationships between the various parts. This analysis could be applied to many types of product, for example an item of clothing where we might identify component parts such as right and left halves of the body, the sleeves, pocket, collar and so forth (Figure 23.1).

In this first stage, the purpose of each of the main parts is defined. Sometimes this is obvious and easy to achieve, while in other instances the purpose might be implicit and dependent on context. Sometimes parts are grouped together to form a larger part, and it's not always obvious which parts should be defined separately. For example an individual bristle of a toothbrush is not really a significant part and neither is one cluster of bristles, because by themselves they do not have a clearly defined function in teeth cleaning. Conversely, the head of a toothbrush can consist of an assembly of various polymers and bristles, and it's perhaps confusing to categorize this as a single

Figure 23.1 Most designs have component parts.
(Shutterstock 42604462)

component. In some products, it can be difficult to assess where one part ends and another part begins. Essentially, component properties deliver functions. These might be technical functions, usability functions, brand functions, etc. Many component properties result from what a component has been made from, its shape or surface finish, and I'll come to this later. But the success of a component also depends on it having a successful interface with other components—that is, how it is arranged and how it relates and works with other components.

Stage 2: define arrangement

With the main parts better defined, the second stage explores their arrangement. Each of the possible arrangements is called a *configuration*. This stage involves the designer in searching for the best way to arrange the parts. As with concept design, sketches can provide a fast and low-cost means of exploring variations but there are many other techniques (CAD for instance) that designers exploit to help them explore arrangements or configurations. Partly, this is a creative activity with the aim of exploring the full range of possibilities, and partly, it is informed by the designer's understanding of the various constraints imposed by practicality or specific instructions in the brief. The designer treads a difficult path where he or she tries not to waste time seeking arrangements that are clearly not going to work, whilst not missing out on opportunities for innovation or radical new thinking, which you should always be open to. Configuration is vital to design. Two types of constraints guide the exploration process. Hard constraints are those that must be satisfied, whilst soft constraints indicate those characteristics that are desirable but not essential. Establishing these is not as easy as one might think. For example, in bicycle design, the

> **"The designer treads a difficult path, where he or she tries not to waste time seeking arrangements that are clearly not going to work whilst not missing out on opportunities for innovation or radical new thinking."**

distance between the saddle and pedal used to be a hard constraint because, it was assumed, the dimensions of the human leg defined the optimum distance. But then someone came up with the idea of the mini-bike, used for tricks and jumps. It had a completely different riding position and turned this hard constraint into a soft constraint.

Figure 23.2a shows a recent model of the innovative Strida bicycle. The configuration of wheels, frame, pedals, handlebars, etc. has some similarities with traditional bicycles, but this one is designed to fold, thus enabling it to be carried or easily stored. The folding mechanism is shown diagrammatically in Figure 23.2b. The cross-member can be disconnected, allowing the frame to fold together because the top of the frame is hinged. Can you identify any other ways this cycle might fold up? A few alternatives are shown in Figure 23.2b. Generating ideas for the arrangement of parts and variations in layout is an engagement in configuration design.

Defining the arrangement of parts has major implications for function. If you get the configuration wrong, the design might not work. Fixing on an arrangement leaves you some flexibility; for example you can still adjust size and form of components, but it is a landmark in the process. Once you have explored the possibilities and fixed on an arrangement, you can move to the third stage.

Figure 23.2a A recent model from the Strida range.
(Copyright Mark Sanders)

Stage 3: define connections

In the third stage, the designer explores how the main parts are joined together. This is a stage concerned with defining *connections*. For some products, it might introduce fixings such as screws or clips. Alternatively, it might involve adhesives or processes such as brazing or welding. Fundamentally it will determine any movement between connected parts and the type of movement allowed. Despite its apparent focus on detail, this is still a creative stage. Innovation in connecting parts might make your product stand out in the marketplace, it might offer superior function or it might simply make it easier to assemble. Partly this is a stage where the design must consider the practicalities of manufacture, though some consideration of this may have been given at an earlier stage. Is a particular artefact going to be made as a one-off, in a limited batch or mass produced? Some manufacturing systems suit some processes more than others; for example it would be difficult to justify making an expensive mould if one only wished to use it to produce a small number of mouldings. The designer needs to trade off the sometimes conflicting requirements for low cost, high quality, flexibility, weight, size and speed. Where possible, it is always much cheaper to buy off-the-shelf fixings to achieve connections rather than design them and have them made for your product. In some cases, creative designing is no more than the successful synthesis of other people's components. Try to reduce the number of parts, perhaps by combining them where appropriate. Injection moulding is particularly good for achieving this. Consider snap-fit parts where relevant, and use subassemblies for efficiency. Assist manufacture by making it impossible to assemble components incorrectly. Specify large tolerances where you can.

Stage 4: define shape, material and appearance

In the fourth stage, the *form* is defined. That is, the sizes, shapes and other properties of a product such as colour and surface finish. Remember we are not only talking about the overall form but the properties of each of the components that make up the complete product. It's still possible to make changes at this stage, but your options are narrower. Decisions at all stages, but particularly at the third and fourth stages, can have a significant influence on the ability to recycle a product. Your specification of component parts, particularly what they are made from and how they are joined together, will determine whether it is worthwhile or even possible to disassemble your design at the end of its life. These decisions also determine whether certain parts can be renewed and whether the user can do this, thus extending the life of the product. While sustainability may have been on the agenda in the concept stage

Figure 23.2b A few of the possible variations for folding such a bicycle. (Copyright author)

of design, it's between concept and detail design that sustainability is decided.

By the end of the fourth stage, a design proposal will have well-defined parts joined together in specified ways. Concept designs that may have been rough or impressionistic have become clear and definite. They can be prototyped, assessed and evaluated. In practice, it is common to find designers, or more usually design teams, going back through the stages in an iterative process. As one stage reveals new problems, the team returns to a previous stage to select an alternative avenue to develop.

In my field—electronic-based consumer and industrial products—it's common for some basic packaging to be explored as part of concept design. I mean by this that we make sure essential component parts would broadly fit inside the product skin, any mechanism would work and that it would be practical and safe for users. Basically I need to establish those hard constraints early in the development process. Other important considerations at this stage are material selection, manufacturing, assembly and sustainability.

case study: the postconcept development of a food thermometer

This example of design concerns a food thermometer to be used in the catering industry. The final product is shown in Plate 28, but the story begins with some requirements and some conceptual CAD exploration.

A number of requirements were set out at the start of the project, and these impacted the layout and the detail design. It was specified that the product should have a high standard of sealing (to the standard specified in IP67, BS EN 60529 and IEC 529), it should be economical to produce and the design should be able to accommodate two completely different types of proprietary thermocouple sockets. It had been agreed at the concept stage that part of the enclosure would be 'overmoulded'[1] with a soft synthetic material to offer protection against knocks, assist grip in wet and greasy conditions and feel pleasant to the touch. It had been a given from the start of the project that the enclosure would be injection-moulded. As is usually the case, the anticipated numbers to be made and the application largely determined the manufacturing process. There is a well-accepted rule that applies here: high up-front tooling costs lead to lower part cost, whilst low up-front costs lead to higher part cost. Of course, there will always be exceptions to any rule, and size can be one of the factors, but in this case, with a five-figure number of units anticipated, injection moulding was the way to go.

The concept proposals had been prepared using three-dimensional (3D) CAD giving photorealistic images, and so we had a good idea of overall size. The concept proposed a printed circuit board (PCB) assembly with a liquid crystal display (LCD) and space to accommodate the thermocouple sockets and a PP3 battery. The first part of the development was to firm up and refine the packaging arrangements. As is often the case, particularly with electronic-based products, concurrent engineering takes place and things get changed. In this project, the specification for the PCB and LCD display changed in the period between concept and the start of detail design, but fortunately the overall space requirement stayed much the same. Significantly, the battery

Tolerance

Tolerance: the allowable variation in a specified size.

In preparing a design for manufacture, the dimensions of each component are specified by a smallest dimension and a largest dimension. The difference between these two dimensions is called the *tolerance*. When designers specify tolerances, they are estimating how precisely a component needs to be made to deliver its intended function. However, they should balance this with difficulties of manufacturing the component to that tolerance.

It might be necessary to specify a very small variation in, say, a plastic component of a drug infusion pump, where performance is vital, but designers should question whether this level of accuracy needs to be built into a child's plastic toy. Reducing the specification for tolerance beyond certain levels leads to a steep increase in manufacturing costs.

A key challenge for manufacturing engineers is to develop manufacturing methods where tolerances can be controlled. If parts are going to be assembled, they must all be made within their designed tolerances, otherwise the assembly will not function properly.

type changed from PP3 to two AA batteries so the product could be slimmer. The crucial components in any battery-powered product, and particularly with user-replaceable batteries, are the battery contacts. A set of proprietary U-shaped contacts that fit over the side wall of the battery compartment were chosen, modelled and put in place.

Fixings, sockets and seals

We knew from past experience that the best method for achieving a good level of sealing between the two halves of the casing was to use evenly spaced screws. These were located, as basic cylinders, inboard of the PCB, this being the widest component. The detail design of the seal was still to be resolved. There was some discussion about the type of screws to be used: M3 or M3.5 size locating into moulded-in brass inserts (they are sometimes inserted after moulding too)

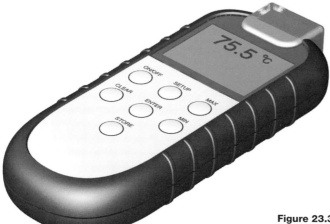

Figure 23.3 Early conceptual CAD model of the food thermometer casing. (Copyright author)

because these are best for repeated disassembly, or thread-forming screws, which are more appropriate for once-and-for-all assembly. Since this product would not be taken apart in normal use, the latter was selected. As well as being cheaper, they are usually a better solution for recycling. Seven thread-forming screws, appropriate for use with polycarbonate, were specified using O-ring seals under their heads. There was to be one brass insert used, however, for the battery compartment door because, whilst battery life would be long, the batteries would need to be changed from time to time. In addition, the battery compartment door needed to be clamped against the seal.

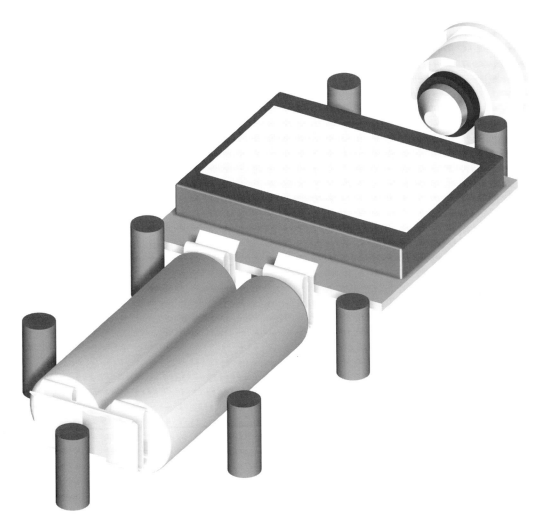

Figure 23.4 CAD representation of the layout of the major internal components: Lumberg cylindrical connector, PCB with LCD display with allowance for components on underside, battery contacts plus batteries and screw bosses. (Copyright author)

One interesting packaging problem remained: how to accommodate two alternative types of connector sockets into the basic case design. Both were widely used proprietary sockets to suit different thermocouple plug types, but neither incorporated any form of sealing. One type, the Lumberg socket, has a cylindrical threaded metal body with an inner plastic moulding to hold the contacts. The other type, known as subminiature, has a rectangular plastic body housing the metal contacts. These are shown in Figures 23.5 and 23.6. The solution devised was two moulded cartridges, each

designed to suit its socket type but with the same external dimensions where they interfaced with the two case halves. The cartridges also functioned as containers into which sealant could be poured and allowed to set during assembly.

It was known that in use the Lumberg plug was often tightened up with the aid of a hand tool, so it was necessary to design a strong location of the socket in the casing to prevent it turning. The subminiature socket needed to be located against the plug being inserted and withdrawn, so a plastic pin was used to locate it in the cartridge.

Figure 23.5 Cartridge to suit Lumberg socket. Note keyway to locate socket to cartridge and similarly cartridge to top moulding. Top and bottom mouldings shown without overmoulding. (Copyright author)

Figure 23.6 Cartridge to suit the subminiature socket. It is introduced from inside and located by pin from below, sealant added and cap fitted. Note hole for cable exit. (Copyright author)

Material selection

Material choice had a significant influence on detail design. As already indicated, strength, ruggedness and good sealing together with economical manufacture were major requirements of the design. Polycarbonate was chosen as the material for the enclosure because of its good mechanical properties, excellent impact resistance and its availability in transparent grades. The latter property was significant because, for simplicity of construction, we could mould the whole enclosure in clear material with no separate windows.

> **"A quality feel can comprise of many factors: solidity, good power-to-weight ratio, attractive surface finish and graphics, attention to detail and how parts fit together."**

Whilst polycarbonate is a relatively expensive plastic material, in this instance it proved to be a cost-effective solution because of its many good properties. Cheapest is not always best. Much of the exterior surface is covered by a combination of the overmoulding, the membrane control panel and graphic labels. It was known from a previous product that there would be good adhesion between the overmoulded synthetic rubber and the polycarbonate body.

Quality feel is a vital, if sometimes intangible, product characteristic today, particularly in a professional handheld instrument. It is sometimes overlooked in the drive to reduce costs but it can make a big difference at point of sale, inspiring confidence when compared with flimsy, creaking competition. A quality feel can comprise of many factors: solidity, good power-to-weight ratio, attractive surface finish and graphics, attention to detail and how parts fit together. Good feel and good looks work together to convey quality.

Figure 23.7 reveals the overmoulded top and bottom mouldings, membrane switch panel, labels, battery door and fixing screws. The disk shown beneath the PCB is a sounder that sits on a resonating chamber in the bottom moulding. The holes in the chamber are sealed by the self-adhesive label below, and the label also covers

the heads of the two fixing screws. The battery door covers four fixing screws, leaving just one fixing screw visible at the rounded end.

Materials and process

We knew that, in this instance, to stand any chance of getting a good seal performance, the mouldings would need to be strong and sturdy to resist any tendency to distort when screwed tightly together to compress the seals. So the wall thickness in key areas of the polycarbonate mouldings was set at three millimetres. This might seem generous compared to consumer products of a similar size—say, TV remotes or portable phones, where wall thicknesses of around two millimetres or less are commonplace—but those products do not have to withstand immersion in water. Areas of the moulding where no compression was needed were given slightly thinner walls. It is good practice when designing mouldings to avoid large and sharp changes in wall thickness as this creates moulding flow problems. The designer should also be mindful that during the moulding process, the molten plastic should flow from thicker areas to thinner areas rather than the other way around; therefore, the position of the 'gate' is a factor in most moulding design. The gate is the point where the material is injected into the moulding cavity and with most small, higher-volume products, the gate position will be around the periphery of the moulding. With larger mouldings, the gate is usually towards the centre of the moulding and is often disguised or covered up on the final product. Another advantage of a thicker-walled moulding is that it makes the design of internal features adjacent to the outside wall (typically ribs or bosses) much easier. To avoid the bane of mouldings, those unsightly hollows or sink marks,

Figure 23.7 Exploded view showing relationship between electronic components and mouldings. (Copyright author)

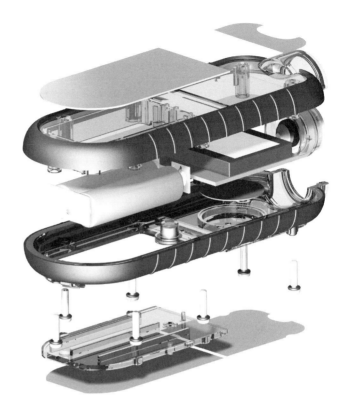

the general rule of thumb is that the thickness of the features should be no more than two-thirds of the thickness of the outside wall. Most of the major suppliers of plastic materials can provide design guidelines about this and other factors that need to be taken into consideration when designing mouldings.

It seemed logical to use the overmoulded material to provide the seal between the two halves of the casing. So a V-shaped seal profile was designed into the top half of the casing, operating on the flat polycarbonate sidewall of the lower casing. The seal profile continued around the periphery of the bulge that accommodates the connector cartridge in the top half of the casing, with a similar half-circle seal in the bottom half to

make a circular seal. Also the overmould material formed three feet—one at the rounded end and two near the connector end—for stability and grip on smooth surfaces. The battery compartment was protected with a seal around its periphery, but it was also necessary to ensure it was screwed up tightly before the instrument would operate, so the battery door was designed with a moulded pin that penetrated the bottom casing and operated an interlock switch on the PCB, all inside the battery compartment seal. An O-ring seal inserted into the bottom moulding provides sealing around the screw hole in the battery door, and the screw itself is held captive by a fibre washer. The battery door is reinforced with ribs for maximum strength.

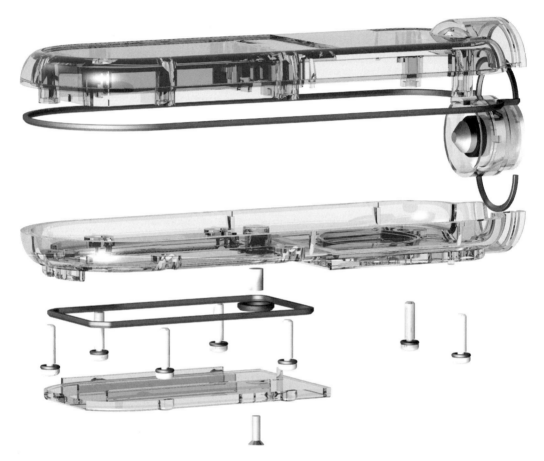

Figure 23.8 The various sealing components of the food
thermometer (no overmoulding shown). (Copyright author)

Figure 23.8 reveals a number of sealing components, but the main seals around the periphery
and cartridge are part of the overmoulding process. The battery door seal is a separate item,
and the seals around the battery door screw and
the seven fixing screws are O-ring seals.

Modelling and manufacturing

The client already had some experience working
with a manufacturer in China, so, when finalised,

the 3D CAD files were forwarded to the manufacturer. File transfer systems remain something of a
black art, and any design office sending out work
needs to have effective procedures for checking
that the files have been received in good order
and that the format can be opened and read.

Rapid prototyping, for example using the technique of vacuum casting to create highly accurate
3D models, was not carried out for this product. Partly this is because the mould tooling was

relatively inexpensive but also because the mate-rials used for rapid prototyping are quite limited. In this instance, it was not possible to test char-acteristics such as mechanical strength because the models would differ significantly from the final injection-moulded components. This was a shame, because in this project, we really wanted to test the clamping performance of the screws and the effectiveness of the seals. Rapid proto-typing can be an extremely useful tool in product development, but on occasions the limitations of the materials used, and sometimes the precision, can give misleading results.

After a relatively short space of time, the first-off mouldings arrived back in the design office. Finish and colour were not perfect, but the mouldings were good enough for testing to begin. Sealing seemed to be quite promising, with very little ingress of moisture into the cas-ing when immersed in one metre of water. How-ever, when the assembly underwent a drop test, one metre onto concrete, the proprietary battery contacts fractured. Bearing in mind the crucial role the battery contacts played in this product, it was decided to change to conical spring-type contacts. This meant that the battery compart-ment part of the mouldings needed to be modi-fied to accommodate the new contacts, mainly a redesign of the ribs to retain the new contacts. With these modifications to the mouldings com-pleted, further tests were satisfactorily carried out. At the same time, the moulders provided preproduction samples of the colour and finish to the overmoulding in final form. With the de-sign of the thermometer enclosure completed, attention turned to the design of the probe and, in particular, the probe handle to form an inte-grated whole in terms of shape and colour. A

bench stand was also designed that allowed the thermometer enclosure to be used in a near-ver-tical position and incorporated storage for the probe (Plate 28).

Being Lean

We may be familiar with the notion of lean production (less time, less stock, less material), but if we take the approach seriously, it can change our whole culture of work. In a book titled *The Machine That Changed the World*, the authors provide this warning:

> Lean production changes how people work but not always in the way we might think. Most people—in-cluding so-called blue-collar workers—will find their jobs more challenging as lean production spreads. And they will certainly become more productive. At the same time, they may find their work more stress-ful, because a key objective of lean production is to push responsibility far down the organizational lad-der. Responsibility means freedom to control one's work—a big plus—but it also raises anxiety about making costly mistakes.
>
> Lean production calls for learning far more pro-fessional skills and applying these creatively in a team setting rather than in a rigid hierarchy. The paradox is that the better you are at teamwork, the less you may know about a specific, narrow special-ity that you can take with you to another company or to start a new business. What's more, many employ-ees may find the lack of a steep career ladder with ever more elaborate titles and job descriptions both disappointing and disconcerting.[1]

[1] J. P. Womack, D. T. Jones, and D. Roos (1990), *The Machine That Changed the World*, New York: Rawson Associates/Macmillan, pp. 13–14.

developing your skills and knowledge

Different organizations have different ways of carrying out design depending on their size, specific field and complexity, but their processes broadly follow the stages outlined above. In reality it is inevitable, unless you are very lucky, that changes to the concept will need to be made once you begin to develop your design. You find that bits won't fit or can't be made—at least within the budget you have. In these circumstances, a balanced judgement will need to be taken as to what is essential in the original concept, what you'll fight tooth and nail to retain and what can change without destroying the concept. Maybe the change might even enhance the concept.

As part of a design team, it's also sensible to listen to valid comments and criticisms from other people from different disciplines. Establishing mutual respect is vital in design teams. An inexperienced designer, or an experienced one for that matter, cannot be expected to know all there is to know about materials or manufacturing processes but it is essential to have a working knowledge. Other members of the design team may be able to help and visits to manufacturing facilities can be useful because you can see the actual processes in operation and talk to the people involved. Help is also often available from material and component suppliers who can advise on specification and use of their products. Find opportunities to build up your fund of knowledge for current and future projects.

Although this chapter has focused on some detail development, it's vital to remain alert and creative. Designers need to move between an approach which opens up possibilities and an approach which closes them down, from generating ideas to evaluating them. This iteration between overview and detail, between divergent thinking and convergent thinking and from exploration to specification is as important in detail design as it is in concept design.

CHAPTER SUMMARY

- While concept design might be a very enjoyable stage of the design process, it's the activities that take place after concept design that largely influence the success of a design.
- Understanding how components of a design can be configured and detailed is vital in the professional practice of design.
- Taking a design from *concept* to *layout* is a process of *embodiment*.
- There are four stages in creating a layout: define the main parts, define arrangement, define connections and define shape, materials and appearance of all parts.
- Component properties deliver functions such as usability, brand reinforcement and performance.

- Using off-the-shelf components might limit your design but will save money and time.
- Detail design is the precise specification of all components such that they can be manufactured and assembled.
- Find opportunities to develop your knowledge by talking to experts and visiting manufacturers and suppliers.

chapter 24

developing your intellectual property

claire howell

ABOUT THIS CHAPTER

Design is not just about creating *things*, it's about creating *ideas*. Ideas are the lifeblood of design. Design ideas are highly valuable, and a whole industry has grown up to help creators, and the businesses they work for, protect their ideas from unauthorized exploitation.

This chapter is about the intellectual property that underpins design outputs. It applies across the whole spectrum of design, from the creations of a fabric designer to the innovations of those who develop engines for Formula 1 racing cars. The chapter provides explanations and definitions as it helps the reader to navigate the complex world of rights and responsibilities within intellectual property. A number of vital tools are introduced, including copyright, registered designs, patents, trademarks and licensing. Collectively they make up the most valuable toolbox you might ever own in your design career.

> **"Design is not just about creating *things*, it's about creating *ideas*. Ideas are the lifeblood of design."**

---

what is intellectual property?

When we talk about intellectual property (IP), we are referring to creations that have come from the intellect, ideas that have been composed in the mind and captured in some tangible form. Music, art, design and inventions can all be identified as intellectual property. In many societies, it is felt that these creations benefit us all and should be encouraged. To reward creators for their effort and to stimulate more innovation, laws have been made to give creators some control or rights over their innovations. We call these property rights. So, just as a farmer has a property right over an apple

he has grown, a creator has a property right over her music, design or invention. However, creating music and making money from it is not like growing and selling apples. If someone steals a farmer's apple and eats it, the apple has gone, it no longer exists. The farmer has been deprived of his property forever; he can no longer sell it to make money. However, if someone copies a design or a piece of music, it's still there. The author has not been deprived of the music, but she has been deprived of the chance to make money by selling it. Intellectual property rights (IPR) are, broadly, rights to stop others from copying or using the creator's work without the creator's consent. Although you are given

Figure 24.1 Protecting intellectual property stimulates innovation. (Getty BU006006 RF)

these rights by law, it is up to you to enforce them; the state will not do it for you. Each country has its own laws, but 153 nations, including emerging economic powers such as Brazil, China and India, have signed up to a World Trade Organization agreement. They agree to minimum standards of IP protection and so there is some similarity of IPR across all these countries. However, this does not mean that national IPR rights are valid in all these countries. You must always check the law of the country where you want to do business.

The main IPR in the United Kingdom are *copyright, rights in design, patents* and *trademarks*. There are also associated rights which protect *trade secrets* or *confidential* information and guard against *passing off*; more on all these later. Performers may also have rights in their performances. As a designer the main rights that you have in your work would be *design right* or *registered design* (called *patent design* in the USA and China) and *copyright*. In rare circumstances, you might also find that your work may be eligible

Inventions and Patents

Inventions and patents are vital concepts in design.

Invention: An idea or concept for a new or improved device, product or process; something that previously did not exist.

Patent: Legal protection for an invention that is proved to be new, is not obvious and is capable of being applied as a practical product or process.

For an invention to qualify for a patent—giving the inventor a monopoly right for a limited period to exploit the invention—it has to fulfil four conditions:

1. It must be new—the invention must never before have been made public anywhere in the world.
2. It must involve a so-called inventive step—when compared to what is already known, the invention should not be considered as obvious to someone knowledgeable in the subject.
3. It must be capable of industrial application—the invention must take the form of a practical device, a new material or an industrial process. It should be described in sufficient detail (e.g. in words and drawings) for a third party to be able to reproduce it.
4. It must not be 'excluded'—for example scientific discoveries, computer programs and artistic works cannot be patented under UK law.

From: R. Roy, *Design and Designing* (T211), The Open University, Blk 3 (2010), p. 26.

for a *patent* (or in other countries a *petit patent* or *utility patent*). If you start a business, you might use a trademark to protect the name or logo of your product.[1]

IPR protects different things and are obtained in different ways. Some need to be registered and payment made while others arise automatically and are free. Some last indefinitely while others last only a short time. They can be sold or licensed or you can raise money by using them as security for a loan. Most importantly, IPR can vary from country to country.

copyright

Copyright in the United Kingdom dates back to 1662. It was formulated as a consequence of the invention of the printing press and the new ability to easily re-create the work of others. Today it protects literary, dramatic, musical and artistic works and arises automatically. You don't have to register it or pay anyone to retain it.

Copyright springs into life the moment you express something in tangible form—that is, in a way that others can see or reproduce. Recording a piece of music electronically would be sufficient. You cannot get copyright for a vague idea, only for the way that you have expressed the idea. The expression must be your own and not copied from another. If you see the film *Star Wars*, a space adventure between the forces of good and evil, and then write your own story based on that idea, you are not infringing copyright. Providing you do not copy what the script writers and filmmakers actually created—that is, their expression of the idea—there is no infringement. You will gain your own copyright for your original work because it is your expression that is being protected. Copyright in Europe for dramatic, artistic or literary work lasts for the life of the author plus seventy years and for broadcasts and sound recordings for fifty years. In some countries, such as China, all copyright lasts fifty years and in India sixty years. Shakespeare can now be copied without infringement because his work is out of copyright. Copyright protects all sorts of creative works. The works don't have to be artistic or beautiful, so it covers, amongst other things, lists, design drawings, computer

Figure 24.2 Copyright can protect design sketches.
(Copyright Morgan Motor Company Ltd)

programmes, films, broadcasts, databases and Web pages. You cannot have copyright in mere ideas, facts or algorithms.

Copyright is a right to stop another copying or communicating your work to the public. Posting another's work on the Internet would be copyright infringement. Remember, it is only protection against copying. It will not protect you if someone creates an identical work

> "Copyright springs into life the moment you express something in tangible form—that is, in a way that others can see or reproduce."

independently. If we stand side by side in Trafalgar Square or Times Square and take photographs of the city, our photographs may look identical but there has been no copying. We each own the copyright in our own photograph. Artistic copyright is of great interest to designers. It protects creations such as sculptures, paintings, photographs, diagrams, plans and even sketches. These works don't have to be of any particular artistic merit and much modern art, although regarded by many as lacking charm, will still attract copyright protection. Some types of craft are also included as artistic works for copyright purposes.

Although, in general, copyright lasts for a considerable period of time, if a design is industrially

Figure 24.3 A design at the concept phase is initially
protected by copyright. (Copyright Morgan Motor
Company Ltd)

exploited (i.e. where more than fifty items of the
article are produced), the period of protection is
reduced to twenty-five years from the end of the
year of first commercial exploitation. So designers
beware.

Ownership of copyright

In most countries, it is assumed that the author,
the person who created a work, is the owner of
the work. If a work is created by more than one
person but you can tell which person created
which bit—for example one person wrote the lyrics to a song while another wrote the music—each
person will own his or her copyright separately in

each part of the work. If the contributions cannot be separated, they will be regarded as joint
authors and will both be entitled to a share of any
benefits derived from the exploitation of the work.
The copyright protection clock begins from the
death of the last to die. However, in many countries, if a work is created during the course of
employment, as part of a job the creator was employed to perform, the work will belong to the employer and only the employer will be able to sell or
license the work to another without the consent of
the employee and without the employee getting
any further benefit from the sale. But if someone
who is employed to sweep floors creates a poem

when at work, he would not lose his right to be regarded as owner of the copyright because he could not be regarded as being employed to create poems. The creator, not the employer, would own the copyright in the poem. In China and Brazil, there is an assumption that the employee, not the employer, owns the copyright to outputs, but the employer in China does have a prior right to exploit the work for the purposes for which it was created.

Infringing copyright

If you take someone's drawing and use it in your advertising literature, you will have infringed copyright. However, if you have not copied it exactly but changed aspects, will you still be infringing? The question to be asked is whether you had taken a 'substantial' amount of the work. This is not just about the quantity of the work that you have taken but the importance or the quality of what you have taken. You may have used only a small amount of the work—for example the smile of Leonardo da Vinci's *Mona Lisa* (assuming it was still in copyright)—but if that is a very important part, it will be regarded as a substantial part of the author's skill and labour and you will be infringing. You may still be infringing if you reproduce the work in a completely different form. By writing a play, you could be infringing a story in a book if you take a substantial amount of the plot. If you want to use another person's photograph in your advertising, just contact the person and ask if you may use it; he or she might give you permission for free.

The Berne Convention and Universal Copyright Convention apply to copyright. World Trade Organization members have agreed to comply with these conventions. Although it is not a legal requirement to attach your name, the © notice and date you created your work, doing so warns people that it is yours and they are not to copy it without permission. It is worthwhile to keep a dated copy of any potentially important work at a solicitor's office as evidence. If someone accuses you of infringing her work and you can prove that you created your work before she created hers, you cannot have infringed. In the USA, registration with the Copyright Office is advisable because you cannot sue for infringement unless the work has been registered.

design rights

Design rights in the United Kingdom date back to 1787. Design right does not protect how your product works, just how it looks. Take, for example, the case of someone who has created a design of a new teapot.

The designer would need to ask himself whether his teapot—or part of it, such as the spout—looks different from other teapots or spouts? Understandably, the designer probably wouldn't be able to answer with any certainty because so many teapot designs are already available. But there are resources to help designers answer such queries. One of these is the Web site of the Office for Harmonization in the Internal Market, a European agency set up to assist companies to work with trademark and design legislation.[2] You can use the search function to enter words that describe your own design field. For example you can enter the word 'teapot'. Design law can be rather complicated. I'm going to unpick four types of design right that are in force in the United Kingdom. There is quite a lot of overlap between the types, and there are similar rights in other continents.

Figure 24.4 Protecting IPR in a teapot design. (Getty 56961127 RF)

Registered design

A registered design right protects the visual appearance of your product. There is a UK variant and a community variant in registered design, but they differ in detail only. They protect not only shape but ornamentation including the lines, contours, colours as well as the texture and materials that you make your product from. You may also register, for a fee, a pattern or logo as a design. Registering your design will stop anyone using a similar design for commercial purposes even if they didn't copy yours. The amount of design freedom you have in designing your product, whether it be a teapot or some other output, is taken into account when assessing how different it has to look. All teapots have to have quite a lot in common in order to function as teapots, so some visual similarity is to be expected. The right lasts for up to twenty-five years but you must pay renewal fees every five years.

To be eligible for registration the design must, first of all, be new. This means that no identical or similar design has been publicly available in Europe before registration. The question to bear

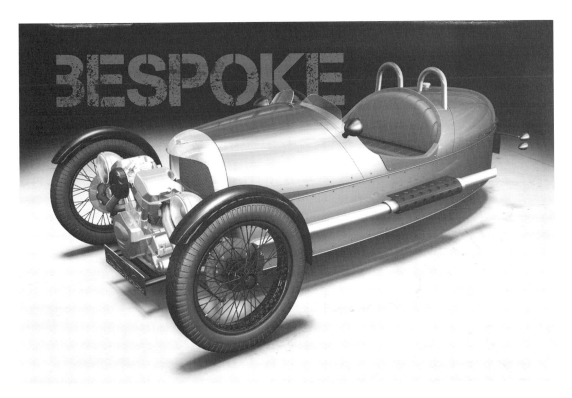

Figure 24.5 You can register not only the overall shape of a product but any new aspect of the design, such as the shape of the lights on this car, or ornamentation. (Copyright Morgan Motor Company Ltd)

in mind is: would it remind an 'informed user' of an existing design? An informed user is taken to mean a person who has experience of similar products. You have a year's grace period to test the market before you lose novelty. In this time, your product will be protected by *unregistered* design rights (explained below). The second requirement for registration is that the design has 'individual character'. Individual character means that the overall impression the design gives to the informed user is different from the impression the informed user gets from existing designs.

Registering a registered community design (RCD) does not protect the way a product works or its function. You would need to consider patenting to protect the functional aspects of your product. In addition, to further competition and prevent the monopolization of the production of spare parts, you may not protect aspects of the designs that 'must fit' or 'must match' some other product.

Unregistered UK and community design rights

An unregistered community design (UCD) lasts for three years from the time a design is made publicly available. There are the same requirements as for a registered community design, but it only protects against copying, not independent creation.

It is a useful right if your product has only a short life expectancy, often the case in the fashion industry. UK unregistered design right is similar to copyright arising automatically. This right protects the original shape or configuration of an artefact and only applies to three-dimensional products, such as the spout of the teapot referred to earlier. It would not protect a two-dimensional pattern or logo. This right lasts for ten years from first marketing.

Why register?

Registered design generally lasts a significant period of time—twenty-five years rather than ten for UK unregistered design right or three years for unregistered community design. It will also apply to two-dimensional designs. Importantly, it is easier to take legal action if you have registered your design. You get a numbered certificate proving your intellectual property and there is no requirement to prove copying if your rights are infringed. Also beneficial is a one-year grace period available before registering to confirm that your product is worth protecting.[3]

Ownership of design rights

If either the RCD or UCD were created by an employee acting in the course of his or her duties, the design would belong to the employer. If the work was commissioned, just as with copyright, the designer, not the commissioner, owns the design rights but an implied licence may be given to the commissioner to use it. However, to confuse things, both the employer and the commissioner have ownership of a UK design right. Where the creation of designs is concerned, it is a good idea to take advice and draw up a signed contract where ownership is agreed.

Infringing design rights

By copying an item of furniture, you could be infringing the design right as represented in the original drawing. A complete copy would clearly infringe, but if you only take some aspects, one would need to ask the same questions as with copyright: has a substantial amount been taken, does it create the same overall impression as the original design on the informed user and does it differ in material details? It is also an infringement to commercially deal with, sell, keep or import an infringing product.

RCD and UCD have protection in all European countries. The Hague Agreement has forty-eight countries as signatories, not including Brazil, where novelty need not be proven. Many commonwealth countries recognize UK rights, although in India the right only lasts for up to fifteen years. Neither the USA nor China offers design registration but they do offer design patents. These apply to three-dimensional functional designs for articles of manufacture as long as they are new, original, non-obvious compared to any previous designs and ornamental, not being primarily functional. In the USA, a design patent lasts fourteen years and no payment is required. A one-year grace period is available.

patents

Patents can be traced back to fifteenth-century Venice, where they were used to protect the secret processes of Venetian glass making. Patents protect inventions that are new and innovative; there must be an 'inventive step'. Also they must be capable of industrial application and must not be on the list of excluded things. You must apply for and have a patent registered for a fee.

Patents are one of the most well-known forms of IPR. If you have a UK patent, it is a very strong protection stopping others from using, making or importing your invention for up to twenty years; you must, however, pay renewal fees every year. In this period of monopoly, you can become the market leader so that even when the patent expires, you are still the pre-eminent player in your field, able to charge a premium for your product. Patents can be used to protect inventions or a new solution to a technical problem, how a product works or how a process is used, what something is made of or how it is made. A patent protects a solution to some problem.

Patenting is not easy. It takes up to four years and can be very expensive. The novelty demanded in patent law is more stringent than that needed for design rights. 'New' in European patent law means that it has not been known by anyone, at any time, anywhere in the world. Even one person being told about your invention, if not told in confidence, can ruin your chances of obtaining a patent as novelty will have been destroyed. This stringent test of newness is because a patent is a complete monopoly over a new and potentially very useful product or process.

Although others may not copy or use your invention until it enters the public domain—either after twenty years or if you stop paying the fees—they may benefit from its publication, which occurs eighteen months after you filed the application. By searching one of the databases, such as the free one offered by the European Patent Office,[4] or that of the United States Patent and Trademark Office,[5] which levees charges, others can learn about your idea in great detail. You may think this might help them copy your hard-won achievement, but in most instances it simply stops competitors wasting time working on the same idea. Of course,

your invention may spark further innovation from other inventors, and in this way your patent can benefit society at large. Alternatively, others may want to license your invention, a good way for you to make money from your patent.

Not only must your invention be new, it must involve an inventive step. This means that it must not be something that is an obvious development compared with what existed before. Of course in some areas, especially in the high-tech industries, defining what constitutes an inventive step may not be easy. A patent examiner will pose the question 'would such a step be obvious to a skilled person with reasonable knowledge in that field?' The invention does not have to be earth-shattering, just sufficiently different. Incremental improvements can be eligible as long as they would not be obvious. Finally, you must be able to prove that the invention is capable of industrial application. This just means that it can be made or used. It is not sufficient to have the idea of a time machine; you must have developed a description of a time machine that could be constructed and actually transport a person from one time to another (preferably, but not legally necessarily, depositing them still breathing and relatively sane). However, some things are excluded from patentability, including ideas and knowledge that should be freely available for all to use, such as scientific discoveries, mathematical methods or things that you could not stop others from doing such as ways of performing a mental act or playing a game. The most important exceptions in Europe, but not Brazil, are methods of doing business and computer programs. However, there may be ways of patenting computer programs if there is a technical effect. Business methods may be protectable in other countries, such as the USA, where a patent was granted for Amazon's 'one-click' shopping cart.

It is very important that designers, inventors and innovators seek legal advice when applying for a patent. Patent claims must be written in a very specific way, to give the creator greatest protection and stop others from patenting something very similar. There is a substantial difference between patents in most of the world and those in the USA, where patents, called *utility patents*, are not granted to the first person to file an application but to the first person to make the invention. It is essential for patent protection in the USA to keep signed and dated log books of all your inventions as evidence of your claim to priority.

Ownership of patents

In the United Kingdom, the inventor owns the patent unless it was created in the course of his or her employment, when it would be owned by the employer. In China, employees have the right to claim ownership. Frequently independent contractors will own inventions because they don't have the status of employee. Where invention is the joint work of two or more people, both will be named on the application and they will be regarded as joint inventors. In some work, there can be problems in determining who the inventor or inventors are. In many research activities, invention is a team effort and it can be difficult to pin down exactly who generated specific creations and when they did so. The questions to ask are (1) what is the inventive concept? and (2) who had the key ideas? It is for this reason that it is vital to keep a log book of your inventive activities, with entries dated, so that you can track the development and source of your ideas.

Infringing patents

Filed patents can be found easily by using a free database such as the one offered by the European Patent Office. If a product that fits the essence of the description is produced without consent, it will infringe. Ignorance is no excuse. It is common for someone accused of patent infringement to retaliate by claiming that the patent is invalid so they cannot be infringing. Such cases can become very expensive and in the United Kingdom, unlike in the United States, the loser has to pay the legal costs of both sides. It is preferable to try to reach an agreement but only after seeking legal advice. There are some defences to patent infringement. For example you may use a patented product or process either privately or for experimental purposes as long as you do not try to exploit the invention for commercial use.

Dyson's Inventive Step

In October 2009, the United Kingdom's *Daily Telegraph* ran a story about how the bladeless fan, the Air Multiplier designed by Dyson Ltd, bore a close similarity to a design developed nearly thirty years earlier by the Japanese company Tokyo Shibaura Electric. It was because of this similarity that the Intellectual Property Office (IPO) required Dyson to resubmit its application for a worldwide patent.

The ruling by the IPO noted that Dyson's Air Multiplier 'cannot be considered novel or cannot be considered to involve an inventive step'. Although the Japanese patent had expired, Dyson was unable to file a new patent because it was judged there was no change or improvement.

Dyson's counter claim was that the design of the Air Multiplier differs in many respects, particularly in the way an aerofoil feature creates a so-called Coanda effect, to improve efficiency in the way air is projected outwards by the fan ring.

The article in the *Daily Telegraph* can be found at www.telegraph.co.uk/technology/news/6377644/Dyson-fan-was-it-invented-30-years-ago.html.

Before you go down the patenting route, you must ensure that it is worthwhile. Not only must people want your invention, but you should check that there is a large enough market to recoup your investment plus make the profit you require.

There are various ways of getting patent protection. You can apply at your national patent office, which will protect you in that country. If you intend to market your product elsewhere, there is nothing stopping someone there from making and selling your invention unless you also register there. You can apply for a patent in each individual country though the European Patent Convention or the Patent Co-operation Treaty via the World Intellectual Property Organization for worldwide protection.

trademarks

The oldest registered trademark in the United Kingdom is the one created by the Bass brewing company which was first registered in 1876 (see www.bass.com). A trademark is a distinctive sign which identifies a particular supplier of goods or services. You must apply to have a trademark registered and there is a charge.

For those intending to bring a product to market themselves and not merely license it to another, a trademark is a useful marketing tool that helps customers recognize the origin of the goods. For those seeking to register a trademark, it is wise to check a trademark office Web site to ensure that a similar sign has not already been registered by another trader for that type of good or service. A trademark can be words, a logo, a shape or even a jingle. Since there are no unfair competition laws in the United Kingdom, you may have to rely on 'passing off' controls (discussed below) if you have not registered your mark and someone uses it on similar goods or services.

A registered trademark will stop all other traders using the same or a confusingly similar mark in their business for the same or similar goods. A UK trademark can be registered at the UK Intellectual Property Office for a class of goods for a fee. You may renew it every ten years indefinitely. However, if you do not use it for five years (three years if you have registered a mark in China), it may be revoked. If you have a registered trademark, you can put the ® symbol on your goods, but doing so without registration is a criminal offence. If you use a mark but you have not registered it, you may put the ™ (trademark) symbol on your goods.

People often want a trademark that describes their goods accurately or indicates that their goods are superior in some way. But to be registered, marks must be distinctive. It is felt that descriptive or laudatory words, such as 'best', should be free for all traders to use and should not be monopolized indefinitely by one trader. A fruit and vegetable seller would not be able to register the word 'orange', whereas a telecommunications corporation can do this because it is not descriptive of the goods or services being sold under the mark.

Infringing trademarks

A trademark is a sign of origin. Infringement will occur if consumers would be confused by the similarity of the marks. There would be no confusion, however, if, although the marks were identical, they were used on different types of goods. For example, in the United Kingdom, the name Marigold is used as a trademark for rubber gloves and butter. Both can be registered as a trademark because customers would not be confused into buying rubber gloves when they intended to buy

butter. However, there are some trademarks, such as Rolls-Royce, that are regarded as so specially well known that no other traders are allowed to use them even on different types of goods where no confusion is likely to arise.

Registering in the UK at the Intellectual Property Office will give you protection in the United Kingdom and a community trademark will give protection in the whole of the European Union.[6] Registering via the World Intellectual Property Organization will provide protection in more than seventy countries, including the United States and China. Beware, however, that registering a company name or Internet domain name does not give you the exclusive right to use those names or give you an automatic right to register them as trademarks.

other protection for intellectual property

Passing off

People are often confused into buying the wrong product due to similarities not in the sign or logo on a product but in the packaging. This can not only reduce profits but can harm the reputation or goodwill of a business, particularly if the mistaken goods are of inferior quality. In the United Kingdom, this is called 'passing off'. A business must be able to demonstrate that it has established 'goodwill'; that means that customers recognize on seeing the packaging that the goods come from it. The look of the packaging is key here. If a claimant can also prove that customers have been misled into buying the wrong goods, it may be able to claim damages and prevent the infringer using that look in the future. This is, however, quite expensive to prove.

Confidentiality and trade secrets

Designers frequently need to involve others in the development process. For example, prototyping a design can often be the only way to prove a principle works but getting outside assistance with prototype construction leaves the creator's intellectual property vulnerable. It is wise for creators to obtain a signed confidentiality agreement whereby the outside agent agrees not to use the information given to it for any purpose other than the one agreed.

If you can't or don't want to patent your invention, you may be able to protect it by keeping it secret, as was the case with the Coca-Cola recipe. But this method of protection will only be successful if it is difficult to find out what your inventive concept is by reverse engineering. It also assumes that no employees will leave and divulge the secret to their new employers. It is essential that if you talk to anyone about an innovation before you have filed for a patent, any discussion about the inventive concept be conducted under a confidentiality agreement.

Trade secrets are secrets of an employer, such as a new design, a manufacturing processes or lists of customers, where it is absolutely essential that the information be kept confidential in order to give the employer a competitive advantage. The employer must have made reasonable

attempts to keep them secret by entrusting only a few select employees with the key knowledge. All parties to such trade secrets should be bound by strict confidentiality agreements. In China, unlike in the United Kingdom, specific anti-unfair competition laws forbid false advertising, slander and the revealing of trade secrets.

Licensing

An IPR licence allows a person to use the specified IPR for a period of time in a particular geographical location for a particular purpose. Such licensing can be of real benefits to creators without access to investment funds. Getting others to manufacture, distribute and market your design means you don't have to be concerned with creating and running a business, investing time and money in buying machinery, hiring and managing employees, ordering raw materials and producing products. At the same time, licensing your IPR to another to exploit will mean that you will receive money from your creation, either a fixed sum or agreed royalty payments.

Licensing may exclude use by all others, by all others except the owner or the owner may retain the right to license as many people as he or she wishes to use the IPR. How exclusive the licence is will be reflected in the cost of the licence. People are less likely to pay to use your IPR unless you have registered it in some way. And don't forget, you may also want to license other peoples' IPR for use in your own products. It's wise to get some legal advice when agreeing licences so that there is no ambiguity as to what rights you are granting or receiving.

If you can prove an infringement of your IPR, you can be awarded compensation. You may receive damages (an assessment of how much you have actually lost due to the infringement) or an

account of profits (a sum based on an assessment of how much the infringer has gained because of the infringement). You may also get an
injunction to stop someone from infringing your
IPR in the future.

know your tools

This chapter has suggested that there exists a
range of tools for the protection of intellectual
property rights. Some of the more significant tools
have been outlined. These tools offer protection
to you and others from unjust exploitation of creative, new and valuable ideas. We live in a time
when protection of intellectual property is a hot
topic. There are some people for example, in the
music-sharing community, who believe protective
legislation should be relaxed. There are others
who believe that effective protection leads to an
improvement in the goods and services available
to us all. Whatever your viewpoint, you need to
be aware of the international competitive environment within which you will bring your own creative

Figure 24.7 The intellectual
property rights toolbox is
potentially the most valuable
set of tools a designer can own.
(Shutterstock 13831546)

outputs. Much of the legislation seeks to help and protect creative individuals and businesses, but some of it will restrict what you might want to do. Understanding IPR tools can be a significant benefit to designers as they seek to forge a profitable career in a hostile commercial world. The IPR toolbox is potentially the most valuable set of tools a designer can own.

CHAPTER SUMMARY

- IPR protects new ideas captured in tangible form from unauthorized exploitation.
- The main IPR are copyright, rights in design, patents and trademarks.
- Some IPR arise automatically while others must be registered for a fee.
- IPR can be owned jointly by the people who created the work, but if they were created during the course of employment, when the employee was doing what he or she was employed to do, IPR will usually be owned by the employer.
- IP can be a business asset with real value. You can sell, license, mortgage or give away your IPR, but it must be protected.
- It is up to you to enforce your rights against infringers but in a dispute it is usually better to negotiate than to go to court.
- You must ensure that you do not infringe others' IPR, and if you do find you have infringed, make sure you get legal advice immediately.
- Confidentiality is important, especially if you think you may be able to get a patent for a new invention or when you are in negotiations with people who may want to license or manufacture your product.
- Most IPR are territorial, so if you wish to exploit your creations in other countries, your rights must be protected there.

Background

In Part VI, the professional practice of design has been shown to increasingly rely on collaboration, teamwork and interdisciplinary working. It can be frustrating but it's the only way you are likely to arrive at a design that resolves the often-conflicting demands of usability, production, cost and marketability, all within a strict time schedule.

This project invites you to address a set brief and to involve twenty-three other people at some point in the creation of the design proposal. There are two outputs you need for a successful conclusion to this project: (1) a solution to the design brief and (2) a diagram communicating the contribution of all twenty-four participants in this project.

You can set your own time scale. You might want to complete it over a day, or you might want to spread it over several weeks.

The Project

Design a child's toy that makes learning fun.

Guidelines

This is a project that stretches your ability at working with a large number of other people. These people don't need to be experts in any particular field, so this might make a good project for a whole class of students. Having said this, there are clearly different types of problems to be solved, and different people should play different roles. If you prefer, you can run this project yourself and bring in the help, opinion and advice of twenty-three other people as you need it. It's important that the design proposal created by your team appeals to children. You need to define an age group you will design for. Your design will need to be produced at reasonable cost, and it must deliver some valuable learning. Achieving this will require research and development and hence the involvement of all twenty-four people. Your design proposal might be presented as a drawing, a computer-aided design model or as a three-dimensional construction.

The design of the diagram of the team's activities or responsibilities will also need to be carefully considered. How will you represent the organization of the group? Do you need to reveal the stages of development or the iterations between team members?

part vii

design futures

introduction to part vii

Many readers will have career aspirations in the world of design and designing, and the final part offers some reflection and advice on this. The four chapters reiterate the importance of key design skills introduced in earlier chapters, such as working to a clear plan, turning problems into opportunities and using visual representations to picture and simplify complex situations. This part provides pointers to help readers design their own future. But, just as the reader is designing his or her career path, the design world is changing and with it the processes and practices of designing.

Today designers are called to work across disciplines and to find ways around outdated lines of demarcation. As Brigid O'Kane points out in Chapter 25, it's insufficient to merely work as a group; today teams of teams must collaborate with a clear shared goal and the capability to build shared understandings. In Chapter 27, Jon Hewitt characterises some key changes taking place in commercial design. He suggests that design thinking needs to be converted to design leadership, and it's this that must guide the career planning of young designers. He appeals for readers to visualize their career aspirations as a road map to assist with reflection on direction, timing and stage gates.

At the heart of much design thinking is a significant complexity. One only has to look at design projects for creating large buildings, consumer products or Web-based services to get an insight to the complexity of activities and responsibilities by all those involved. Such design work might appear very simple and logical to some people, but this apparent simplicity is, in reality, synthesized complexity. Future designing is likely to become more complex, and those who wish to enter a career in design need to demonstrate their ability for resolving complex problems and being able to manage complex processes. It's for this reason that complexity is given a chapter in this collection. Theo Zamenopoulos and Katerina Alexiou reveal both the theory and the application of complexity science today and suggest that it forms one of the new domains for design attention.

Successful design thinkers can become a valuable catalyst in the transformation of the workplace by harnessing their ability to translate information and their skill in creating representations. And it's not just designers who are adopting new thinking. Engineers, managers and technologists recognize the demands of the new landscape of work and are challenging for the leadership of design. But the authors of Part VII suggest that designers have some significant competences that enhance their potential for design leadership. First, they have the potential to support bridges of understanding in increasingly complex and disparate commercial environments, and second, their ability to iterate between foci brings a vital holistic perception to situations of design, innovation or development. As the final chapter documents, this includes the ability to switch between problems and solutions, the integration of the virtual and the physical, the capacity to act as arbiter between users and producers and the competence to iterate between concept and detail. Collectively, design thinking is shown to exploit a unique, flexible lens with which to stimulate creativity, scrutinize designs as they are brought into being and oversee processes of development as ideas are turned into marketable outputs. Today design thinking is more than a collection of cognitive tools and approaches. Design thinking has come of age as design intelligence.

chapter 25

building bridges to new realms

brigid o'kane

ABOUT THIS CHAPTER

This chapter is about collaboration within design practice. It is a major factor in almost all successful companies, consulting firms and start-up businesses today and is likely to become even more important in the future. In this chapter I'm going to illustrate its importance by referencing one key relationship in one key industry: the relationship between industrial designers and engineers in the design of vehicles and transportation systems. If this isn't your intended career path, don't stop reading! If you are going to be an excellent designer, you need to understand and apply good collaboration skills, and this chapter has something for all disciplines. Poor collaboration can be incredibly disruptive to the design process and will almost always compromise the final product. Collaboration isn't easy and it can take a little bravery, vision and creative thinking to achieve it.

A vehicle is one of the most complex products to design and put into production. The design process incorporates knowledge and expertise from many different disciplines, including colour and trim, materials science, parts suppliers and marketing. Through collaboration, design teams seek to absorb, reconfigure and apply this knowledge in many different ways, including creating a visual form, defining assembly and materials and generating effective marketing. The knowledge base of engineers and designers increasingly overlaps as today's design process requires more creativity and greater attention to science and technology. Input from both disciplines is essential, but achieving an appropriate balance at various points in the process is not straightforward. This chapter explores strategies for encouraging powerful interactions between industrial designers and engineers to produce successful, innovative products in vehicle design.

---

the need for collaboration: why silos don't work

Often groups of individuals may believe they are collaborating simply because they interact with one another or because their product passes through various departments. We might see this in a wide range of commercial or public-sector organizations. However, in reality, group members might work in their own silos, areas of safety where the problems of collaboration are not allowed to encroach. All teams are vulnerable to this silo mentality. At its worst, it leads to people adopting a strategy of completing their responsibility in one silo and passing work on to people in another silo, sometimes referred to as 'throwing it

Figure 25.1 Silos are independent spaces, even if they are connected. (Shutterstock 66675382)

over the wall' because it suggests that responsibility for decisions ends once an output is passed along to the next person. This is not collaboration and it's not teamwork.

True collaboration as a design team requires participants to engage with the problems of other participants throughout the design process. The benefits of such collaboration are not limited to design. Effective collaboration can energize all departments in an organization. When individuals step up to this challenge, and strive for excellence in team relations, there is usually a marked improvement in product quality plus the fostering of a culture of innovation across the whole organization. Team pride brings with it a new sense of satisfaction and integrity for the participants, and

> **"True collaboration as a design team requires participants to engage with the problems of other participants throughout the design process."**

these can be powerful conduits for stimulating innovation.

People involved in developing products generally want to work together in collaborative teams because they see potential they cannot achieve alone. However, despite seeing the potential gains, they may lack the understanding to lead or participate in

Convergent and Divergent Thinking

In the 1950s, the U.S. psychologist, J. P. Guilford argued that creative problem solving was related to a mental ability he called *divergent thinking*.[1] This enables people to diverge from what is known to produce novel ideas. He concluded that divergent thinking comprised separate abilities which he called fluency, flexibility and originality. *Fluency* is the ease with which individuals produce many different responses to a problem. *Flexibility* is the ability of an individual to alter his or her mental set and to produce ideas outside of the usual categories. *Originality* is the ability to generate novel, unusual or ingenious ideas.

Guilford contrasted divergent thinking with another mental ability that he called *convergent thinking.* He argued that both were essential to creativity. Convergent thinking is needed after divergent thinking has created many ideas. It employs logic and information in order to converge on a single idea or solution.

Divergent thinking has much in common with Edward de Bono's concept of *lateral thinking*—ways of breaking out of familiar patterns and solutions by thinking laterally or sideways.[2]

From: R. Roy, *Design and Designing* (T211), The Open University, Blk 3 (2010), pp. 43–44.

[1] J. P. Guilford, 'Creativity', *American Psychologist* 5 (1950), pp. 444–54.

[2] E. de Bono (1977), *Lateral Thinking: A Textbook of Creativity*, Harmondsworth, Penguin.

successful collaborations. Alternatively, an organization might lack the necessary cultural characteristics that allow team working to flourish. Establishing a culture for effective collaboration is not easy, and there are many instances in commercial practice where old practices still dominate. Even in today's unforgiving world of design, there still exist examples of the silo mentality, and designers can find themselves confronting obstacles to effective collaboration. Within the automotive industry, some teams work in collegial harmony and are able to effortlessly reach a consensus in problem solving. Other teams are hostile, egotistical and, in some ways, profoundly unethical. This behaviour creates a wake of missed opportunities. It can even encourage more positive and productive team members to leave an organization, which ultimately weakens both the team and the company further.

thinking styles

The construction of teams that can confront the design challenges of today and tomorrow is likely to bring together individuals with very different thinking styles. Some people have a developed ability to work amidst uncertainty and might even thrive where there is chaos. Others may prefer a thinking style characterized by order and strategy. Examining thinking styles or traits in the context of design and engineering can assist effective collaborative team working.

Some people are not put off by incompleteness; in fact, they might deliberately seek open-ended solutions. They can display a spontaneous, intuitive style of dealing with information that delights in the process of exploration and discovery. Design education has traditionally fostered this, combining it with strong visual skills. It's a thinking style that focuses on the qualitative, as opposed to the quantitative, and it suits some types of practitioners very well because it meshes with aesthetic inquiry and creativity. This thinking style is closely associated with *nonlinear* learners (Figure 25.2a), whose progress in education or early practice is characterized by periods of time with no apparent advancement interspersed with big leaps forward. Again, design education has been largely shaped both by and for people with this type of thinking style. They can bring novel approaches to a product development team or offer new conceptual visions. But remember we are talking about thinking styles here and not the professions of the people who possess these cognitive preferences. There are examples of creative, intuitive engineers who display nonlinear learning, as we shall see shortly.

Product design and development requires people who can conceptualize product potentials in a broad sense—who have command of 'blue sky' or 'outside the box' thinking. Such breadth of perception can lead to innovation, but of course it can also generate irrelevant or impractical ideas. This style of creative thinking has been termed *divergent* thinking. That is, from a given starting point, the practitioner tries different directions in order to generate many alternative ideas. Ideally the starting point will be a stimulating and provocative catalyst (Figure 25.3a). When this strategy is combined with a capacity for making visual images, the

process can result in a diverse range of ideas that are easily communicated to others in the form of sketches or other quick, pictorial representations. Some have called this capacity 'design thinking', but real design thinking harnesses and integrates some very different capacities and thinking styles with the ones I've just introduced.

As noted above, there is also a very different thinking style that thrives on order and strategy. People who prefer this thinking style display characteristics of rational, systematic and objective ways of working. They frequently find roles in the analytical rather than the creative aspects of design and development and typically feel at ease with both quantitative and qualitative data. People with this thinking style are frequently *linear* learners (Figure 25.2b). It's easier to plot the path of their learning. It's steadier and less erratic than nonlinear learning. Significantly, nonlinear learning is more amenable to being examined by objective tests and exams. For people with this thinking style, new discoveries can

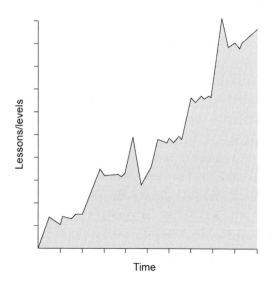

Figure 25.2a Nonlinear learning. (Copyright author)

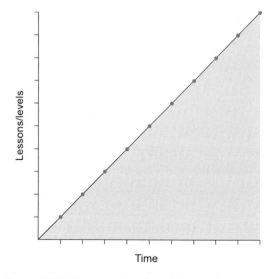

Figure 25.2b Linear learning. (Copyright author)

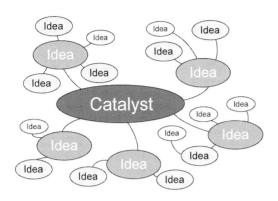

Figure 25.3a Divergent thinking. (Copyright author)

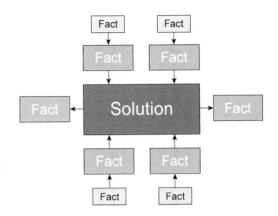

Figure 25.3b Convergent thinking. (Copyright author)

arise from outcomes that are not in accord with what was anticipated. In contrast to the potentially erratic process of divergent thinking, this seeks a direct path from problem to solution through the accumulation of information. This is the practice of *convergent* thinking (Figure 25.3b), which is rational, orderly, empirical and logical. Practitioners with this thinking style are more likely to focus on performance, technology, structure and manufacturing and frequently prefer specificity in communication by exploiting, for example, technical language or unambiguous images.

bridging perceptual gaps

Partly our preferred thinking style evolves from the education we are exposed to but it is also influenced by personal cognitive preferences and professional development. Our thinking style can be very strongly embedded in us. We have created cultures to justify and perpetuate thinking styles, but their existence can act as a barrier to collaborative working—particularly if we associate

thinking styles with the domains or professions that must interact in many design projects today. In the creation of vehicles, for example, it's easy to imagine the two thinking styles as representing design and engineering. Design authors Jonathan Cagen and Craig Vogel suggest there exists a 'perceptual gap' between the designer and the engineer (Figure 25.4), and indeed there is in many industries today. They reveal a separation between what the engineer focuses on (e.g. cost, timing, quantitative ergonomics, manufacturing) and what the designer is more likely to be interested in (e.g. visual order, qualitative ergonomics, cultural trends). They define this perceptual gap as 'the differences in perspectives that team members have that stem from discipline-specific thinking'.[1]

Others who have studied modern industrial practice suggest that, increasingly, both thinking styles are found in design and engineering. The perceptual gap may still exist between people with different thinking styles, but, in contrast to Cagen and Vogel's visualization, the gap is as likely to be found within domains as between them. Despite such differences, modern industrial

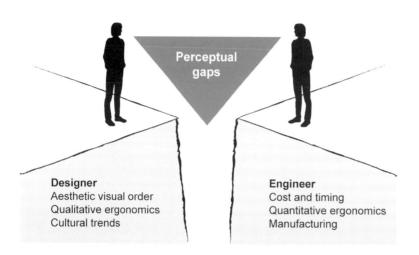

Designer
Aesthetic visual order
Qualitative ergonomics
Cultural trends

Engineer
Cost and timing
Quantitative ergonomics
Manufacturing

teams must embrace people with different thinking styles because they provide essential and complementary skills and practices. The differences between thinking styles can be very helpful in creating innovative products where team members constructively evaluate the product from their own perspective. Quite often the polarities in thinking bestow creative energy to the momentum of joint efforts. Productive collaboration is high-performance, and I have named such positive exchanges as *creative friction*.

An example of creative friction occurred at General Motors (GM), where the disciplines of design and engineering display evidence of the thinking styles. This example concerns the integration of light-emitting diode (LED) technology into vehicle headlights. Engineering initially created large components that had to be placed at the extreme corners of the vehicle, compromising the overall aesthetics. When designers made this problem known, the engineering team repackaged the components, enabling the repositioning of the headlights to the desired area. As a result, this repositioning actually improved some of the safety qualities of the headlights.

Of course, differences between thinking styles can also be disruptive, resulting in major conflicts that negatively affect the overall quality of a product. At these times, collaboration is corrosive. It causes breakdowns in progress and compromises the goal. I refer to this nonproductive approach to collaboration as *uninspired friction*. It stifles the development process. For example when engineering the trunk (boot) of a car, a specific volume or interior space needs to be maintained depending on the vehicle category. In one case, to achieve this goal, engineering insisted that the deck-lid location needed to be higher. The designers adamantly opposed this because it changed the vehicle proportions. Engineering was unwilling to explore moving the inner walls of the trunk in an attempt to increase the volume while keeping the deck-lid in a lower position. So the end result was a vehicle that looked more stout and heavy. This was a direct compromise to the brand identity, which was described as being sleek and lean. Small adjustments such as these, if made repeatedly on parts of a vehicle, can dramatically alter its visual and other aesthetic qualities and potentially seriously diminish sales.

Understanding this perceptual gap between participants in design and development processes is critical to effective collaboration. Individuals who are aware of these differences learn to appreciate, respect and trust the unique contributions of fellow team members. While perceptual gaps can exist between any of a team's components, such gaps are still common between design and engineering. The *hairball* and the *cube* (Figure 25.5) is a playful representation of the differences between designers and engineers. This idea emerged from a conversation I had in 2007 with Wayne Cherry, retired vice president of design for General Motors worldwide. In Figure 25.5, designers are represented by the hairball and engineers by the cube. Introducing such a representation to a collaborative group can ignite lively conversations while opening channels of constructive communication. Such light-hearted and fun interactions can really help to stimulate innovation. However, it's not the hairball or the cube that's ultimately important here but the linking lines

between them—the bridge between the two elements. This bridge is a vital metaphor to establishing a shared space for mutual understanding.

A bridge of understanding is a catalyst for dialogue; it encourages crossing over into other domains while establishing a home base. It offers a point of balance and a middle ground, and it enables team members to build relations. Distinguishing similarities, as well as differences, within multidisciplinary teams is valuable not only for balance but also for building team unity. Such a bridge can provide clarity by establishing a common language, ground rules and mutual respect. One of the first steps in establishing common ground is through shared learning experiences so that designers and engineers are able to understand and appropriately respond to differences in thinking. Examples of these kinds of experiences include workshops and off-site visits to compare competing products, experiences which are further discussed later in this chapter. Achieving shared knowledge and understanding

Figure 25.5 The hairball and the cube. (Copyright author)

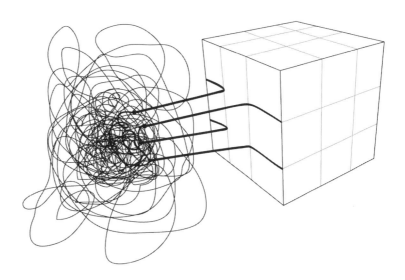

can dramatically reduce the uninspired friction between the two disciplines and help create a strong bridge for effective collaboration.

finding common ground in the collaborative process

Creating conditions that can support the co-working of engineers and designers across all stages of the design process can be challenging since the process itself often goes through enormous transitions. However, such interaction is necessary to ensure that each discipline has continuous input influencing the product. Breakdowns in communication, or simply the failure to schedule it into the process, can be catastrophic in transport design. For example if engineers develop a vehicle package without input from designers, the overall vehicle proportions could be overlooked. Since proportion is one of the most important characteristics in market acceptance of new vehicle design, this oversight can lock in undesirable aesthetics from the earliest stages of the process. A recent discussion with Dave Lyon, executive director of interior design for North America at General Motors, revealed the importance of collaborative practice.[2] For years, the prevailing culture at the GM Design Center in Warren, Michigan, excluded designers from some key early stages in the creation process. Engineering would write vehicle specifications and find suppliers who could produce parts at low costs. Encouraging suppliers to minimize costs succeeded in reducing overall vehicle costs, but it also often yielded unattractive assemblies with poor quality. When designers were finally given the product brief detailing these specifications, it was usually too difficult, too costly or too late to make changes. This

has been a common model in many industries where engineering and marketing make decisions based on short-term finance rather than long-term product quality. In this model, the concerns of design are not heard simply because they are not involved in decision-making early in the process. Take, for example, a vehicle interior door handle. This can be configured into door systems in many different ways. At one time, engineering at GM preferred to mount door handles on the door panels and then add trim around each one. This was a great way to engineer an inexpensive part that was easy to assemble, but this method resulted in visible gaps around the door handles—it was an unmistakable indicator of poor quality and design. Many competitors achieved consistent gaps of only one millimetre around their door handles, so GM had to examine why its product was so poor. It turned out that every time GM designers began a vehicle project, they were tied to one particular type of door handle assembly that had been specified by engineering. Since engineering and marketing could not understand why designers would want a door handle that was ten dollars more expensive than what they had already specified, their working relationship was characterized by frustration and dispute. Even today you can still find examples of such conflict in a wide range of industries, including manufacturers of consumer appliances, toys, luggage and numerous others.

In General Motors' case, this inability to confront problems in detail design went beyond the door handles. Some parts had to be given large radii, and feature lines were intentionally shifted from part to part to disguise alignment problems. Overall, this approach had a major negative impact on consumers' perceptions of vehicle quality. Design became a process of trying to disguise the flaws rather than a demonstration of harmony between process and product. While the story at GM is very different today, at that time the silos of design and engineering did not support the type of collaboration that could have addressed the problems of the vehicle assemblies. Anne Asensio was appointed executive director of design, interior design, quality and brand character with the mandate that the interior quality problem be fixed. Understanding the importance of collaboration, she met with her counterpart in interior engineering, John Calabrese, who was also concerned with the lack of quality. Collaboratively they had the ability to produce world-class interiors, and they understood that organizational changes were needed to bring this about. From that point, a collaborative culture was established. A new procedure for writing vehicle specifications was created, bringing together the expertise of designers and engineers. Both parties were willing to actively collaborate to improve quality and innovation in new vehicles, but it was the discipline and commitment to change that truly transformed the teams.

To achieve their goals design and engineering managers held weekly forums with project updates. Regular, structured meetings supported the necessary cultural change. They began to set new standards, create new processes, discuss concerns and make decisions together. One result of this collaborative activity was the collective agreement that mounting door handles to door panels was no longer acceptable. Together designers and engineers developed new definitions of requirements and innovative responses in the form of product ideas. Multiple examples of this kind of collaborative success rippled through entire vehicle platforms. New teams improved the fit between parts, minimized gaps, improved finish quality and added value through options to make vehicles competitive within specific market segments.

exploring the bridge

Good collaboration, such as that developed at General Motors, depends on successful navigation of the bridge between the hairball and the cube (Figure 25.5), but the story doesn't stop there. Figure 25.6 presents this bridge as having its own distinct character. It is a combination of the intuitive thinking of the hairball and the rational thinking of the cube. We might characterize bridge thinking as 'creative order'.

This creative order, or bridge thinking, is vital to product development. It may not be required continually, but at key decision points it is essential. Sometimes bridge thinking comes about through successfully integrating design and engineering. At other times, bridge thinking is a capacity of certain gifted individuals. I want to explore this in a bit more detail.

The erosion of the notion of silos and their replacement with a more unified model of collaboration reveals how the different styles of thinking introduced at the beginning of this chapter coexist today. Figure 25.7 presents four realms: the *creative designer's realm,* the *analytical engineer's realm,* the *analytical designer's realm* and the *creative engineer's realm.* These realms can only hope to caricature the real people the model seeks to portray, but it does illuminate some important qualities and strengths of participants within industrial processes. A healthy system embraces contributions from all four quadrants.

The creative designer is a design expert. He or she needs creative 'play' time, individually or as part of a group. The creative designer needs to

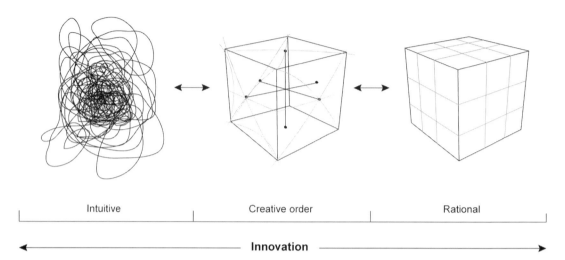

Figure 25.6 Thinking styles of the hairball and the cube, with creative order between. (Copyright author)

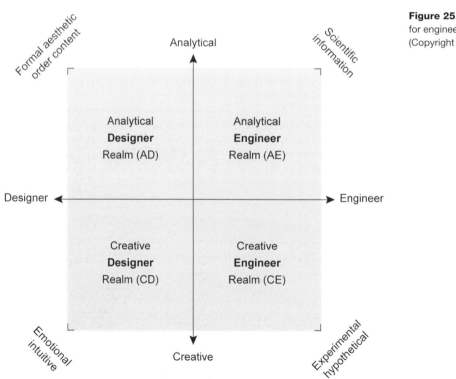

Figure 25.7 Different realms for engineers and designers. (Copyright author)

be able to disengage from aspects of engineering to explore the boundaries of the problem and the possible solutions. Harnessing creativity is the goal here. When successful, it can provide almost visionary outputs. The analytical engineer is an engineering expert. When working with extreme focus, he or she can display the same level of passion and inspiration as the creative designer.

This intense focus provides opportunities for technical invention and discovery that can inspire radical innovation. Both groups need command of their own realm but must be aware of the bridge across to the realm of the other. If creative designers continuously ignore analytical engineering, then difficulties will arise in bringing a product to production. Likewise, if analytical engineers work in complete isolation from creative designers, they might create products that are functional but less successful in the marketplace. When these two groups bring ideas from their particular quadrants to the team, their ideas are more likely to be accepted if a common ground for understanding is in place. They need buffer quadrants that support the type of creative order provided by the bridging stage in Figure 25.6.

Analytical designers and creative engineers provide this buffer of creative order. They are people who have a functional understanding of, and an interest in, design and engineering. They have the ability to see value and importance within each discipline and cross over from one discipline to the other with little or no effort. Theirs is a very valuable role today. Creative engineers and analytical designers are hybrids who cope with the creative application of information in modern product development. They usually do not possess the extreme characteristics of creative designers or analytical engineers, meaning they are neither a hairball nor a cube. However, these individuals help function as a bridge during collaborative efforts. Analytical designers and creative engineers are beneficial in many situations. They are translators, facilitating communication in diverse teams and bridging the gaps in understanding that can arise.

However, the team environment and the lure of interdisciplinary situations can distract the analytical designer or creative engineer. Ideally, these individuals should have an area of expertise either in

Figure 25.8 Some designers are interpreters or translators, bridging gaps in understanding. (Copyright Brigid O'Kane)

> "Analytical designers and creative engineers are translators, facilitating communication in diverse teams and bridging the gaps in understanding."

design or engineering. Without such a focus, analytical designers who forget that they are designers can get wrapped up in technical aspects of the engineering and ultimately sacrifice advancements of design. Similarly, engineers can get sidetracked by visual details. There is a danger that hybrids will have too much flexibility and forget what they should be focusing on, neglecting their discipline-specific tasks.

workshops and team building

Activity workshops are one of the most effective ways to establish common ground between design and engineering. They can be tremendously empowering, even if the outcomes can be alarmingly unpredictable. Designer-hosted workshops for engineers can be structured in many different ways, perhaps offering insights to the design process, reviewing content in a project brief that is deemed important from the designers' perspective, examining criteria commonly used to judge excellence in design or engaging in model building or other hands-on activities. For example designers might demonstrate the fundamentals of drawing, giving engineers the tools to aesthetically design using traditional methods such as pencil and paper or more contemporary approaches using a graphics tablet and computer for digital sketching. These interactions stretch

people's awareness. Such workshops expose engineers to the subtleties of, for example, using form, colour or line to visually unify assemblies. They foster an understanding of how aesthetics are important in vehicle marketing. Such workshops leave participants with a shared appreciation for design quality.

Engineer-hosted workshops for industrial designers also offer many possibilities. One approach is to engage designers with engineering software. Of course, this requires some investment in training, but it can reveal insights into engineering priorities and processes. Designers who participate might never again use the software, but the experience can foster an appreciation of the engineering workflow and can create a deeper understanding of what exactly engineers do. Designers get to see firsthand how seemingly minor changes can have significant consequences for time and resources. Such workshop experiences usually ease tensions and uninspired frictions that may have existed. During workshop activities, it is critical that team members interact. The main purpose of such workshops is to facilitate insights into the other's realm and to reveal how team members with different backgrounds can contribute to a shared goal. When working with designers and engineers, it is helpful to incorporate creative activities of exploration that would appeal to designers and activities that have a more rational approach to applied knowledge, which engineers will better relate to.

In my interview with Dave Lyon, he described how such workshops and other collaborative activities form an important part of team building at GM. Every quarter, designers and engineers travel to the GM proving grounds in Milford, Michigan, where together they spend time analysing competitor vehicles and conducting comparisons of

Figure 25.9 University of Cincinnati students from industrial design and mechanical engineering disciplines collaborating under the direction of Professors Brigid O'Kane and Sam Anand. (Photo copyright Brigid O'Kane)

Mass Customization

Henry Ford's innovation in production line assembly in the early twentieth century had one clear disadvantage: it reduced variety. It depended on each vehicle using the same set of components, so each Model T car, for example, was almost identical to the next. Since this time, the quest for manufacturing engineers has been to devise a system that has the advantages of Ford's principle whilst allowing a range of products to be assembled on a single manufacturing line. This has been the search for mass customization.

Mass customization offers the potential to personalize products to suit the specification of individual customers whilst still producing in large numbers. Mass customization of products allows customers to choose options from a suite of possible features, and the manufacturer can deliver these by selecting from a range of alternative components and subassemblies. In theory, it stimulates demand by allowing consumers to have a product tailored to their wishes and which is different to that purchased by others.

In adopting mass customization, a company has to be assured that there is sufficient consumer demand for an extended variety in product range to warrant the investment in the technologies and systems required to support mass customization. These include computer-controlled machines, quality control and computerised planning and scheduling of manufacture.

For example designers and engineers are paired up to experience the exhibition together. While walking around the showroom floor, designers and engineers share their differing perspectives. It encourages a dialogue about issues of structure, product image, reduced mass, fuel economy or new visions for the future. Experiencing the show side-by-side develops shared perceptions that cannot be replicated simply by meeting afterwards. Spending time outside the immediate bubble of their normal work and looking at what is out there in the world is a great way to learn and, as Dave Lyon puts it, to 'share what we see'. In addition to the physical design of vehicles, electrical engineering is evolving at a rapid pace. In an effort to keep up with these advancements, General Motors' electrical engineers and designers attend consumer electronics shows together and return with different perspectives and ideas for new strategies. 'We come back from these shows and want to rework everything we are currently working on,' said Lyon. 'Designers could only make these kinds of significant changes because we walked through the show with engineering so they could see the value in adjusting the plans.'

the projects they are working on. At one such meeting, the teams of designers and engineers returned to the problem of gaps such as those around headlights, trim panels and doors. It provided a focus for dialogue and creative thinking. Other sessions looked at how interior specifications were generated, how parts were purchased from suppliers and the basic pricing system for the entire vehicle. GM creates additional opportunities for team building at the North American International Auto Show, which has long been an annual event attended by those in the industry.

the organic growth of innovation

Innovation is an increasingly powerful component of successful products. Without innovation, we are simply editing what has been done before or re-creating what already exists. Innovation is not to be confused with incorporating new technology or methods into the process. Innovation is looking at a product from a completely new point of view and from that creating a new product that is novel or unexpected. Striving to push the use of, for example, new software, within the develop-ment process may result in better methods, but it may mask a need for real innovation. Often the root of this is close at hand, as Thomas Walton points out. 'Technology makes a difference, but it is the human dimension that ultimately determines the nature and extent of that direction.'[3] Bridging the differences in individuals and facilitating com-munication forges a common ground that can be infused into collaborative teams to establish and cultivate a culture of creativity that is ultimately manifest in innovation. Once this common ground is established, it takes work, planning, open chan-nels of communication and continuous effort to bring about effective results.

Healthy collaborative systems embrace the four design and engineering realms presented in Fig-ure 25.7. They can unite organizational expertise into one vibrant organism. This system naturally fosters the *organic growth of innovation* (Figure 25.10). One way to achieve this arrangement is to organize the design development process to allow

appropriate opportunities for *team-specific activi-ties* and *discipline-specific activities*. Team-specific activities would include both designers and engi-neers, while discipline-specific activities would in-clude only designers or only engineers. In either case, activities would vary depending on the stage of the design development process. Creativity should be encouraged for all team members when working collaboratively and individually. When team members anticipate and expect creative input from each other, regardless of discipline, the prospect for innovative thinking increases.

Feedback loops within the design process are critical for evaluating teams and products. Pow-erful team working can develop when feedback mechanisms constructively capture and utilize information from team interaction. Such mecha-nisms should be compatible with group dynam-ics but do not need to be elaborate or costly. Sometimes all that is needed is a simple survey, a conversation between collaborative partners or acknowledgement for a job well done.

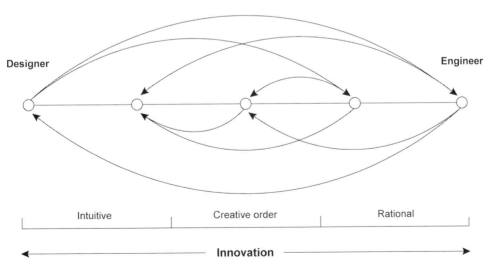

Figure 25.10 Organic growth of innovation. (Copyright author)

the importance of leadership

The greatest challenge in collaborative practice is overcoming the many differences between disciplines. These differences provide some of the most significant difficulties in managing today's design processes. Good communication between disciplines is key and should be grounded in a solid understanding of oneself and others. Hopefully, this chapter has alerted you to begin this inquiry. Comprehending the characteristics of designers and engineers helps you avoid misconceptions and aids communication. But probably the most important lesson is the need for good leadership. This is vital if people are to navigate between the thinking styles referred to earlier. There's a desperate need for leaders who are also bridge thinkers.

Leaders of collaborative teams must be flexible, giving teams opportunities to change and adapt to unexpected situations and outcomes. These unpredictable happenings are more likely to occur when individuals have different ways of thinking and operating. Vision and courage are needed to preserve what works and to eliminate or change what does not work. An effective leader of collaborative teams must be mindful that methods of distributing information can influence how it is received. When leaders distribute documents to team members, they should present the information in formats that suit the different styles of thinking. Leading collaborative teams can be refined through experimenting with different approaches. Empowering team members to contribute information is vital. Note that General Motors' designers are now involved in development from the earliest stages. They contribute to specifications and use images to convey subtle visual characteristics that might otherwise be overlooked when others apply the specification. These detailed images aid understanding of the specifications and

lead to their complete fulfilment, thus contributing to product quality. The ideas of collaboration, communication and leadership incorporated in this chapter are synthesized in Figure 25.11. This figure represents a new and desirable process model for collaborative team working. It suggests an environment that fosters regular interaction between members. It values the realm of individuals and the unique contributions they might be able to make, but it also represents balance and leadership. It seeks to bring about a workable, creative mix of disciplines, stimulating crossover and a movement of individuals outside their comfort zones. Such a continuum of expertise powerfully supports interdisciplinary teams and drives excellence in innovation.

solutions to new challenges

Transportation designers and engineers are addressing challenging issues facing humanity. Solutions for current and future challenges cannot be developed in isolation. Interdisciplinary teams of engineers and designers, as well as representatives from a multitude of different fields, are key. We are inextricably linked. The support infrastructure may be present, but can organizations and individuals grasp the opportunity? As David Muyres and Geoff Wardle pointed out recently: 'The working culture of design offers unrivalled levels of facilitation that allow multi-disciplinary teams to develop valid solutions for the future.'[4]

In addition to the contrast in thinking styles previously discussed, designers and engineers face other challenges to the collaborative process. When developing products in transportation and many other disciplines, team members will face barriers presented by different cultures, lifestyles, time zones, attitudes and behaviours.

Engineers' Realm

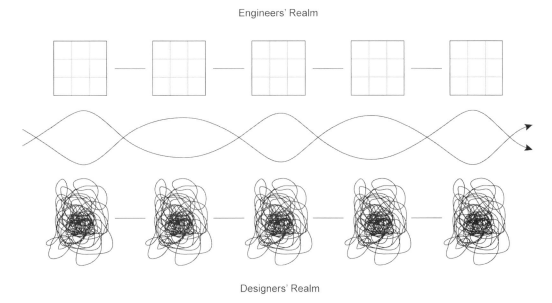

Designers' Realm

Figure 25.11 The new model for collaborative practice—
a continuum of expertise. (Copyright author)

Figure 25.12 Build bridges to new realms.
(Shutterstock 32185006)

Overcoming these differences and any associated prejudices for the sake of a successful collaboration on any scale can be transformative. Good resources exist to guide our design processes and practices, but ultimately it is up to us as practitioners to develop our skills and bring about change.[5] Collaboration skills can enable us to effectively operate across barriers. Designers, particularly, need to develop skills for building and crossing bridges into different realms and disciplines. They need to be individuals prepared to use these bridges to build partnerships that enhance and develop innovative processes and products.

CHAPTER SUMMARY

- Commercial design today is largely a team process requiring collaboration between a variety of participants. Poor collaboration stifles innovation. Building bridges of understanding is essential to successful collaboration.

- One of the key relationships in transport design, as well as many other disciplines, is that between designers and engineers. These professions display distinctly different knowledge bases and thinking styles. Perceptual gaps can exist between them.

- Some designers and engineers have developed hybrid characteristics. Analytical designers and creative engineers are two hybrid types. These individuals can help facilitate positive team interactions.

- Workshops provide a valuable technique for building bridges between design and engineering because they help to foster understanding and trust.

- Bridge thinking leadership is vital to assist members of interdisciplinary teams in achieving successful collaboration.

chapter 26

complexity: what designers need to know

theodore zamenopoulos and katerina alexiou

ABOUT THIS CHAPTER

Architects, engineers, urban designers, product designers, interface designers—in fact, designers from all fields—increasingly use the word *complexity* to characterize both their design activity and its outputs. This chapter examines the phenomenon of complexity and reveals some profound implications for design and designing today. In a broad sense it reflects on reality, but more specifically it proposes that complexity science underpins a new scientific approach to what designers do and how they do it. This chapter explains why designers need to understand the ideas and tools of complexity science, integrating them with perhaps more familiar creative and analytical processes of design. It identifies distinct types of complexity that can be recognized in design projects and suggests how the designer might deal with these in practice. Embracing knowledge of complexity and applying it through practical design skills is vital to anyone seeking to work in the design professions of the twenty-first century.

---

complexity in design problems, processes and products

The activity of design and its outcomes, in the form of various environments, artefacts and systems, are frequently complex. Whether your interests lie in, for example, film, product, graphic or automotive design or the domains of architecture or engineering, the outputs of these professions today are nearly always complex assemblies of numerous component parts. A design output may be complex in terms of form, user interface or behaviour, but it may also be complex in terms of its construction, manufacturing or assembly.

The characterization of design activity as complex has arisen partly because design problems can be ill-defined or messy and partly because creative thinking is required. Design problems are open to different interpretations, they can be addressed by different approaches and they can have different but equally satisfactory solutions. Design activity is also complex because of the many stakeholders involved in a particular project and their different views on what the end result should be. The process of uncovering the needs and wants of different stakeholders and the processes of communication and negotiation needed in order to arrive at a design specification are themselves complex. Take for example the design of the iconic Sydney Opera House.

Figure 26.1 Sydney Opera House (Jorn Utzon).
An example of design complexity. (Getty 94123541 RM)

The knowledge for resolving this architectural project was distributed across a variety of experts, including architects, engineers, material scientists, acoustics experts, planners, politicians and many others. Other local stakeholders included the anticipated end users of the building. Within different stakeholder groups there is frequently evidence of conflicting goals, differences in requirements and alternative views on constraints such as cost and functionality.

You can see such complexity in many domains. Take, for example, Formula 1 car design, where the criteria for success and, more generally, the design problems are typically more closely defined than in architecture. Here creative development is guided by prescribed rules and regulations. Even so, the search for successful innovation requires the design and engineering teams to make new interpretations of the rules so as to bring about new visions. It requires creativity of analysis as well as creativity of synthesis. The success of the Brawn Formula 1 team in 2009 was exactly due to the ability of the team to creatively overcome the constraints defined in the brief and make new interpretations of the design problem. Many examples of design are the result of this co-evolution of problems and solutions. The complexity of designing stems from the very nature of design activity, which requires the definition of problems together with potential solutions.

Wicked Problems

Any design problem can be difficult and tricky to re-solve. Some design problems have been termed *wicked* problems—not only because resolving them is so hard but because even understanding the problem is difficult! Wicked problems are a small but significant class of design problems, as Ken Friedman points out:

Of all design problems in any field or subfield of de-sign, wicked problems constitute the smallest class. Much design work is routine work. This is why it is easy to delegate so much studio production work to junior designers and inexperienced members of a design team.

...Nevertheless, wicked problems are among the most visible problems. This is because wicked problems tend to stand out against the background of other, less visible problems. This is a natural out-come of the fact that wicked problems generally in-volve many stakeholders. In contrast, large classes of problems of the kind known as *tame problems* generally involve relatively restricted issues. More-over, these problems often affect a small group of stakeholders or a single client. Some tame problems are so restricted in scope and so simple in scale that any solution satisfies nearly everyone involved.

...The wickedness of wicked problems is par-tially defined by the competition of interests among stakeholders whose interests conflict with the inter-ests of other stakeholders in the same problem.[1]

[1]Ken Friedman, quoted in *Design and Designing* (T211), The Open University, Blk 1 (2010), pp. 106–7.

towards a science of complexity

In the above examples complexity is presented as an inner quality of the design process, the design environment and the design artefact, but context is vital too. Perceptions of complexity, and its influ-ence in design, have changed over recent decades. Robert Venturi's book *Complexity and Contradic-tion in Architecture*, published in 1977, reflects a postmodern emphasis on diversity and ambiguity in design.[1] This arose in contrast to the modernist emphasis on order, simplicity and technical ratio-nality. However, Venturi's notion of complexity was some distance from the scientific notion of com-plexity. The scientific study of complexity has a long and diverse history that can be traced back to cybernetics, systems theory and information the-ory. In the period of postwar reconstruction, there emerged an international interest in systems. Both the natural world and the artificial world of design artefacts were seen to be composed of systems that hold and manipulate information. An interest in the static properties of systems was rapidly over-taken by studies of system instabilities, unpredict-able behaviour and how interacting components organize themselves. Complexity was seen as a key concept in the construction of new knowledge about systems, their structure and behaviour.

With the popularization of concepts such as chaos and fractals came a new and broader inter-est in complexity science. One famous example is the discovery of the Lorenz attractor, a struc-ture generated by a series of equations devel-oped to represent and predict the weather. The visual representation of this structure resembles a butterfly (Figure 26.2a). It provides a means of demonstrating the behaviour of *nonlinear dy-namical systems*; the two wings constitute two attractors for the behaviour of such a system. Although we know the existence of the two tra-jectories around the two attractors, we cannot predict which trajectory the system will follow at any given time. In other words, in such systems small variations in the initial conditions may lead to completely different final states, and their behaviour is unpredictable. This notion was popularized as the 'butterfly effect'. Other inspiring examples from the early days of complexity science include computer-generated images of fractal structures (Figure 26.2b) and experiments of symmetry breaking and spontaneous pattern formation in chemical systems (Figure 26.2c).

Charles Jencks, another architectural theorist and designer, picked up on such theoretical advances in complexity science in his book *The Architecture of the Jumping Universe*.[2] For Jencks the knowledge generated by complexity science revealed a different view of the world—a dynamic, creative, unpredictable and exploding universe. He considered that this new worldview could offer a new language and a new aesthetics for building and architecture. The new aesthetics was characterized by complex patterns, folding surfaces, skewed angles and twisted, fluid forms, as exemplified by works of architects such as Peter Eisenman, Daniel Libeskind and Frank Gehry (Figure 26.3 and Plate 29).

Can complexity as a scientific discipline offer insight to design practice with its attendant practicalities and pressures? Surely scientific knowledge and practice aims to discover *how the world is*, while design knowledge and practice

(a)

Figure 26.2 (a) The Lorenz attractor (Copyright author); (b) a fractal image, part of the Mandelbrot set (Copyright author); (c) spontaneous patterns formed in a Petri dish experiment (Belousov Zhabotinsky reaction, image by Stephen Morris). (Copyright Stephen Morris, www.physics. utoronto.ca/nonlinear)

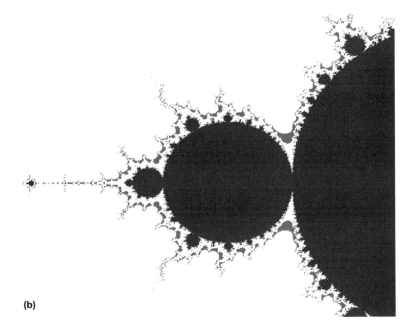

(b)

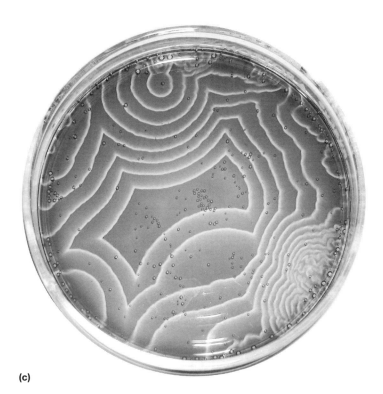

(c)

Figure 26.3 Interior of the Jewish Museum in Berlin, by Daniel Libeskind. (Photo copyright author)

aims to intervene in reality and propose *how the world should be*. Of course, scientists study design: the nature of design activity, the perceived problem, the properties of a designed artefact or the values and behaviours of potential users. Science helps us analyse, model and resolve design matters. But more recently, complexity science has enabled designers to understand the core processes of our design thinking and design actions. It has provided a bridge between problems, processes and products.

The following sections have two objectives: to introduce some basic concepts and methods of complexity science and to illustrate these with real examples from design practice and design research. In working towards these, we highlight some useful further readings to illustrate why it's important to embrace concepts and methods of complexity science in design and designing.[3]

reality and types of complexity

Complexity science aims to create scientific theories and methods in order to describe and explain the origins and effects of complexity. Complexity is a concept used to understand reality, and it takes a specific position about the nature of reality, as well as the nature and limits of our knowledge. Just like any other branch of the sciences, complexity science applies well-defined strategies or methods to create explicit knowledge about some aspect of reality. When we talk about explicit knowledge, we mean knowledge that can be expressed or is describable in some language, whether a natural language such as English, a mathematical language or a computer program. For instance, knowledge for the most efficient emergency evacuation of a building can be captured in a set of instructions. Figure 26.4 diagrammatically presents the processes of observing, measuring, evaluating and acting that characterize the creation of objective reality through the construction of representations of reality.

A successful representation of reality is important, as it can be used to predict, manage and make decisions about the world in which we live and work. This is where complexity science holds an important key.

One of the cornerstones of complexity science is the recognition of the importance of interrelationships and interconnections for the understanding and characterization of a variety of physical, social or technical systems. Such interrelationships and interactions are common in design. They exist within systems (e.g. parts of a mechanical product, activities within a building or traffic flows within a city) but also between systems (e.g. between products, between products and users, between buildings in a neighbourhood or between cities). So the aim of complexity science is to understand systems, and it does this by looking at their underlying organization. It looks at interdependencies as well as interactions or exchange of information at different levels. Thus it might examine interaction between components of a system or between a system and its environment. Complexity scientists suggest there are common principles that underlie the organization of different systems (physical, biological, social, cultural), and thus complexity science is, by definition, a cross-disciplinary science.

> "Complexity scientists suggest there are common principles that underlie the organization of different systems (physical, biological, social, cultural), and thus complexity science is, by definition, a cross-disciplinary science."

To further the discussion we distinguish between four types of complexity:

- structural complexity
- behavioural complexity
- computational complexity
- epistemological complexity

Figure 26.4 Scientific inquiry: a dialogue between objective reality and representations of reality. (Copyright author)

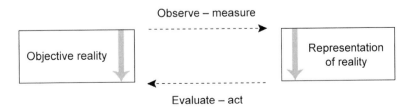

Structural complexity

Herbert Simon was perhaps one of the earliest design theorists to grasp the significance of complexity science and to see the significance of interdependencies. His work on complexity has made important contributions to fields as diverse as economics, organizational theory, artificial intelligence, cognitive psychology and computer science. Simon characterized complex systems as follows:

> By a complex system I mean one made up of a large number of parts that interact in a non-simple way. In such systems, the whole is more than the sum of the parts, not in an ultimate, metaphysical sense, but in the important pragmatic sense that, given the properties of the parts and the laws of their interaction, it is not a trivial matter to infer the properties of the whole.[4]

Simon emphasises the hierarchical structures that often characterize such systems. He draws our attention to the organization of systems in interrelated subsystems, which are not necessarily subordinate to each other but form a whole because of the intricate relationships developed among them. So there are special properties derived from the grouping and interaction between parts that cannot be understood by studying the parts in isolation. This characteristic applies to a great number of natural and artificial objects, such as human bodies, machines, buildings, cities and social structures. For Simon, hierarchical structures are 'signatures' of complexity, which represent robust, successful solutions generated by evolutionary processes.

Most systems that we call complex, such as the human brain or the Internet, have a particular organizational structure. Typically, components with very few interdependencies are very common, while components with a very large number of interdependencies are very rare. For example urban systems display this characteristic in the relationship between big and small plots of land, buildings, roads and so on. It is generally thought that such structures are the outcome of long evolutionary processes. Identifying such signatures of complexity gives rise to the possibility of recreating or managing complexity in different systems. Knowing, for example, which structures make a network adaptive, robust or resilient to external forces, facilitates redesign or development.

Behavioural complexity

Another way to think of reality is as a dynamic structure of interdependent and co-evolving components. The interest lies in the behaviour rather than structure of a system. Researchers into behavioural complexity seek to understand how components, which can be as diverse as physical or mechanical entities, people and social groups, organize themselves, generate new structures or create transitions from one structure to another. A particular focus is often placed on those transitions that realize a change from a random organizational structure, where independencies between components are very loose (and components have many degrees of freedom), to a well-ordered organizational state, where a clear pattern, form or function can be observed. An example is the transition from water to ice; as water, the molecules display loose interdependencies, while as ice, the molecules have strong interdependencies. The process that realises the transition from a random to a well-structured organization is called *self-organization*, and the observable outcome or phenomenon is called *emergence*.

An interesting sociotechnical example of self-organization is the well-documented case of the Millennium Bridge in London.[5] The engineers that designed the bridge used well-tested models and codes of practice to predict its behaviour. However, the behaviour of the bridge on the opening day was quite unexpected. When a large number of people walked over it, the bridge started to sway sideways in a very dramatic way, and the engineers feared that it would collapse. What happened? To a certain degree, the unpredictable behaviour of the bridge was the result of an oversimplification in the underlying assumptions of the behavioural model of the bridge. The designers didn't include in their models the lateral forces that our feet exercise on a surface when we walk. In most cases, such lateral forces are too small to be taken into account. Indeed, it is a common practice in bridge design to consider only the vertical forces. But this simplification is not the whole story. Initially people walked across the bridge in an unorganized way, as each person naturally has a different pace. As the bridge started to wobble, people subtly reacted by making lateral steps to balance themselves. The random and unorganized marching of people became more coordinated as each person adjusted his or her step to fall into line with the swaying of the bridge. The tiny movement of the bridge co-evolved, and finally synchronised, with the walking patterns of the visitors. A dangerous sway emerged, which we might call an organizational structure. There are two important lessons for designers in this example of behavioural complexity. First, it reveals how simple rules can define complex behaviour that is difficult to predict and, second, how highly complex interactions in space and time can generate some form of order.

Computational complexity

It can be convenient to think of reality as a very large computing machine that, given an event (expressed by an input) and following some laws or rules (expressed by the *computer program*), generates some results (the consequence of the events). Using this metaphor, the computer program is our *explanatory theory* enabling us to understand how reality works.

Consider the following illustrations of configurations. Figure 26.5 depicts a set of two simple shapes $S = \{S_1, S_2\}$.

Using this set S, it is possible to generate a family of configurations. The following two configurations are two examples of this family:

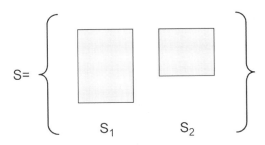

Figure 26.5 A set that consists of two simple shapes. (Copyright author)

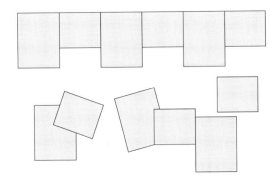

Figure 26.6 Two possible configurations produced through composition of shapes in the set illustrated in Figure 26.5. (Copyright author)

Most people would say the first configuration is more ordered than the second configuration. Why? Because the first configuration can be generated by applying just two rules of composition over an initial shape (an input), as seen in Figure 26.7.

In contrast, the second configuration can be characterized as random because it is not possible to generate it with the application of rules. The description of the configuration is not compressible. There are no successive applications of the same rule. The number of composition rules that generate it is as big as the configuration itself.

Most successful designed artefacts have configurations which are neither very simple nor random but complex enough to offer diversity in form and function. Finding the appropriate level of complexity for an artefact is one of the key pressures in design, and it seems that complexity science might offer effective help to designers.

Epistemological complexity

While the notion of epistemological complexity may seem complicated, in essence it means that complexity can be defined relative to an observer. In contrast to the previous type, here the paradigm states that reality cannot be understood and defined objectively. Our understanding of reality relies on our subjective perceptions and our unique skills and abilities. Researchers in this camp consider that complexity must be studied not as an independent quality of an observed reality but as a quality that arises relative to an observer or creator. For instance according to Casti, the complexity of an observed system is a relative quality that is determined by the coupling of the observed system with an observer; the finer the capacity to discriminate details of the structure or behaviour of an observed object, the more complex the object appears in the mind of the observer.[6] In this sense, a stone is a more complex

Start

Rule 1: Compose $S_1 + S_2$

Rule 2: Compose $S_{1+2} + S_{1+2}$

Repeat rule 2

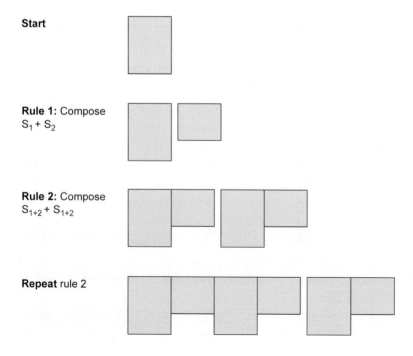

Figure 26.7 The rules of composition of the first configuration seen in Figure 26.6. (Copyright author)

object in the eyes of a geologist than it is in the eyes of an unskilled observer. Such a viewpoint holds that complexity is a function of our own limitations.

Herbert Simon introduced the concept of *bounded rationality* to describe the idea that humans are not perfectly rational beings but are limited in their ability to optimally solve a problem or take an optimal decision.[7] This is not only due to limitations in the capacity of the brain to grasp all the necessary knowledge required to solve a complex problem but also due to practical constraints arising from the availability of information and resources, including time. This is particularly true of design problems, which typically are not well defined or structured, thus presenting no obvious route to progress. The concept of bounded rationality has had a significant impact on the way human behaviour is perceived, and it has inspired a wide range of applications in domains such as computer science and engineering. It was also a formative influence on distributed artificial intelligence and multiagent systems.

The idea that intelligence can be the product of interactions between low-level, and perhaps nonintelligent, parts is quite prominent in new approaches to complex adaptive systems, swarm intelligence and evolutionary robotics. It also informs our understanding of high-level attributes or abilities such as creativity, language and sociality. Design research in this field seeks to understand and reproduce the way multiple interconnected elements coordinate themselves through their capacity to interact and adapt to each other and to their environment. These scientific ideas and applications are influencing design theory, but they also offer a new set of tools and methods for supporting design practice and the solving of today's design problems.

what can complexity science do for design?

This section reviews different ways in which complexity science can be used to support design thinking, practice and research. The first part is concerned with methodologies used to represent and capture the complexity of different aspects of design, including the complexity of design artefacts, design processes or design environments. The second part is concerned with methodologies used to analyse reality. The third part is concerned with methodologies used in order to synthesize some aspect of reality.

Representing complexity

One of the core challenges for design is the representation of the complex interconnections that exist in artefacts and processes. A useful tool for representing a system of interconnections is graph theory. Graph theory is a branch of mathematics that studies the properties of networks. It generates representations such as that shown in Figure 26.8.

This representation is constructed using a set of dots (called nodes) and a set of lines between dots (called edges). This simple mathematical construction can be used to represent many different phenomena in design—for example the interconnectivity of components in consumer products, the social structure of a design team or relationships between design processes and actions.

Back in the 1970s, Lionel March and Philip Steadman used graph theory to represent the morphology and spatial relationships in buildings plans (see Figure 26.9).[8] The proposed method can be used to create systematic encodings of families of plans, and it is important for design

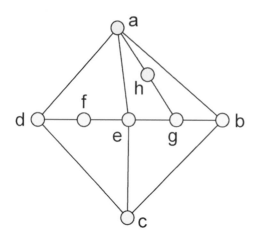

Figure 26.8 An example of a graph representation, using nodes and edges to indicate the structure of a system. (Image copyright Chris Earl/Open University)

because it can support the evaluation and generation of alternative plans. For example Figure 26.9 might allow us to scrutinize adjacency of rooms or help us minimize journeys between those rooms most used. Using such graphs, we can study intrinsic characteristics and properties of designed artefacts. Graphs allow designers to systematically describe the role of each component in an assembly. Graph representations also can be used to capture different attributes of a design — not only spatial or structural relationships but also morphological and functional relationships, such as flows of energy from one mechanical or electric part of an engine to another. For example in Figure 26.9, room number 2 and room number 5 are less connected to the overall configuration — that is they have only two links/connections — whereas all the other rooms have three or four connections. Such systematic observation about the connectedness between rooms supports design evaluation — for example understanding which rooms have better privacy or are better suited as

gathering spaces. The simplified representations of graphs are especially useful where designs result in complex configurations. In architecture this is particularly the case with hospitals and other large public buildings.

The use of such graph representations has also been applied in studies of social network analysis. Design teams have been studied as examples of complex networks with characteristic structures and rules of interaction. For instance Schadewitz and Zamenopoulos examined the kind of community that developed between remotely located design students using the social networking tool Facebook.[9] The use of graphs to plot community structure revealed the existence of particular social roles such as that of 'broker'. In social network theory, this notion has been termed 'betweenness' and is a measure of the number of times a particular participant is involved in the transmission of information in a certain context. In Figure 26.10, the person with the highest betweenness measurement (Nic) occupies the central ring. Two other participants (Paul and Bibi) also adopted a broker role and appear in the graph with high degrees of betweenness. The adoption of the role of broker is important for preserving the connectivity of the network. It is hypothesized that the existence of such brokers is important for creating a sense of community and facilitating communication, exchange of ideas and creation of a common understanding of the content and context of a distributed design task.

Methods for representing complexity are therefore important for understanding the principles and underlying attributes of design artefacts, processes and environments. Next we explore how complexity science can be used to support design analysis.

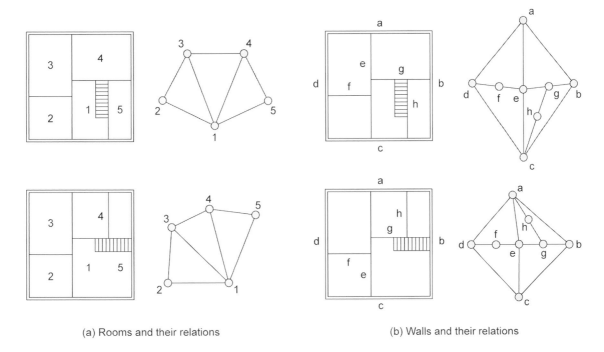

(a) Rooms and their relations   (b) Walls and their relations

Figure 26.9 Graphs used to represent spatial relationships in room plans. On the left are graphs created by representing rooms as nodes and links between rooms (through openings or doors) as edges. On the right are graphs representing walls as nodes and links between walls as edges. (Image copyright Chris Earl/Open University, *Design and Designing*, Blk 4, pp. 45–46, 2010)

Complexity as a tool for design analysis

Complexity science uses simulation extensively as a method for analysing complex systems through a process of modelled reconstruction. Today most simulation is computer-based and consists of implementing a model of some real or imaginary system. Two complementary approaches to computer simulation are contrasted here. The first (predictive) focuses on generating hypotheses about the behaviour of a system, and the second (explanatory) focuses on generating hypotheses about the working principles or rules that determine the behaviour of a system.

Computer simulation as a predictive tool

This type of simulation uses real-world data. By running the simulation one expects to match the behaviour or outcomes of a real system. The guiding principle in this case is that if the simulation replicates behaviour or outcomes faithfully, then it can be used to make predictions about the real system in the future. Modelling for prediction requires a careful encoding of observed qualities in the simulation program, plus verification and validation through comparison with the real world. This type of simulation is valuable to designers, because it allows them to generate 'what

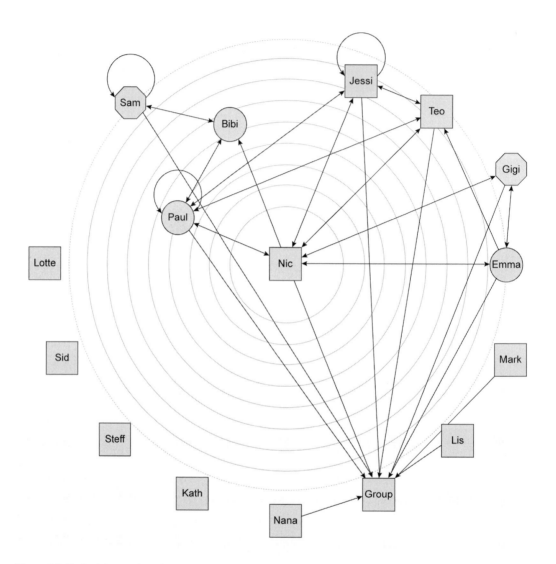

Figure 26.10 Social network analysis of the degree of 'betweenness' among participants in a team design task. People with higher betweenness appear towards the centre of the network. (Copyright author)

if' scenarios. It allows us to study the effects of our design proposals. For instance consider that one is interested in understanding the implications of a certain urban design decision on the traffic of a city. A simulation will use real data—for example how people travel from one place to another or their places of origin and destination. Then different parameters of interest are defined (e.g. closure of a certain road or changes in the topology of the road network) and applied to the model. Once the simulation is run, it facilitates observations about predicted behaviours (e.g. people's movement, traffic load). By adjusting parameters one can formulate predictions and 'what if' scenarios about the object of interest. TRANSIMS is a computer tool for complexity analysis in precisely this field. It was originally developed at the Los Alamos National Laboratory but has since been applied in the United Kingdom. TRANSIMS simulates road network usage using sample data about individual travellers within a city. Travellers are located in sets of zones defined by where they park their cars or begin the pedestrian part of their journeys. TRANSIMS can be used to explore different situations or scenarios—for example what happens if there is an accident in a certain location or a new road or a bridge is constructed. A snapshot of a typical representation from TRANSIMS is shown in Plate 30.

Computer simulation as explanatory tool

Simulation has also been used in science, particularly social science, to explore and explain

phenomena. It can be used to generate would-be worlds, alternative scenarios or hypotheses about the workings or rules of systems under study. Such simulations might not exploit real-world data because sometimes it's just not available. Simulation constitutes a kind of experiment that helps explore relationships and develops understanding. Agent-based social simulation in particular builds on simple rules and assumptions to generate complex behaviours or structures. Scientists have used this kind of simulation to explore the principles of growth of spontaneous settlements and model the diffusion of innovations in societies.

Complexity as a tool for design synthesis

In contrast to the processes of analysis in the previous section, simulation can also be used to synthesize new realities, and thus it has a

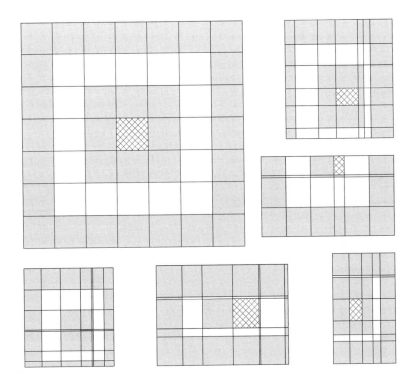

Figure 26.11 Generic building plans generated using neural networks. Grey represents internal spaces, white represents external spaces or corridors and cross-hatching represents light wells or courtyards. (Copyright author)

potentially vital role in design. One contemporary method that has attracted much attention is the application of artificial neural networks. Artificial neural networks are computational analogues of biological neural networks. They seek to simulate how the brain works. The fundamental unit of an artificial neural network is an artificial neuron, which receives inputs and calculates outputs on the basis of a simple function. Information is stored in the weights of the connections between neurons. These weights among neurons change according to a process of learning or adaptation. What is interesting for design is that artificial neural networks can be used as a method for recognizing and generating forms and patterns. Here, knowledge required to synthesize the description of an artefact is not explicitly represented. Instead, design descriptions emerge through a process of collective adaptation of the weights connecting the neurons, that is, as a product of memory and experience. Neural networks have been used to model the design process and generate room and building layouts as shown in Figure 26.11.[10]

Another computer-based technique for exploring, synthesising and optimising shapes and structures, and one that is seeing increased application, is simulations of evolutionary processes implemented in the form of genetic or evolutionary algorithms. These are computational techniques that take initial populations of representations

> **"Few who enter the design professions in the next decade will escape the influence of complexity science."**

and evolve new and better representations by applying the general principles of inheritance, mutation and selection. They have been used in a variety of domains, including mechanical engineering, structural engineering, architecture, product design and art. Figure 26.12 shows one example from the field of product design. In this a family of related mobile phones has been generated.

Complexity is a characteristic of today's design processes and designed products. Few who enter the design professions in the next decade will escape the influence of complexity science. This chapter has taken a look at reality and some future strategies for understanding the realities to come. As noted in the introduction, the priority for designers is not to seek to become experts in complexity but to demonstrate an ability to combine new analytic and synthetic tools of complexity science with traditional sensibilities for understanding the needs of future consumers, creative thinking and prototype building.

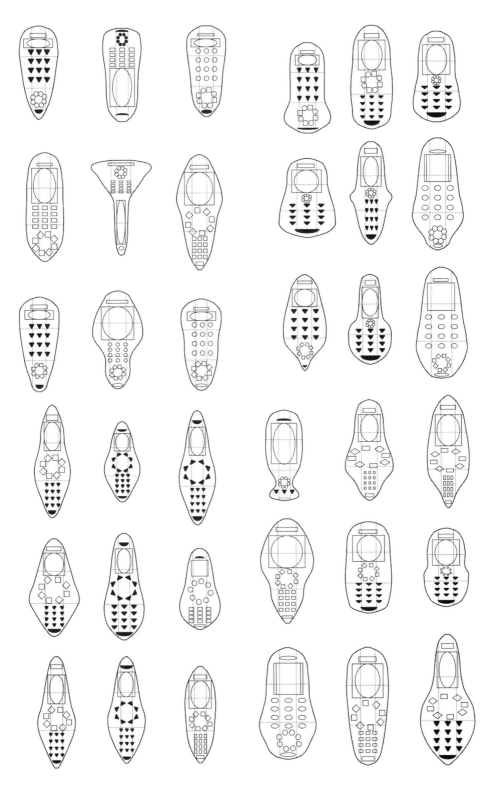

Figure 26.12 A population of mobile phone designs generated using a genetic algorithm. (Image copyright Hong Liu and John Hamilton Fraser with permission from Elsevier)
From: H. Liu, M. Tang, and J. H. Frazer, 'Supporting Evolution in a Multi-agent Cooperative Design Environment', *Advances in Engineering Software* 33/6 (2002), pp. 319–28.

CHAPTER SUMMARY

- Complexity is an interdisciplinary science focused on the study of highly interconnected systems whose parts interact with each other and adapt to one another.

- Design is increasingly characterized by complex interrelationships and interactions. Complexity lies at the core of modern design products and design processes.

- Complex interrelations exist within systems (e.g. between parts of a mechanical product, activities within a building or traffic flows within a city) but also between systems (e.g. between products, between products and users, between buildings in a neighbourhood, between cities).

- Complexity of systems can be examined from four viewpoints: structural, behavioural, computational and epistemological.

- There are three main ways in which complexity science has been and can be used in design. The first is to *represent* complexity in various aspects of design (the design artefact, the design activity or the environment of design). The second is to reconstruct complexity in order to *analyse* the behaviour and working principles of a system. The third is to reconstruct complexity in order to *synthesize* new realities and new design products.

chapter 27

managing design:
a road map to a career

jon hewitt

ABOUT THIS CHAPTER

Design is changing. Change is in the nature of design; it's part of its DNA. This chapter looks at changes in the organization and management of design within the consumer electronics industry today, but it also exposes some important general features in the relationship between design and industry that all students of design should be aware of. It explores the changing role of those who seek to contribute to design through employment in industry or consultancy, and therefore this chapter is relevant to a wide variety of students considering a career in design. The chapter reflects on new design priorities for individuals and corporations, and it examines responsibilities and opportunities when working in a design department, covering areas such as management and strategy. The content draws on the author's own experiences and observations working in several design studios for global brands in the consumer electronics sector. The chapter uses the notion of a road map to help readers visualize and plan their own career directions and targets.

---

the organization of design

The importance of team working in design today is indisputable. A number of authors in this book have contributed to this compelling case. But less has been said about the management of design teams. Currently project teams working in the design and manufacture of consumer electronics tend to adopt a core team approach to the management of live projects. This model places a project manager at the centre of the team (see Figure 27.1). Outside the hub are four specialist roles, which concern the leadership of hardware, software, business and design. Beyond these, further project roles are defined, such as personnel who have responsibility in quality, manufacture and electrical hardware. The way the core team is assembled depends on the organization, but, in general, the closer to the centre a role is located, the greater is the influence over decisions and outcomes. Companies that take design seriously tend to locate senior designers very close to the hub, reporting directly to the project manager.

Issues within a programme of design and development, including general progress, are typically discussed in weekly project meetings, with specific gatherings called to resolve outstanding issues. Above the project team sit others who have more strategic concerns dealing with, for example, direction, policy or product portfolio. Of course, those responsible for design have a foot in both camps because they are dealing with both

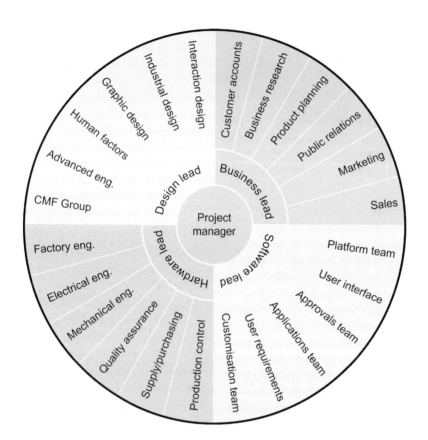

Figure 27.1 Project management model typical in the consumer electronics industry. (Copyright author)

the 'now' and the 'next'. This position helps to steer project decisions but also puts a fair amount of responsibility in the lap of designers not only to help steer the direction of the company but to also ensure that the agreed direction is realized in the right way. The next section focuses on the upper left quadrant of Figure 27.1, which, collectively, we can call the design studio.

design studio

As you can see from Figure 27.1, a typical design studio is made up from various specialist discipline groups. The particular mix will depend on the specific industry and sector the various specialist groups are situated in.

Within consumer electronics, specialists in graphic design; industrial design; interaction design; human factors; colour, material and finish; advanced engineering and layout design are generally represented in some capacity. Integrating the contributions of these specialist groups helps to unify product concepts into cohesive design solutions in accordance with the design direction. A brief summary of each group and its role within live projects is given here.

Graphic design

This group works on product graphics, packaging and communications design. Typography, printed matter and logo application might also appear under the umbrella of responsibility of this group.

Figure 27.2 Managing the integration of various design disciplines helps to enrich the end product. (Getty 879064-001 RM)

Personnel are usually required to follow the direction of the brand and corporate identity guidelines.

Industrial design

This group handles the physical side of design proposals along with the broader product experience. Industrial designers help steer projects by pulling design elements together. Generally these individuals form part of the core team, becoming the point of contact for other members of the project team and the organization for all matters relating to design on live projects.

Interaction design

This group is concerned with the interface between the user and the device, the goal being to create a seamless link between the two. Increasingly, this interface exploits digital technologies. Interaction designers work closely with the software team to ensure that future operating system releases can incorporate new ideas. Likewise, the link between industrial and interaction design is very close, fusing physical and digital worlds to ensure that the user interface is as intuitive and pleasurable to use as possible.

Human factors

This group aims to maximize ease of use and functionality of products. Working closely with industrial designers and engineers, human factors specialists bring expertise on human abilities, both physical and mental, and the techniques to investigate these. They might consider areas such as anthropometrics, cognitive processes, key sizes, legibility of graphics and perceived qualities. They will take the point of view of able-bodied and less able users. Where required, the human factors group also initiates user testing to establish the validity of usability concepts.

Colour, material and finish

This group develops and monitors global and market trends of colours, materials and finishes. The group's work is concerned with the physical characteristics of products, and their proposals inform industrial design. Members of the team handle colour variants of products after initial launch, and they liaise with the advanced engineering section, creating and realising new finishes and materials.

Advanced engineering

The advanced engineering group develops mechanical layout concepts (space envelopes), mechanisms and advanced interfaces. The team forms an integral part of product feasibility studies and plays an important role in bringing about the transition of a project from concept to prototype. Advanced engineering can consist of a wide range of experts and researchers from various branches of engineering. They might implement advanced materials, processes and technologies or monitor developments. A subgroup of advanced engineering is the surface modelling team. This team takes data about product surfaces from industrial designers and recreates this data in the digital applications used by the engineers. They also help resolve technical matters with the engineering team around issues such as tooling, assembly and processes.

new pressures, new trends

This precise design studio structure may not be seen in every organization. Clearly organizations differ in size, the resources (including financial resources) they have access to. Nevertheless, some key common characteristics impinge on the management of design today. Highly influential is the fact that design teams are having to become multiskilled, combining a diverse range of design backgrounds from various fields or industries. Diverse teams can bring an innovative or fresh perspective, new market insights or new approaches. In smaller organizations, it's not unusual for designers to be required to undertake multiple roles. Whether you work in a small or large organization, designing today requires flexibility, the ability to adapt and the skills of applying emerging methods and approaches.

> **"Whether you work in a small or large organization, designing today requires flexibility, the ability to adapt and the skills of applying emerging methods and approaches."**

Gone are the days when design was simply concerned with getting consumers to purchase a product. Today design must anticipate the complete product life cycle and the user experience at each stage in this life cycle. This includes the marketing of a product and its purchase through to materials recovery and ultimate disposal. Essentially this means a closer integration of the specialist services represented in Figure 27.1. That is, in consumer electronics, design must become more integrated with the other three quadrants—business, hardware and software. More than ever before, designers must be the representatives of the intended users at the inception and development stages. Designers must be acutely sensitive of the user experience created by their ideas. Defining the right user experience requires many different skills, knowledge and sensitivities. We need to understand the implications arising from the way something looks, feels, sounds or changes during its use. Our aim must be to produce objects such that the consumer is at one with a device's functionality. There must be a seamless harmony between product and user. Consumers have a right to expect a high-quality experience from their products and brands from the first point of contact to the last. Achieving this has eroded some old boundaries between specialisms. Effective design teams are today less segmented. They are both more flexible and more coherent.

Today designers are expected to apply their creativity to define new approaches, new interpretations and new ways of investigating problems as well as coming up with innovative solutions. In the twenty-first century, the need to demonstrate transferable design thinking is challenging the traditional focus on the development of artefacts. This is particularly true in the consumer electronics industry, where a designer has to question whether a design brief must lead to a physical object. Could it, for example, lead to a service, an application, a database or a Web site instead or as well as an artefact? That's not to say that every brief now requires complete 'blue sky' thinking.

However, there seems to be an increasing amount of projects searching for a solution that does not have a predefined deliverable. This approach to business creates new opportunities for innovation and opens the way for designers to lead the creation of business models for economically viable revenue streams.

product road maps

This section focuses on the upper right quadrant of Figure 27.1. This is where business thinking leads but liaises closely with design. Product planning helps to manage the product portfolio, working closely with the design team to monitor markets, technologies, user needs and pricing. This activity often leads to the construction of a road map of products, outlining requirements for devices against estimates for cost and development time (see Figure 27.3). Such road maps need to be read in conjunction with formal business plans since all potential products need to give an adequate return on the development costs, unless there are strategic business reasons to make a loss. The design team will discuss and compare the road map against its vision of what the company should put in its folio with a view to producing a clear lineup of devices for the coming months. The road map is a live document, constantly being updated relative to market changes, customer demands and competitor pressures.

Product marketing manages the promotional side of the product throughout its lifetime. The creation of associated materials such as packaging, point-of-sale publicity, TV and film adverts and magazine exposure are all coordinated by this team. Design must successfully interface with this team, briefing them on what

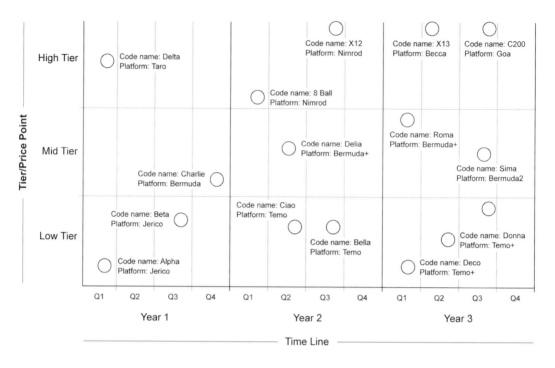

Figure 27.3 Generic product road map for a three-year period. (Copyright author)

the product is about, ensuring they have a clear understanding of the design story and intent. Depending on the company, it's not unusual for the design team to approve and give art direction to the photography and resulting product images to be used by the product marketing department.

Customer accounts look to specific customer requirements and needs, feeding them into the development process. This group defines core features and needs that a product should fulfil in order to get onto the shelves at the right price. These core features and needs are used to help define a specification and support a project's business case. Managing customers at the early stages of development has become crucial to any programme's success. Without enough demand, a product will not be economically viable, which can result in development being stopped.

Figure 27.1 also displays two other quadrants that together might broadly be categorized as engineering. These are the hardware and software development groups. These groups help to realize a design concept, helping to take an idea from a concept through prototyping phases and into mass-produced reality. The engineering teams also conduct a significant amount of testing, working with quality specialists to ensure a design complies with performance targets and industry standards. The contribution of hardware and software to the overall success of electronic consumer items cannot be overstated. However, the bottom line is that the four quadrants of the model must work together effectively, with the common goal of producing great products.

live projects

A designer's involvement at the start of any live project is normally quite intense. It is important to establish the right direction for concept creation, ensuring that all parties are aligned and in agreement about what is required. Once a concept has been defined and agreed upon, it needs to be supported by the project team to ensure the design intent is maintained throughout. Terrific amounts of energy can be expended to define a product, partly because it is normal for design rules and technologies to change from one project to the next. It is also normal for products in higher tiers—that is, the more expensive products—to include characteristics that have not been attempted before by the manufacturer. Pulling these various elements together into one object can be a taxing yet rewarding process for all those involved. Having defined a product, the involvement of designers ramps down, but there is still a need to oversee the development. While questions will certainly arise, in general, the resource demands on the creative team will be less.

Every design program contains elements of risk. Introducing a new concept into mass production can be unpredictable, and failure can result in heavy financial consequences. Add to this the demands of releasing a product on an agreed date and it's possible to see how pressured scenarios can arise. Managing, quantifying and controlling these risks is key to designing, manufacturing and launching a successful product. Generally, to maintain a good quality of product it is necessary for performance targets to be set for the team in each area of development. These targets can range from the electrical performance (e.g. brightness of a display), how the product performs when used in certain environments (e.g.

in high humidity) to the level of defects permitted in manufactured and finished components. To establish and sustain a brand it's important to maintain high performance levels because these build equity. Consumer confidence in the level of quality that can be expected from a product can be a major factor in buying decisions. Maintaining quality levels as manufacturing, technology and user requirements evolve becomes a balancing act of risk versus reward.

> **"Managing, quantifying and controlling risk is key to designing, manufacturing and launching a successful product."**

Another characteristic of live projects is the potential conflict between innovation and stability. By its nature, design is a progressive medium, and the field of consumer electronic products, particularly, is renowned for innovation—for example in miniaturization, functionality and user benefits. Clearly, innovative features can lead to competitive advantage. However, the unpredictability introduced to a program by new technologies, new interactions and new processes offers a stark contrast with the stability needed for a product to meet performance targets and quality levels. Commonly projects and platforms are planned based on previous programmes unless they are totally new. If a team is introducing a new program, then a significant amount of design and feasibility work is completed prior to project initiation to ensure the outcome is more quantifiable and thus more predictable. Such studies can indicate obstacles and problems that might lie ahead, but they are just one more variable in the

Figure 27.4 Maintaining high levels of performance in a product helps to build brand trust and equity. (Getty 112052059 RF)

mix. Ultimately, any work put into a project can be shaped by agreed completion schedules, deadlines or design-specific deliverables.

As a result of the application of large and diverse teams of individuals in design projects is the potential for splits and divisions. Even where cooperation and collaboration are sought, there are often very good reasons for teams to become segmented. This, in turn, places great strains on the networks and can result in people looking inwards to their own respective area rather than looking outwards towards the shared goal of creating a great product.

internal projects

As well as live projects in design studios, there are also internal projects that function as forerunners to future or anticipated live work. Both are outward facing, but internal projects provide an opportunity for design teams to explore directions away from the pressures of live projects. These might particularly focus on design and brand strategy, future and exploratory projects and design language and experience.

Design and brand strategy

This type of internal project is concerned with planning the future of a brand, considering where to allocate company resources and budgets to yield the best results or enhancing the position of the company in the market.

Future and exploratory projects

These explore possible future designs and experiences. Briefs are generally written by senior members of the design department and the senior leadership team. A successful outcome from this sort of project conveys the ethos behind a product or how it will enhance users' lives. Business cases can also form part of the conclusion, substantiated by a rationale and point of view from the studio. Results are presented to business leaders with a view to using some of the design work as a steer towards the company's future strategy and development.

Design language and experience

This type of project is concerned with the characteristics of a company's end product. Leading questions are posed, such as: How does the company define itself through the experience it creates for the end user? How does this experience remain timeless? How are current products perceived in the market—is this in line with company expectations? The results of this type of study aim to set a general direction for design outlining core principles that form the foundation for the objects themselves. The aim is not to create a rule book but to create a set of principles that ensure continuity of work as the design language unfolds over time.

Many internal projects go on to become live projects, and these provide the means for a company to communicate its design intent to the outside world. They bear the fruits of all the hard work put into the design explorations. However, there are no guarantees that projects that have transferred from internal to live will be launched. It's not unusual for such projects to be modified or even cancelled at the development stage.

an example from practice

Some recent live work by the author reveals how characteristics of design and development coexist today. One project for a major communications company required the integration of an antenna in a mobile phone. In this instance, several viewpoints needed to be considered. Understandably, engineering was concerned predominantly with performance, and this was a major influence on the space allocated. Generally, the larger an antenna, the more effective it is, but there are considerations other than performance that govern the acceptability of a product, including materials, form and finish. Clearly no one wants a device that doesn't function, but the designer needs to balance the various requirements and opportunities, and this will include determining how well a product functions, how the components will be grouped and how the unit will be manufactured.

Simulations, models, theoretical studies and prototypes are created to give an indication of how any given mix will perform—although this can give rise to as many questions as answers. These usually get resolved by healthy debate and discussion. In some situations, it is normal for the designer to present several different models alongside the performance projections to help all project members understand the ramifications of decisions.

What is important to note is that the designer is vitally important at these tricky development stages. The approach must be an informed balance between driving for the best design, which results in pushing performance limits, and being sympathetic to the risks being undertaken by those involved. Deliver nothing and the company could suffer significantly. Delivering something that does not sell can be equally expensive and also damage the brand. The attitude and character of the team plays a significant role; good team management and leadership are vital to modern practice.

in-house or consultancy?

The nature of projects worked on by internal and external design teams can differ. Larger corporations tend to have studios that handle the 'now' and the 'next' areas of design, whereas external agencies can offer fresh ideas, unaffected or influenced by directions being studied in-house. Due to the sensitivity and business advantage attached to design strategy, senior in-house personnel generally manage the latter type of work.

As you might imagine, working for a consultancy can expose a designer to a wide variety of briefs. Consultancy size and specialism will dictate the nature of projects undertaken, but in general there is a broader scope of work available. Within bigger in-house teams, design groups tend to be divided into product categories. One of the benefits of working as a design employee of a product

manufacturer is the opportunity to contribute over the full development spectrum, from end to end, in creating product innovation. Typically, you can expect to be involved in defining the user experience, the creation of initial concepts, ensuring the execution meets the design intent and guiding marketing in conveying the appropriate story behind the design. This can yield a true sense of fulfilment for the designer.

As an in-house design employee in a corporate studio, personnel development tends to be more structured and ordered. Career milestones can appear to be much clearer than those in the consultancy sector, but job security in both depends on performance. Both sectors seek to empower design staff to become competent at managing multiple projects, to lead with creativity and vision, to be effective communicators and to possess a blend of people skills to enable them to collaborate with personnel from the boardroom to the factory floor. Many designers must face a career-defining question sooner or later: whether to follow a design path that is more technical or specialist in its nature or whether to take the managerial path, where they will oversee more projects but in less depth. Individuals need to examine their own preferences and take the counsel of colleagues. Might you prefer to liaise with fewer people on fewer projects but in greater depth? Or do you prefer working with more people on more projects guiding the direction? In some ways, this choice is similar to that of a consultancy compared to an in-house team. The pressures towards specialism exert a considerable force in career choices in design. As previously discussed, larger design teams tend to be split into several disciplines. For example mechanical and industrial design is frequently split between departments. The sheer volume of work required to design and manage both elements makes it almost impossible for one individual, or a small team, to manage in the tight time scales of practice today. Team working between groups of specialists and managers has become the norm.

design, strategy and process

Most companies look to maximize revenue by taking various approaches to their innovation and market strategies. The economics and resourcing of a project team in consumer electronics is expensive, with teams being sizeable. Businesses need to think strategically, and they need to consider how to get a good return on project investment. In consumer electronics, the financial outlay on software and hardware can be significant. Developing a software platform, for example, is a lengthy process requiring a lot of time, resources and forethought. Purely mechanical objects usually require smaller teams, and, as such, they can result in much cheaper projects. One of the prime development expenses is the cost of people's time, and much effort goes into achieving efficiency. The goal is to reduce the financial outlay needed for development programmes. In consumer electronics, the software platform can make up a significant element of the development costs, and the management task here is frequently to create a scalable and adaptable operating system allowing multiple projects to be launched from it, recouping expenditure and improving profit.

Alliances and open-source operating systems are common, opening the door for collaboration between companies. The considerable benefits to this way of working include increasing the size of the available resource pool. Also, the opportunity for the platform itself to gain a foothold in the market can be enhanced, because releasing a number of products through several companies can outperform a single manufacturer. But adopting a common platform means differentiation, and individuality of the user experience becomes harder. Also, the platform might be linked to certain types of technology (e.g. screen size and aspect ratio), and this forces those using the software to produce devices that use a standard size of component, resulting in look-alike devices. The platform approach can be economically attractive because it can facilitate an organization releasing multiple products based on the same core printed circuit board. This allows a company to squeeze more out of the platform development, but such tiering is complex to manage. Teams need to balance many variables, including cost, functionality and physical size. The forms of those products sharing a common platform normally need to be fixed in key dimensions and shapes, but even this limitation can be turned to advantage by allowing the creation of families of related products. An alternative approach is to minimize core functionality changes and differentiate by modifying the mechanics. From the consumers' point of view, separation from other platform models can be gained by changing the appearance of the user interface or by simply making cosmetic changes to colour, material or finish.

While multiple hardware variants have become the norm in many types of consumer products, particularly in mid- to low-market price points, the more recognisable products are those that are not spun into multiple variants. Products that are clear in their design and functionality, offering the user a more in-depth connection, as opposed to those trying to be a jack of all trades, tend to be successful in the more expensive tiers of

Figure 27.5 Development time lines and costs for multiple products can be reduced by taking a platform approach to software. (Getty 102761393 RF)

consumer electronics. Perhaps in the future, we will see a tailored approach used more frequently across product price points. Considering current software development trends and constraints, it's difficult to see how the time and finance taken to develop an operating system can be radically reduced. For this reason, open-source operating systems and open applications development seems to be a model that has some way to run yet. In this respect, user experience is becoming a key measure in the commercial battleground, particularly regarding shared software platforms.

The end user is looking for much more than just the veneer of a product. Today all manner of devices need to engage and connect with their owners and users in more and more ways, transforming from the cold, passive tools they perhaps once were to become more helpful, more active objects that enrich lives.

mapping your own career

Earlier in this chapter, I introduced the notion of a road map as a device to assist organizations to understand the business they were in and where they intend to go. Such a road map might have a significant role within a wider business plan. In this section, I want to encourage you to create a road map for yourself, but instead of focusing on new product development, your road map will focus on your career direction and aspirations. There is no particular model for you to follow, but, like other maps, yours should be graphic and reveal various landmarks and important routes in your career planning. Put simply, the map should show where you are now and where you want to get to with a few key stages in between.

Consider Figure 27.1 and Figure 27.3 again. Although these have been constructed to portray the context of electronic consumer products, they are easily adapted to portray other contexts, such as fashion design or graphic communication. Your versions of Figure 27.1 might contain more or fewer sections and present different specialist contributions, but design is likely to figure prominently. It introduced four key quadrants or sections. Perhaps you anticipate a career in the design-led section, but don't neglect opportunities in the other specialist areas. Consider opportunities to work at the interface between these sections, perhaps acting as an interpreter between specialist services such as interaction design and software creation. Perhaps your map will chart a route towards one of the specialist design services shown on the circumference of Figure 27.1, or, alternatively, perhaps you're attracted to a role near the hub, maybe even being a project manager. Two of the key skills I have alerted you to are team working and the ability to perform a number of roles. Your map should try to show where you have already picked up parts of these skills and where you might develop your competences further.

Revealing Design Thinking Through a Portfolio

Teaching design through studio practice, self-directed learning, tutorials and collaborative projects, as is usual in universities and colleges, means that evidence of process as well as final product is required for assessment. Typically students are required to collect evidence of their design thinking process in some form of portfolio. The contents of a portfolio can vary enormously, but typically the work would be highly visual, including photographs, digital images, plans and sketches.

Assessment of a portfolio includes evaluation of evidence of the thinking process the designer has been through to arrive at a solution as well as those representations that seek to illustrate and explain the proposed solution. Such design thinking is valuable and transferable, meaning design thinkers can play effective roles in the team working of many organizations.

Traditionally the portfolio was a physical collection of outputs, but today most designers will have an e-portfolio of their work in digital format. This can be made available online for people to browse, to assist with communication with clients, for feedback by colleagues and for use in interviews. E-portfolios facilitate content that was difficult to contain in traditional portfolios such as video and animations.

A number of companies, such as Coroflot (www.coroflot.com/), offer online portfolio space, making it easy to showcase your most recent work and track interest.

In this chapter, I've contrasted employment in a manufacturing company with employment in a consultancy. Again, your map might seek to reveal your preferred goal and the route you might take. It would be perfectly acceptable for your map to reveal that you want experiences in both. This chapter also has suggested that there are new pressures on designers to apply their creativity in new ways, to make creative new interpretations

Figure 27.6 The author leading a design studio class.
(Copyright author)

of what is needed and wanted by society and to define new approaches. What are your landmarks in creative thinking, and where would you place them on your road map? Is transferable design thinking your destination or a stage on a longer journey?

Younger and less experienced designers are generally mentored throughout the early stages of their development to ensure projects and their associated workloads are managed effectively. Use your map to reveal what mentoring experiences you need to progress along your preferred route.

The Crit

Most models of design education at the undergraduate level involve students in critical appraisals or 'crits' of work. This is a seminar in which tutors and fellow students offer feedback on work. Each student will present his or her work and seek to justify such things as direction, interpretation of the task, progress and innovation. Essentially each participant communicates his or her design thinking to colleagues and tutors, and questions are expected from all. Participation in the critical appraisal of the work of others is just as important as defending your own work.

While crits can seem hostile at times, the aim is to assist each presenter and to enrich the learning of the community. These seminars can take place at the end of a project or during the progress of a project. Typically the expectations develop in scale and complexity as students move through their design studies. Partly crits prepare students for professional work where they will present their work to clients or managers, but crits also develop the vital reflective and evaluative capacities of design thinking.

CHAPTER SUMMARY

- Commercial design project teams require a core of management expertise supported by specialist contributions. Get to know where you want to locate yourself on a map of your own design field.

- Designing today requires flexibility, the ability to adapt and the skills of applying emerging methods and approaches.

- Designers must be acutely sensitive to the user experience created by their ideas.

- Design is a process of managing risk as companies seek potential rewards. It frequently has to find a path between innovation and stability.

- The strategic goal is profitability. Look for opportunities to make efficiencies and economies. In consumer electronics, this includes collaboration between companies and the development of platforms with multiple uses. However, the most successful brands display great clarity in design, function and user experience.

- Constructing a road map of your career intentions can help you visualise, plan and achieve your own goals. Document your landmark skills and use the map to chart what new skills you need.

chapter 28

motivation and the learningscape of design

steve garner and chris evans

ABOUT THIS CHAPTER

Designers, engineers, architects and artists are trained to deal with conflicting requirements and opportunities; in fact, their ways of investigating problems and prototyping ideas are frequently aimed at exposing hidden but influential conflict, bringing conflict out into the open. To achieve this requires a familiarity with a multidimensional landscape of design and designing. It's a landscape that has similarities with the environment of some digital games in that it is not one landscape but many. One of these landscapes can be characterized as an arena for conflicting forces that drive design. Another concerns the skills and knowledge with which designers undertake design activity. But there is a third and neglected landscape concerning the understanding and development of motivation in design. This chapter is about learning across this three-dimensional landscape or 'learningscape' and particularly the importance of motivation.

Effective movement around the learningscape is vital for practising designers and students alike, because design is a dynamic process of resolving problems. It's a process that involves learning, generating, testing and evaluating, and it takes place amongst the shifting sands of society, culture and technology. However, the pathways for movement around the learningscape are not clear, and they demand the application of motivation if movement is to be effective. It's here that there are opportunities for improvement. There are lessons here for those who believe they are effective design thinkers and for those who create the learningscapes for the education of future design thinkers.

---

working between consumers and producers

Users have become a powerful force in design today, and the market exerts great influence on the strategic decisions taken by companies. Market success is held up as an indicator of design success. It is for this reason that companies spend so long getting to know their markets, eliciting feedback and communicating with users. Designing today is less about what an organization chooses to impose on a particular market and more to do with responding to particular opportunities or market conditions. Understanding the needs and wants of markets can mean getting to know the requirements of individuals within markets. However, in most situations, it's the producer who pays for the design service, and his or her agenda is more likely to focus on the profitability of the organization. So, just as users must influence the earliest formulation of the design brief, so must the issues of supply chains, production and distribution be represented.

The designer's location between the producer and consumer emerged in the industrial revolution of the eighteenth century and was brought into sharp focus in the early twentieth century, particularly in the United States. Since this time, the designer's role as interpreter between users and producers has been adopted in a global model of service. In essence the designer is charged with the responsibility of guiding a company to create outputs that people are willing to buy at a price that is greater than the unit cost of production. The perennial problem in design is how to add value while reducing cost, and frequently this demands more than finding an agreeable middle ground. In some situations, user or market priorities must dominate. Apple and Sony, for example, have developed reputations for anticipating market trends and creating new types of products that are pleasurable to own and use.

In other situations, it has been appropriate for manufacturing innovation to dominate, such as Toyota's pioneering application of design for manufacture.[1]

The designer today is expected to occupy the zone between consumers and producers and to challenge the boundaries on both sides in a search for appropriate resolution. To do this, designers need particular abilities, many of which have been the subject of chapters in this collection. For example designers need to be able to work with problems that are not clearly defined, they need to be creative and good communicators, they need to be efficient in finding out information through appropriate techniques, they need to work effectively in multidisciplinary teams and they need to have a grasp of the specialist knowledge of other

---

Designing the Future

In 2010 the Institute for the Future, an independent nonprofit organization based in California's Silicon Valley, published a ten-year forecast titled *The Future Is a High-Resolution Game.* Here's their summary of the book:

> The next decade will be one where we become both the gamers and the creators of the game itself. The goals of the game are clear: *Happiness*—what we really want out of life; *Resilience*—a way to respond better, adapt more quickly, and find steadiness amidst perturbation; and *Legacy*—crafting a world worth leaving for the next generation, the next hundred years of play. But the rules are less obvious. Do we follow the old rules of the past century, and compete to grow? Or do we create new rules for a new era? This is a game where we, the players, must choose the rules. Never before has humanity been able to encounter the future in such detail, to measure the forces of change at such vast scales and yet still fill in the details with such fine grain.[1]

The Institute for the Future identifies five key forces facing humanity: carbon, water, power, cities and identity. The institute suggests that, for each, we might take one of four alternative paths: growth, constraint, collapse and transformation. These frame an agenda for the future design professions.

---

[1] For more information on this ten-year forecast, see www.iftf.org/tyf

---

participants in design and development. Standing between the opposing forces of consumers and producers is just one of a designer's many intermediary roles.

a landscape of forces

All designers stand between alternative opportunities. These are shaped by forces often outside the control of designers, and they give rise to tensions. For most designers, their service is a process of finding appropriate emphases between opposing opportunities to create outputs that represent an agreeable resolution of the tensions. Note that we don't say 'compromise'. A compromise suggests a rational but perhaps mechanistic approach to trading-off requirements against each other. Designing is very different because it applies creative thinking to reframe problems and uncover innovative ways to resolve conflict. It challenges preconceived notions of what might be needed, and it can lead to unexpected ideas. Successful designing can result in an output that is greater than the sum of its parts. It's a form of arbitration where the outcome is agreeable to all stakeholders.

While some of the tensions arise from *who* a designer represents, other tensions are rooted in *what* designers do. For example there are pressures on designers to uncover problems and generate solutions, to deconstruct issues and to reconstruct them, to ensure an output looks right and works right. In addition to this, design has acquired a responsibility to not only resolve today's problems but to help anticipate tomorrow's problems. Then there are some opposing strategies for how designers might operate, such as being systematic or intuitive, using two-dimensional representations or three-dimensional ones and working in the digital/virtual world or the physical world. If one adds to these further questions concerning when, why and where design should be applied, a picture emerges of a designer standing within a circle of opportunities and pressures (see Figure 28.1).

This landscape of questions was mapped by the ancient Greeks but perhaps is best known through the poem by Rudyard Kipling titled 'I Keep Six Honest Serving Men'. The first verse begins:

> I keep six honest serving-men
> (They taught me all I knew);
> Their names are What and Why and When
> And How and Where and Who.
> I send them over land and sea,
> I send them east and west;
> But after they have worked for me,
> I give them all a rest.[2]

The basis of all successful design and development is rooted in such questions. Each leads to further avenues of questioning. The circle represented in Figure 28.1 can make significant demands on one's thinking because, to be effective, you need to be both creative and systematic. While there's no guarantee that the perfect answer is waiting to be discovered, the circle of questions does help to resolve the conflicts and illuminate the opportunities. It can help you create an effective overview of the task in hand.

The how and why questions are becoming increasingly important in design. As pressures increase on organizations to anticipate market demands, new approaches to information gathering and interpretation are required. Design is increasingly part of a holistic problem-finding process. Also, there are growing expectations for design to play a role in helping society, both locally and globally, to recognize and respond to new important forces. The emerging priorities for ecological awareness and, more generally, the need for sustainability and fairness in production and consumption have reshaped society's perception of the role of designers. Their role as arbiters between individual choice and social responsibility has highlighted the moral and ethical dimensions

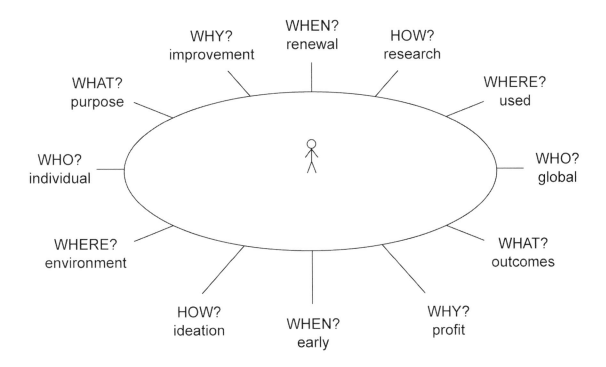

Figure 28.1 The landscape of a design project is illuminated by questions. (Copyright author)

to designing today. This wider, transformative role for design has led some, such as David Orr, professor of environmental studies and politics, to suggest that the aim of education should be a form of design intelligence:

The challenge to us as educators is to equip our students with the practical skills, analytic abilities, philosophical depth, and moral wherewithal to remake the human presence in the world. In short order, as history measures these things, they must replace the extractive economy with one that functions on current sunlight, eliminates the concept of waste, uses energy and materials with great efficiency, and distributes wealth fairly within and between generations. We will have to recast the systems by which we provision ourselves with food, energy, water, materials, and livelihood, and by which we handle our wastes. These, in turn, imply the need to design organizations that are capable of ecological design. The particular skills of ecological design necessary to a future that is sustainable and spiritually sustaining are in turn means to a still larger end of fostering hope in a world of growing despair, and anger, and its offspring, terrorism, whether by individuals, organizations, or governments.[3]

Whether you believe that the ecological agenda is the primary force in design or just one of a number of forces, the what, why, when, how, where and who questions of Figure 28.1 have huge implications for the future role of designers. They are reshaping the skill sets required of designers and are recasting the whole landscape of design career opportunities.

building the learningscape

Figure 28.1 suggests that the designer exists at the centre of the what, why, when, how, where and who questions. While every designer might have cause to ask these questions, it's clear that their responses will differ depending on their particular context and the forces operating at any particular time. In some design projects it might be necessary for the producer issues to dominate. In other

projects it might be appropriate for the designer to fight for recognition of global implications of decisions. And of course designers differ in their skills. Some are better at a research-led analytical process while others might be better suited to creative ideation. If we were to develop the diagram presented in Figure 28.1 to plot a representative sample of designers working today, we might very well create the sort of distribution shown in Figure 28.2.

It reveals designers distributed across the whole of our landscape. We might discern clusters that indicate some shared preferences for certain mixes in ways of dealing with the pressures and opportunities, but generally people will reveal great variety in the ways they choose

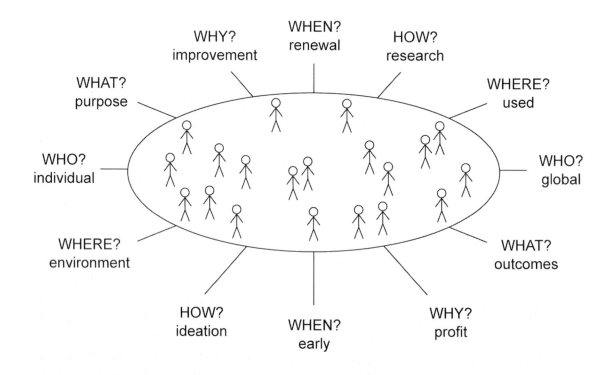

Figure 28.2 A sample of designers distributed across the landscape of Figure 28.1. (Copyright author)

to apply their design thinking. There is no best or most intelligent place to be. In fact, design intelligence might be defined as an ability to place yourself at a particular location and be able to justify it until it becomes beneficial to move to another location. Such movements might need to take place frequently, or conditions might dictate stability. Developing your design intelligence so that you know where to place yourself in this diagram at any given stage, and indeed at any given moment, of a design project is vital. It's vital because it means you understand the active forces and the emphasis you give to them. To develop your design intelligence means working with other landscapes, and to reveal these we shall develop Figure 28.2 to include a landscape of skills and knowledge.

Skills and knowledge

Education places a lot of emphasis on skills and knowledge, and these dominate the teaching in many subjects, including design. Design skills can include an ability to exploit computer-aided design in idea generation or communication, it can include a competence for safe working with resilient materials and it can include an ability to uncover design issues amongst complex real-world situations. Knowledge, on the other hand, has been defined as 'the acquaintance with facts, truths and principles'.[4] Using the same examples again, knowledge can include an appreciation of the different principles behind building digital models, knowledge of a taxonomy of materials and an ability to distinguish between qualitative and quantitative research approaches. While being conceptually different than skills, knowledge is inextricably bound up with skills in a symbiotic relationship.

Skills and knowledge are partly unique to each design domain. That is, the skills and knowledge

of a High Street fashion designer will be different than those of a mass-market car designer. Also the skills and knowledge of these two examples might be very different than, say, those fashion or car designers who work on exclusive one-off designs. Also it's possible to identify some shared or generic skills and knowledge across design professions, and this collection has begun to reveal these, such as an ability to make representations and an ability to allow problems and solutions to co-evolve. Skills and knowledge are so distinctly different from the forces at work as revealed in Figure 28.2 that we need to modify our representation and add a whole new layer (Figure 28.3).

The development of Figure 28.2 is liberating because it provides space for the development of skills and knowledge that is both connected to the driving forces of design and separate from them. Figure 28.3 suggests that we can, at any time during a design task, move upwards to the skills and knowledge layer. We might do this because we need some new skill or knowledge relevant to the task, or alternatively we might immerse ourselves in some learning simply to increase our portfolio of skills and knowledge or for recreation. This might be particularly useful in, for example, learning to draw, where sometimes we need to have the space to experiment and make mistakes away from the pressures of employing our developing skills and knowledge in design. But there's a second, powerful potential for moving into this upper layer. The skills and knowledge developed for one purpose can help address the problems and opportunities presented subsequently. That is, you can descend from the upper layer to arrive at a different point than the one you ascended from. By doing this you can move around the

Skills and knowledge

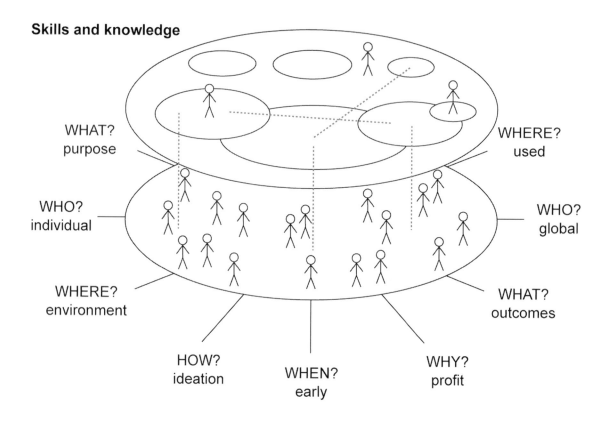

Figure 28.3 A two-layer model introducing skills and knowledge. (Copyright author)

model, acquiring skills and knowledge and applying these to resolve design problems that are subject to dynamic forces and which present multiple opportunities. Acquiring skills and knowledge can help designers reframe the active forces that shape their perceptions of where they are and what they need to do. The model is applicable at the career level too. For example a person developing his or her skills and knowledge of new polymers in furniture design might find that these same skills and knowledge open up opportunities for creating special effects in the film industry. Similarly, a person with skills and knowledge of the creation of letter forms

> **"The skills and knowledge developed for one purpose can help address the problems and opportunities presented subsequently."**

in graphic communication might develop some critical powers highly transferable to curating exhibitions in museums or galleries.

It's impossible to convey every possibility, but the movement upwards from the lower level to the

Figure 28.4 Design skills and knowledge can be surprisingly transferable across fields such as product, graphic, film and advertising design. (Getty 109717859)

upper level and then back down again offers a rich potential for developing design competence. As Clive Mockford, managing director of consultancy Engineering Creatives, points out:

> That's what a designer does. He or she moves between the chaotic, creative processes and the ordered, systematic processes in order to progress a design. It's a process of many sidesteps as well as forward and backward steps. In fact this may be the only way to proceed given the ever-changing context in which new products and systems are created.[5]

There's even scope for playfully moving between the levels to see where it takes you. But this isn't the end of the story. The model needs one more layer, and this concerns motivation.

motivation

Those leading design education place great emphasis on developing skills and knowledge, and yet many expect students to automatically possess the necessary motivation for operating across the landscape of today's design practice. Sometimes those who create design education assume their students must have the same drive and enthusiasm as themselves, while others assume that a hunger for success in the form of assignment grades or career opportunities is sufficient motivation. Clive Mockford highlights the same misconception in professional practice:

> You might imagine that most designers are motivated by money but in my experience the most powerful rewards are those associated with being part of successful innovation; working as part of a team to successfully get a product into the marketplace where it's well received. It's an emotional reward rather than a financial reward. This is another reason why it's hard for undergraduate design courses to give students realistic experiences—the assessments create false reward systems.[6]

There is frequently a rigorous search for enthusiasm at the point of entry onto design degrees, which is why many universities still insist on interviewing design candidates; but once admitted to a degree programme in one of the many and varied design fields, the development of motivation is left largely to the individual. However, motivation is not some optional add-on. It has a function equal in significance to the whole landscape of skills and knowledge. Figure 28.5 provocatively illustrates this. Motivation is not a passive force; it can be understood, shaped and developed. In fact, designing demands a constant refreshing and renewal of motivation, and this has implications for design curricula and the sort of learning experiences that are created for students.

If Figure 28.3 represented a dynamic and adventurous journeying between two levels, then the

> "Motivation is not some optional add-on. It has a function equal in significance to the whole landscape of skills and knowledge."

addition, in Figure 28.5, of a third level concerning motivation provides a valuable opportunity to understand this important force in design thinking. Figure 28.5 is more than a multilevel landscape— it is a model of design thinking, design action and design learning. We emphasize design learning because all designing is about learning, whether in professional practice or education. The model presented in Figure 28.5 is nothing less than the learningscape of design. One might assume that navigation around this learningscape was easy and straightforward, and, for some, it is. However, one of the drivers to movement is motivation, and to understand its significance, we need to take a closer look at motivation and its role in learning.

Studies by educational psychologists have confirmed that what people learn, and how much they learn, are influenced by the learner's motivation. Some studies have focused on learning by children in schools and have not been design-specific. Such studies provide some general reasons why we should value motivation and how we might develop it. They reveal, for example, the significance of practical tasks for enhancing motivation and, conversely, the negative influence of anxiety over potential failure. Other studies have focused on teaching and learning in design, and they reveal a vital need to spend time on motivation as well as developing skills and knowledge. In response, design programmes have sought to introduce learning tasks that are relevant and meaningful to students and that are interesting and appropriate in complexity and matched to learners' abilities. Project work, and particularly live projects with external agencies or clients, has traditionally been a key motivational device for allowing students to exercise personal choice and control.

The value of motivation is a question that rarely presents itself outside of design pedagogy discussions, but it should concern every student of

Skills and knowledge

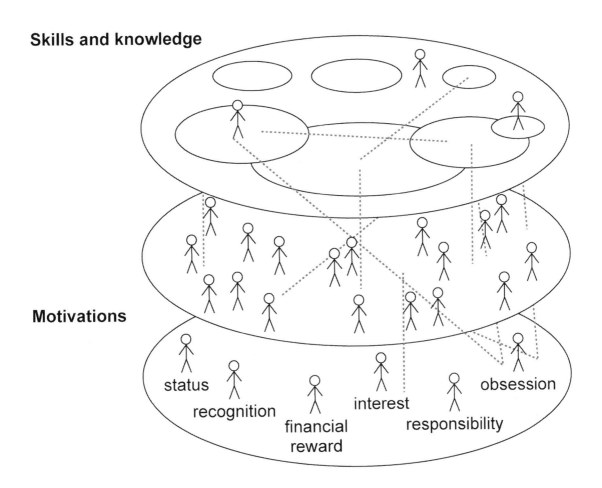

Motivations

status

recognition

financial
reward

interest

responsibility

obsession

Figure 28.5 Motivation underpins design education and
design practice. (Copyright author)

design. Having motivation enables individuals to navigate the design learningscape represented in Figure 28.5. Partly it provides the energy to move between levels. This energy might manifest itself as enthusiasm to engage with chosen skills or knowledge or curiosity to explore unknown or un-developed skills and knowledge. Motivation also provides the energy to persevere with skills and knowledge when their value is not clear or their application is without direction. Given that the value of motivation is widely accepted, it seems strange that strategies for developing motivation are so thin on the ground. Skills and knowledge are the subject of numerous resources, and while students engage with this level of the learning-scape model they are well provided for. However, those students who dive down to the motivation layer of the model, out of necessity or desire, to replenish or develop their motivation find a paucity of resources and expectations to be self-reliant.

So there's a need in design education for learn-ers to appreciate the importance of moving down

Figure 28.6 Design projects in collaboration with professional practice have traditionally proved highly motivating for students. (Getty 87881783)

the model, to enhance their motivation, which in turn will equip them to navigate the learningscape with direction and vigour; but there is an equal responsibility for teachers to provide resources for those students who seek to understand the significance of motivation and the techniques for developing and applying it. There are four key needs in design education.

Embrace failure

There is a need to unpack failure and to let an understanding of failure guide assessment. Tim Brown of the design consultancy IDEO is widely reported as saying that design is a process of trying to 'fail faster', and by this he means that design thinking progresses by testing ideas and either rejecting them or developing them. As designers we need to be hungry for failure! But we also know that failure can be hugely demotivating. Fear of failure can create barriers in all learning. This can be resolved in design if we frame the criteria for success as controlling failure, of generating and testing conjecture through modelling rather than the limited type of success embodied in the defence of a selected proposal. It's a success criteria that focuses on process as much as product. Digital models provide ideal environments for safe failures, but we persist in limiting the digital realm to the creation of beguiling representations of an imagined reality.

Challenge and risk

Motivation is enhanced by challenge and intellectual risk, but the nature of the challenges and risk placed before design students is too closely controlled. The reasons for this control are understandable: the demands of closely defined curricula, the requirement to focus on particular skills and knowledge, the pressure to assess students against particular learning outcomes and the need to offer consistent experiences to large student cohorts have combined to impoverish the nature of the challenge and risk. Compared to the challenge and risk in professional practice, the preparation on degree programmes can seem limp. Challenge needs to be supported by the development of strategy.

Strategy for managing

Many designers display a natural ability to exploit simplifications to make complicated tasks understandable and manageable. After all, design models are no more than simplifications to assist the understanding of problems or the communication of ideas. Feeling able to manage is particularly important where design tasks present ambiguity or conflict between forces. Motivation is enhanced if we feel we have a strategy for dealing with the complexity or ambiguity of tasks. This might be something simple such as breaking a job down into manageable chunks or into a sequence, but it also includes understanding the processes that have proved effective for other people. We might distil key lessons from expert designers, but we might also learn much from those who don't seek to wear the label of expert.

Self-evaluation

Motivation relies on an ability for self-evaluation. If an individual is unable to measure his or her own performance in relation to that of others, then he or she learns to rely on the opinions and judgements of peers and tutors. Independence and well-founded resilience are vital in order to cope with conflict and confidently defend proposals. Traditionally, universities have not been very good at developing students' ability for evaluating their own performance, but self-evaluation is not only empowering, it has become a key skill for employment in today's creative industries.

Who Needs Design History?

The study of the history of design has long been part of design education, but who needs it? Why look backwards when surely design and designing are about looking forwards?

Design history is the study of the tangible and the less tangible things we humans have made, and it can include the study of the processes we apply to create and develop designs. Some design historians believe that we should note the contribution of certain design experts. Perhaps they pioneered work with a new material or demonstrated a new priority. Perhaps their designs sold in vast numbers or appear in major museum collections. Other design historians say this perpetuates the myth of the designer as 'hero'. In contrast, they appeal for education to expose the wider social and cultural context of design, examining the consumption of design as well as its supply. Wherever your sympathies lie, as a designer you need to have an opinion on design history.

A study of our human design past can achieve much. It can help us develop important critical and reflective skills, it can stimulate our creativity and it can remind us that we are not the first to face difficult dilemmas or the first to try to make our world more usable, beautiful or sustainable. It can help us to perceive new relationships between technology and culture and between the individual and society. Design history can help us make sense of our own design contribution to the broad network of human development.

challenging the forces suppressing motivation

The design professions, ranging from communication design to urban planning, face radically new responsibilities concerning their ability to act as interpreters and transformers of conflict. As a recent article by New Zealand architect Shannon Joe points out:

> The pace of change in the 21st century continues to increase with the world demanding more knowledge and skills. We are moving into a world of seamless interconnection and complexity. Society is confronted with an evolving 'learningscape' where typical models of tertiary education are now being developed into a more hybrid and holistic model.[7]

The design professions already look for new graduates who can operate confidently at the interface between opposing forces, and the skills and knowledge required are set to increase. But skills and knowledge without motivation are little use for anything other than routine design. In situations that demand design leadership, motivation can be more valuable than skills and knowledge.

This chapter has made a case for prioritising the development of motivation in young designers. This is all the more urgent as forces conspire to erode motivation by swamping design tasks with conflicting information. Designing is a learning task as much as a creating task, so designers need support for the agile navigation of the world of design that has been characterized as a learningscape. We need learning experiences that tap into students' natural motivations but which professionalize motivation to create a resilient, informed and sustainable capacity. Since motivation is not one distinct force but is shaped and coloured by numerous cognitive forces and emotions, it seems logical that any attempt to develop motivation should acknowledge its diversity. For example it might be necessary to work on curiosity through investigative tasks. These might tap into a designer's emerging ability to communicate. Other approaches to developing motivation might focus on attitudes or beliefs, personal interests or the nature of obsession.

This chapter suggested that there exists a form of design intelligence—an exercising of design thinking skills—that is well-suited to addressing some of the conflicts in today's world. Design intelligence recognises the ubiquity of designing, the role of the past in the creation of the future and the potential for design to be a problem-causing phenomenon as well as a problem-solving one. Design intelligence helps us address the what, where, when, how, who and why questions of design, but it is a capacity built on potentially fragile foundations of motivation, attitudes, values and beliefs. Design intelligence isn't robust and resilient; it can be hesitant and fragile, but it is essentially optimistic, inclusive, reflective and creative in the way it frames and seeks to resolve conflict.

Figure 28.7 Design practice requires motivated navigation of the learningscape. (Getty 73666825)

CHAPTER SUMMARY

- Conflict is the lifeblood of designing because it stimulates and focuses the co-working of critical and creative thinking.
- The designer today operates amidst conflicting forces.
- Skills and knowledge provide part of the designer's armoury, but they are inadequate without motivation.
- One needs motivation to drive the navigation of the learningscape of design.
- Motivation is a fragile phenomenon influenced by notions of failure, challenge, risk, strategies for management and self-evaluation.
- Design programmes in our universities need to find ways for students to develop motivation at a time when forces act to suppress this.

Background

A recent forecast has suggested the global snack food industry will be worth over US$300 billion by 2015.[1] The industry embraces an immense range of foods catering for widely differing markets, such as snacks for children and those who are health conscious or who don't eat certain products. As well as addressing our hunger, snack foods are part of our social interaction, for example at sports events or while watching a film. But the food is only part of the story—there are related industries in, for example, snack food packaging, eating utensils, storage, retail, transport and graphic communication. The industry is not without its critics—there are concerns the industry contributes to obesity and that it can have impacts on farming and the developing world.

This project invites you into the world of design in the snack food industry. It seeks to help you achieve an excellent product and to improve your design process. Just like the best gold is rated as 24-carat, this project aims to help you achieve 24-carat design and designing.

The Project

Create a new snack food product based on a vegetable. This product must appeal to a sufficiently large market so as to attract investment for further development. Once you have a new snack product, you can take the project in any of several directions as outlined in the guidelines below. You may set your own time frame for this project, but keep a log book, blog or diary for the whole process.

Guidelines

The product: Use your design thinking skills to generate creative ideas for new markets. Where are the future snack markets: takeaway lunches, travel snacks, breakfasts? A snack doesn't need to be dry—it might be liquid. This might be a cold snack or a hot snack or a combination of the two. The main constraint is that the snack must be based on a vegetable. Expect to be challenged on the sustainability of your proposal.

As stipulated above, you need to steer this project in your own preferred direction. For example you might want to create an advertising campaign for the food or a Web-based education resource. Alternatively, you might want to create the packaging, the graphic design or point-of-sale materials. Another direction would be to explore the storage and serving of the snack at home, its incorporation into a lunchbox or the creation of innovative eating utensils. Perhaps you might prefer to use your design skills to reduce the impact of consumption through an idea for reuse or recycling. Remember the advantages of digital and physical modelling.

The process: Use your log book, blog or diary to document your process, including your investigations, ideas and developments. Just as in a diary, note down your feelings as you review your work. At the end of the project, create a single diagram that communicates your process. Where are your strengths and weaknesses in designing? Which chapters in the book do you find most stimulating for improving your design process and why?

notes

chapter 1

1. J. Lave and E. Wenger, *Situated Learning Legitimate Peripheral Participation* (Cambridge University Press, 1991).

2. E. Wenger, *Communities of Practice: Learning, Meaning and Identity* (Cambridge University Press, 2007).

3. Ibid.

4. S. Bailey, *Harley Earl* (Trefoil Publications, 1990).

5. *Car Design News,* www.cardesignnews.com (accessed 19 April 2011).

6. H. E. Gardner, *Frames of Mind: The Theory of Multiple Intelligence* (Basic Books, 1993).

7. M. Tovey, 'Designing with Both Halves of the Brain', *Design Studies* 5/4, pp. 219–28.

8. E. de Bono, *Lateral Thinking: A Textbook of Creativity* (Word Luck Educational Press, 1970).

9. H. Pringle, *Diagonal Thinking,* www.ipa.co.uk/Content/Diagonal-Thinking-Introduction (accessed 19 April 2011).

chapter 2

1. Widely cited quotation by Nolan Bushnell, for example www.ideachampions.com/weblogs/archives/2010/11/25_awesome_quot.shtml (accessed 30 April 2011).

2. T. Brown, 'Design Thinking', *Harvard Business Review* (June 2008), www.ideo.com/images/uploads/thoughts/IDEO_HBR_Design_Thinking.pdf (accessed 30 April 2011).

3. Hasso Plattner Institute of Design at Stanford University, http://dschool.stanford.edu/ (accessed 30 April 2011).

4. H. Dubberly, *How Do You Design? A Compendium of Models* (Dubberly Design Office, 2004).

5. Hasso Plattner Institute of Design at Stanford University, *Design Thinking* (Stanford University Press, 2007).

6. A. Osborn, *Applied Imagination: Principles and Procedures of Creative Problem Solving* (Charles Scribner and Sons, 1953).

7. J. H. Flavell, 'Speculations about the Nature and Development of Metacognition', in F. E. Weinert and R. H. Kluwe, eds, *Metacognition, Motivation and Understanding* (Lawrence Erlbaum Associates, 1987), pp. 21–29.

8. C. Dweck, 'Unboxed—If You're Open to Growth, You Tend to Grow', *New York Times* (6 July 2008), www.nytimes.com/2008/07/06/business/06unbox.html (accessed 30 April 2011).

9. G. Claxton, *What's the Point of School?* (One World Publications, 2008).

10. B. Edwards, *Drawing on the Right Side of the Brain* (Penguin Putnam, 1979).

11. R. J. Sternberg, *Handbook of Creativity* (Yale University Press, 1999).

12. D. Pink, *A Whole New Mind* (Riverhead Books, 2005).

13. 'IDEO's Ten Tips for Creating a 21st-century Classroom Experience', *Metropolis* (18 February 2009), www.metropolismag.com/story/20090218/ideos-ten-tips-for-creating-a-21st-century-classroom-experience (accessed 30 April 2011).

14. W. Berger, *Glimmer: How Design Can Trans-form Your Life, Your Business, and Maybe Even the World* (Random House of Canada, 2009).

chapter 3

1. J. C. Jones, *Design Methods* (John Wiley, 1997).
2. E. Sanders, 'From User-centered to Partici-patory Design Approaches', in J. Frascara, ed., *Design and the Social Sciences: Making Connec-tions* (Taylor & Francis, 2002).
3. D. Koberg and J. Bagnall, *The Universal Trav-eller: A Soft-systems Guide to Creativity, Problem-solving and the Process of Reaching Goals* (Crisp Publications, 2003).
4. T. Leblanc, 'Evolved Design Thinking and the Impact on Education and Practice. New Perspec-tives in Design Education', in A. Clark et al., eds, *E&PDE 2008* (Artyplan, 2008), pp. 547–52.
5. J. Carroll, ed., *Scenario-based Design: En-visioning Work and Technology System Develop-ment* (John Wiley & Sons, 1995).
6. M. Buchenau and J. F. Suri, 'Experience Pro-totyping', in D Boyarski and W Kellogg, eds, *De-signing Interactive Systems: Processes, Practices* (ACM Press, 2000), pp. 424–33.
7. K. Krippendorff, *The Semantic Turn: A New Foundation for Design* (CRC Press, Taylor & Fran-cis, 2006).
8. J. D. Novak and A. J. Cañas, 'The Theory Underlying Concept Maps and How to Construct and Use Them', *Technical Report IHMC Cmap-Tools 2006–01 Rev 01–2008* (Florida Institute for Human and Machine Cognition, 2008), http://cmap.ihmc.us/Publications/ResearchPapers/TheoryUnderlyingConceptMaps.pdf (accessed 30 April 2011). S. Stoyanov and P. Kommers, 'WWW-intensive Concept Mapping for Meta-cognition in Solving Ill-structured Problems', *International Journal of Continuing Engineering Education and Lifelong Learning* 16/3–4, 297–316.
9. See for example http://compendium.open.ac.uk/institute/ (accessed 30 April 2011).
10. E. Rosch, 'Principles of Categorization', in E. Rosch and B. B. Lloyd, eds, *Cognition and Cate-gorization* (Erlbaum Associates, 1978), pp. 27–48.

chapter 4

1. '"Power by the Hour": Can Paying Only for Performance Redefine How Products Are Sold and Serviced?' Knowledge@Wharton, 21 Feb-ruary 2007, http://knowledge.wharton.upenn.edu/article.cfm?articleid=1665 (accessed 20 April 2011).
2. K. Ulrich and S. Eppinger, *Product Design and Development* (McGraw-Hill, 2004). J. Cagan and C. Vogel, *Creating Breakthrough Products: Innovation from Product Planning to Program Ap-proval* (Prentice Hall, 2002).
3. J. R. Giard, *Design FAQs* (Dorset Group, 2005).
4. P. Checkland and J. Poulter, *Learning for Ac-tion: A Short Definitive Account of Soft Systems Methodology, and Its Use with Practitioners, Teachers and Students* (John Wiley & Sons, 2006).

chapter 6

1. E. Hill, *The Language of Drawing* (Prentice Hall, 1966).
2. R. Arnheim, *Visual Thinking* (Faber & Faber, 1969).
3. See for example the work of Betty Edwards, particularly her book *Drawing on the Right side of the Brain* (Souvenir Press, 1979).
4. For a fuller discussion of this capacity of drawing, see T. Rosenberg, 'New Beginnings and Monstrous Births: Notes Towards an Appreciation

of Ideational Drawing', in S. Garner, ed., *Writing on Drawing* (Intellect Books, 2008).

5. 'Lateral thinking' was a term coined by Edward de Bono in the 1960s. For further information, see his books *Lateral Thinking, Creativity Step by Step* (Harper & Row, 1970) and *Serious Creativity: Using the Power of Lateral Thinking to Create New Ideas* (Harper Business, 1992).

chapter 8

1. J. Bruner, *Acts of Meaning* (Harvard University Press, 1990).

2. M. D. Dickey, 'Game Design Narrative for Learning: Appropriating Adventure Game Design Narrative Devices and Techniques for the Design of Interactive Learning Environments', *Educational Technology Research and Development* 54/3 (2006), pp. 245–63.

3. G. Frasca, 'Ludology Meets Narratology: Similitude and Differences between (Video) Games and Narrative', www.ludology.org (accessed 30 April 2011).

4. J. Juul, 'Games Telling Stories? A Brief Note on Games and Narratives', *Game Studies: The International Journal of Computer Game Research* 1/1 (2001), www.gamestudies.org/0101/juul-gts/ (accessed 30 April 2011).

5. R. Rouse, *Game Design: Theory and Practice* (Worldware Publishing, 2001), p. 232.

6. C. Crawford, *Chris Crawford on Game Design* (New Riders Publishing, 2003).

7. C. Vogler, *The Writer's Journey: Mythic Structures for Writers,* 3rd edn (Michael Wiese Productions, 2007).

8. *Wizard of Oz,* Victor Fleming, dir. (Metro-Goldwyn-Mayer, 1939) [film].

9. C. G. Jung, *The Collected Works of C. G. Jung,* H. Read, M. Fordham, and G. Adler, eds (Pantheon Books, 1953).

10. Vogler, *The Writer's Journey.*

11. A. Rollings and E. Adams, *Game Design* (New Riders Publishing, 2003).

chapter 9

1. D. Norman and S. W. Draper, eds, *User Centered System Design: New Perspectives on Human–Computer Interaction* (Lawrence Erlbaum Associates, 1986).

2. K. Vredenburg, S. Isensee, and C. Righi, *User-centered Design: An Integrated Approach* (Prentice Hall, 2002).

3. J. Rubin and D. Chisnell, *Handbook of Usability Testing: How to Plan, Design, and Conduct Effective Tests,* 2nd edn (John Wiley, 2008).

4. Vredenburg, Isensee, and Righi, *User-centered Design.*

5. International Organization for Standardization, *ISO/IEC 13407: Human-centered Design Processes for Interactive Systems* (ISO, 1999).

6. C. Wilson, ed., *User Experience Re-mastered: Your Guide to Getting the Right Design* (Morgan Kaufmann, 2010), p. 31.

7. C. Courage and K. Baxter, *Understanding Your Users: A Practical Guide to User Requirements Methods, Tools, and Techniques* (Morgan Kaufmann, 2005).

8. J. Blomberg and M. Burrell, 'An Ethnographic Approach to Design', in A. Sears and J. Jacko, eds, *Human–Computer Interaction: Development Process* (CRC Press, 2009), pp. 71–94.

9. E. B-N. Sanders, 'From User-centered to Participatory Design Approaches', in J. Frascara, ed., *Design and the Social Sciences: Making Connections* (Taylor and Francis, 2002), pp. 1–8.

10. C. Rohrer, 'When to Use Which User Experience Research Methods', www.useit.com/alertbox/user-research-methods.html (accessed 21 April 2011).

11. See, for example, U.S. Department of Health and Human Sciences, 'Research-based Web Design and Usability Guidelines', www.usability.gov/guidelines/ (accessed 21 April 2011).

12. J. Nielsen, 'Heuristic Evaluation', in J. Nielsen and R. L. Mack, eds, *Usability Inspection Methods* (John Wiley, 1994), pp. 25–62.

13. J. S. Dumas and M. C. Salzman, 'Usability Assessment Methods', in R. C. Williges, ed., *Reviews of Human Factors and Ergonomics,* vol. 2 (Human Factors and Ergonomics Society, 2006), pp. 109–40.

14. For more on this, see S. G. Hart and L. E. Staveland, 'Development of NASA-TLX (Task Load Index): Results of Empirical and Theoretical Research', in P. A. Hancock and N. Meshkati, eds, *Human Mental Workload* (Elsevier Science, 1988), pp. 139–83.

15. For more on this, see R. M. Taylor, 'Situational Awareness Rating Technique (SART): The Development of a Tool for Aircrew Systems Design', in AGARD Conference Proceedings-478, *Situational Awareness in Aerospace Operations* (Advisory Group for Aerospace Research and Development, 1990), pp. 3/1–3/17.

16. J. R. Lewis, 'Usability Testing', in G. Salvendy, ed., *Handbook of Human Factors and Ergonomics,* 3rd edn (John Wiley, 2006), pp. 1275–1316.

17. Rubin and Chisnell, *Handbook of Usability Testing.*

18. Dumas and Salzman, 'Usability Assessment Methods'.

19. Lewis, 'Usability Testing'.

20. Dumas and Salzman, 'Usability Assessment Methods'.

chapter 11

1. S. Kelly, *Plurality and Unity in the Modes of Wonder, All Things Shining,* http://allthingsshining book.wordpress.com/2010/09/07/plurality-and-unity-in-the-modes-of-wonder/ (accessed 12 April 2011).

2. S. Kelly and H. Dreyfus, 'Notes on Embodiment in Homer: Reading Homer on Moods and Action in the Light of Heidegger and Merleau-Ponty', *Moving Bodies* 4/2 (2007), p. 21.

3. Ibid., 9.

4. F. Martin-Juchat and G. Verney-Carron, 'Construire Une Ambiance De Bien-Être Dans Les Parcs De Stationnement: Une Démarche Intégrée Architecture, Art, Design', in J. F. Augoyard, ed., *Faire Une Ambiance* (A la Croisee, 2008).

5. H. Wotton, 'The Elements of Architecture', in H. F. Mallgrav, ed., *Architectural Theory,* vol. 1: *An Anthology from Vitruvius to 1870* (Blackwell, 2006), p. 90.

6. J.N.L. Durand, 'Precis of the Lectures on Architecture', in H. F. Mallgrav, ed., *Architectural Theory,* vol. 1: *An Anthology from Vitruvius to 1870* (Blackwell, 2006), pp. 336–37.

7. Interview with Adriaan Geuze, 'The Enterprising Civil Engineer', *After Zero* 18, C-Lab, The Columbia Laboratory for Architectural Broadcasting, Columbia University. http://c-lab.columbia.edu/0151.html (2008).

8. D. Orr, 'A Meditation on Building', *Chronicle of Higher Education* (20 October 2006), http://chronicle.com/article/A-Meditation-on-Building/17359 (accessed 12 April 2011).

chapter 12

1. C. Peterson and M.E.P. Seligman, *Character Strengths and Virtues: A Handbook and Classification* (Oxford University Press, 2004).

chapter 13

1. J. M. Olson, 'Come Bearing Gifts: Practical Advice for Designers Working on Organizational

Change', Design Management Institute (2011), www.dmi.org/dmi/html/publications/news/view points/nv_vp_jmo.htm# January (accessed 12 April 2011).

2. M. Dziersk, 'Ten Things to Demand from Design Thinkers', *Fast Company* (22 May 2009), www.fastcompany.com/blog/mark-dziersk/ design-finds-you/ten-things-demand-design-thinkers (accessed 12 April 2011).

3. I. Mootee, '10 Design Thinking Principles for Strategic Business Innovation' (19 February 2008), http://mootee.typepad.com/innovation_ playground/2008/02/10-design-think.html (accessed 12 April 2011).

4. R. Martin, *Director* magazine (April 2010), www.director.co.uk/ONLINE/2010/04_10_roger martin.html (accessed 12 April 2011).

5. C. Zott, R. Amit, and L. Massa, 'The Business Model: Theoretical Roots, Recent Development and Future Research', IESE Business School Working Paper WP-862 (2010).

6. M. W. Johnson, C. M. Christensen, and H. Kagermann, 'Reinventing Your Business Model', *Harvard Business Review* (December 2008), pp. 51–59.

7. T. Brown, 'Six Sigma and Design Thinking' (10 September 2009), http://designthinking.ideo. com/?p = 387 (accessed 12 April 2011).

8. T. Brown, 'Design Thinking', *Harvard Business Review* (June 2008), www.ideo.com/images/ uploads/thoughts/IDEO_HBR_Design_Thinking. pdf (accessed 12 April 2011).

9. A. G. Lafley and R. Charan, *The Game-Changer: How You Can Drive Revenue and Profit Growth with Innovation* (Crown Business, 2008).

chapter 15

1. See, for example, Wikipedia, 'Brand', http:// en.wikipedia.org/wiki/Brand (accessed 23 April 2011).

2. D. Ogilvy, www.ogilvy.co.uk/ (accessed 23 April 2011).

3. IHS Global Insight, 'Country & Industry Forecasting', www.ihsglobalinsight.com/ (accessed 23 April 2011).

4. A. Cooper, *The Inmates Are Running the Asylum: Why Hi-Tech Products Drive Us Crazy* (SAMS, 1999).

5. Range Rover, 'Photos and Videos', www. landrover.com/gb/en/rr/range-rover-evoque/ photos-and-videos/ (accessed 23 April 2011).

chapter 16

1. Usina Escritório de Desenho, www.usin adesenho.com.br (accessed 22 April 2011).

2. J. C. Jones and D. G. Thornley, *Conference on Design Methods* (Oxford University Press, 1963).

3. G. Bonsiepe, *Teoria y práctica del diseño industrial* (Gustavo Gili, 1978).

4. L. Bucciarelli, 'An Ethnographic Perspective on Engineering Design', *Design Studies* 9/3 (1988), pp. 159–68.

5. For a discussion of design as a knowledge-intensive business service, see I. Miles, 'Innovation in Business Services: Knowledge-Intensity and Information Technology', PICT International Conference, London (1995).

chapter 18

1. See Chapter 1 of P. Hawken, A. B. Lovens, and L. Hunter Lovens, *Natural Capitalism* (Earth-scan, 1999).

2. See *Waste Strategy Annual Progress Report 2007/08,* Department for Environment, Food and Rural Affairs, http://archive.defra.gov.uk/environ ment/waste/strategy/strategy07/documents/ waste-strategy-report-07-08.pdf (accessed 18 December 2011), p. 5.

3. See Josh Brooks, 'Recession Blamed as Recycling Exports Rise 22% in a Year', *Packaging News* (4 August 2009), www.packagingnews. co.uk/environment/news/924742/Recession-blamed-recycling-exports-rise-22-year/ (accessed 29 April 2011).

4. According to the U.S. Geological Survey (see S. M. Jasinski, *U.S. Geological Survey, Mineral Commodity Summaries* [January 2009]), the global reserve base of phosphate rocks is 47 billion tons. It is assumed that one-third of this is phosphorous (P205), thus equating to 7 billion tons of phosphorous. Dissolved in the oceans, which have total mass of 1.3 times 1,018 tons, this gives five parts per billion, compared to the current concentration of phosphorous in seawater of sixty parts per billion (see Open University, *Seawater: Its Composition, Properties and Behaviour* [Oxford University Press, 1989]).

5. Global Humanitarian Forum, *Anatomy of a Silent Crisis, Human Impact Report: Climate Change* (Global Humanitarian Forum, 2009).

6. Ibid.

7. Committee on Climate Change, *Building a Low Carbon Economy: The UK's Contribution to Tackling Climate Change* (The Stationery Office, 2008). http://www.theccc.org.uk/pdf/TSO-ClimateChange.pdf (accessed 18 December 2011), p. X111.

8. Sometimes the manufacturing stage is subdivided into a raw material extraction stage and a production stage. Separate stages for shipping and distribution may also be included in the life cycle assessment.

9. *SimaPro* LCA software is a product of PRé Consultants. A demo version can be downloaded from www.pre.nl.

10. M. Goedkoop, A. De Schryver, and M. Oele, *Introduction to LCA with Simapro 7* (PRé Consultants, 2007).

11. See Chapter 15 in D.J.C. MacKay, *Sustainable Energy: Without the Hot Air* (UIT, 2008).

12. Goedkoop, De Schryver, and Oele, *Introduction to LCA with Simapro 7.*

13. S. Aumônier, M. Collins, and P. Garrett, *An Updated Lifecycle Assessment Study for Disposable and Reusable Nappies* (UK Environment Agency, 2008).

14. See Chapter 6 in N. Stern, *A Blueprint for a Safer Planet* (Bodley Head, 2009).

chapter 19

1. E. O. Wilson, *The Diversity of Life* (Belknap Press of Harvard University Press, 1992).

2. Department for Environment, Food and Rural Affairs, *e-Digest of Environmental Statistics* (DEFRA, 2006).

3. U.S. Environmental Protection Agency, *Municipal Solid Waste Generation, Recycling, and Disposal in the United States: Facts and Figures for 2008* (EPA, 2009).

4. N. H. Stern, *The Economics of Climate Change: The Stern Review* (HM Treasury, 2006), http://www.hm-treasury.gov.uk/sternreview_index.htm.

5. N. Morris, 'Climate Change Could Force 1 Billion from Their Homes by 2050', *The Independent on Sunday* (29 April 2008), www.independent.co.uk/environment/climate-change/climate-change-could-force-1-billion-from-their-homes-by-2050–817223.html (accessed 23 April 2011).

6. E. Datschefski, *The Total Beauty of Sustainable Products,* Design Fundamentals (Rotovision, 2001).

7. W. McDonough and M. Braungart, *Cradle to Cradle* (North Point Press, 2002).

8. D. Summers, D. Carrington, and agencies, 'Government Pledges to Cut Carbon Emissions by 80% by 2050', *The Guardian* (16 October 2008), www.guardian.co.uk/politics/2008/oct/16/greenpolitics-edmiliband (accessed 23 April 2011).

9. L. Ramrayka, 'The Rise and Rise of the Ethical Consumer', *The Guardian* (6 November 2006), www.guardian.co.uk/society/2006/nov/06/5 (accessed 23 April 2011).

10. Waste & Resources Action Programme, www.wrap.org.uk (accessed 23 April 2011).

11. Institute of Grocery Distribution, 'Packaging Reduction', www.igd.com/index.asp?id=1&fid=1&sid=5&tid=48&cid=187 (accessed 23 April 11).

12. 'Think Ink: The 2005 U.S. Ink Jet Cartridge User Survey', *Recharger Magazine,* in partnership with Lyra Research (2005), http://rechargermag.com/articles/2005/08/18/recharger-lyra-team-to-offer-report-on-ink-cartridge-buyers.aspx (accessed 20 December 2011).

13. 'Functional Sales of Washing', Electrolux, *Towards Sustainable Product Design,* 6th International Conference, Netherlands (2001).

14. eBay Inc., 'Who We Are', www.ebayinc.com/who (accessed 23 April 2011).

chapter 20

1. V. Papanek, *Design for the Real World: Human Ecology and Social Change* (Pantheon Books, 1971).

2. N. Whitely, *Design for Society* (Reaktion Books, 1994). B. Mau and the Institute Without Boundaries, *Massive Change* (Phaidon Press, 2004).

3. J. Ehrenfeld, *Sustainability by Design: A Subversive Strategy for Transforming Our Consumer Culture* (Yale University Press, 2008), p. 58.

4. P. Senge, C. O. Scharmer, J. Jaworski, and B. S. Flowers, *Presence: An Exploration of Profound Change in People, Organizations and Society* (Doubleday and Society of Organisational Learning, 2005).

5. S. Walker, *Sustainable by Design, Explorations in Theory and Practice* (Earthscan Ltd, 2006).

6. Ibid., p. 37.

7. Statistics from the Campaign for Dark Skies (2010), http://www.britastro.org/dark-skies/environmental.html?7O (accessed 26 April 2011).

8. NASA, 'Visible Earth' project, http://visibleearth.nasa.gov/view.php?id=55167.

9. Author's correspondence with Kate Lyndon, the Design Collective, Civic Twilight (26 September 2010). See www.civiltwilightcollective.com (accessed 26 April 2011).

10. Author's correspondence with Christopher Borroni-Bird, General Motors' director of advanced technology vehicle concepts (23 September 2010).

11. SafePoint Trust, www.safepointtrust.org (accessed 26 April 2011).

12. M. Koska, '1.3 Million Reasons to Reinvent the Syringe', *TEDGlobal* (July 2009), www.ted.com/talks/marc_koska_the_devastating_toll_of_syringe_reuse.html (accessed 26 April 2011). A. Turner, 'Used Needles Are Causing a Health Crisis in India', *The Sunday Times* (22 March 2009), www.timesonline.co.uk/tol/life_and_style/health/article5931974.ece (accessed 26 April 2011).

13. 'Pig 05049', Index: Award 2009, http://www.indexaward.dk/index.php?option=com_content_custom&view=article&id=375:pig-05049&catid=9:winners-2009&Itemid=293&Itemid=293 (accessed 26 April 2011).

14. E. Steele-Saccio et al., 'Bright Orange', GOOD (22 November 2006), www.good.is/post/bright-orange-2/ (accessed 26 April 2011).

chapter 21

1. L. Watson, *Lightning Bird: The Story of One Man's Journey into Africa's Past* (Simon & Schuster, 1983), p. 201.

2. Ibid.

3. For example see the excellent M. Ashby and K. Johnson, *Materials and Design: The Art and Science of Material Selection in Product Design* (Elsevier Ltd, 2010).

4. D. Farrelly, *The Book of Bamboo: A Comprehensive Guide to This Remarkable Plant, Its Uses, and Its History* (Sierra Club Books, 1984).

5. D. Pye, *The Nature and Aesthetics of Design* (Barrie and Jenkins Ltd, 1978), p. 64.

6. S. Braddock Clarke and M. O'Mahony, *Techno Textiles 2: Revolutionary Fabrics for Fashion and Design* (Thames and Hudson, 2005), p. 74.

7. C. Lefteri, *Materials for Inspirational Design* (RotoVision, 2006).

8. S. Lee, *Fashioning the Future: Tomorrow's Wardrobe* (Thames and Hudson, 2005), p. 188.

9. J. M. Benyus, *Biomimicry: Innovation Inspired by Nature* (Harper Perennial, 2002), p. 135.

chapter 22

1. See K. Krippendorff, *The Semantic Turn: A New Foundation for Design* (Taylor & Francis, 2006); and K. Krippendorff, *Redesigning Design: An Invitation to a Responsible Future* (1995), http://repository.upenn.edu/cgi/viewcontent.cgi?article=1046&context=asc_papers (accessed 28 April 2011).

2. See J. J. Gibson, *The Ecological Approach to Visual Perception* (Houghton Mifflin, 1973).

3. See A. A. Moles, 'The Legibility of the World: A Project of Graphic Design', *Design Issues* 3/1 (1986).

4. N. Sawasdichai, 'User Goal-Based Approach to Information Search and Structure on Web Site', PhD thesis, Illinois Institute of Technology, Chicago (2004).

5. See P. Welsh and C. Palames, *A Brief History of Disability Rights Legislation in the United States* (1995), www.udeducation.org/resources/61.html (accessed 28 April 2011).

6. See Interprofessional Projects Program at Illinois Institute of Technology, http://ipro.iit.edu (accessed 12 February 2011).

7. See S. H. Poggenpohl and Keiichi Sato, eds, *Design Integrations, Research and Collaboration* (Intellect Books, 2009). See, in particular, 'Collaborative Infiltration in a Media Organization' (Ch. 8), 'A Complex Model for International and Intercultural Collaboration in Health Information Systems' (Ch. 12), and 'Innovative Collaborative Design in International Interaction Design Summer Schools' (Ch. 11).

8. See S. H. Poggenpohl and D. R. Winkler, eds, 'Communication Design Failures', a special issue series, *Visible Language* 43/2–3 (2009) and 44/1 (2010).

9. See S. H. Poggenpohl, 'Design Literacy, Discourse and Communities of Practice', *Visible Language* 42/3 (2008).

10. G. Melles, 'PhD Design International Overview', LISTSERV archive for PHD-DESIGN, www.jiscmail.ac.uk/lists/phd-design.html (posted 15 June 2007).

11. M. Polanyi, *The Tacit Dimension* (Peter Smith, 1983).

12. K. van der Waarde, 'Visual Communication for Medicines: Malignant Assumptions and Benign Design?' *Visible Language* 44/1 (2010).

chapter 23

1. There is a wide range of informative videos on the technique of overmoulding on the Internet. Enter the US spelling 'overmolding' into your search engine or directly into YouTube (www.YouTube.com).

chapter 24

1. For a comprehensive analysis of UK intellectual property law, see David I. Bainbridge, *Intellectual Property*, 8th ed. (Pearsons, 2010).

2. Office for Harmonization in the Internal Market, http://oami.europa.eu/ows/rw/pages/index.en.do (accessed 29 April 2011).

3. For information on how to register a design, see the UK Intellectual Property Office Web site: www.ipo.gov.uk/ (accessed 29 April 2011).

4. European Patent Office, http://ep.espacenet.com/ (accessed 29 April 2011).

5. United States Patent and Trademark Office, www.uspto.gov/ (accessed 29 April 2011).

6. You can register either at the national IP office or via the Office of Harmonization for the Internal Market at https://secure.oami.europa.eu/ctm/ (accessed 29 April 2011).

chapter 25

1. J. Cagan and C. M. Vogel, *Creating Breakthrough Products: Innovation from Product Planning to Program Approval* (Financial Times/Prentice Hall PTR, 2002).

2. Telephone interview with Dave Lyon (28 December 2009).

3. T. Walton, 'Exploring How Technology Is Changing the Landscape of Design', *Design Management Journal* 14/2 (2003).

4. D. Muyres and G. Wardle, 'Futurama 2.0: Mobilizing America's Transportation Revolution', *OnGoing Transportation* (August 2009), www.ongoingtransportation.com (accessed 27 April 2011).

5. For example see O. Ocvirk, R. Stinson, P. Wigg, et al., *Art Fundamentals Theory and Practice*, 9th ed. (McGraw-Hill, 2001); and M. Stewart, *Launching the Imagination: A Comprehensive Guide to Basic Design* (McGraw-Hill, 2002).

chapter 26

1. R. Venturi, *Complexity and Contradiction in Architecture* (Architectural Press, 1977).

2. C. Jencks, *The Architecture of the Jumping Universe*, rev. edn (Academy Editions, 1997).

3. A good place to begin is K. Alexiou, J. Johnson, and T. Zamenopoulos, *Embracing Complexity in Design* (Routledge, 2009).

4. H. Simon, 'The Architecture of Complexity', *Proceedings of the American Philosophical Society* 106/6 (1962), pp. 467–82.

5. See, for instance, the short documentary on YouTube: www.youtube.com/watch?v=gQK21572oSU.

6. J. L. Casti, 'On System Complexity: Identification, Measurement, and Management', in J. L. Casti and A. Karlqvist, eds, *Complexity, Language, and Life: Mathematical Approaches* (Springer-Verlag, 1986).

7. H. Simon, 'Bounded Rationality and Organizational Learning', *Organization Science* 2/1 (1991), pp. 125–34.

8. L. March and J. P. Steadman, *The Geometry of Environment* (Methuen, 1971).

9. N. Schadewitz and T. Zamenopoulos, 'Towards an Online Design Studio: A Study of Social Networking in Design Distance Learning'. *International Association of Societies of Design Research 2009* (Korea Society of Design Science, 2009).

10. K. Alexiou and T. Zamenopoulos, 'Artificial Design and Planning Support: Interactive Plan Generation and Coordination in Distributed Decision-Making', in *Design and Decision Support Systems in Urban Planning: Proceedings of the 6th International Conference* (Eindhoven University of Technology, 2002), pp. 1–11. T. Zamenopoulos and K. Alexiou, 'Structuring the Plan Design Process as a Coordination Problem: The Paradigm of Distributed Learning Control Coordination', in P. Longley and M. Batty, eds, *Advanced Spatial Analysis: The CASA Book of GIS* (ESRI Press, 2003), pp. 407–26.

chapter 28

1.   See Toyota, 'Lean Deployment: Toyota Production   System',   www.leandeployment.com/
pages/toyota-production-system.php.
2.   See Rudyard Kipling, 'I Keep Six Honest Serving Men', www.kipling.org.uk/poems_serving.htm.
3.   D. W. Orr, 'Ecological Design Intelligence',
Resurgence (September/October 2004), repub-
lished at www.ecoliteracy.org/essays/ecological-
design-intelligence (accessed 14 July 2011).
4.   www.dictionary.com (accessed 14 July 2011).
5.   Unpublished interview with Clive Mockford,
managing   director,   Engineering   Creatives   (24
March 2009).

6.   Ibid.
7.   Shannon Joe, 'The Learningscape', Warren
and Mahoney (22 February 2011), www.warren
andmahoney.com/en/perspectives/the-learning
scape/ (accessed 14 July 2011).

24:7 project 7: 24-carat designing

1.   'Global Snack Foods Market Expected to
Reach $334 Billion by 2015', *Quality Assurance
and Food Safety* (6 April 2011), www.quality
assurancemag.com/qa-0311-snack-foods-fat-
global.aspx.

further reading

Ashby, M., and Johnson, K., *The Art and Science of Material Selection in Product Design,* Oxford: Elsevier, 2010.

Benyus, J. M., *Biomimicry: Innovation Inspired by Nature,* New York: Harper Perennial, 2002.

Boradkar, P., *Designing Things: A Critical Introduction to the Culture of Objects,* Oxford: Berg, 2010.

Braddock Clarke, S. E., and O'Mahony, M., *Techno Textiles 2: Revolutionary Fabrics for Fashion and Design,* London: Thames and Hudson, 2005.

Braungart, M., and McDonough, W., *Cradle to Cradle,* London: Vintage, 2009.

Bringhurst, R., *The Elements of Typographic Style,* Seattle: Hartley and Marks, 2005.

Brown, T., *Change by Design: How Design Thinking Creates New Alternatives for Business and Society,* New York: Collins Business, 2009.

Cross, N., *Design Thinking: Understanding How Designers Think and Work,* Oxford: Berg, 2011.

Fry, T., *Design Futuring: Sustainability, Ethics and New Practice,* Oxford: Berg, 2009.

Goleman, D., *Primal Leadership: Learning to Lead with Emotional Intelligence,* Cambridge, MA: Harvard Business School Press, 2004.

Hudson, J., *Process: 50 Product Designs from Concept to Manufacture,* London: Lawrence King, 2008.

Krug, S., *Don't Make Me Think! A Common Sense Approach to Web Usability,* 2nd edn, Berkeley, CA: New Riders, 2005.

Lefteri, C., *Making It: Manufacturing Techniques for Product Design,* London: Lawrence King, 2007.

Lefteri, C., *Materials for Inspirational Design,* Hove, East Sussex, UK: RotoVision, 2006.

Maeda, J., *The Laws of Simplicity (Simplicity: Design, Technology, Business, Life),* Cambridge, MA: MIT Press, 2006.

Norman, D., *Emotional Design: Why We Love (or Hate) Everyday Things,* New York: Basic Books, 2004.

Norman, D., *The Psychology of Everyday Things,* New York: Basic Books, 2002.

Ocvirk, O., Stinson, R., Wigg, P., et al., *Art Fundamentals Theory and Practice,* 9th edn, New York: McGraw-Hill, 2001.

Poggenpohl, S. H., ed., *Graphic Design: A Career Guide and Education Directory,* New York: AIGA Press, 1993.

Pye, D., *The Nature and Aesthetics of Design,* London: Barrie and Jenkins, 1978.

Quick, T., *Successful Team Building,* New York: AMACOM American Management Association, 1992.

Robinson, D., and Garratt, C., *Introducing Ethics: A Graphic Guide,* Thriplow, UK: Icon Books, 2009.

Samara, T., *Design Elements: A Graphic Style Manual,* Gloucester, MA: Rockport, 2007.

Schell, J., *The Art of Game Design: A Book of Lenses,* Burlington, MA: Morgan Kaufmann, 2008.

Schuler, D., and Namioka, A., eds, *Participatory Design: Principles and Practices,* Hillsdale, NJ: Lawrence Erlbaum, 1993.

Scott, B., *The Art of Project Management,* Sebastopol, CA: O'Reilly Media, 2005.

Sparke, P., *The Genius of Design,* London: Quadrille, 2009.

Stewart, M., *Launching the Imagination: A Comprehensive Guide to Basic Design,* New York: McGraw-Hill, 2002.

Stickdorn, M., and Schneider, J., *This Is Service Design Thinking: Basics, Tools, Cases,* Amsterdam: BIS Publishers, 2010.

Sudjic, D., *The Language of Things. Design, Luxury, Fashion, Art: How We Are Seduced by Objects around Us,* London: Penguin, 2009.

index